Ancient Tiwanaku

Nearly a millennium before the Inca forged a pan-Andean empire in the South American Andes, Tiwanaku emerged as a major center of political, economic, and religious life on the mountainous southern shores of Lake Titicaca. Beginning in AD 500 and for the next five centuries, Tiwanaku influenced vast regions of the Andes and became one of the most important and enduring civilizations of the pre-Colombian Americas. Yet for centuries, the nature and antiquity of Tiwanaku remained a great mystery. Only over the past couple of decades has archaeological research begun to explore in depth the fascinating character of Tiwanaku culture and the way of life of its people.

ANCIENT TIWANAKU synthesizes a wealth of past and current research on this fascinating high-altitude civilization. In the first major synthesis on the subject in nearly fifteen years, John Wayne Janusek explores Tiwanaku civilization in its geographical and cultural setting, tracing its long rise to power, vast geopolitical influences, and violent collapse. The author frames the study with a novel theoretical approach that emphasizes Tiwanaku's striking environmental setting in relation to its profound cultural diversity, vibrant daily rituals, and dynamic political history. He concludes that the Andean past sheds important light on current national ideologies and global geopolitics.

JOHN WAYNE JANUSEK is associate professor of anthropology at Vanderbilt University. He is the author of *Identity and Power in the Ancient Andes: Tiwanaku Cities through Time* and several chapters in *Tiwanaku and its Hinterland: Archaeology and Paleoecology of an Andean Civilization, Vol. 2.* He has conducted archaeological research in the Andes for the past two decades.

Case Studies in Early Societies

Series Editor
Rita P. Wright, New York University

This series aims to introduce students to early societies that have
been the subject of sustained archaeological research. Each study is
also designed to demonstrate a contemporary method of
archaeological analysis in action, and the authors are all specialists
currently engaged in field research. The books have been planned
to cover many of the same fundamental issues. Tracing long-term
developments, and describing and analyzing a discrete segment in
the prehistory or history of a region, they represent an invaluable
tool for comparative analysis. Clear, well organized, authoritative,
and succinct, the case studies are an important resource for
students, and for scholars in related fields, such as anthropology,
ethnohistory, history, and political science. They also offer the
general reader accessible introductions to important archaeological
sites.

Other titles in series include:

Ancient Mesopotamia
Susan Pollock

Ancient Oaxaca
Richard E. Blanton, Gray M. Feinman, Stephen A. Kowalewski,
Linda M. Nicholas

Ancient Maya
Arthur Demarest

Ancient Cahokia and the Mississippians
Timothy R. Pauketat

Ancient Puebloan Southwest
John Kantor

Ancient Middle Niger
Roderick J. McIntosh

Ancient Jomon of Japan
Junko Habu

Ancient Egyptian Civilization
Robert Wenke

Ancient Tiwanaku

John Wayne Janusek
Vanderbilt University

CAMBRIDGE UNIVERSITY PRESS
Cambridge, New York, Melbourne, Madrid, Cape Town, Singapore,
São Paulo, Delhi

Cambridge University Press
32 Avenue of the Americas, New York, NY 10013-2473, USA

www.cambridge.org
Information on this title: www.cambridge.org/9780521016629

First published 2008

Printed in the United States of America

A catalog record for this publication is available from the British Library.

Library of Congress Cataloging in Publication Data

Janusek, John Wayne, 1963–
Ancient Tiwanaku / John Wayne Janusek.
   p.   cm. – (Case studies in early societies)
Includes bibliographical references and index.
ISBN 978-0-521-81635-9 (hardcover) – ISBN 978-0-521-01662-9 (pbk.)
1. Tiwanaku culture.   2. Tiwanaku Site (Bolivia)   3. Andes Region –
Civilization.   4. Andes Region – Antiquities.   I. Title.   II. Series.
F3319.1.T55J35   2007
980 – dc22   2007001318

ISBN   978-0-521-81635-9 hardback
ISBN   978-0-521-01662-9 paperback

For Wolfgang and Julia, my family in La Paz

Contents

Figures

Text Boxes

Acknowledgments

I am indebted to many friends, colleagues, and students. Extended thanks go to Alan Kolata and Arthur Demarest for proposing the idea of a Tiwanaku book for this series. Gratitude is owed the two anonymous colleagues who reviewed the prospectus, and profound thanks go to Rita Wright, the series editor, for her ongoing support and suggestions. Simon Whitmore and Beatrice Rehl graciously waited as deadlines came and went. Many thanks are owed their formidable patience and good faith.

Most profound acknowledgments are owed my many dear colleagues whose research is summarized in the following pages. Working with them in the Andes over the past two decades has been an exciting ride: frequently exhilarating, at times maddening, often on the brink of insanity. They are a group of sincere humans I refuse to live without. Inextricably intertwined with my own research and interpretations are those of Juan Albarraćín, Sonia Alconini, Matt Bandy, Deborah Blom, Nicole Couture, Martin Giesso, Paul Goldstein, Carlos Lemuz, Donna Nash, Claudia Rivera, Alexei Vranich, and Ryan Williams. Equally deserving are close senior colleagues: David Browman, Tom Dillehay, Clark Erickson, Christine Hastorf, Bill Isbell, Alan Kolata, the late Max Portugal and Carlos Ponce Sanginés, Katharina Schreiber, and Chip Stanish. I thank my students Randi Gladwell, Arik Ohnstad, Jennifer Zovar, Adolfo Perez, and Maribel Perez for sharing their insights.

A host of close colleagues deserve recognition for offering reviews, thoughts, images, articles, unpublished manuscripts, or a patient ear. They include (but are not limited to): Karen Anderson, Brian Bauer, Robin Beck, Leo Benitez, Marc Bermann, Jose Capriles, Amanda Cohen, Beth Conklin, Anita Cook, Francisco Estrada-Belli, William Fowler, Mary Glowacki, Sabine Hyland, Liz Klarich, Pat Knobloch, Erick Marsh, Jerry Moore, Mike Moseley, Jeffrey Parsons, Wolfgang Schüler, Scott Smith, Tiffiny Tung, Steve Wernke, and Jason Yaeger.

I would especially like to thank the many Bolivian archaeologists and community members who facilitated the research that went into this book. In particular, leaders and community members of Chojasivi,

Korila, Quiripujo, Lukurmata, Tiwanaku, Icla, Iruhito, and most recently Qhunqhu Liqiliqi deserve special recognition. Archaeologists Cesar Kalisaya and Felipe "Papi" Choque, my *compadre*, generously offered their advice and expertise, while Oswaldo Rivera and Javier Escalante, successive directors of the National Direction of Archaeology in La Paz (DINAR), facilitated professional support.

I am grateful to the private and governmental agencies that funded portions of the research summarized here. They include the National Science Foundation (BNS-9021098, BCS-0514624, and others to Alan Kolata), the Fulbright-Hays Foundation, the National Geographic Society (7700-04), the Wenner-Gren Foundation for Anthropological Research, the H. John Heinz Cheritable Trust and Howard Heinz Foundation, the Curtiss T. and Mary G. Brennan Foundation, Vanderbilt University's Discover Grant and Faculty Development programs, and the Universidad Mayor de San Andrés in La Paz.

To those who helped with final editing I owe more limbs than I possess. They include Randi Gladwell, Arik Ohnstad, Jennifer Ohnstad, Steve Wernke, Tiffiny Tung, Ryan Willams, Joel Zovar, and Abigail Levine. I am also grateful to those who allowed me to reproduce or adapt their original artwork or photos: Marilyn Bridges, Sergio Chavez, William Conklin, Javier Escalante, Alan Kolata, Kenneth Garrett, Danielle Kurin, William Isbell, Augustine Llagostera, Linda Manzanilla, Gordon McEwan, Stella Nair, Jean-Pierre Protzen, Heiko Prümers, Clare Sammels, Wolfgang Schüler, Johann Reinhard, and Margaret Young-Sanchez.

1   Unveiling Tiwanaku's Mystery

"History is messy for the people who must live it."

– Michel-Rolph Trouillot, 1995:110

Some fifteen hundred years ago in the brisk Andean high plateau, or *altiplano*, Tiwanaku became one of the most important and influential centers in the Americas (Figure 1.1). Perched at a skyscraping 3,800–4,000 meters above sea level, the altiplano strikes contemporary sensibilities as cruelly cold and supremely challenging. For many, it is a remote place one visits to purchase colorful alpaca clothing or to test one's endurance climbing perilous peaks. One is tempted to think that the altiplano could not have fostered one of the earliest, most enduring, and fascinating civilizations of the ancient world. Yet it did, as abundant ongoing research confirms.

Tiwanaku emerged at approximately AD 500, about the time Imperial Rome was being submitted to memory. It collapsed at around AD 1100, not long after King John signed the Magna Carta in foggy Runnymeade, England. By any historian's calculation, six centuries is a long time, and this cultural and political longevity begs explanation.

In this book, I explore Tiwanaku's long history and unique character. I summarize vast bodies of past and recent research to demonstrate that its endurance stemmed from an ancient cultural inheritance, social and ideological tolerance, extensive economic ventures, unparalleled religious prestige, and vast popular appeal. It ultimately succumbed to severe environmental stress, continental political shifts, and its own strategies of state consolidation and class formation. This study of Tiwanaku's rise and fall offers an extraordinary case study of state legitimacy and fragility, and of cultural uniformity and diversity. It suggests caveats regarding the potential legacy of the civilizations we live in, hold dear, and routinely celebrate or criticize today.

Much about Tiwanaku remains a mystery. The site's original name may have been the native term *chucara* (Anello Oliva 1998 [1631]:60),

Figure 1.1 The altiplano. The Eastern Cordillera is in the background.

"sun's home" in Pukina, or *taypikala*, "central stone" in Aymara (Cobo 1990[1653]:100). The first invokes a key celestial-symbolic icon of later Andean imperial religions and the second the monumental stonework that shapes the identity or "soul" of people from the modern town of Tiahuanaco. Today, Tiahuanaco natives are nicknamed, partly in fun, *kalawawa*, or "stone babies." Both names may have been employed, for they resonate with Tiwanaku's ancient past. *Chucara* may refer to the solar elements of Tiwanaku religious ideology, and *taypikala* to Tiwanaku's place at the center of a long-lived Andean civilization and between diverse cultural and geographical realms. Like the Inca empire several centuries later, the Tiwanaku state proselytized an innovative and highly prestigious religious complex. Rulers and commoners together promoted a cosmology in which the center, as the social and ceremonial axis of the civilized world, mediated society, nature, and the cosmos.

In this chapter, I introduce Tiwanaku by delineating a history of research into its character and chronology. I then outline current knowledge regarding culture history in the Lake Titicaca Basin, Tiwanaku's heartland (Figure 1.2). I introduce Wari, an expansive state centered in the Ayacucho Basin of Peru that interacted and occasionally clashed with Tiwanaku. Next, I outline the theoretical underpinnings of the book and my approach to Tiwanaku and prehispanic history in the region.

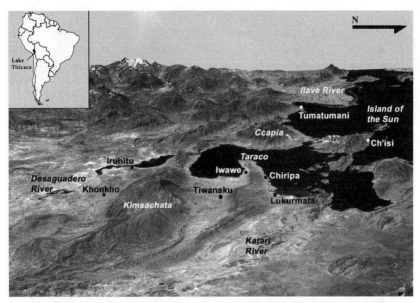

Figure 1.2 The southern Lake Titicaca Basin showing key sites (base map by Arik Ohnstad). The southern part of the lake highlighted here is known as Lake Wiñaymarka.

A History of Tiwanaku Research

Fifty years ago, knowledge of Tiwanaku hinged on myth and yarn. Tiwanaku has been appropriated to an array of political, intellectual, and industrial projects. Its monuments have been buried, defaced, decapitated, and blown up. In early historical periods, carved stones from monumental constructions were mined to build residences, tombs, churches, and mills in Tiahuanaco, nearby towns, and La Paz (Cobo 1990[1653]; Lizárraga 1909[1605]; Squier 1878:274). The long history of Tiwanaku's cultural appropriation begins with the Inca. Located in the lucrative Inca province of Collasuyu, and a three-week trek from the royal capital in Cuzco, Tiwanaku boasted enigmatic sculptures and massive architectural ruins that inspired "great admiration" and awe in its visitors (Molina 1916[1553]:13). Just as many inhabitants of Western civilization think of the Near East, the Inca considered Tiwanaku their place of cosmic and ethnic genesis.

Inca Legitimacy and Colonial Chronicles (1535–1800)

Early writers concur that Inca royalty considered Tiwanaku and nearby Lake Titicaca the places where the heroic creator deity Viracocha once

fashioned the then-current incarnation of the Andean cosmos. In a fascinating twist, these accounts attribute the origins of Andean cultural diversity and the original definition of the Andean landscape to Tiwanaku.
Numerous chroniclers (e.g., Betanzos 1996[1551–1557]; Sarmiento de
Gamboa 1999[1572]) recounted a myth in which Viracocha first fashioned Andean society at Tiwanaku or on the nearby Island of the Sun.
According to Sarmiento (1999:34), Spain's first official Andean historian, Viracocha then "went to a place now called Tiahuanacu [*sic*] . . . and
in this place he sculpted and designed on a great piece of stone, all
the nations that he intended to create." He provided each "nation" its
language, clothing, hairstyle, music, dances, and signature crops. Each
group was to enter the earth, travel underground, and spring forth like
a plant near a particular feature – whether a tree, lake, spring, cave,
or mountain – that would henceforth be its principal *huaca*, or sacred
place.

Viracocha then charged the two individuals to remember the name of
each group and its place of origin. Together, the three traveled north by
northwest. One followed the Western Cordillera hugging the Pacific coast,
the other the rugged Eastern Cordillera overlooking the eastern valleys,
or *yungas*. Viracocha himself followed the highland route in between. The
purpose of their journey was to "call forth" from the earth – essentially,
to harvest – all of the diverse nations or ethnic groups of the Andes that
Viracocha had fashioned. Their synchronized journeys defined the three
major environmental zones of the Andes: the dry Pacific coast, the humid
eastern valleys, and the highland sierra. In this manner, Inca imperial
ideology implicated Tiwanaku in the creation of Andean social and geographical diversity, and more important, in its cultural unification.

A few early chroniclers visited the altiplano and wrote tantalizing but
brief descriptions of Tiwanaku's ruins. They include the young Spaniard
Pedro de Cieza de León, "a common soldier with an uncommon eye for
detail" (D'Altroy 2002:11). Cieza visited Tiwanaku in 1549, just sev-
enteen years after Francisco Pizarro and his band of *conquistadores* had
captured the Inca ruler Atawallpa. Cieza described the massive temple
known as Akapana as a "man-made hill, built on great stone foundations"
as well as the "finely built" walls of the Kalasasaya, which, according to
some natives, had inspired Inca imperial architecture. He marveled over
several great "stone idols" near the buildings, "of human size and shape,
with the features beautifully carved, so much so that they seem the work
of great artists or masters" (1959[1553]:283). Cieza also noted that the
Inca used Tiwanaku as an architectural model and that Manco Capac,
son of the last legitimate Inca ruler, Wayna Capac, had been born at
Tiwanaku (1959:284; also Cobo 1990:105). Yet when he asked whether

the Incas had built the monuments, the natives "laughed at the question, repeating... that they were built before they reigned" (1959:282–284). Cieza surmised that Tiwanaku was the "oldest antiquity" in the Andes.

It appears that the Inca had merely claimed ancestry to the ancient kings of Tiwanaku to legitimize their rule, by proclaiming the site a sacred place of cosmic origin and by emulating its impeccably crafted monuments. The question thus remained: Who created Tiwanaku?

Armchair Archaeology: Naturalists, Explorers, and Enthusiasts (1800–1945)

Scholars seriously turned to this question again following Bolivia's independence in 1825. The prior 150 years of Spanish Colonial rule had produced a hiatus of inquiry into Tiwanaku, most likely due to the cumulative social unrest that characterized the south-central Andes during this time. In the decades following Spanish arrival thousands of natives perished yearly, whether in battle or by succumbing to new diseases such as smallpox and measles. By the 1560s Spanish administrators were forcibly relocating native populations to Potosí, in the central altiplano, as cheap labor to mine silver. Lands were left desolate and scores of workers died daily due to collapsing shafts, physical exhaustion, and mercury poisoning. After 1570, the Spanish imposed radical resettlement programs (*reducciones*) to facilitate effective administration in the Andean countryside. They built central pueblos in an attempt to eradicate local ties to landscape and promote cultural amnesia among native populations, and to facilitate privately run *haciendas* where natives worked as indentured servants.

A salient sense of native history and social identity reemerged slowly in the seventeenth century. By the mid-eighteenth century, increasing social tensions and a series of minor rebellions fostered full-blown revolts led by native and *mestizo* revolutionaries such as Tupac Amaru, in southern Peru, and Tomas Katari, in the Bolivian altiplano. These messianic movements refashioned ancient myths and symbols to challenge the Spanish imperial regime, leading European administrators and writers to consider the Andean countryside a dangerous place inhabited by rebellious Indians.

Meanwhile, on the progressive winds of the European Enlightenment, new intellectual disciplines promoted the objective study of natural and human history. As biological and cultural evolution became influential conceptual paradigms, social thinkers tended to categorize societies according to their degree of "civilization." Hand in hand with such protoanthropological writing went an interest in discovering the ruins of past civilizations around the world, especially those considered reminiscent of Europe's past cultural patrimony. In light of its enigmatic architectural wonders, Tiwanaku was interpreted as an exotic, ancient center of Andean civilization. Yet, for many of this intellectual temperament, people from distant cultures, continents, or even galaxies were considered responsible for building and inhabiting Tiwanaku.

Nineteenth-century explorers and "armchair archaeologists" produced some of the first detailed descriptions and speculative interpretations of Tiwanaku's monuments. In 1799, the Bohemian naturalist Tadeo Haenke wrote an illustrated account of sites in the Lake Titicaca basin, and created one of the earliest sketches of Tiwanaku's megalithic Sun Portal (Ponce 1995). More comprehensive descriptions followed the influx of foreign diplomats and naturalists after Bolivia's independence. Particularly astute in this era was the French naturalist Alcide Dessalines d'Orbigny (1944[1839]), who visited Tiwanaku in June 1833. D'Orbigny defined Tiwanaku's principal temple complexes – the Kalasasaya, Akapana, and Pumapunku – and interpreted the central image of the Sun Portal as a religious and political ruler (Figure 1.3a). His work helped inspire the first national museum, for which Bolivian President José Ballivián commissioned "excavations" to collect Tiwanaku relics (Albarracin-Jordan 1999).

Many explorers recognized in Tiwanaku the ruins of a center that had thrived long before the Inca. The German naturalist Alexander von Humboldt (1878:372) admonished his European audience to visit "the center of an ancient civilization." Still, Tiwanaku remained a mystery, in no small part because of what many considered its intractable environment. The British naval cadet Clemens Markham (1862) considered Tiwanaku the political and intellectual center of a "megalithic empire" that had stretched across the Andes long before that of the Inca. Perplexed by the high altitude of the ruins, however, he speculated that the altiplano had been located hundreds of meters lower than it was during his own time. The North American Ephraim George Squier (1878), President Lincoln's Commissioner to Peru, also was struck by Tiwanaku's stark environment and poor soils. He took the first photographs of the site, made maps of its structures, sketched its monumental sculptures, and described the ruins, estimating their expanse at 3 square kilometers (Figure 1.4a). Because of Tiwanaku's altitude and "harsh" setting, and for lack of "any traces of habitations," Squier concluded that it had been but a pilgrimage center consisting of isolated monumental structures. As he put it (1878:300), "Tiwanaku may have been a sacred spot or shrine, the position of which was determined by an accident, an augury, or a dream," but it had not been "the seat of dominion."

A

B

Figure 1.3 Two Victorian views of Tiwanaku's ruins: (a) Alcide D'Orbigy (adapted from Parejas and Reyes de Parejas 2002); and (b) Leonce Angrand (adapted from Prümers 1993).

A common thread linking the thought and writing of many nineteenth-century adventurers, a thread remarkably vital today, is the idea that native Aymara-speaking "Indians" could not have built Tiwanaku's magnificent monuments. Several writers proposed far-fetched speculations in support of overtly racist assumptions. Francis de Castelnau favored the idea that Egyptian pharaohs built Tiwanaku, not the "imbicilic race that inhabits the country today" (Castelnau 1939:56[1850–1851]).

Leonce Angrand (1866; Prümers 1993) speculated that peripatetic Toltec immigrants from the Central basin of Mexico first built Tiwanaku (Figure 1.3b). In a similar vein, the Marquise de Nadaillac argued that, indeed, a Nahuatl speaking race, perhaps the Mexica-Aztec, founded Tiwanaku (1939:75[1883]). Others were more equivocal. If Squier believed that "the civilization of ancient Peruvians was indigenous" (1878:569), the location of Tiwanaku's "beautifully cut stones" among the "wretched" and "impoverished" Aymara struck him as incongruous. Such ideas live on in remarkably popular, supremely ill-researched New Age notions that Tiwanaku was founded by enlightened Egyptians or Atlanteans (Bellamy 1948; Hancock 1996). On the ludicrous, if entertaining end of the spectrum is the notion that Tiwanaku was inspired by aliens from outer space (von Däniken 1971)!

The supreme embodiment of Victorian mythology was Arthur Posnansky (1914, 1945), an eccentric Austrian who lived and worked among Tiwanaku's ruins for much of the first half of the twentieth century. If for him native altiplano communities had descended from the ancient Qolla, they were now "completely devoid of culture" and "live a wretched existence in clay huts which seem...the caves of troglodytes" (1945, Vol. 1:33). Like others, Posnansky believed that climatic conditions had been much more favorable in the distant past. "Climatic aggression," Posnansky argued (1945, Vol. 1:2), fostered Tiwanaku's decline and its subsequent cultural diffusion as the "Cradle of American Man." Despite recent scientific research that roundly challenges such ideas, Posnanky's quasi-racist speculations continue to fire upper and middle class imaginations and amateur speculation around the world (as testified by a quick surf through the World Wide Web).

Early Archaeology (1890–1958)

More rigorous interpretations of Tiwanaku emerged around the turn of the nineteenth century. Max Uhle, who first visited Tiwanaku in 1894, laid the foundation for systematic archaeological research in the Andes (Figure 1.4b). Before setting foot in the Andes, Uhle collaborated with Alphonse Stübel (1892) to describe and illustrate Tiwanaku's monumental constructions. They considered the Kalasasaya an "American Stonehenge," and suggested that it was one of several isolated structures that together formed an early religious site of paramount regional influence. Unlike many adventurers, Uhle believed that the builders of Tiwanaku had been ancestors of the altiplano's Aymara-speaking communities, but that memory of greatness had withered upon the civilization's eclipse (Stübel and Uhle 1892:62). He later defined a pan-Andean "Tiahuanaco

Figure 1.4 Two Victorian views of the Sun Portal: (a) Ephraim
Squier approaches the monument on horseback (after Squier 1878)
and (b) Max Uhle leans against it (after Stübel and Uhle 1892).

Style," later termed the Middle Horizon (Rowe 1960), that predated Inca style by centuries.

Adolph Bandelier, Uhle's contemporary, visited Tiwanaku in 1894 and then left to conduct excavations on the nearby Islands of the Sun and Moon (1910). Bandelier broke the mold and suggested that Tiwanaku had incorporated several thousand inhabitants, inferring that it had been a city as well as a ceremonial center (1911). He observed that prehispanic dwellings, much like those inhabited at the time of his visit, had been earthen buildings consisting of adobe bricks or hard-packed *tapia*; impermanent materials that long since had eroded onto the landscape. Bandelier admonished archaeologists that they had concentrated exclusively on Tiwanaku's striking monuments, neglecting the "more modest features" that truly illustrate "the mode of living of the people" (1911:221). Like Uhle, Bandelier believed that the native Aymara-speaking community members who inspired this insight were descendants of Tiwanaku's original inhabitants.

By the turn of the century, the Andes had gained popularity among educated circles in North America and Europe as an exotic, rugged region. Scores of foreigners embarked on the long journey to Tiwanaku to gain firsthand experience of ancient ruins and, in some cases, to assemble precious collections for export to home countries. Such activity fed on and promoted looting. As Alan Kolata and Carlos Ponce surmise, such "expeditions . . . took on a transparently neocolonial character in which Bolivian citizens played auxiliary roles, or none at all, and crates of irreplaceable objects were shipped overseas without so much as an inventory" (2003:23). In the early twentieth century, amateur enthusiasts such as Colonel Diez de Medina and Fritz Buck (Querejazu 1983; Sagarnaga 1987) amassed massive collections of archaeological artifacts. A few decades later, national response to this cumulative activity would profoundly affect the course of Bolivian archaeology.

Tiwanaku suffered a particularly egregious moment of destruction in 1902–1903, when a railway joining La Paz with Lake Titicaca was built right through the site. The construction crew mined hundreds of Tiwanaku's finest ashlars and monuments to build railway platforms and bridges, exploding the larger stones with dynamite to make a level rubble fill. To one of many protests, a cynical crew member replied, "So much the better that these stones have endured to serve two civilizations" (*my translation*; Arguedas 1911:236, cited in Ponce 1995:117).

Georges de Créqui-Montfort, the recently-arrived director of an inter-disciplinary French scientific mission to the south-central Andes (Créqui-Monfort 1904), sought to stop the destruction. Part of his intent in studying Andean natural and human history was to conduct excavations at Tiwanaku. In 1903, when by circumstance Créqui-Monfort was left without a project archaeologist, George Courty (1910), originally assigned as project geologist, took the helm and led excavations in the Sunken Temple (or Semi-subterranean Temple), Putuni, Chunchukala, and Kalasasaya. Courty's excavations revealed the incredible richness and intricacy of Tiwanaku's monumental constructions. Yet he had never been trained in archaeological methods. His crew tore through intact buildings, damaged carved sculptures, and completely dismantled the Putuni's extraordinary, multicolored staircase entrance. After finishing excavations early in 1904, the crew left fragile walls and floors exposed to heavy rains and looting (Figure 1.5). Ironically, Créqui-Monfort's well-intended project, which remains largely unpublished, in the end was regrettable.

Between 1930 and 1958, foreign-led archaeological research commenced in earnest at Tiwanaku and in nearby sites and regions. Trained archaeologists prospected little-known regions and excavated isolated units at key sites, seeking to establish local chronologies and reveal elements of prehispanic culture history. In the Lake Titicaca Basin, archaeologists began to forge a coherent regional chronology. Some offered insights into Tiwanaku's prehispanic character, and others began to define its cultural precursors and successors. A common theme was the extraordinary complexity of Tiwanaku's cultural deposits, and by extension, the difficulty of interpreting Tiwanaku history based on simple reconnaissance or limited excavation.

Key figures during this time included Wendell Bennett, Stig Rydén, and Alfred Kidder II. Wendell Bennett (1934, 1936), of the American Museum of Natural History, excavated Tiwanaku in 1932 and nearby sites, including Chiripa, Lukurmata, and Pariti Island in 1934. Bennett excavated nearly a dozen test units in and around Tiwanaku's monumental core, based on which he defined a cultural sequence that he interpreted as constituting Tiwanaku's Early, Classic, and Decadent phases. Today, we know these phases as Late Formative, Tiwanaku IV, and Tiwanaku V. Bennett's isolated units perforated the superimposed lenses of midden that constitutes much of the site of Tiwanaku. He found no clear evidence for prehispanic dwellings at Tiwanaku, and so decided that Tiwanaku was "a major ceremonial center, rather than a city or large village" (Bennett and Bird 1964:138; also Bennett 1934:480). After excavating seven isolated units in 1938, Stig Rydén echoed Bennett in suggesting that the site had housed abundant "ritual meals" rather than vast populations (1947:158–159).

By 1950 archaeologists had outlined Tiwanaku's place in Andean prehistory and had begun to explore the complexities of its expansion and distant interactions. Some were beginning to notice that the so-called Tiahuanaco Style was diversified. Berkeley graduate student Dwight

Wallace (1957) made the critical suggestion that Bennett's Classic-Decadent distinction might better reflect contemporary styles or polities rather than successive chronological phases. Drawing on contemporary research in Peru (Bennett 1953; Rowe, Collier, and Willey 1950), he suggested that Uhle's broadly defined Tiahuanaco Style had glossed several cultural configurations. By 1970, the Andean Middle Horizon was thought to comprise two dominant civilizations: Tiwanaku and Wari. Dorothy Menzel (1964, 1968, 1977) and Luis Lumbreras (Lumbreras 1974), adopting a traditional interpretation of Tiwanaku, interpreted Wari as an expansive state inspired by Tiwanaku's religious ideology and ceremonial prestige.

Other North American archaeologists considered Tiwanaku a major Andean urban center. In a seminal essay on Andean urban settlements, John Rowe listed Tiwanaku as a prehispanic city (1963:7–9). Edward Lanning (1967:116) took the old pilgrimage idea to task in a popular book summarizing Andean culture history. Not long after, University of Michigan archaeologist Jeffrey Parsons (1968:244) briefly visited Tiwanaku and noted that artifacts littered the ground far from the visible monuments. He considered Tiwanaku a past urban center with a peak population of perhaps ten thousand souls.

The Era of Nationalist Archaeology (1958–1980)

Archaeology emerged as an official discipline in Bolivia during the late 1950s. In 1957–58, in the wake of a turbulent agrarian reform, Carlos Ponce Sanginés and a group of dedicated colleagues institutionalized Bolivian archeology. The inauguration of Bolivian archaeology coincided with the rise to power of the left-led National Revolutionary Movement (MNR). Integral to the new order, Ponce and his colleagues drew up itemized agendas for a staunchly "National Archaeology" (Ponce 1961, 1978a, 1978b, 1980) in ideological opposition to the "Neocolonial Archaeology" of Europe and North America. Putting this ideology into practice, Ponce and colleagues effectively impeded North American and European research at Tiwanaku until the early 1980s. In line with MNR political ideology, in which indigenous leaders were enlisted as the "bases" of revolution, Ponce proposed a direct historical link between Tiwanaku and contemporary Aymara communities. Tiwanaku was now considered Bolivian cultural patrimony and the Aymara represented the nation's glorious past.

Ponce and colleagues made many important contributions to Tiwanaku studies. First, Ponce sought to turn the tables on emerging interpretations of the Middle Horizon. He strove to demonstrate that

Figure 1.5 Exposed west wall of the Sunken Temple, with the Akapana in the background (after Posnansky 1945, Vol. 1).

Tiwanaku had been the densely populated center of an imperial state that extended its control across much of the Andes via military conquest. He estimated that Tiwanaku had reached an extent of some 4.2 square kilometers and had housed perhaps one hundred thousand people (Ponce 1981). He directed state-funded research programs in Tiwanaku's monumental core in the 1960s and 1970's, excavating and "curating" the Sunken Temple and Kalasasaya (Figure 1.6).[1] The ambitious and heavily criticized reconstruction of these complexes succeeded in aggrandizing them as monuments worthy of an optimistic national spirit. Ironically, as Lanning pointed out, it served to strengthen the popular idea that Tiwanaku was primarily a ceremonial center.

Second, Ponce and colleagues argued that Tiwanaku had developed over a long prehispanic history that originated in formative Wankarani and Chiripa cultures. At the heart of Ponce's chronology is a three-stage evolutionary sequence that, much like V. Gordon Childe's narrative for the rise of Mesopotamian civilization (1936), grounds Tiwanaku cultural expansion in increasing surplus and the rise of cities. According to Ponce (1980, 1981), Tiwanaku had persisted as a self-sufficient hamlet for several centuries, until AD 1–100. On the basis of excavations in the Kalasasaya, he divided this long era into two phases: Tiwanaku I and II. Agricultural intensification during these phases, according to him, had fostered population growth, economic specialization, and sociopolitical hierarchy. Following early urbanism in Tiwanaku III, the city experienced a period of "mature" development in Tiwanaku IV. At this point, Tiwanaku began to establish secondary urban centers in nearby regions. During the final Imperial Stage, or Tiwanaku V, Tiwanaku expanded vastly and by military might outside of the Lake Titicaca Basin.

Multinational Archaeology (1980–Present)

Following a Bolivian warming toward international research in the 1980s, intensive research on Tiwanaku commenced in earnest. Much of this research has been collaborative; projects have involved researchers and students from multiple continents and numerous institutions. In Tiwanaku and its immediate hinterland, the multidisciplinary effort known as Project Wila Jawira coordinated large-scale excavations at Tiwanaku sites, vast regional surveys in surrounding landscapes, and investigations of past productive systems and climatic conditions (Kolata 1996a, 2003a). Such intensive and widely cast research was in keeping with Alan Kolata's mission (2003a:3), as general director, of clarifying

---

[1] The Sunken Temple refers to what Ponce (1980, 1981, 1990) and others (Kolata 1993a) term the "Semi-subterranean Temple."

Figure 1.6 The west balcony wall of the Kalasasaya at the time of its reconstruction (photo by Gregorio Cordero Miranda, courtesy of Alexei Vranich and the Dirección Nacional de Arqueología, Bolivia).

"the relationship of Tiwanaku as a total cultural phenomenon to its surrounding environmental matrix."

Synthesizing much of this research, Kolata's (1993a, 2003b) interpretive vision encompasses three interwoven focuses. First, he interprets Tiwanaku political economy as a balanced, state-managed *troika* consisting in the exploitation of lake resources, extensive herding of llamas and alpacas, and most importantly, intensive farming of raised field systems in the low *pampas* or plains near the lake shore. Second, Kolata interprets Tiwanaku cities as intensely hierarchical centers of elite power and authority that embodied a compelling, conservative, and sacred cosmology. Third, he interprets Tiwanaku influence outside of its heartland as consisting of direct colonization and more indirect but unequal clientage relations that turned on the cyclical movement of massive state-run llama caravans (1992, 1993b). Championing Ponce's position, Kolata interprets Tiwanaku as a highly centralized, autochthonous state with densely populated cities that thrived most critically on intensive, centrally controlled farming and herding.

Ongoing research in the south-central Andes both refines and challenges aspects of this model. It encompasses four trajectories that together provide novel perspectives on cultural development in the south-central Andes. First, new research collectively indicates that Tiwanaku influence was highly strategic rather than territorial and contiguous. In many regions, it was predicated on trade, cultural influence, or religious proselytism rather than political hegemony and control (Janusek 2004a; Stanish 2002). New research encourages consideration of intricate and flexible models of regional integration. David Browman (1978a, 1980, 1981, 1997a) considers Tiwanaku a federation based on "economic and theological ties rather than political expediency" (1981:416–417). Rautaro Nuñez and Tom Dillehay (1995[1979]; also Dillehay and Nuñez 1988) consider Tiwanaku a magnet trade hub for cyclical llama caravan networks that had thrived for centuries before state emergence. Such research casts a critical eye on traditional models of states and statecraft, and inspires multicentered rather than strictly "core-periphery" models of state development and hegemony.

Grounded in such insights and with ample bodies of new data, archaeologists working in the Tiwanaku heartland now stress the roles of local groups and communities in Tiwanaku political economy and sociopolitical organization. It is now clear that intensive farming and herding developed out of the local knowledge and skills of early lake-adapted communities (Erickson 1985, 1988, 1992, 1993; Janusek 2001; Stanish 1994, 2003). Clark Erickson suggests that, in most regions, state control over intensive farming was minimal. Regional studies in the Tiwanaku heartland indicate that for several centuries, local leaders and communities had managed such enterprises (Albarracin-Jordan 1996a, 1996b; Janusek and Kolata 2003, 2004). Juan Albarracin-Jordan interprets heartland settlement networks as consisting of "nested hierarchies" of semiautonomous communities integrated by religious ideology more than by political hegemony. Research in Tiwanaku's two heartland urban centers, Tiwanaku and Lukurmata, further complicates traditional ideas. Marc Bermann's (1994, 1997, 2003) research in Lukurmata indicates that local households and communities responded to regional conditions and temporal shifts that transcended state rise and collapse. State incorporation, he argues, was just one moment in the long historical trajectory of the community.

Drawing on extensive excavations at Tiwanaku and Lukurmata, I (Janusek 2002, 2003b, 2004a, 2004b, 2007a) argue that Tiwanaku was an incorporative religious, economic, and sociopolitical phenomenon that successfully forged a vast and coherent cultural identity out of profound social diversity. Tiwanaku, Lukurmata, and their respective hinterlands followed different historical trajectories and maintained discrete identities throughout the dynamic phases of state rise, consolidation, and collapse.

A third research trajectory explores the meaning and history of monumentality at Tiwanaku. Kolata interprets Tiwanaku as a tightly organized cosmogram attuned to celestial cycles such as the sun's daily path and aligned with prominent mountain peaks such as Kimsachata to the south and Illimani to the east (Kolata 1996b; Kolata and Ponce 1992). Linda Manzanilla's excavation in the Akapana (1992) reveals a long history of ritual activity spanning the entire Tiwanaku Period (Alconini 1995). More recent research indicates that Pumapunku was an extensive monumental complex with a complicated local history (Escalante 1997; Portugal Ortiz 1992; Vranich 1999). Other monumental complexes were integrally linked with elite residences or "palaces" (Couture 2002; Kolata 1993a). Tiwanaku incorporated several such complexes, each with distinct architectural configurations, life histories, and religious meanings. Monolithic portals, including the intricately carved Sun Portal, facilitated movement into and between them (Protzen and Nair 2000, 2002).

Specialized analyses offer further insight into Tiwanaku's cultural foundations and political economy. Ceramic analyses provide a stylistic chronology for the prehispanic Lake Titicaca Basin (Albarracin-Jordan and Mathews 1990; Bandy 2001; Janusek 2003a; Lemuz 2001; Stanish and Steadman 1994) and indicate that pottery was socially and ritually sententious (Janusek 2002, 2003a, 2005b). Faunal analyses point to the increasing significance of large camelids – and especially llamas – in altiplano diet and political economy (Webster 1993; Webster and Janusek 2003). Archaeobotanical analysis of carbonized plant remains indicates that altiplano diets also included tubers, quinoa, beans, and maize (Wright, Hastorf, and Lennstrom 2003), and that diet differed significantly among communities and ethnic groups. Lithic analysis locates the sources of highly valued stones such as basalt and obsidian, and suggests that certain specialties, such as crafting obsidian arrow points, were driven by state demands (Giesso 2000, 2003). Bronze metallurgy also was a highly specialized craft industry involving complex and diversified alloys that served monumental construction and elite adornment (Lechtman 1997, 1998, 2003). Bioarchaeological analyses of human remains reveals fascinating patterns of human migration and body modification and confirms that Tiwanaku was both imperial and yet socially and culturally diversified (Blom 1999, 2005).

An Overview of Tiwanaku Cultural Development

Ongoing research in the south-central Andes provides a framework for understanding the chronology of prehispanic cultural development in the Lake Titicaca Basin and its environs. The rise of complex society and the history of Tiwanaku's rise and fall occurred over several successive periods. The four periods discussed in this book span nearly three thousand years. Archaeologists identify historical periods by noting changes in characteristic material correlates such as artifacts, architecture, productive systems, spatial organization, and settlement patterns. Measuring history requires both relative and absolute chronological methods (Figure 1.7). That is, archaeologists seriate, comparing material styles across contexts (among regions, sites, or areas within a site) to determine contemporaneity, and employ radiometric measurements to locate particular contexts in an objective time frame. Chronology provides archaeologists a shared idiom for discussing cultural developments in a world region.

The Early-Middle Formative Periods

The Early-Middle Formative periods span 1500–200 BC and correspond with the Initial period and Early Horizon of the standard central Andean chronology. As yet little known, the Early Formative defines the first permanently settled villages in the Lake Titicaca Basin and a shift from the preceding Late Archaic period (~5000–1500 BC) to sedentism and agropastoral resource strategies. Diet now included modest proportions of domesticated plants and animals; yet, most communities still hunted, foraged, and fished. Early Formative sites were relatively small and tended to cluster near natural springs and streams above low marshy flatlands or *pampas*. People began crafting and using pottery to cook, store, and serve food, and some regions, such as the Taraco Peninsula, gave rise to early religious art and ceremonial structures (Bandy 2001; Beck 2004a).

Beginning around 800 BC, the Middle Formative was characterized by the development of two regional cultural complexes, the first complex societies, and a widespread ritual tradition known as Yayamama. Centered in the northern basin, Qaluyu comprised sites with distinctive decorated pottery and platforms with sunken courts. Inhabitants of Qaluyu sites cultivated high-altitude crops, herded camelids, and harvested river and lake resources. They established settlements in warmer, subaltiplano valleys and cultivated long-distance trade routes to acquire valued mineral resources such as obsidian. Far more is known about Chiripa in the southern basin. Chiripa communities clustered near lake edges and emphasized lacustrine pursuits in diversified local economies that also included farming, herding, and hunting. Particularly dense Chiripa settlement emerged on the Taraco Peninsula, where large sites incorporated ceremonial enclosures and monumental platforms with sunken courts. Elaborate pottery served ritual events and communal consumption.

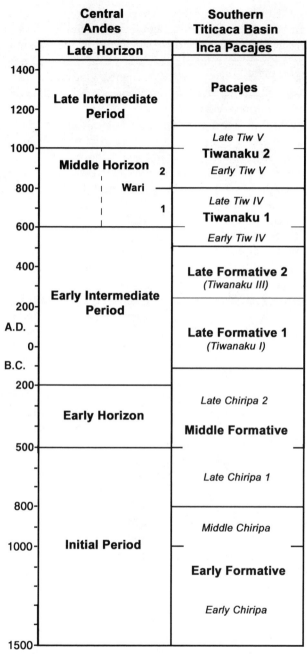

Figure 1.7 Chronological chart for the Central Andes and the Lake Titicaca Basin.

Qaluyu and Chiripa were characterized by networks of interacting communities, and many important settlements emerged in areas outside of their immediate zones. Large sites participated in the Yayamama ritual tradition, a pan-regional religious ideology manifested in sunken courts, stone sculptures, and ritual paraphernalia. Questions addressed in Chapter 3 include: What were these complexes? What integrated them, and what distinguished them?

The Early-Middle Formative witnessed significant cultural development across the south-central Andes, where communities interacted via long-distance trade networks facilitated most critically by llama caravans. Important cultural developments are coming to light in Potosí and southern Bolivia, northern Chile, southern Peru, and the eastern Andean valleys of central Bolivia. A particularly early and long-lived culture known as Wankarani coalesced before 2000 BC just south of the Lake Titicaca Basin. Wankarani consisted of interlinked, semi-independent communities that were particularly adept at herding and trading, harvesting river resources, and cultivating some of the driest salt-encrusted soils in the Andes. Cultural continuity at Wankarani settlements throughout the Formative is astounding. While ritual was well-developed, Wankarani communities, unlike those in the Lake Titicaca basin, emphasized household and intracommunity rites.

The Late Formative Period

Until very recently the Late Formative was a chronological black hole in our knowledge of cultural development in the Lake Titicaca Basin. It corresponds roughly with the Central Andean Early Intermediate Period. Ongoing research, summarized in Chapter 3, is finally amending this situation. Archaeologists have defined two clear phases for the Lake Titicaca Basin, Late Formative 1 and 2 (200 BC–AD 250 and AD 250–500; Bandy 2001; Janusek 2004b; Lemuz 2001; Stanish 2003). In Late Formative 1, the Pukara polity emerged out of the Qaluyu cultural complex and came to predominate in the northern basin. Archaeologists disagree on whether Pukara was an interaction network, a federation, or a state (Lumbreras 1981; Mujica 1978; Stanish 2003). Many sites within and just beyond the Pukara heartland most likely were quasi-independent ritual-political centers. What is clear is that trading expanded, especially in the acquisition and movement of valued consumable items and highly valued materials such as obsidian, and communities intensified their herding and farming strategies. Pukara culture also correlated with innovations in ceramic and metal technology, especially in objects destined for adornment and ritual. Pukara groups influenced and interacted with communities in warmer valleys to the east and west, and with inhabitants of rising political-ritual centers in the southern basin.

Many polities developed out of Chiripa culture in the southern Lake Titicaca Basin. As I write, archaeologists are illuminating cultural development in the region. No regional polity comparable to Pukara developed here until AD 200, after Pukara's regional influence had begun to wane. Numerous ritual-political centers, each the head of a multicommunity polity, arose in the region, including Palermo in Juli, Ckackachipata in Ccapia, Lukurmata in the Katari Valley, Kala Uyuni on the Taraco Peninsula, Khonkho Wankane in Machaca, and Tiwanaku in the Tiwanaku Valley. Most new centers were located at the peripheries of Middle Formative political communities, indicating that the transition from Middle to Late Formative involved dramatic political change. As they did in the northern basin, communities here expanded trade networks and intensified herding and farming activities. The most important sites, now located near inland floodplains or spring-fed marshes (*bofedals*), interacted, allied, and competed with one another. Ceramic, lithic, and metal technologies experienced significant innovation, but the fruits of the most skilled production were destined for exclusive groups and ceremonies. By AD 300, largely high-status groups were acquiring decorated pottery for local rituals and wrought bronze objects for personal adornment. This would change significantly under Tiwanaku's emergent regime, circa AD 500.

Cultural development continued in regions adjacent to the altiplano, though they were inextricably linked to concurrent changes in the altiplano. Some archaeologists interpret evidence for altiplano stylistic influence in the subaltiplano valleys of southern Peru, northern Chile, and central Bolivia as evidence for altiplano colonization. Ongoing research questions such assumptions. Some archaeologists point out that stylistic similarities across the south-central Andes point to multicentered interaction and influence (Goldstein 2005; Nuñez and Dillehay 1995). Vibrant interregional interaction gave rise to vital local cultural developments, including the Alto Ramirez communities of northern Chile, the Huaracane culture of southern Peru, and the strategic trading hubs of Mizque, Bolivia. New evidence highlights the problems inherent in assuming an altiplano-dominated perspective of south-central Andean prehistory.

The Tiwanaku Period

Toward the end of Late Formative 2, Tiwanaku emerged out of networks of interacting and fluid polities as the primary cultural, political, and ceremonial center in the Lake Titicaca Basin. Chapters 3 through 6 discuss some of the likely processes behind this profound transformation. Yet the question remains: Why Tiwanaku? To varying degrees, environmental shift, changing trade routes, competitive political practices, and a vibrant ritual cult each played a part. Ongoing research suggests that Tiwanaku's rise and initial expansion were grounded more profoundly in consensus and cultural affiliation than coercion or militarism. Tiwanaku's early success, in great part, was its ability to incorporate geographical and social diversity through a flexible, elegant cosmology and prestigious goods and practices that gave each group good material, ideological, and affective reasons for being part of the polity.

Archaeologists now consider the Tiwanaku Period as consisting of two principal phases, what I term from here on Tiwanaku 1 and 2.[2] It corresponds with the central Andean Middle Horizon. Tiwanaku 1, dating to AD 500–800, begins with the sudden appearance of a new range of elaborate, decorated red-slipped ("redware") pottery. In a sharp break from Late Formative 2, virtually everyone now had access to elaborate ceramic vessels for household consumption and feasting. Settlement patterns formed a four-tier settlement hierarchy in Tiwanaku's immediate core zone, defined here as the Tiwanaku and Katari valleys and the Taraco Peninsula. Nevertheless, clear settlement clusters and regional boundaries suggest that local communities remained largely intact (Albarracin-Jordan 1996a; Bandy 2001; Janusek and Kolata 2003). Tiwanaku agriculturalists intensified farming, which included the expansion of raised field systems ingeniously adapted to the marshy pampas so prevalent near lake shores in the basin. Herding and the exploitation of domesticated camelids for meat, wool, and transport also intensified precipitously. Yet fishing, hunting, and harvesting lake resources such as *totora* reed, remained critical to the productive strategies of many local communities. Integrating these diverse economies, in part through an effective calendar system, was critical to Tiwanaku's success as a sociopolitical and ideological enterprise.

In Tiwanaku 1, Tiwanaku expanded into a bustling urban center, as did Lukurmata in Katari, which remained for at least three hundred years a primary regional center and Tiwanaku's "second city." Urban inhabitants were differentiated by kin ties, occupation, ethnicity, and increasingly

---

[2] The phase names I and other archaeologists typically employ are "Tiwanaku IV" and "Tiwanaku V," following Ponce's chronology (Tiwanaku I–III corresponding with the Late Formative; see Janusek 2003a). I use Tiwanaku 1 and 2 in this book because Ponce's designations do not make sense in the present context, and because these terms parallel advances in the chronology of Tiwanaku's contemporary, Wari.

through time, social status. Although Tiwanaku's highest elites included castes of priests, dynasties of kings and their factions most likely ruled Tiwanaku. Tiwanaku rulers and architects planned and built massive ritual complexes such as the Akapana and Pumapunku, each an integrated temple ensemble that expressed common ideological principles, if in very distinct styles. Regional centers in the core and beyond can be identified by the presence of more modest monumental complexes with similar spatial and architectural patterns. Nevertheless, Tiwanaku monumental complexes differed significantly within Tiwanaku and among such local centers.

Tiwanaku presence beyond the core was highly complex and strategic. It ranged from periodic interaction and local diasporic movement to state political hegemony, forming an intricate polity that looked in plan like a discontinuous and multiplex web rather than a contiguous nation with "hard" political boundaries. Interaction between Tiwanaku and other centers was multidirectional and operated at various social scales; if Tiwanaku colonized and influenced local cultures, local cultures "colonized" the Tiwanaku center and fostered its local cultural and political development. Tiwanaku leaders were particularly interested in lands that produced a particular range of highly valued goods. Outside of the altiplano heartland and its productive farmland, vast pasturage, extensive salt pans, and other resources, Tiwanaku leaders sought minerals such as obsidian and sodalite and lowland crops such as maize and coca. Altiplano groups colonized warm valley zones, such as Moquegua, Peru, and Cochabamba, Bolivia, expressly to cultivate and process valued lowland crops on a grand scale. Trade networks intensified ferociously as age-old caravan routes became veritable highways linking distant peoples and places. Yet Tiwanaku was an incorporative political and religious formation that meshed creatively and profoundly with local political and ideological systems. Colonization in many cases was not a result of centrally directed "geopolitical pragmatism" (Goldstein 2005:47) but the voluntary movement of local communities to valley lowlands or other highland areas, where they resided as "expatriate" communities dedicated to a variety of productive enterprises.

Tiwanaku 2, spanning AD 800–1100, began with the creation of a more tightly centralized political economy. Though difficult to prove, this transformation may have corresponded with the rise of new dynasty. Much of Tiwanaku itself was renovated in a massive program of urban renewal that left much of the core devoted to elite activity and state-sponsored ceremonies. Elite residences such as Putuni were refurbished, enlarged, and essentially converted into modest palaces, demonstrating that Tiwanaku society was now supremely class-riven and hierarchical.

Critical changes occurred outside of Tiwanaku, both in the heartland and in many peripheral regions. Lukurmata waned as a regional center as most of the Katari Valley pampa was turned into a raised-field farming estate. Tiwanaku ceremony and pilgrimage intensified at ritual sites such as the Island of the Sun, and the Moquegua Valley was reorganized as an integrated province to more effectively produce vast quantities of maize to support elite-sponsored ceremonies in the core. Tiwanaku ruling and elite groups, it appears, now developed transformative strategies of state control and appropriation to assert greater control over key resources and local socioeconomic networks. Such transformations, in tandem with a deteriorating climate after AD 1100, eventually helped precipitate state collapse.

Tiwanaku and Wari

Tiwanaku interacted intensively with Wari, the other major highland Middle Horizon state. Wari was a parallel but entirely distinct cultural and political phenomenon centered in the central Andes, in the mountainous sierra of Ayacucho, Peru. Wari thrived at about the same time as Tiwanaku. As discussed in Chapter 7, Wari emerged out of Warpa, an early cultural complex punctuated by local ceremonial-political centers such as Ñawimpukyo (Leoni 2004). Like Tiwanaku, Wari drew on multiple cultural influences, including Nasca iconography and Tiwanaku ideology. It differed from Tiwanaku in many respects, including its overall manner of establishing political hegemony, an emphasis on sierra mountain slope terracing, the construction of well-planned and tightly controlled regional centers, and in its key ceremonial structures and ritual practices.

Wari experienced two phases of cultural development, Wari 1 and 2, which correlate well with, and were closely tied to, Tiwanaku's two successive phases of cultural development. Dating to AD 600–800, Wari 1 involved imperial expansion on a vast scale and the establishment of political and economic hegemony in diverse environmental zones of what is now Peru. Dating to AD 800–1000, Wari 2 witnessed political consolidation, productive intensification, and the development of a tightly controlled infrastructure. Most researchers consider Wari an imperial state that incorporated vast regions (Isbell 1987; Isbell and McEwan 1991; Isbell and Schreiber 1978; Lumbreras 1974, 1981; Schreiber 1992, 2001). While this clearly was the case, Wari shared often overlooked cultural parallels with Tiwanaku, such as a profoundly religious foundation, highly strategic and discontinuous territoriality, and great social and ethnic diversity. Yet, Wari and Tiwanaku imperialism and ideology differed remarkably. Unintentionally, and downplayed in later histories, Wari appears to have paved the route for Inca imperial expansion some four centuries after its collapse.

Cultural similarities and differences crystallized in Tiwanaku-Wari border zones, most notably in the dry, warm valleys of southern Peru. Clients, colonists, and affiliates of both Tiwanaku and Wari sought key mineral and consumable resources in valley zone such as Arequipa and Moquegua. Whereas Tiwanaku colonists settled naturally fertile lower valleys, Wari colonists occupied mountaintops and slopes in the upper valleys overlooking them (Feldman 1989; Williams and Nash 2002). While Tiwanaku colonists harvested corn to produce mass quantities of maize *chicha* or beer (Goldstein 1993a, 2003), Wari colonists developed irrigated terraces and cultivated orchards to produce mass quantities of *molle* berry *chicha* (Goldstein and Carter 2004; Tung 2003). The two states developed much like distinct nations or ethnicities. In Tiwanaku and Wari 1, the two polities came in contact and maintained an overall relationship of tense *détente*, most likely punctuated by periodic conflict. In Tiwanaku and Wari 2, international relations in local regions appear to have warmed, facilitated by cooperative trading strategies and inclusive elite-sponsored feasts and ceremonies (Williams and Nash 2002). Yet whatever cozy alliances characterized Tiwanaku-Wari relations eventually disintegrated. Sometime after AD 1000 Tiwanaku settlements were destroyed and Wari sites were abandoned, whether at the hand of one or the other or of local or neighboring populations.

Post-Tiwanaku

By AD 1050, Wari had collapsed and Tiwanaku was in trouble. As discussed in Chapter 8, Wari and Tiwanaku disintegration had something to do with their mutual development and interaction. The twelfth through fourteenth centuries were a chaotic time throughout the Andean highlands. Middle Horizon states disintegrated and households, communities, ethnic groups, and polities adapted to profoundly shifting social and environmental conditions. Tiwanaku collapse was a drawn out process in which monumental complexes were submitted to memory, elite palaces were razed to the ground, and key icons of elite ancestry and power were ritual mutilated and destroyed. In the following Late Intermediate Period, groups abandoned old nuclear centers, built refuge locales in the mountains of ethnic border zones, abandoned raised field systems to pursue more diversified careers, created mortuary rites that involved aboveground burial towers, and designed new brands of material culture. Altiplano communities initiated a cultural revolution that encompassed a new non-Tiwanaku cosmology grounded in a sociopolitical landscape of hierarchical but decentralized federations and polities. It was this cultural landscape that the Inca would encounter, conquer, and claim to be their mythical home during the fifteenth century.

A Theoretical Perspective for Andean Studies

Guiding any interpretation of past human societies are particular sociopolitical contexts, theoretical underpinnings, and individual perspectives. Indeed, multiple critical interpretations of a past civilization are possible (Chapman 2003). In approaching a vast, enduring, and complex civilization such as Tiwanaku, we cannot hope to explain everything in one fell swoop any more than a person in the past, even a divine king, had a coherent idea of what was Tiwanaku. In advancing a plurality of perspectives (Wylie 2002), I do not support an extreme relativism in which all interpretations are good and legitimate. I advance an *epistemic relativism* (Bhaskar 1978:6), which recognizes that any understanding, including our deepest notions of what constitutes a person, family, and society-indeed, your very sense of self -is rooted in specific times, cultures, and conditions. Without abandoning objectivity or empirical research we recognize that reality is plural and all knowledge socially constructed (Berger and Luckmann 1966; Bourdieu 1990; Marx 1986[1888]), and that, as Sartre concluded (1992:400), "no point of view on the totality is conceivable."

Since the 1950s, most archaeological interpretation of long-term change in the Anglo-American tradition has focused on abstract, general processes. In *cultural evolution* models, cultural change followed regular pathways of development in which "simple" egalitarian societies gradually become more hierarchical and differentiated. One influential lineage (e.g., Service 1975) proposed that egalitarian bands developed into big-man societies headed by charismatic "networkers," which, in some cases, developed into hierarchical "paramount" chiefdoms and states. Many archaeologists studying the reasons behind these transformations focus on the operation of metahuman social or environmental *processes*, which are considered to externally impact human thought and activity. Cultural ecologists view social change and state formation as products of social adaptation to changing natural environments, while systems theorists, who view complex societies as highly integrated systems of internally differentiated subsystems, treat their transformations as the outcomes of social or environmental stresses. In a different vein, many structuralists view social institutions and built environments – including cities, monuments, and modified landscapes – as the material expressions of shared mental templates, and change as the outcome of social conflict or external change (such as environmental shift).

Emphasis on process or structure pushes us beyond the idea that past societies were homogeneous archaeological cultures of shared, static activities and values. We no longer view cultural change as inevitable, whether gently guided by the divine will of an omnipotent deity or as heroic narratives limited to the great achievements of a "few good men." Yet overemphasizing process leaves us wondering where the messiness of history fits in; about the place of intricate and volatile cultural revolutions that characterized, say, waves of decolonization and ethnogenesis in Latin America and Africa; and about the people who make history daily, respond to environmental change, constitute social systems, and think cultural templates. History and humanity become helpless pawns determined by abstract but unstoppable teleological, environmental, social, or cognitive forces. In some cases, metahuman "systems" and "structures" are breathed a life of their own and treated as living beings. Pointing out what should be obvious, Anthony Giddens (1979:7) notes that "social systems have no purposes, reasons, or needs whatsoever." Societies are created and reformulated, if sometimes violently, through human activity and via relations among groups of people and their built and natural environments. Indeed, as Trouillot's introductory quote affirms, and as we know in a practical sense, history is messy, and immediate, for its subjects.

In interpreting Tiwanaku, I adopt a perspective of practice theory that emphasizes the myriad ways humans *dwell* in the world (Ingold 1993; also Barrett 2000; de Certeau 1984). This involves perspectives of the microscale of human behavior and history that we cannot always directly "see" in the dirt but indirectly infer in the broader history and character of past civilizations. At base is a recursive approach that views cultural traditions and social structures as both the deep generators and hard consequences of human thought and action. Pierre Bourdieu (1990:53) calls these dynamic traditions "structuring structures" because they simultaneously guide and result from day-to-day activity. We all go about life working, relaxing, or perhaps procrastinating, but both following routines and improvising – say, taking a new route home from work or changing a career or hometown – but usually not wanting to radically change things. So for the most part, society and the cultural logic that informs our decision to retrace an old route or forge another is continually remade. We all know quite a bit about the world we inhabit; we have mastered complex routines such as driving, shopping, or reading the newspaper. We do not need to think about these things too much; they are part of our tacit knowledge and shape our common sense. This knowledge is specific to our place, time, and culture.

Yet we know more. We have a more penetrating understanding of society and the world that Giddens (1984) calls *discursive knowledge*. We have opinions, political views, ideas for positive change, or cynical views of humanity that we regularly air, even if most often in our heads or among our dearest friends (see Gramsci 1971:323–377). Empowered with both tacit masteries and such penetrating knowledge, and applying such masteries and knowledge to new domains and circumstances throughout our lives (Sewell 1992), our actions continuously elicit changes, if largely in local communities and contexts, in relation to unforeseen circumstances, and sometimes with unexpected consequences.

Further, as we follow routines or forge new routes, the world around us changes. Our thoughts and activities, if guided by shared ideals, engage a dynamic and potentially volatile world of other people with discursive knowledge and improvised activities, of ever-shifting circumstances, and of cultural and environmental shifts. Some circumstances and human actions are more potent than others, such as Mount Vesuvius's eruption over Pompeii on a normal day in August, AD 79; or the destruction of the World Trade Center in New York on another such day in September, 2001. Such catastrophes do not happen in a vacuum. Like everyday activities, their impact is shaped by their cultural and historical situations, and those situations, grounded in a specific permutation of human relations, define the impact and significance of such events. The world changes as we constantly re-create and refashion it but also in ways that we cannot always predict.

In following and manipulating cultural traditions, human activity is eminently social. It occurs in "hard" communities such as families, institutions (such as a school or workplace), and political organizations. It also engages "softer" or more imagined social fields such as ethnicities (Anderson 1983) and intertwined "communities of practice" in which specific roles, identities, and occupations are learned (Lave and Wenger 1991). Any such community or field is both hard and soft to the extent that it inhabits physical places, involves concrete activities and purposes, and yet motivates activity even though one does not always interact with its members and environment. Each differentiates itself from others via habitual practices, religious ideals, and cultural values. Yet in any society, people participate in and identify with multiple such communities. In them they develop values, identities, roles, status, and positions of power (Holland et al. 1998). Throughout people's lives, as they learn more and more about the various logics and quirks of the disciplines, institutions, or communities they engage and inhabit, they change them. No communities or institutions would be quite the same without you and your relations with those whom you love, work with, or fight. Given particular situations and people, and the actions and relations they engender, societies may endure generations or transform profoundly.

Such a practice approach has important consequences for understanding complex societies and long term history. Archaeologists (including me) sometimes treat past societies as material things themselves. Types and scales of society such as household and state are sometimes attributed too much "noun-ness" (Geertz 1980). They are treated as essential, static entities. A practice approach discourages essentialism and encourages critical attention to human diversity, recurring practices, and the historical dynamics constituting a society. A past household, we might agree, was a minimal co-residential group with corporate functions and shared tasks, including production, consumption, distribution, and social reproduction. Yet households around the world are dynamic even in a single generation, experiencing regular cycles of expansion, fission, and trauma (Hirth 1993; Tourtellot 1988). Further, households are not homogeneous, egalitarian entities with singular goals. They are continually constructed, eminently conflictive domains of individuals differing in age, gender, role, and power; each with unique agendas and interests (Hendon 1996; Joyce 1993; Wright 1991). In many societies, the concreteness attributed to a household forms part of a broader ethnic or state ideology that affords such groups symbolic unity and coherence (Gillespie 2000). For example, it is a highly idiosyncratic Western ideology that fuels the popular equivalence of nuclear family and household as a "natural," primordial group.

States notoriously present themselves as concrete, enduring entities of homogenous citizens with common experiences and goals and a shared past and future. Reflecting and reiterating current national ideologies, many archaeological models take too literally "the *idea* of the state" (Corrigan and Sayer 1985:7) and its lofty messages of impenetrability, generosity, and morality. In the past, as in the present, state rites (like the Memorial Day parade in the United States) and symbols (such as a flag) promoted emotional attachment to a powerful sense of community (Kertzer 1988). Through recurring activities and ongoing projects, the people who formed past states produced patterns amenable to archaeological detection, including a shared material culture of techniques, styles, material culture, and activities. Attention to the *cultural practices* (*sensu* Pauketat and Alt 2005) that produced such material culture emphasizes that polities such as Tiwanaku were both political organizations and imagined communities that were always under construction and in flux. Their futures were at no moment certain or secure.

Preindustrial, or *archaic states*, consisted of individuals and groups with highly diverse motivations, identities, interests, and roles, many of which transcended the limited domains of a state's immediate political boundaries and interests. Many states, archaeological research demonstrates, were intricate and dynamic confluences of interaction networks and social relations among populations differentiated according to class, ethnicity, territory, lineage, gender, and ancestry (Brumfiel 1994; Crumley 1987; Feinman 2000; Joyce, Bustamente, and Levine 2001). A state's unifying symbols and material culture served to maintain hegemony, but these symbols and materials were variously interpreted among local groups and appropriated for specific interests; in some cases, as in later Tiwanaku, to counterhegemonic ends. This may well happen when popular contradictory consciousness has intensified (Gramsci 1971:333) and when "contradictions between the world as represented" in state ideology and "the world as experienced" day-to-day "become ever more palpable" and "insupportable" (Comaroff and Comaroff 1991:26).

A broad insight entailed in such a perspective is that all human societies incorporate both egalitarian and unequal relations and hierarchical and nonheirarchical institutions. Acknowledging this encourages more intricate accounts of local trajectories of cultural development and nonessentialized interpretations of complex societies. For example, ethnographic research documents "complexity" – social ranking, craft specialization, and surplus production – in what cultural evolutionists would consider egalitarian bands in Australia and on the North American California coast (Arnold 1996). By the same token, many states incorporate egalitarian ideologies and their accompanying relations and leveling mechanisms. If religion and iconography in Classic Maya polities and Mesopotamian city-states celebrated rulers and kingship, the same media, and their corresponding *dominant ideologies*, downplayed such figures in the Mesoamerican state of Teotihuacan. In the contemporary United States, where statistics confirm an alarming trend in which the "rich get richer and poor get poorer," political ideology emphasizing democracy and equality and a social etiquette proclaiming that "we're all middle class," *still* shape citizens' everyday practical consciousness and social interactions.

A corollary is that state centralization, today as in the past, is a complex and often fragile balance of centripetal and centrifugal forces, of diverse societies and ideologies, and of dominant values and local interests (Stein 1998). Even the most despotic states incorporate social diversity and some degree of heterarchy (Crumley 1987, 1995), by which I mean multiple local hierarchies and nodes of social power that are perhaps complementary in role but potentially conflictive in interest. Today, cities interact and compete in this way (consider competition for tourists and businesses via "cultural" sites and skyscrapers!). Resistance to or at least nonidentification with elite power and centralizing forces, whether overtly expressed politically or more covertly expressed in local "hidden transcripts" (Scott 1990), stylistic expressions, and religious attitudes, is endemic to hierarchical systems. In the United States, consider the enduring "rebel flag," local militias, and more subtle local expressions of identity in regional dialects, clothing styles, body mutilation, and "small-town" rituals.

Armed with local resources (such as a "right to vote"), tacit masteries, and penetrating political views and other discursive knowledge, all people have some power in society. A successful and enduring regime *must* seek popular resonance with its dominant ideologies, interests, and values, and emotional or spiritual attachment to its cultural and religious expressions. The most successful strategies foster popular consensus and emotional attachment in the sense that dominant ideologies and their "truths" are internalized as "natural" common sense, the "right" and civilized way to live, or perhaps the way the world has been and should remain. When such conditions are breached, or when a regime's legitimacy erodes, groups will seek cultural coherence and social resonance through a variety of subtle and, perhaps ultimately, not so subtle means. In conjunction with major environmental or ideological shifts and historical circumstances or events, a social order may change profoundly and rapidly. Such a volatile juncture, I argue, characterized Tiwanaku state collapse.

An important element in such a practice perspective is a focus on human-landscape interrelations. We can sift out two dimensions of these dynamic relations. First, as some early Tiwanaku explorers realized, environments both limit and shape cultural processes and characteristics. In the high altiplano, where warmth, oxygen, and rain are in relative demand, some such conditions are evident. Societies are further affected by environmental shifts, most notably recurring climatic cycles (such as El Niño events on the Pacific coast) and more severe thresholds that may catalyze major changes in a society or world region (Kolata 2000; Moseley 2001). To be sure, human societies can adapt creatively to changing natural conditions and periodic catastrophes. Yet landscape conditions and environmental cycles and transformations shape human livelihoods and values.

Second, physical spaces are social places that constitute meaningful and in may cases sacred landscapes. Archaeology always has attended to space, whether considering networks of cities and villages or the locations of farming and irrigation systems. Yet landscape is often thought to provide a passive, a *priori* backdrop for human action and cultural development (Knapp and Ashmore 1999; Smith 2003). In the past as today, humans transformed, experienced, and afforded meaning to the landscapes they inhabited. Their identities and memories were inscribed in them, whether they were largely "natural" or entirely anthropogenic. And such places were not limited to what we normally consider "archaeological sites." Outside of the settlements where humans dwelled were other meaningful places, including majestic mountain peaks, mineral sources, farming lands, pasture fields, and well-trodden roads that facilitated trade and pilgrimage.

Human-landscape relations are dynamic, interactive, and intimate. Landscapes must be learned (Rockman 2003) in dynamic communities of practice. Knowledge regarding resource locations, productive potential, and climatic cycles and thresholds must be transmitted and augmented over generations to facilitate cultural adaptation. In the Andean altiplano, such knowledge facilitated the development of large-scale irrigated farming systems known as "raised fields" that turned vast floodplains into agricultural breadbaskets, and that even today shape climatic conditions and cultural uses (see Chapter 5). Past societies tended to attribute religious importance to natural features and cycles, giving rise to sacred landscapes that figure prominently in myth, ritual, and pilgrimage. Settlements and monuments incorporated key elements of such features and cycles, thereby appropriating their essential elements and timeless rhythms to the rhythms of social life and ritual. In Tiwanaku as in other Andean societies, the sky, mountains, water, and specific vegetation figured prominently in urban planning, architectural construction, and religious ideology. In turn, the ritual and symbolism of Tiwanaku monuments shaped social identity, state formation, and knowledge of the landscape and its resources.

A practice perspective that emphasizes the variable means by which humans dwell and act in the world, views the past as the product of culturally guided human activity and intimate human-landscape relations. In focusing on the long term, we do not accept that change just happened, that tribal societies inevitably evolved into states, or that day-to-day events and human intentions were insignificant. As Trouillot alludes in the opening quotation, long-term history is the product of what would seem infinite events, actions, and relations; all guided by particular masteries and apprehended according to the knowledge of a given time, place, and culture. Cultural continuity results from ceaseless social reproduction and recurring environmental cycles. Yet, history is cumulative. Occasionally, societies reach social thresholds, or times of pervasive tension, contradictory consciousness, and volatility engendered by any conjunction of social, economic, or ideological conditions. Such conjunctions may foster major transformations, especially in tandem with major historical events, regional circumstances, or environmental shifts. They characterized key junctures in Andean prehistory, including the emergence of formative societies, Tiwanaku's rise to power, and ultimately, its collapse.

The Chapters That Follow

In the following chapters, I elaborate a narrative of Tiwanaku history and culture drawing on past and ongoing research in the Lake Titicaca Basin and its environs. My theoretical perspective simply guides this narrative. Increasing numbers of researchers and research projects in the south-central Andes have given rise to multiple intriguing perspectives and interpretations. Interest in Tiwanaku has generated an exciting and collaborative atmosphere of intellectual interest, interaction, and debate. Encouraging this setting are impressive technological advances in archaeological methods and the growth of scientific subdisciplines. They include: archaeobotany or the study of carbonized plant remains; bioarchaeology, the study of past human remains and their chemical and genetic characteristics; geophysical survey, which detects buried features from the surface; and Geographical Information Systems analysis, which provides detailed computer models for past changes in social-landscape interactions. It is an exciting time to research and learn about this enigmatic yet remarkable civilization.

The rest of the book follows a roughly chronological trajectory. Framing each chapter is a more general thematic issue that develops this theoretical perspective. Chapter 2 discusses current geographical and social characteristics of the Lake Titicaca Basin and results of paleoenvironmental research in its environs. Chapter 3 examines the rise of social complexity in the south-central Andes by focusing on the Formative period formations that preceded and ultimately produced the Tiwanaku state. Chapter 4 is a case study of archaic urbanism that focuses on the shifting ceremonial, economic, and social characteristics of the central city. Chapter 5 discusses relations of society, landscape, and production in Tiwanaku's cultural and political heartland. Chapter 6 treats the various forms of interaction and influence that joined diverse regions into a politically integrated, culturally coherent imperial state. Chapter 7 delves into Tiwanaku's peer-state Wari and its changing interactions with Tiwanaku. Chapter 8 engages Tiwanaku collapse and the generation of new social, political, and cultural conditions in the Titicaca Basin and beyond. It was the legacy of Tiwanaku and its successor societies that first the Inca, then the Spanish, and later other Western explorers and researchers would encounter and document. In Chapter 9, I offer some conclusions and directions for future research.

Tiwanaku was a project of political integration that lasted centuries. Its primary center was a place of social, economic, and ritual encounter for communities of diverse origins, languages, and ethnicities. While in this and other respects it was like some other past civilizations, Tiwanaku was in many ways like no other. In comparing civilizations, we find that general concepts such as household, ethnicity, and state, while heuristically necessary and useful, put inordinate emphasis on categorical types, broad evolutionary trajectories, and metahuman processes (Yoffee 2005). This often obscures the unique history and character of particular social phenomena. Tiwanaku was an archaic state and yet a distinct example of the type. In Andean research specifically, the Inca imperial model has been imposed on pre-Inca Andean polities such as Tiwanaku. Such analogies have been useful. Nevertheless, most recent research in the south-central Andes reveals cultural patterns and political processes very different from those that had been developing in the central Andes from as early as the Foramative Period. Ongoing and future research across the continent promises to shed valuable new light on affinities, interactions, and variability among its remarkable civilizations.

2   Land and People

The Andes form a challenging and rugged land of contrasting landscapes and dynamic environments. Their natural setting influenced human lives and societies, conditioning the production and procurement of food, the directions of interaction and trade networks, and the trajectory of cultural development. Reciprocally, for hundreds of generations native Andeans worked, traversed, and transformed the landscapes they inhabited. By the time the Spanish set foot on the Pacific coast in the 1530s, much of the Andes was anthropogenic. Ancient ruins and thriving cities sprawled over coastal plains and mountain valleys, roads and paths linked distant settlements, extensive caravan routes crisscrossed the high sierra and altiplano, and terraces sculpted steep mountain slopes into productive farmlands. The Tiwanaku, like more recent native Andean peoples, viewed natural and social worlds as a conjoined reality in which human, natural, and spiritual forces interwove and interpenetrated in all aspects of life. Such a view shaped cosmology, social relations, ritual practices, and political developments in the south-central Andes.

Environment and Landscape

Background

It is difficult for many of us in our hyperspeed, digitally driven, concrete-and-steel metropolises to imagine life in a world inextricably bound to the practical rhythms of farming and herding. Over several centuries, Western minds and daily routines have been alienated from nature. Our daily environments are largely human-wrought. Remnant bits of nature are obsessively divided up and excessively manicured as lawns, parks, preserves, and subdivisions that are eminently "safe." Nature is a nostalgic symbol that, paradoxically, conjures both the domesticating hand of development and the romantic allure of exploration. It is not an imperative but a recreation, and increasingly it disappears. How rare that in the prehispanic Andes nature was the supreme source of life and power.

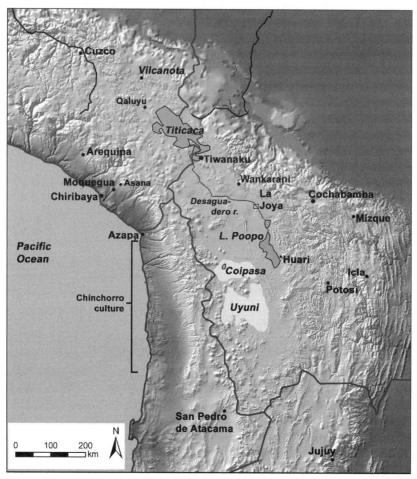

Figure 2.1 The south-central Andes (base map by Steve Wernke).

The Andean chain of South America consists of three broad zones, as narrated in the Viracocha origin myth; the arid Pacific coast, the mountainous highlands, and the humid eastern slopes, or *montaña*, which grade into the vast tropical basins of the Orinoco, Amazon, and Paraná rivers (Figure 2.1). Geologically, it is a volatile world region rife with periodic tectonic and volcanic activity. As part of dynamic global geological movements, a westward bound continental plate clashes with and rises over an eastward bound oceanic sea floor (the Nazca plate). Millions of years of such movement, begun in the Miocene epoch (23 to 5 million years ago), have caused the compression and buckling that continue to form

Figure 2.2 Llamas graze on the high *puna*.

the Andes. Framing the landform are two parallel chains: the undulating Western ("black") and rugged Eastern ("white") cordilleras.

The smaller Vilcanota range joins the two cordilleras in what is now southern Peru. North of Vilcanota, the sierra highlands of the Central Andes consist of long parallel and shorter perpendicular ranges that form alternating high grasslands, ideal for pasturage, and intermontane basins, amenable to farming. South of Vilcanota, in the south-central Andes, the cordilleras part widely to form the altiplano. The altiplano is an immense mountainous plateau (3,800–4,000) some 800 km north-to-south. Dominating the northern altiplano is the Lake Titicaca drainage basin. The southern altiplano consists of drier grasslands and salt flats, residues of extensive lakes that have been receding since the Pleistocene (Lavenu 1992). Drainage proceeds slowly north-south via the Desaguadero River, which flows from Lake Titicaca toward Lake Poopó and the arid salt pans of Uyuni and Coipasa.

Like many ecological boundaries, the Vilcanota range and its La Raya pass, which joins the central and south-central highlands, were of great importance to prehispanic Andean societies. For the Inca, it was the source of their sacred river, the Urubamba. Every June, as part of Inca solstice rites, ritual specialists known as *Tarpantay* would make a pilgrimage to the place in reverence to Inti, the sun (Zuidema 1999). Such ritual significance overlaid and elaborated earlier practices. As the ecological divide between sierra maize-growing and altiplano tuber/quinoa-growing societies, Vilcanota had for centuries formed a key cultural boundary. During the Middle Horizon, it marked the volatile border zone between the Tiwanaku and Wari states.

Landscape, Dwelling, and Production

The Andean highlands of southern Peru and northern Bolivia are most likely where Andean camelids were first domesticated, and it formed the zone of their greatest concentration and importance upon the arrival of Europeans (Figure 2.2). Highland Andean civilizations such as Tiwanaku were agropastoral rather than simply agrarian, meaning that herding and farming formed conjoined elements of their productive regimes. Tall and slender llamas, most important during life as pack animals, and shorter and squatter alpacas, highly prized for their fine and fluffy wool, were domesticated as early as seven thousand years ago. Their gregarious behavior and tendency to form male-dominated herds rendered them highly amenable to human management and breeding. Their wild counterparts are the large gúanaco and the petite vicuña, respective progeny of wild ancestors of the llama and alpaca (Wilson 1999:84). Hunted nearly to extinction for its soft pelt, the vicuña grows extremely fine brown-and-white wool that Inca rulers had woven into colorful royal tunics. After death, llamas and alpacas provide meat for human consumption, bones for ornaments and tools, and blood and fat for religious ceremonies. Even today, few things are more powerful than a llama or alpaca sacrifice as a plea for community well-being and fertility in farming and herding (Text Box 2.1).

Hemmed in by two cordilleras, the altiplano extends from southern Peru through western Bolivia and into northern Chile and Argentina. Life here turns on the imperatives of altitude, sun, and rain. For centuries, livelihoods have been attuned to its environmental conditions and seasonal cycles. The altiplano comprises two altitude zones, the *suni* plateau of 3,800–4000 meters, and the higher mountainous *puna* of 4,000–4,800 meters. While *suni* lands can be cultivated, the *puna*, beyond the upper limits of most farming, are dedicated to grazing camelid herds and growing "bitter" potatoes. The year is defined by the annual alternation of a rainy season, from December through March, and a longer dry season running from April through November. The Titicaca region of the northern altiplano receives 700 millimeters of rainfall on average, far more in most years than the drier, salt-choked southern altiplano. Rain tends to fall in periodic, potentially catastrophic downpours during the rainy season. Vegetation primarily consists of tough alpine grasses ranging from

Box 2.1 Wilancha!

Few activities stir the contemporary imagination more than sacrifice. In the Andes, blood sacrifices, or *wilanchas*, are potent ritual practices (in Aymara, *wila* means blood). Camelid blood was among the most powerful offerings the Inca made to immanent forces of the earth, mountain peaks, and sky. Archaeological evidence for llama sacrifice indicates that as much held for their Tiwanaku and Wari predecessors. *Wilancha* traditions continue today in many Andean communities, intimately meshed with various Christian religious values and practices. *Wilanchas* are key moments in recurring calendar feasts that mesh society, religion, and economy.

In the canton of Jesus de Machaca, Bolivia, *wilancha* is the central ritual task of an annual June Solstice ceremony that involves a long sequence of ritualized activities. In the past two decades, native Andean communities have vitalized June solstice as "Aymara New Year." An ongoing reconstitution of native identity casts *wilancha* as the blood offering of one or more vital llamas in dedication to a particular community and its landscape over the course of an impending annual cycle. In Jesus de Machaca, the ritual has come to recur on the archaeological site of Khonkho Wankane, an ancient ritual-political center located in a community that was historically considered one of two complementary "heads" (literally and figuratively) of the region.

Wilancha enacts both the spiritual power and "totalizing" import of Andean ritual. As the sun rises over the crest of the Kimsachata range on the morning of June 21, a sacrificer slices open the neck of a selected llama, collecting its blood in a cup that is then sprayed eastward over an ancient stone monolith known as Tatakala, toward the rising sun and, to festive squeals, over nearby participants and observers. A ritualist simultaneously makes prayers to the major *achachilas* or sacred mountains of the surrounding eastern and western cordilleras, to which the sacrificial offering is dedicated to ensure the llama's spiritual replacement in local corrals and a good year for the encompassing community.

Yet there is more to a *wilancha* than meets the gore-turned eye. *Wilancha* in Jesus de Machaca is what the anthropologist Marcel Mauss would call a "total social fact." It is a recurring ritual practice that, much like past Tiwanaku rituals (see Chapter 4), wove together multiple strands of human activity and meaning. *Wilancha* is when representatives of each community in Jesus de Machaca gather to share news and gossip. It is also an opportunity for entrepreneurs to make a little cash by setting up kiosks selling hot cups of delicious boiled corn drink, or *api*, and fried bread. Local ceramic specialists, representing a long-term Machaca tradition, sell their wares to locals, tourists, and archaeologists. Most dramatic, by the afternoon, community members gather to elect their *mallku*, or native leader, for the coming year. Usually, such elections involve vitriolic shouting and debate. Always, it ends with feasting, dancing, and drinking, accompanied by music played by community groups on native instruments.

soft *ch'iji* to hardy *ichu*, which provides forage for camelids and building materials for humans. It includes resinous shrubs such as *thola*, which burns hot as fuel. Despite its challenges, Titicaca fostered the cultivation of numerous crops, including tubers such as potatoes, *oca*, *ulluco*, and *mashwa*; grains such as quinoa and *cañiwa*; and legumes such as *tarwi* with seeds that are extremely high in protein, and Nuñas, or "poping beans."

Over millennia, Andeans devised sophisticated ways to intensify cultivation. They devised ingenious, intensive farming and herding systems, each adapted to unique environmental conditions (see Chapters 5 and 7). They also devised ways to store key resources over the dry season and for long periods to alleviate potential drought, hail, and frost. Storage over lean times was critical. To this end, denizens of high altitudes devised complex technologies to produce eminently storable, essentially manufactured foods. These include freeze-dried potatoes, known as *chuño* and *tunta*, and sun-dried and salted llama and alpaca meat, or *charqui* (Figure 2.3). These manufactured goods helped allay chronic high-altitude stressors such as cold and hypoxia, or low oxygen tension, both of which oblige people to eat more. They also helped mitigated episodic climatic fluctuations that causes drought and pestilence.

At the heart of the northern altiplano, and presently divided between Peru and Bolivia, is the Lake Titicaca Basin. The entire drainage area covers over 50,000 square kilometers and includes diverse landscapes ranging from windswept mountainous *puna* to sun-baked lacustrine flatlands. When describing the region, researchers tend to emphasize its aridity and homogeneity. It is not only potentially productive but also naturally diverse, differing from one valley to the next and even within a given valley (in some cases significantly) because of variable geomorphological, climatic, hydraulic, soil, and altitudinal conditions. In lakeside valleys such as Tiwanaku and Katari, in the Tiwanaku heartland, three juxtaposed environmental microzones were of greatest importance for humans (Albarracin-Jordan 1999; Bandy 2001; Janusek and Kolata 2003). These are the rocky upper piedmont, generally 3,860–4,600 meters above sea level and dedicated to grazing; the lower piedmont of foothills and alluvial fans, at 3,820–3,880 meters, which are intensively occupied and farmed;

Figure 2.3 Paulino Lifonzo and his wife make *chuño*, or
"freeze-dried" potatoes.

and the valley bottoms or pampas, usually below 3,840 meters, which are
in many cases waterlogged (and "spongy") and provide farm land and
pasturage today. South of the lake region there is generally less rainfall
and other water, rendering most areas away from rivers and streams arid,
sandy, and nonproductive. To the east and west, the cordillera slopes give
rise to high *puna* grassland zones cut by deep, intermittent streams fed
by mountain glaciers and springs. These stark lands are mostly dedicated
to seasonal herding.

The lake itself, covering some 8,500 square kilometers, provides rich
aquatic resources. Such resources include various genres of edible waterfowl, including ducks, geese, gulls, wrens, herons, ibises, and skinny-
legged pink flamingos, which periodically flock by the hundreds along the
cold shores of Titicaca. They also include various useful aquatic plants,
including algae, submerged plants such as *lima*, and extensive stands of
totora (Figure 2.4). *Totora* is a tuberous, edible reed that flourishes along
the marshy littoral shores. Andeans cultivate *totora* to thatch house roofs,
weave shirts, twine ropes, and build watercraft. They even sing beautiful
songs about it. The lake and nearby rivers also include a rich native fish
flock. Native fish comprised two genre; two species of catfish of the genus
Trichomycterus, which live in shallow waters, and several pupfish species

of the genus *Orestias*, including the *umantu*, *carachi*, and sardinelike *ispi*. In 1940, overambitious North American fishery experts introduced rainbow trout, which "transformed the lake's ecosystem profoundly and irrevocably" (Orlove 2002:134). Trout effectively replaced the largest native fish species, the *umantu* (*Orestias cuvieri*) and irrevocably changed traditional fishing practices.

South of the Lake Titicaca Basin and away from the southbound Desaguadero River, the lake's primary drainage, the altiplano is colder and drier. Farming is a risky enterprise, and much of the altiplano is characterized by barren salt pans left by ancient, retreating lakes. In the Atacama Desert of northern Chile, to the west, ferocious winds drive massive sand dunes across the horizon. Here, early societies inhabited spring and river-fed desert oases such as San Pedro de Atacama, and human livelihoods and worldviews revolved around seasonal mobility, or transhumance, and herding. By fourteen thousand years ago, humans were hunting camelids for their meat and fat, and by seven thousand years ago, they began domesticating llamas and alpacas (Fernández 1974). As of thirty-five hundred years ago, llamas and alpacas formed a cornerstone of altiplano economy. The animals were carefully tended, their wool was spun into clothing, their meat and fat were consumed, their dung was used for fuel, and their bones were fashioned into tools. By three thousand years ago, juvenile and adult llamas were being sacrificed in elaborate religious ceremonies, and thus had become central to Altiplano religious ideology.

Beyond the cordilleras, the south-central highlands descend into series of lower, warmer valleys, or *yungas*. To the west, the altiplano rises gently but persistently toward the peaks of the Black Cordillera, an old range with bleak, rolling, steppelike *puna* grasslands that support groves of native *kiswara*, blue mountain lakes, and spongy moors, or *bofedals*. The snow-capped range itself is largely devoid of permanent human occupation and in many places vegetation. Aside from hunting and grazing, it offered outcrops of valued minerals such as copper, silver, and obsidian. The mountains descend gradually toward the Pacific coast, severed by a series of rivers that cut deep gorges through them in their descent toward the coastal plain. These corridors formed highways for moving people, goods, and ideas between highland and coast. They widen and shallow near the ocean, fanning out to form green, isolated hot valley oases amidst some of the most arid and desolate valleys in the world. Dependable cultivation in the valleys depends on intricate, well-tended irrigation systems. During the Middle Horizon, their cultivation produced cotton and a host of tropical fruits and vegetables, including chili peppers, gourds, fruits such as *pacay* and *lúcuma*, and *molle* berries.

Figure 2.4 Harvesting *totora* from the lake (a) to fashion reed boats (b).

Perhaps the most important valley cultivar by the Middle Horizon was maize. Maize does not grow well over 3,400 meters above sea level. It grew well in low, protected valley bottoms and hillslopes of the Peruvian sierra, where Wari and later Inca built extensive terraces to enhance its production. Some small species, cultivated for Inca state temples and rituals, flourished in isolated pockets on the shores of Lake Titicaca and on the Island of the Sun (Garcilaso 1966[1609]:81–82; Murra 1975). Yet it was in warm coastal valley bottoms where, fed by cool mountain water via irrigation networks, maize was most intensively sought and farmed. First cultivated on a small scale during the early Archaic (around 5000 BC, and most likely following gourds, quinoa, potatoes, and chili peppers), maize from the Middle Horizon and later was harvested in the

Andean sierra and coastal valleys. Highlanders sought it out as a festival delicacy, an "elite" ration for mobile Inca armies, and as the key ingredient in fermented beer, or *chicha*. Termed *kusa* in Aymara, *chicha* has fueled ceremonial feasts for centuries, declining in importance only recently due the increasing popularity of bottled beer and cane alcohol. In hosting lively festivals, which involve heaping plates of food and massive quantities of *chicha*, aspiring and established politicians demonstrated generosity, respect, and *cariño*, or kindness, key elements of leadership throughout the Andean world.

The coast itself is blessed with a continual marine food supply, making Peruvian fisheries some of the richest in the world. The source of this abundance is a continual upwelling of cold water in the northward-moving Humboldt Current, the easternmost portion of the counterclockwise circulation of the southern Pacific Ocean. As the current sweeps north along the coast of Chile and Peru, over a deep offshore trough, it faces and deflects a warmer, southward moving tropical surface current. The upwelling supports rich plankton beds that in turn support the diverse species of fish, shellfish, crustaceans, sea mammals, and fowl on which humans thrived. Until most recently, Peru led the world in anchovy production, yielding 12.3 million tons in 1970 (Bawden 1996:40). Particularities of wind, current, and landmass create the coastal geoclimate. Passing over the cool current the prevailing easterly trade winds gather thick clouds that, when over the warm shoreline, gain moisture-bearing capacity as they move toward the mountains, leaving the coastal plain arid. Except in El Niño years, it is only the high Andean flanks that cause eastward-bound clouds to release their precipitation, feeding the rivers and irrigation intakes that nourish valley farmlands further downriver.

Crossing eastward over the altiplano toward the Eastern Cordillera, one drops suddenly into the foothills of its rugged, spectacular white peaks and into the eastern *yungas*. The transition from altiplano and *puna* to the tropical rain forests of the Amazon basin is abrupt and dramatic (Figure 2.5a). This is a radically diversified landscape of extraordinary ecological variability. The vertiginous upper valleys are known as the *ceja de montaña*, or "eyebrow of the mountains." Water from ancient mountain glaciers and puna moors and springs tumble down steep escarpments and cascade over breathtaking waterfalls to form rivers that cut deeply through the hard rock of the Andean flank, creating steep and perilous valleys to which humans and vegetation alike cling tenaciously. Narrow rocky roads once treaded by trains of long llama caravans – some consisting of hundreds of animals laden with diverse commodities – today facilitate creaking buses and diesel trucks packed to the brim with people and their produce, several of which in any year wind up tumbling tragically

Figure 2.5 View of an eastern Andean valley (a), and coca from the region (b).

down perilous slopes. More than the humid climate, it is the rocky, vertical topography of the eastern valleys that constrains farming. Flat, arable lands are at a premium in the valleys. Native populations sculpted steep mountain slopes into narrow agricultural terraces and consumed the exuberant natural vegetation. For centuries, highlanders sought beans, chili peppers, gourds, and maize from middle valley elevations and fine timber hardwoods (walnut, cedar, and mahogany), jaguar pelts and canines, tropical bird feathers, honey, and diverse fruits from hot valley bottoms.

Among the most precious commodities of the Andean eastern valleys and foothills, aside from maize, were a host of mind-altering, medicinal and ritual plants and herbs. A variety of psychotropic plants and shrubs were grown or gathered in more distant jungles by ritual specialists. Among them were *vilca* (*Anadenanthera colubrine*), used to induce shamanic trances and visions (and depicted in Tiwanaku and Wari iconography; see Knobloch 2000); *Ayahuasca* (*Banisteriopsis* sp.), thought "to free the soul" and induce visions of powerful jaguars and serpents (Wilson 1999:95–96); *Brugmansia*, which provokes severe, violent convulsions followed by a long, dream-enhanced sleep; and the columnar cactus San Pedro (*Trichocereus* sp.), which invokes a hallucinogenic sense of flight that allows specialists to commune with spirits and treat a variety of illnesses. More commonly consumed was the highly nutritional, far less potent analgesic known as coca (Figure 2.5b). Coca has been for centuries the preeminent medicinal and ritual plant of the Andes, and has remained as indispensable for massive community ceremonies and fertility rites as it has for household and human life-cycle rituals.

Use of psychotropic plants goes back to the first inhabitants of the continent (Dillehay 1984; Wilson 1999). By the Middle Horizon, many played key roles in treating illnesses and inducing a "ritual attitude" during ceremonies. Their crushed seeds and leaves were sometimes added to "spike" *chicha* (Knobloch 2000). By this time, some people living in the valleys east of Lake Titicaca, today known as Kallawaya, became specialists in procuring, producing, and traveling great distances to administer such plants and herbs for medicinal and ritual purposes. The Inca held the Kallawaya in such great esteem, as much for their rapid and steady gait as for their medicinal-ritual expertise, that they served as royal litter bearers (Bastien 1978).

Environmental Shift and Paleoecology

Advances in scientific technology and interdisciplinary research over the past twenty years have generated important advances in paleoecology, or the study of ancient environmental patterns and changes. Under the influence of pioneers such as Michael Moseley and his many students, Andean archaeology has benefited immensely through collaboration with geologists, limnologists, climatologists and ecologists.

On long- and short-term time scales, the south-central Andes like the rest of the Andean chain has fluctuated significantly and to profound environmental and social effect. The continual subduction of the Nazca Plate under the South American plate generates ongoing and periodically devastating tectonic shifts. The Andes are still buckling and rising at a rate of about 0.3 mm a year. The same altiplano I returned to in 2007 was some 6 mm higher than the altiplano I first stepped onto in 1987!

Tectonic movement in the south-central Andes and all along the Pacific coast, from Tierra del Fuego through Colombia, produces periodic volcanic eruptions and earthquakes. Over the past millennium, such activity has been intense in sierra regions of the central and northern Andean highlands and the valley and coastal zones north and west of the altiplano. Volcanic eruptions have left thick deposits of gray ash over vast parts of southern Peru, especially in and around Arequipa. Mount Huaynaputina exploded with such force in 1600 that it reduced the volcano to a crater (Moseley 2001:28). Earthquakes affect the altiplano as I can attest, having rocked precariously in Wolfgang Schüler's third-story apartment in La Paz during a severe earthquake in June 2001. Yet like most recent earthquakes, this one, its epicenter in Arequipa, far more severely affected sierra and valley regions. In 1970, a powerful quake centered in the Callejón de Huaylas, Peru, triggered a glacial slide that wiped out two towns and claimed seventy thousand lives. In part to withstand tectonic movement, much past monumental architecture, including Tiwanaku cyclopean and Inca fitted stonework, was built to last.

Of more consistent pertinence and impact in the Andes are climatic fluctuations. We can think of them as occurring over short- and long-term phases and as cyclical recurrences or periodic, high-amplitude events (Bawden 1996; Kolata 2000; Moseley 2001). Human societies in the Andes adapt relatively well to short-term, cyclical variation. The most important recurrence, named El Niño (Christ Child) because it often begins around Christmas, most drastically affects the Pacific coast. In El Niño years, warm southbound equatorial waters replace the deep, northbound Humboldt Current, raising offshore water temperatures, interrupting the normal upwelling of nutrients and microorganisms, and devastating marine life so critical to human coastal societies. In strong occurrences, which may happen once every one or two generations, torrential rains cause violent floods and cataclysmic mudslides that strand vital irrigation intakes, bury channels, fields, and buildings, and destroy roads, bridges, and settlements. Evidence implicates a series of such events in the collapse of Moche, a statelike federation of polities that covered much of the north coast of Peru. Coastal adaptation to such events includes intensive intravalley specialization, techniques for preserving marine resources, and interdependence between groups specialized in fishing and farming.

In the highlands, climatic fluctuations have great effect as alternating phases of relatively high rainfall and drought. Because the Lake Titicaca Basin is so large, small fluctuations in relative rainfall and other hydrological changes substantially affect lake levels. Over the past century, lake level has varied by more than 6 meters (Roche et al. 1991:84). A relatively minor lake rise in the late 1980s flooded vast fields, pastures, and hamlets, rendering the site of Lukurmata a lakeshore port (Figure 2.6). Eight years later the same fields and hamlets were again on dry land and the lakeshore was barely visible from Lukurmata. Local fishers now had to carve long, snaking canals several kilometers long just to get their boats to the lake! Clearly, shifting lake levels was an ongoing concern throughout history. It is particularly severe because the pampas bordering Titicaca, remnants of its large predecessor lakes Minchin and Tauca, rise gradually from the shifting shoreline. A typical 1-meter shift in lake level can move the lake edge 5 kilometers inland, and a 5-meter shift can move it more than 15 kilometers inland in some areas (Binford and Kolata 1996:38). Such shifts can severely affect local production and livelihood as well as regional trade routes and settlement patterns. Populations in the basin have adapted to such normal variation by diversifying production strategies and cultivating alliance and trade with groups in nearby and distant regions.

Research in paleoecology and limnology detects a series of severe, longer-term fluctuations over the past ten thousand years. Recently, members of ORSTOM (Wirrmann, Mourguiart, and Fernando de Oliveira Almeida 1990), Wila Jawira (Abbott et al. 1997; Binford, Brenner, and Leyden 1996; Binford et al. 1997), and other projects (Baker et al. 2001) have cored the southern arm of Lake Titicaca, or Lake Wiñaymarka (see Figure 1.3). Shifts in sedimentation rates and in the timing of lake-deposited mineral and organic deposits reveal much about long-term climatic shifts. Independent evidence for climatic fluctuation comes from the Quelccaya glacier near the Vilcanota range between the Cuzco and Titicaca basins (Shimada et al. 1991; Thompson et al. 1985; Thompson et al. 1988). Here, ice cores reveal a series of fluctuating long-term wet and dry phases. Of particular relevance, they signal a record long-term wet phase in AD 750–1050, Tiwanaku's cultural and political peak, followed by a dry spell of long duration.

Figure 2.6 The flooded Katari Valley in 1986 (photo by Alan Kolata).

In coordination with Quelccaya ice cores, lake studies tell us of a series of successive high and low lake stands, many of which correspond to key cultural phases and transformations (Figure 2.7). Lake Wiñaymarka may have been dry before 1500 BC, at which point it rose rapidly on the order of 15–20 meters to near-modern levels. This rise corresponds roughly with the end of the Archaic and beginning of the Formative periods, and thus with earliest social complexity in the region. The lake experienced long-term drops again in 1000–800 BC and 450–250 BC, respectively, just before and during the Middle Formative (the peak of Chiripa culture). Lake levels were high after Chiripa and then sank once again in AD 100–300, just before Tiwanaku's rise, and then rose after AD 300 and remained high, overall, as Tiwanaku peaked. The lake sank once again on the order of 10–12 meters beginning at around AD 1100, marking the end of Tiwanaku and initiating the Late Intermediate Period. Lake levels remained low until at least AD 1300 and possibly AD 1500, the peak of Inca imperialism.

Correlations between paloecological and archaeological studies indicate that shifting lake levels profoundly affected regional cultural development. During high lake stands, centers such as Chiripa and Lukurmata would have thrived as lakeside fisheries and ports. During phases of pro-longed low lake stands, conditions in the basin were drier and the shores of Lake Wiñaymarka pulled far back, presenting severe challenges for these communities while opening opportunities for others. In the severe, pro-longed low stands of the Late Chiripa and post-Tiwanaku periods, Lake Wiñaymarka all but disappeared, leaving previously inundated regions vast grassy plains.

Society, Landscape, and Cosmos

Contemporary native populations, heirs to thousands of generations adapting to such challenging natural conditions, as well as successive phases of local and external political hegemony, are steadfast and tena-cious. Native-speaking populations make up almost 60 percent of Bolivia and nearly 50 percent of Peru. The dominant native languages are Aymara in Bolivia and Quechua (official language of Tawantinsuyu) in Peru. Today, these two groups are the predominant native ethnicities and lan-guages of the Andean highlands. Over the past half-century, beginning with turbulent agrarian reforms in the 1950s, their identities have become more palpable and their political voices clearer. In October 1992, self-styled Aymara leaders from the town of Tiahuanaco triumphantly scaled and symbolically reclaimed the Akapana platform of the nearby site (Kolata 1996b). As one instance of the transnational remembering of the Columbus Quincentenary, and accompanied by heartfelt speeches, they planted on its summit a colorful, billowing *wiphala*, a recently designed emblem of Aymara ethnicity and symbol of resistance to Bolivian author-ity and global hegemony.

By 2000, political conditions had changed. On a normal August after-noon, natives descended on Tiahuanaco and demanded that the ruins, and a significant portion of the annual proceeds derived from tourism, be turned over to local communities; which had always, they claimed, had the biggest stake in ancient Tiwanaku. This was no simple ceremo-nial gesture. It was an effective and well-planned political appropriation of the past along with its symbolic and material capital. It was a critical juncture in cumulative history, and things here would never be the same for those who call themselves Aymara, Bolivian, or anthropologist.

Ethnic Diversity

Aymara and Quechua communities have adapted to hundreds of years of Western hegemony. Before contact and for several generations thereafter, native political organization was complex and social identity diversified

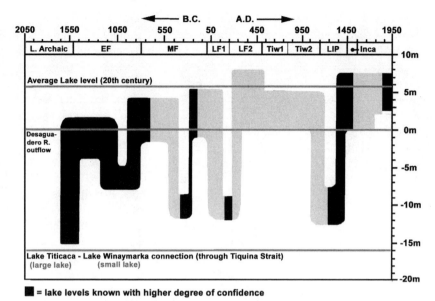

Figure 2.7 Changing lake levels based on four cores and sixty radiocarbon measurements (adapted from Abbott et al. 1997).

in the south-central Andes. Aymara was the language of many societies in the altiplano and in some adjacent valleys. Most Aymara speakers were farmers and herders, emphasis on one or the other economy varying according to cultural and environmental milieu. The deeper history of Aymara occupation in the Lake Titicaca Basin has been under debate. According to some historians, Tiwanaku succumbed to waves of migrating Aymara in the Late Intermediate Period. For Torero (1970, 1987), the Aymara originally immigrated from Ayacucho in Peru and for Bouysse-Cassagne (1986, 1987), they came from the central and southern altiplano. Whatever migration occurred, most archaeologists now see more continuity between Tiwanaku and post-Tiwanaku peoples of the basin (Albarracin-Jordan 1996b; Browman 1994; Janusek 2004a; Kolata 1993a; Ponce 1981; Stanish 2003). Following Max Uhle, most now contend that modern Aymara communities are for the most part descendants of the ancient Tiwanaku. I return to this question in Chapter 8.

Yet Aymara was not the unifying ethnicity it has become. Rather, it comprised many coexisting communities, ethniclike groups, federations, and polities. Aymara-dominated polities in the Lake Titicaca Basin included Colla, Lupaca, and Pacajes. To conquer and formulate Collasuyu, Inca leaders cultivated alliances with Lupaca leaders to defeat their bitter enemies, the neighboring Colla. Dominating the southern basin, loosely centralized Pacajes federations occupied the old Tiwanaku heartland. Further south were communities and polities among which alliances fluctuated over generations and bitter boundary disputes frequently raged (Izko 1992). Following the Andean axis southeast from the lake, one found the Carangas, Soras, and Charcas polities, the Killakas and Qaraqara polities, and further south, the Chicha. While Aymara language predominated, some polities included groups with languages and cultural affiliations other than Aymara, such as Pukina and Uru.

Pukina refers to a linguistic community that is all but extinct. Some claim that Pukina was widely spoken (Espinoza 1980; Torero 1970; Stanish 2003) while others question its geographical extent (Browman 1994). We know very little of its vocabulary because the only known lexicon, compiled by a Jesuit priest in 1590, has since been lost (Stanish 2003:302). Early in the Colonial period Pukina was still spoken in many valleys east of Lake Titicaca, in the highlands west of the lake and its southern drainage, and in pockets of Chuquisaca far to the southeast. For Espinoza (1980), Pukina was Tiwanaku's primary language. Less radically, Kolata speculates that early Pukina farmers allied with Aymara herders to form Tiwanaku's ruling dynasties (1993a). Pukina history, language, and livelihood remain to be explored.

Early Colonial census data identified some 12–25 percent of native population in the south-central Andean highlands as Uru (Mercado de Peñalosa 1965[1583]:335–336; Wachtel 2001). Uru communities currently are scattered along the lake's aquatic axis (Figure 2.4). In Puno Bay, some well-known Uru live on artificial *totora*-raft islands and thrive on fishing and tourism (Orlove 2002). On the arid, salt-encrusted plains west of Lake Poopó, the Uru-Chipaya eke out a precarious living combining fishing and irrigated quinoa farming (La Barre 1947; Wachtel 1994). Uru now distinguish themselves from others as *qut'suñi*, "people of the lake." Since at least the fifteenth century, they have occupied lake edges, the Desaguadero River, and its tributaries further south. While Aymara farmed and herded, many Uru harvested lake and river resources (e.g., *totora* reeds, algae, and birds; La Barre 1948; Métraux and Lehmann 1937; Wachtel 2001). Even today, their knowledge of fish cycles, bird species, and lake fluctuations is astounding.

Yet in the past, being Uru carried little social capital. The Aymara called them *chullpa puchu*, or excrement from the dark, primordial era before "creation" (Wachtel 2001:15). Spanish administrators embraced this view and considered the Uru, as one Jesuit noted, an uncivilized "nation of Indians despised by all" (Bertonio 1984[1612]:Bk. 2, 380).

In part because of such enduring racism, Uru language remains a mystery. Today most self-styled Uru speak Aymara and many farm and herd. Less than 100 years ago, some Uru communities were practicing farming technologies strikingly similar to ancient raised field agriculture (Metraux 1945; Uhle 1895). The depth of Uru history is also an enigma. Many believe that the Uru had a long history in the south-central Andes. Kolata (1993a:240–241) argues that their ancestors were specialists in lacustrine pursuits and formed a low-status segment of Tiwanaku's original population. Others argue that Uru was a census category imposed much later, by the Spanish (Stanish 2003:53–57). To be sure, today's Uru are unlike their prehispanic ancestors. Yet ethnicity is rarely invented. Grounded in traditional practices and collective memory, it can transcend major historical transformations. In Chapter 5, I present evidence for early altiplano aquatic-oriented groups with regional identities and specialties very similar to those of the later Uru.

The rugged valleys bracketing the altiplano were home to numerous communities, languages, and polities. For the most part, their languages and mythic narratives are lost, but archaeology has begun to reveal their ways of life and reconstruct their far-reaching trade networks. These regions were home to societies that interacted intensively with highland groups (Janusek and Blom 2006). Among these societies today are the Kallawaya, who live in the mountainous valleys east of Lake Titicaca (Bastien 1978, 1988; Girault 1987). The Kallawaya form an extensive macrocommunity; many are ritual specialists, native doctors, or diviners. Archaeology indicates that ancestors of today's Kallawaya have inhabited these valleys for hundreds of years (Rydén 1957; Wassén 1972). In Tiwanaku times, Kallawaya healers performed brain surgery ("trepanation") by removing part of the skull with sharp stone knives (Bandelier 1904; Bastien 1978:22). For centuries, altiplano residents have taken their prescriptions, worn their amulets, and drunk their potions, for the Kallawaya have specialized medical and ritual knowledge.

As with Andean landscapes, diversity is a keyword in describing native communities in the south-central Andes. For millennia, people have expressed social identity and community affiliation in highly perceptible ways. Ritual practices, language dialects, house styles, and innumerable other patterns varied in style among groups and regions. People themselves bore some of the most potent visual styles. Style in woven clothing included variability in the techniques, colors, and designs of male tunics and female skirts. More unique were differences in styles of skull modification. Through various techniques, people in the prehispanic Andes modified the shape of their children's heads to conform to local ideas of beauty and identity. Doing so, some explained, allowed their heads to fit into their woven hats (*chucos*), which also varied in shape and design from one group to the next.

Social and Political Organization

Despite substantial regional and ethnic diversity, social organization followed characteristic patterns across the south-central Andes. Polities and ethnicities consisted of nested *ayllus*. *Ayllu* refers most specifically to a social group larger than the household yet smaller than the ethnicity or polity (Abercrombie 1998; Bastien 1978; Izko 1992; Platt 1987; Rasnake 1988). *Ayllus* of the same social scale had similar sociopolitical, economic, and ritual roles. They were kin-based communities each of whose members claimed descent from a common ancestor, though kinship could be fabricated (to include, for example, godparents) or based on blood. Headed by a representative leader, an *ayllu* was a political group that could prove a powerful faction. By the same token, an *ayllu* held lands and herds in common and oversaw the distribution of key resources among its constituent households. Many cultivated specific occupations, whether in subsistence, skills, or craft. *Ayllus* also held certain places and features sacred and conducted rituals in common. Geographically, an *ayllu* tended to form a cluster of villages, hamlets, and nearby fields and resources.

It has proven difficult to isolate and define the *ayllu* for a number of reasons. Particular characteristics of *ayllus* varied according to region and ethnicity. For example, in Killakas inheritance in an *ayllu* followed the father's line (Abercrombie 1998), while in Kallawaya it followed both paternal and maternal lines (Bastien 1978). An *ayllu*'s households and lands frequently were widely dispersed over separate regions and different ecological zones. In addition, *ayllu* was a complex and malleable concept much like our term "community." People used it in reference to multiple nested scales of society. The micro-*ayllu* or "*ayllu* proper," was a corporate group with common resources, rituals, leadership, and ancestry. People also referred to more encompassing groups (such as ethnicities and polities) as *ayllus*, even though they had different roles and domains of action. Macro-*ayllu* identity in Carangas, Izko notes (1992), was potent largely in major festivals and times of external threat (e.g., boundary disputes). Altiplano polities, fluid in composition and alliance, might incorporate hundreds of micro-*ayllus* and many ethnicities or macro-*ayllus*. They were scalar hierarchies of encompassment in which power, identity, and rights to recourses were distributed among so many embedded groupings. Attributing "*ayllu*" to such hegemonic structures afforded their hierarchical relations the intimacy and kinship of familial domains.

Macro-communities and polities routinely consisted of two moieties (also known as *ayllus*), each of which consisted of several micro-*ayllus* and their households (Figure 2.8a). Greater Inca Cuzco consisted of Hanan and Hurin, each associated with several of the royal lineages, or *panacas*, that claimed descent from a deceased and mummified ruler. In parts of the south-central Andes, moieties were termed *alasaya* and *majasaya*. Moiety division drew on the symbolic and practical dimensions of duality and complementary opposition that characterized much of Andean life. An upper moiety (*alasaya*) occupied the north or the dry and mountainous portions of a region. A lower moiety (*majasaya*) occupied the south or low, wetter portions of a region. Moiety division attributed to society and politics the duality that Andeans held dear in other domains of life. Bodies consisted of (horizontally) right and left sides and (vertically) head and feet, households of men and women, landscapes of mountains and plains, earth of land and water, and cosmos of celestial and chthonic domains. In ritual, offerings and libations were made in pairs. The asymmetrical complementarity and potential antagonism of such categories were applied to moiety distinctions. Upper moieties were conceptually male and lower moieties female, upper moieties conceptually right and lower moieties left. Further, moieties involved distinctive practices. Most dramatic were ritual *tinku* battles in which warriors from each moiety faced off and fought, spilling blood as an offering for the well-being of the macrocommunity or polity (Platt 1987; Schüler 1988).

Egalitarian and hierarchical relations were interwoven in Andean societies. Reciprocity was an enduring cultural principal guiding social interaction and activity. The term *ayni*, for example, invoked a relation of balanced reciprocity in which service or goods given on faith would be at some point returned in kind. As a hypothetical example, when household head Anaclo Mamani needed his house roofed or repaired, he asked other community members to offer their help. Some of them already were in debt to Anaclo for a similar service he had provided in the recent past. In turn, Anaclo was expected to show his *cariño* during the event by providing food, coca, and fermented *chicha*. Many a house in the Andes has been built by such a team of raucous, if surprisingly effective, drunken men. At any time, Anaclo had accumulated "social debt" with several other community members and "social credit" with those who were so indebted to him. Social debts could always be tapped and politically manipulated to gain standing or power in society.

Each *ayllu* had a representative leader. Because leadership was distributed across society, political organization was segmented and heterarchical. Leaders of micro-*ayllus* were elected (Figure 2.8b). Leadership in macro-*ayllus* and polities tended to be inherited or to circulate among high status households. Such leaders, *mallku* in Aymara, could be very power-ful. Such a leader and his family often had privileged access to productive wealth, such as coca plantations in warmer valleys (Platt 1987:75). Yet much of a *mallku*'s wealth served not just his family and followers but also his constituency. A leader was expected to demonstrate *cariño* and generosity to promote his legitimacy. If a leader wanted a building con-structed, irrigation systems cleaned, his llama flocks tended, or salt flats mined, he had to formally *beg* his constituents. He had to throw a big feast to coax them. Today this requires troops of bands and dancers, heaping plates of food, and truckloads of beer and cane alcohol. Much of a leader's own wealth wound up continually funding his own legitimacy and posi-tion among his people. An etiquette of reciprocity grounded leadership. Political leaders were considered elder brothers or fathers (Abercrombie 1998; Bastien 1978; Platt 1987) and hierarchical political relations were construed as intimate household relations. In this sense, calling hierar-chical polities "*ayllus*" afforded them the idealized, reciprocal relations that characterized more intimate social domains. Thus, *ayllu* could also be political ideology.

Such patterns gave rise to distinctive settlement patterns. People of a community occupied hamlets and villages that were well distributed across a given landscape. Separating settlements were lands dedicated to farming and herding and linking them were well-worn earthen roads. Roads linked dispersed villages, plots, and shrines to central political and ceremonial centers, or *markas*. Today known as towns or *pueblos*, *markas* were (and still are) the places with which dispersed *ayllu* members iden-tified. They were central places where political reunions and calendri-cal festivals were held. In the largest, macropolity issues were debated and major ceremonies culminated. Following opening rites and offer-ings in local hamlets, *ayllu* members converged on their *marka* follow-ing well-worn paths. Fluctuating in activity and population, these towns were inextricably tied to their rural hinterlands. They were "incomplete," momentarily populous political-ritual centers that anchored the identity of widely flung communities.

Economic Organization

Natural and social characteristics of the south-central Andes gave rise to diverse forms of economy and regional exchange. The market-oriented economies so characteristic of other world civilizations – Mesopotamia, Mesoamerica, and Medieval Europe – never became predominant in the prehispanic Andes. Economic interaction followed different social rhythms, attuned to the diversity of the environment and an ideal of

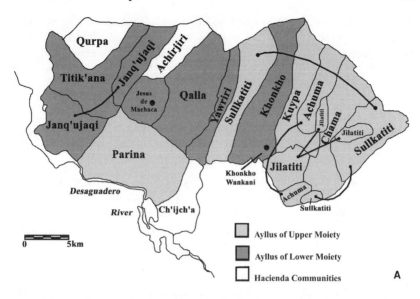

Figure 2.8 Ayllu spatial organization (a) and leadership (b).

familiar intimacy. In broad terms, economic interaction and resource acquisition in the Andes had vertical and horizontal dimensions. Vertical interaction, or verticality, refers to relations between people and resources at different altitudes, and horizontal interaction refers to interaction among societies at similar altitudes. Only in rare instances would a particular family, *ayllu*, or polity maintain one form of interaction with other societies.

A striking characteristic of Andean societies, and an astute strategy for dealing with a diversified environment, is their penchant for maximizing diversity to minimize risk. This held as much for their local productive strategies as it did for their far-flung social relations. In adapting to precarious natural conditions, people tended to forgo maximizing profit to assure community well-being; a heretical business ethic in the culture of late capitalism. This meant establishing a balanced repertoire of highly varied productive techniques, forms of exchange, and social ties.

Forms of verticality in the south-central Andes ranged from direct (kin-based) to indirect (exchange-based) modes of interaction and ecological complementarity (Murra 1972). Highland *ayllus* and polities frequently sought direct access to resources from lower zones via intermarriage, seasonal migration, or colonization. Depending on local geographical and social conditions, direct access could be continuous or discontinuous. In cases of continuous verticality multiple zones were within a few days' walk (Brush 1977; Murra 1972). Community members moved seasonally between zones of different altitudes, residing temporarily in areas outside of their primary place of residence. Continuous verticality was common in communities that straddled high farming and grazing zones and along the eastern slopes where zones varying 3,000 meters in altitude were within a few-day trek. In discontinuous verticality an *ayllu* or polity maintained direct access to resources in zones (usually lower in altitude) that were several days' journey from the primary residence or heartland. By settling distant colonies, a single polity might form a patchwork quilt of noncontiguous farmlands, mineral sources, and settlements. Direct control over distant lands and resources was a primary motive behind the expansion of Tiwanaku and, later, Tawantinusyu. Direct Tiwanaku influence, in fact, did not form a contiguous territory. Rather it was much like a large-scale archipelago stretched across the south-central Andes (see Chapter 6).

Complementing direct and "internal" forms of resource acquisition was a wide range of indirect or trade-based forms of economic interaction. Trade networks spanned both relatively vertical and horizontal dimensions of zonal complementarity. At the heart of Andean trade relations were long, well-trodden llama caravan routes that crisscrossed the highlands. Led by specialized *llameros*, they formed circuits linking the altiplano, coast, and valleys. A peculiar characteristic of Andean trade and exchange was its intimate character. Even long-distance transactions occurred most frequently among friends, *ayllu* members, and fabricated kin (Browman 1990). Particular routes and trading partners were passed down over generations. Even modern European-style markets have been transformed by enduring Andean ideals. Deals occur most frequently between *ayllu* members and *caceras*, or repeat patrons and customers, for whom a discount or "something extra" (*yapa*) is routinely arranged.

Interaction and trade across zones of similar altitude was paramount in the south-central Andes. They characterized relations among groups living in isolated coastal valley oases (Rostworowski 1989). Hand-in-hand with coastal trade went a highly developed artisanry in which a group crafted specific valued goods such as metal adornments or ceremonial pottery. Similar patterns also characterized the altiplano and adjacent highlands. Here, long caravan circuits provided effective distribution via long-distance trade for a wide range of sought-after products (Dillehay and Nuñez 1988; Nuñez and Dillehay 1995). Maintaining good relations with people in other altiplano regions was of paramount significance, especially in light of the risk inherent in local productive ventures. Important centers or *markas* were ceremonial and agropastoral hubs that also framed the directions and end points of caravan routes. As on the coast, altiplano *ayllus* developed specialized occupations as traders, miners, farmers, herders, or craft specialists (Browman 1978a, 1980). Trade ensured that goods produced in a specific region made their way to the people in other zones who needed or desired them.

Andeanists often assume that markets never graced the Andes. Dominating economic research in the Andes has been the so-called substantive idea that economy was thoroughly embedded in predominant social forms. According to this view, there was no market, no free exchange, and no profit motive. Yet, according to sixteenth-century Spanish documents, markets were a real, if subdominant element of Andean culture (Rostworowski 1989). Few have thoroughly explored the nuances of economic interaction in the Andes. In the altiplano, trade and exchange were important elements of major feasts and ceremonies, and they remain so today. In later chapters, I suggest that vibrant "open" economic intercourse prevailed in Tiwanaku ceremonies and feasts.

Cosmology, Landscape, Body, and Ritual

Andean social and economic forms framed a potent cosmology. Enduring cultural principles of reciprocity and intimacy also characterized relations between humans and spirits. These relations were mapped onto prominent natural landscape features, recurring celestial cycles, built environments such as dwellings and *markas*, and human bodies. People across the region considered their own well-being and reproduction and that of their communities, herds, and crops to be the work of ancestral spirits. The spirits of deceased and metaphorical ancestors inhabited the landscape. Andean religion was profoundly animistic.

Certain significant landscape features, including springs, lakes, hills and mountain peaks, embodied powerful spiritual forces and were held sacred by those who resided near or in sight of them. Through periodic pilgrimages, sacrifices, offerings, and libations, each social group – households, micro-*ayllus*, macro-*ayllus*, and polities – paid tribute to a particular network of such ancestral places. These were spiritually salient places that facilitated interaction and rapport between humans and their ancestors, and between the present and mythical past. They were places to influence and experience what Mircea Eliade called the *numinous* (1959:20). Maintaining intimate and reciprocal relations with ancestral spirits was critical for a group's social and economic well-being. If in Judeo-Christian tradition an "original sin" characterizes cosmic origin and human nature (Sahlins 1996), in Andean religion it is an "original gift." Deities and ancestors created and will continue to foster a society's well-being and productivity so long as people continue to pay respect to them through pilgrimage, sacrifice, and offering. Life is the gift that keeps on giving, but also the debt that must continually be repaid.

Social life thrived between the celestial heavens and the murky underworld (Abercrombie 1998; Martinez 1989; van Kessel 1992). Cycling above, the sun, moon, Milky Way, and various constellations established the recurring, predictable rhythms that dictated farming and herding calendars, ceremonial cycles, and camelid and human reproduction. These bodies were associated with mythical heroic personages, now Christianized deities who in a primordial epoch gave rise to humanity and the world. Humans sought to replicate their unalterable rhythms, follow their paths, and harness their generative powers. Deep inside the earth, which was personified by the female force of *pachamama*, lurked the shadowy forces of ancient mythical generations. Just as the celestial realm was beyond the pale of human intervention, so the most ancient depths of the earth were too otiose and abstract to intercede directly in human affairs.

More amenable to human influence were the ancestral forces associated with particular social groups. Social and political relations were mapped onto terrestrial landscapes, and these maps were periodically recalled and reinvigorated through pilgrimage and ritual offerings. Each household had an outdoor shrine that represented and protected it. Hamlets

Figure 2.9 Mount Sajama, near the Bolivian-Chilean border (photo by Wolfgang Schüler).

of closely related households had more powerful representative places, including nearby hills that embodied the distant ancestral spirits of the larger social group. Embodying the ancestral spirits of an entire moiety or ethnic group were prominent mountains (Figure 2.9). Punctuating the horizon and reaching toward the heavens, their peaks mediated earthly and celestial realms. They fostered violent storms that provided rain and the springs and streams that directed life-giving waters to crops, herds, and humans. A society's history and identity palpitated within mountains.

Andean cosmology outlined a pragmatic view of the world and humans' place within it. It incorporated generations of knowledge regarding natural cycles and human-environmental relations. Pilgrimage facilitated an experience of the social maps articulated as abstract cosmic principles, and offerings were practical measures of engaging cosmic forces and summoning their primordial generative powers to the present. Offerings included libations of fermented drinks, traditionally *chicha* and now also cane alcohol and beer. Today, before you drink you must pour a little bit of spirit onto the ground as an offering to *pachamama*. Traditional libations were more complex. Libations opening annual festivals in Killakas were offered in long sequences and were dedicated to places increasingly broader in space, time, and spiritual power (Abercrombie 1998:350– 367). They forged a memory path that defined current social and political relations and conceptually mapped them on the landscape. Offerings also included burnt *misas*, or wrapped and ordained bundles of herbs, coca, first crops, candy, llama fat, llama fetuses, and other elements. Gathered and dedicated under the supervision of a ritual specialist, they evoked the generative forces that ultimately consumed them in fire and smoke (Kolata 1996b:23). More potent were blood sacrifices (*wilanchas*) of specially selected live llamas (Text Box 2.1). In such rites the blood and meat of the sacrificed animal were shared among households. Human sacrifice may have formed a more potent form of sacrifice in the distant past.

The human body was conceived and medically treated according to Andean principles of hierarchy, reciprocity, and natural cycles. The body symbolized the unequal and complementary relations of communities and polities (Bastien 1985). One *ayllu* or region of each moiety represented the head, others the torso, arms, and innards, and still others legs and feet. By the same token, predominant social and ideological concepts applied to the body, bodily functions, and explanations of health and illness. The Kallawaya, specialists in health, medicine, and divination, made this their science. The human body, like the dwelling it inhabited, consisted of three levels. It was vertically divided and yet integrated by the circulation of fluids such as blood, the element of life, and fat, the basis of human energy. Vital fluids, much like water from mountain springs, were reciprocally condensed and centrifugally dispersed in spiral motion within one's *sonqo*, or "heart." Dead and dying humans were characterized by loss of vital circulation; that is, being existentially dry (like mummies). Just as *pachamama* and mountains were fed burnt offerings, one's body was periodically revitalized with *chicha*, coca, and herbs to ensure proper circulation and vitality. Such ideas were given lived expression in the spiraling dances of musicians – first inward and counterclockwise, then outward and clockwise – in festivals that revitalized community identity and relations to landscape and cosmos.

Cosmic principles and recurring cycles ordered the built spaces and social worlds that human bodies inhabited. Across the south-central Andes, moieties were ideally divided along an east-west axis defined by the sun's daily path. This cosmic-social division was replicated in microcosm in the main plaza of a central town, the north side of which was the domain of *alasaya* and the south side *majasaya*. Churches and plazas, forms of European imperialism and public space, were conceived according to native spiritual concepts. Church and plaza came to represent, respectively, masculine and feminine spaces, not least because male priests headed Catholic services and plazas were home to periodic markets that, by and large, were managed by women. In Killakas, houses traditionally were built with their doorways facing east to face the rising sun (Abercrombie 1998). Houses themselves represented the cosmos in miniature (Arnold 1992). In Qaraqara, their foundations were rooted in the earth's chthonic core, living areas afforded social life, and roofs invoked mountain peaks and sky. Houses were further divided into right and left sides, one associated with male and the other with female domains. Conceiving public and private living spaces according to predominant cosmic concepts attributed to them the unequal and complementary relations that characterized social life at all scales.

Cosmic principles also recursively shaped Andean practices of hierarchy and inequality. The Aymara term for sacred peak was the same term for a primary political leader – *mallku*. *Mallku* leaders, so long as they were legitimate, charismatic, and effective, were attributed the ancestral powers inherent in skyscraping peaks. Attributing to leaders such symbolic ancestry afforded them the intimate, complementary roles found in households and *ayllus*. The relations of ancestry and reciprocity idealized in *ayllus* formed an ideology that legitimated political rule and social hierarchy. By the same token, the sacred was amenable to political maneuvering; in fact, politics defined its contours. In the altiplano, an *ayllu* routinely demonstrated a political schism by founding a new sacred place or shrine (Abercrombie 1998:502). Cosmology could also legitimize a politicized past or present. In some cases, the asymmetrical positioning of moieties explained political circumstances by way of cosmological ideals. Lower moieties often were societies that had been conquered or incorporated (via alliance, etc.) as lower-status communities.

Predominant social and cosmic principles even explained important geopolitical boundaries in the south-central Andes. At the time of Spanish contact, a "macromoiety" division of Urkosuyu and Umasuyu subsumed multiple polities, federations, and far-reaching interaction networks in the south-central Andes. The boundary between them, or *taypi*, traversed the altiplano through Lake Titicaca. In rough terms, polities and *markas* to the west formed Urkosuyu and those to the east Umasuyu (Bouysse-Cassagne 1986; Choque 1993; Pärssinen 1992). The dual division drew on shared concepts with more complex social and geographical meanings. *Urko* referred to male beings and activities, solidity, mountains, and the high cold lands associated with herding and cultivating highland crops (e.g., potatoes, quinoa). *Uma* (or "water") referred to female beings and activities, liquidity, the lake, and the warm, wet valleys of the Amazonian headwaters where lowland crops such as coca and maize are grown. Possibly, past Aymara were associated with *urko* and Uru and Pukina with *uma*. Urkosuyu societies tended to maintain close interactions with coastal valleys to the west and highland Umasuyu societies with lower valleys to the east. This was no abstract duality but rather a pragmatic and politicized interpretation of social and economic relations by way of shared and enduring cosmological concepts. The geopolitical boundary passed right through the older Tiwanaku core and most likely had originated during Tiwanaku's reign.

Conclusions

Nature and culture and the worlds of humans and spirits were intimately connected in the prehispanic Andean past. Ideas regarding the cosmos, environment, human relations and bodily health never were precisely the same from one society to the next. Yet because societies began interacting long before Tiwanaku's rise to power – trading valued crops and crafts via long llama caravans, forging political alliances or fighting with other societies, intermarrying or temporarily inhabiting places far from a community's homeland – the south-central Andes formed a vast place of interaction in which, as if in a grand kaleidoscope, many principles and practices were shared. Characteristic values, ideas, and relations continually developed, gained currency, and became "practical consciousness" or common sense. For this reason, they tended to endure.

Many traditional cultural principles and practices remain vital today. Subtly resisting and establishing some purchase over Spanish Colonial, Republican, and global hegemonies, natives have been for centuries appropriating dominant forms (markets, Christianity, etc.) and values (profit motives, education, etc.) to local beliefs and ideals. Such practices can be traced to the most distant origins of complexity in the Andes. Such is the focus of the next chapter, which investigates the rise of complex societies and the processes that led to the crystallization of Tiwanaku culture, religion, and statehood.

3   Early Complexity and Tiwanaku's Ascendance

Some of the thorniest issues in archaeology concern the rise of civilization. Traditional comparative approaches tended to espouse evolutionary perspectives that emphasized the role of either integrative (e.g., central government) or of divisive (e.g., class differences) social institutions in state development (Fried 1967; Service 1975). Even today, archaeologists often emphasize a single process, whether environmental, economic, or ideological, to explain the long-term conditions that fostered state emergence. Many models also remain "unilinear." They interpret state development as a one-way trajectory of increasing political and economic complexity driven by a particular condition or social process. Some models outline powerful explanations for particular cases. Yet early history in the south-central Andes complicates such tidy scenarios.

Archaeologists have been at a loss regarding Tiwanaku's early history. In great part, this has been due to a lack of research into the critical historical phases preceding the state's rise. Complicating this problem have been assumptions regarding the challenging, high-altitude environment in which Tiwanaku developed and thrived. For some early researchers, Tiwanaku's rise was nothing less than a miracle. Until very recently, little of substance had been proposed, let alone debated, regarding the early, long-term trajectory of Tiwanaku state development. Over the past two decades, research projects have produced exciting new finds, a working chronology, and intriguing interpretations for the millennium preceding Tiwanaku's rise. Every year new discoveries change our ideas regarding early complexity in the south-central Andes.

In this chapter, I outline the early history of the Lake Titicaca Basin and its environs. I focus on the natural shifts and cultural practices that played roles in the trajectory leading to Tiwanaku's rise to power. The development of complexity and state institutions was a pan-regional process with a long history, so it is important to begin with the transition to so-called formative cultures. I discuss the fascinating Early-Middle Formative complex societies of Chiripa and Qaluyu in the Titicaca basin and Wankarani to the south. Next I turn to dynamic Late Formative political developments, including Pukara in the north and several multicommunity polities in the south. Toward the end of the formative, the Tiwanaku state emerged out of a long history of dynamic sociopolitical and integrative religious traditions.

We find that no process single-handedly drove state emergence. Complexity and statehood emerged out of shifting conjunctions of social, ideological, and environmental forces in relation to often-unpredictable historical circumstances. Further, complexity did not develop uniformly or in a unilinear manner in the south-central Andes. It emerged out of broad interaction networks and cultural affiliations that, through material and ideological exchanges, linked societies with distinct local identities, productive concerns, sociopolitical systems, and worldviews. I begin with the Late Archaic and Early Formative periods. By then Andean societies had developed many characteristic skills, strategies, and principles to deal with the tectonic cultural changes soon to come.

The Rise of Formative Cultures

The transition from Archaic to Formative lifestyles varied in time and character in the south-central Andes. In some places it occurred between 2200 and 1500 BC. In others, groups maintained archaic adaptations well into the Late Formative. In general, the transition involved a profound shift in livelihoods from transhumant occupations, in which groups moved seasonally between different altitudinal zones, to one in which groups lived in relatively permanent villages (if with seasonal camps). From an evolutionary perspective, this shift is considered the hallmark of a jump from "bands" to "tribes," or from hunters and foragers to sedentary farmers. It is thought to coincide with early cultivation, the domestication of camelids, pottery production (to process, store, and serve foods), and incipient complexity, or "ranking."

In reality this "Neolithic Revolution," as V. Gordon Childe termed it, involved highly complex shifts in productive strategies. Facing shifting climate, resources, and human interactions, groups assimilated new strategies to old livelihoods, and cumulatively old livelihoods were transformed. In the Lake Titicaca Basin the transition involved an increasing emphasis on a wider range of economic strategies that included gardening and herding as well as hunting, fishing, and foraging (Stanish 2003:100). It also involved a shift from transhumant seasonal residence to permanent settlement, fostered by a cultural emphasis on balanced reciprocity among groups in adapting to more specific but risky and unpredictable environments (Aldenderfer 1998:55).

Such transitions were as conceptual as they were material. Archaeologists tend to emphasize the environmental and material dimensions of

Figure 3.1 The high *puna*.

similar transitions around the world. Yet they involved profound shifts in the principles and ideals that guided human productive strategies and daily practices (Bradley 1998). These included new views of human-natural relations, the significance and spirituality of particular places, and the composition and symbolism of kin and community. As humans began to transform and manipulate their environments and its products, a deep sense of human power and efficacy in the domestication of nature took root. Characteristic elements of Andean religion now developed: animism, ancestor veneration, shamanic human-spirit relations, and an experience of landscape as sacred and transcendent.

Three elements of the Archaic to Formative transition bear further discussion: first, early sedentism did not always involve full reliance on domesticated plants or animals; second, in many regions groups already had developed complex interaction networks with other zones; and third, religious ideals and ritual practices were well-developed by the end of the Late Archaic.

Archaic groups moved seasonally. In the Lake Titicaca Basin, groups spent the austral summer (November–March) at *puna* camps hunting wild camelids and deer (Figure 3.1), and the austral winter (April–October) at lower altitudes nearer to the lake (Aldenderfer 1989; Santoro and Nuñez 1987). Other regions supported different seasonal adaptations. In the southern altiplano, groups moved seasonally from the coast to *puna* and back from austral winter to summer (Ravines 1967, 1972).

In the highlands of northern Chile, groups may have moved in triangular fashion among *puna*, desert oases, and coast (Hesse 1982; Rivera 1991). In each case, cycles of movement and seasonal residence focused on exploiting local wild resources and on manipulating key plants and animals. By the end of the Archaic, highland groups were exploiting a vast range of ecological niches and intensifying their use of crops such as wild quinoa. Communities began to establish residential settlements and satellite camps in key resource zones (Aldenderfer 1998:55). Gradually, reciprocal interaction among neighboring groups supplanted transhumance as a predominant mode of resource acquisition in the region.

Means of acquiring exotic resources were well developed by the Early Formative. Evidence for continual movement and regional interaction is found among Late Archaic communities throughout the south-central Andes. Archaic sites in the southern altiplano and nearby *puna* of northern Chile yield coastal products such as marine shell and shark tooth (Aldenderfer 1998:54; Arellano 2000). Settlements and cemeteries affiliated with Chinchorro, a cultural complex on the Chilean coast, included goods from the tropical lowlands, across the altiplano (Rivera 1991, 2002). These included crops such as manioc and sweet potato, paraphernalia for storing and ingesting hallucinogenics, and head ornaments with feathers of tropical birds. In the Lake Titicaca Basin, Late Archaic–Early Formative communities on the Island of the Sun obtained nonlocal lithic materials such as basalt and obsidian, the latter from the distant, temperate Colca Valley in Arequipa (Stanish 2003:104–105). The trade and interaction that produced such patterns must have varied greatly in form. Groups may have acquired exotic goods indirectly, over several smaller circuits of trade or barter in what Colin Renfrew terms "down-the-line trade" or directly via long-distance trade or transhumance.

A striking characteristic of Archaic and Early Formative Andean communities is their precocious religious life. Communal ritual activity in the Andes predates 12,000 BC, judging evidence from Monte Verde in southern Chile. Here, Tom Dillehay (1997) and an interdisciplinary research team discovered an oddly shaped building associated with shallow pits with burnt offerings and remains of medicinal plants. By 5000 BC, communities of the coastal Chinchorro complex had begun to prepare complex mortuary practices for the deceased. Mummification procedures became more complex between 5000 and 2000 BC, advancing technically from the disarticulation of deceased individuals to the use of incisions to remove decomposing body organs (Arriaza 1995; Rivera 1991). Each body was reconstituted as a permanent material symbol by creating simulacra of surface features, body parts, and a mask of black or red-coated clay plaster. Mummified individuals were buried in cemeteries, each of which appears to have represented a particular kin group or community. Curating and venerating deceased family and community members, as well as burying them together, were elemental in Chinchorro religious ideology.

Other Late Archaic and Early Formative communities engaged in distinctive ritual practices. A rock shelter on the banks of the upper Rio Asana, over a moor (*bofedal*) in the high sierra (3,450 meters above sea level), was a locus for ceremonial activities between 3500 and 3000 BC (Aldenderfer 1991, 1998). Structures at Asana consisted of prepared clay floors with elevated platforms bounded by trenches that may have supported wooden frames. Associated with the structures were cairns, split boulders with specular minerals, plastered basins with superimposed burning events, and small twig enclosures. In and around basins and hearths were bits of pulverized bone, miniature projectile points, and small stone figurines. The complex was renovated several times over five centuries. Mark Aldenderfer hypothesizes that it served as a group shrine; a sacred space for intimate offerings and periodic ceremonial gatherings.

The Archaic-to-Formative transition bore profound cultural transformations. Communities became more entrenched in particular settlements and developed a sense of permanent place. They intensified reliance on resources in specific locales, fostering the cultivation of crops such as quinoa and tubers and the domestication of animal species such as llamas, alpacas, and guinea pigs. Religion, with roots in the earliest human settlements, developed an emphasis on ancestral ties to a particular society and landscape; not so surprising in that tenure and inheritance, whether largely in land or in animals, were increasingly important concerns. Within these parameters, societies changed following distinctive rhythms and attuned to local physical conditions, cultural practices, and historical circumstances. One of the earliest cultural complexes to emerge from archaic roots was Wankarani, located in the central Andean altiplano.

The Middle Formative

Wankarani

Wankarani culture emerged in the dry regions north of Lake Poopó before 2000 BC. Sites affiliated with Wankarani clustered in the middle and lower Desaguadero basin. Today they are highly visible on the altiplano as tell-like mounds of continuous occupation rising up to 6 meters high. Material culture diagnostic of Wankarani changed very little over several centuries, suggesting that many elements of life and everyday activity remained fairly consistent throughout the Early-Middle Formative. Early on, archaeologists noted that significant material patterns distinguished

Wankarani from other altiplano complexes, including nondecorated ceramic vessels, abundant stone hoes, and tenoned effigy llama heads hewn of volcanic stone (Metraux and Lehmann 1937; Ponce 1970; Walter 1994[1966]; Wasson 1967). Dwellings and ritual structures were circular (Figure 3.2). Wankarani communities maintained a coherent cultural identity grounded in distinct productive strategies, domestic architecture and practices, and rituals.

Wankarani societies consisted of autonomous villages rather than cohesive polities. Sites were widely dispersed and regularly spaced across any given region of the middle-lower Desaguadero basin. Settlements were small and surpassed 2 hectares only in exceptional cases, and smaller sites tended to cluster around larger settlements, suggesting regular fissioning from large progenitor villages (McAndrews 2001, 2005). According to Tim McAndrews, groups moved out of old settlements and established new villages when social tensions became intolerable. Social pressures may have involved local population growth and resource competition or competition among ambitious lineage or ritual leaders. Apparently, Wankarani societies had little tolerance for over hierarchical human relations. Rather they collectively formed a widely flung cultural landscape and regional interaction network characterized by sociopolitical heterarchy.

Ongoing excavations in La Joya indicate that Wankarani communities consisted of nested social groups (Bermann and Estevez 1995). Any village housed groups of circular dwellings and their adjacent activity spaces. By the Middle Formative period, groups of two to four dwellings clustered in bounded compounds. Several compounds, in turn, formed broader neighborhoods. Such a nested organization bespeaks a segmental, embedded community organization. Each compound formed a basic household group or extended family, while a neighborhood housed an entire clan or lineage segment. Such an organization is reminiscent of the segmental order of more recent altiplano societies.

The Wankarani site of La Barca offers evidence for significant status differences (Rose 2001a, 2001b). A major privilege here was access to the best portions of camelid meat. Painstaking analysis of faunal remains revealed that some groups had better access to the torso, haunches, and limbs of llamas and alpacas: those with the prized beef. The same groups had greater portions of lithic tools made of minerals procured from distant groups and regions. These materials included basalt, a durable volcanic stone ideal for agricultural tools, and obsidian, a dark volcanic glass used to make sharp knives and arrow points. Basalt derived from natural outcrops at Querimita, some 150 km to the south, and obsidian came from sources far north of La Joya. The same high-status groups also used elaborate serving vessels with incised decoration. Differences in access to

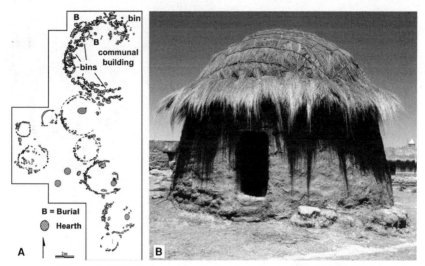

Figure 3.2 Wankarani structures (a) (adapted from Rose 2001a) and a recent Uru-Chipaya dwelling (b) (photo by Alan Kolata).

valued goods at La Barca were most palpable between residential neighborhoods, that is, between clan or lineage segments. Status and wealth differences characterized entire social groupings rather than particular households and individuals.

Ritual was an important part of life in Wankarani communities. Tenoned camelid heads adorned Wankarani village ceremonial places, though their precise role in Wankarani religious life remains unclear (Figure 3.3). Household debris included fragments of ceramic trumpets, one crafted in the Yayamama style popular around Lake Titicaca (Bermann and Estevez 1995). Wankarani rituals also included the burial of anthropomorphic figurines, grinding stones, and basalt stone hoes under living spaces. Most likely, household members conducted such offerings at key moments in the life cycle of a dwelling or its resident group. If ritually carved camelid effigy heads belie a preoccupation with the viability of herds and herding, subhousehold offerings point to preoccupation with domestic reproduction and agricultural production.

Wankarani communities also built and maintained discrete ritual buildings. Each household had a circular ceremonial structure for periodic ceremonies dedicated to recently deceased ancestors (Figure 3.2a). Serving more encompassing neighborhoods were larger circular sunken structures for the occasional ritual observances of an entire clan or lineage segment. Rituals conducted in these places were charged moments in which a group's past was remembered and its identity revitalized and reproduced.

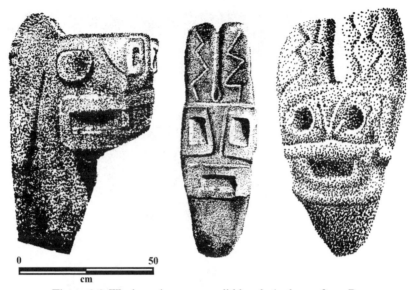

0   50
                   cm

Figure 3.3 Wankarani stone camelid heads (redrawn from Ponce 1970 and Portugal Ortiz 1998b by Jennifer Ohnstad).

By the Middle Formative, Wankarani communities comprised agropastoral groups who were particularly adapt at herding. The limited food crops amenable to cultivation in the dry and salt-encrusted soils of the region included quinoa and a variety of tubers, including *papa luqi*, the bitter potato from which *chuño*, the infamous but eminently storable "freeze-dried" potato is elaborated. Households managed much of their own surpluses. Their harvest was stored in bins and pits in Wankarani house compounds. Some products, including "wild" foods (fish, river fowl, and *vizcacha*) and salt, were undoubtedly exchanged for other goods in more distant communities. Crops, salt, and crafted items moved across vast exchange networks that reached as far as desert oases in northern Chile (Rivera 1991) and the Cochabamba valley of Bolivia (Gabelman 2001). Such networks were facilitated by caravans led by herders who cultivated friends and clients in such places. Status differences in Wankarani communities most likely followed differential involvement in such long-distance trade networks.

Chiripa

Chiripa was a distinct cultural complex that thrived along the southern edges of Lake Titicaca and its nearby tributaries and drainages from 1500 to 200 BC (Figure 3.4). Archaeologists divide Chiripa's long chronology

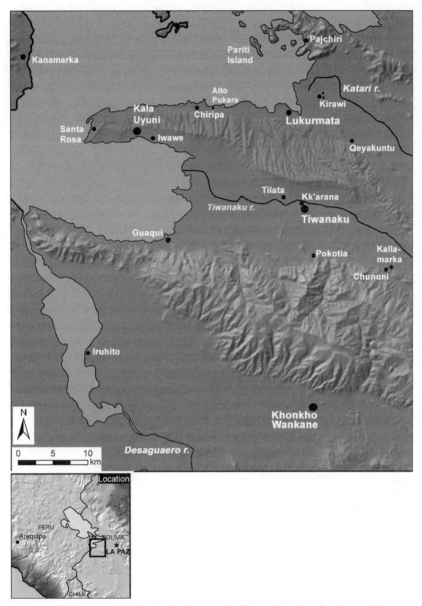

Figure 3.4 Chiripa and other major Formative sites in the southern Lake Titicaca Basin (base map by Steve Wernke).

into Early, Middle, and Late phases, the last corresponding with the Middle Formative Period. Years ago, archaeologists knew that Chiripa comprised distinctive cultural patterns, including earthen platforms with central sunken courts, elaborate stone sculptures, and decorated fiber-tempered ceramic wares (Bennett 1936; Browman 1978a, 1978b, 1980; K. L. M. Chávez 1988; Hastorf 2005; Kidder 1956; Kolata 1993a:69; Ponce 1970, 1980; Portugal Ortiz 1998a). Most considered the site of Chiripa, on the shores of the Taraco Peninsula, as its most important center.

Early excavations at Chiripa exposed a platform mound some 5 meters high that incorporated a trapezoidal ring of rectangular buildings (Figure 3.5a). Although early archaeologists referred to the buildings as "houses," more recent research indicates that they were intimate storage and ritual chambers (Figure 3.5b; K. L. M. Chávez 1988; Hastorf 2003). The monumental complex was covered and reconstructed at least three times during Middle and Late Chiripa, in each case reemerging with greater architectural elaboration and height (Bandy 1999, 2001:126–133; Hastorf et al. 2001:86). Buildings in the platform's final incarnation were highly elaborate and colorful. They had internal niches, storage bins, sliding doors, yellow clay floors, and adobe walls plastered and painted in rich hues of white, yellow, green, and red. Some walls depicted abstract designs (K. L. M. Chávez 1988:18–19; Conklin and Moseley 1988:160–161). The buildings surrounded a deep sunken court fixed with sculpted panels and roughly hewn limestone and sandstone slabs, some of which depicted carved mythical figures.

Chiripa's final platform complex was the latest in a long history of monumental construction in the Early and Middle Formative periods. The earliest buildings on the Chiripa platform were more vernacular, less elaborate, and probably built piecemeal. Similar buildings characterized the Middle Chiripa site of Alto Pukara, just 4 kilometers east of Chiripa (Figure 3.6). Excavations here exposed a raised platform that supported an open plaza bounded by two such buildings, one of which contained a fire pit where offerings presumably were burned (Beck 2004a). This complex was buried at the beginning of Late Chiripa, just when the final platform complex was built over early buildings at Chiripa. At this time, ritual on the peninsula may have shifted to concentrate primarily or solely on Chiripa itself.

Platform complexes were but one form of built ceremonial space at Chiripa and its affiliated sites. Excavations at Chiripa revealed two extensive sunken courts with prepared clay floors that served communal gatherings and ceremonies (Hastorf et al. 2001). Similar courts were found at Chiripa-affiliated sites in the nearby Tiwanaku Valley

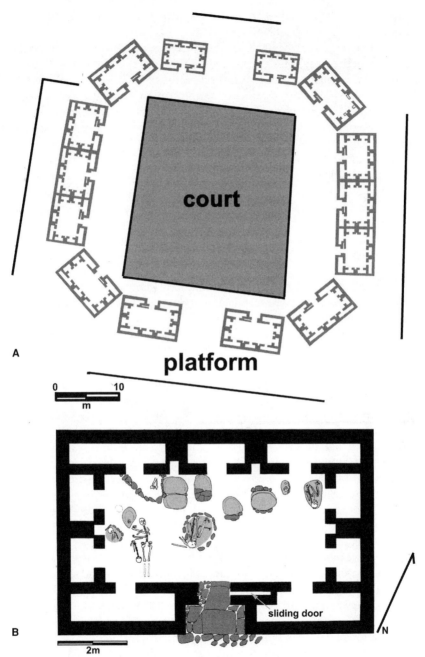

Figure 3.5 The Chiripa mound (a) (adapted from Hastorf 2003) and one of its ritual structures with sub-floor burials (b) (adapted from Bennett 1936).

and on the Copacabana Peninsula (Albarracin-Jordan 1996a:105–110; Chávez and Chávez 1997; Mathews 1992:149, 558).

Chiripa may have been the primary center of Chiripa culture. Still, it was not the only important center on the Taraco Peninsula, and the peninsula, in turn, was one of several regions in the Titicaca Basin that supported major Chiripa centers. On the Taraco Peninsula alone, where sites tended to form clusters consisting of two site sizes, three other sites were as extensive as Chiripa. Two of these and a few smaller sites also had monumental platforms (Bandy 2001:133–136). Sites with monumental platforms also occupied inland valleys where Chiripa settlement was sparser (Albarracin-Jordan and Mathews 1990:58–73; Janusek and Kolata 2003; Kolata 1993a:63–64). Dense Chiripa settlement emerged in several regions of the Titicaca Basin, including Copacabana, Santiago de Huata, and Titimani. Chiripa settlements even spilled down into the eastern *yungas* (Faldín 1991, 1995; Paz Soria 2000), indicating that interaction between distinct altitudinal zones was an important element of Chiripa society.

Particularly important Chiripa ceremonial centers occupied Copacabana Peninsula and the nearby Island of the Sun. In Copacabana, Sergio Chávez and the late Karen Mohr Chávez revealed a densely settled landscape focused on relatively large sites with monumental architecture and communal ceremonial spaces (Chávez and Chávez 1997). Major centers on the peninsula were densely clustered and spaced on average some 6 kilometers from one another. As at Chiripa and other major centers of the Chiripa complex, monumental complexes included extensive courtyards or plazas and raised platforms with deep sunken courts. The Chávez's reconstructed one particularly well-preserved sunken court at Ch'isi, on a high outcrop overlooking the shore (Albores 2002:105). Also densely occupied was the north part of the nearby Island of the Sun, where the Titikala or sacred Inca "stone of the puma" formed a natural outcrop that, like the Ch'isi temple, overlooked the lake. If the two regions were not yet considered places of cosmic and human origins, they already formed important social and ritual landscapes during the Middle Formative.

Ritual was an important element of life in Chiripa society. It fostered values that shaped common bonds within a community and shared identities across broader regions. Many emphasize the increasing elaboration of mortuary rituals and group ancestors during Middle and Late Chiripa times (Beck 2004b; Hastorf 2003). This is manifested in the increasing elaboration of platform buildings in Late Chiripa, the niches in which may have originally housed wrapped mummy bundles as did similar niches in Pukara a few centuries later. In the 1930s, Wendell Bennett determined

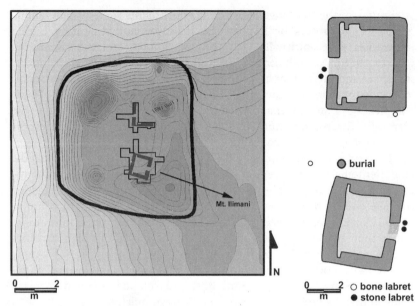

burial

0 2
m

0 2   ○ bone labret
m   ● stone labret

Figure 3.6 The site of Alto Pukara and its ritual chambers (adapted from Beck 2004b).

that humans were buried underneath these buildings (Figure 3.5b). One included thirteen subfloor burials that included offerings of decorated pottery and individuals adorned with gold and copper jewelry (Bennett 1936:432–433). At Alto Pukara, the skull of a human buried under one early building was covered with hematite, a blood-colored mineral that metaphorically afforded "life" to the deceased individual (Beck 2004b). Such buildings most likely were ancestral shrines for formative communities. Each building housed the deceased ancestors of a suprahousehold group, and as the focus of its periodic rituals and the repository of its most sacred objects, came to represent that group.

Ritual buildings themselves were treated as symbolic ancestors (Hastorf 2003). They were positioned on prominent places of the landscape, whether along visual pathways with ancient peaks as at Alto Pukara, or on human-made platforms that mimicked such peaks and appropriated their generative power, as at Chiripa. Such buildings endured cycles of construction, use, and ritual interment. At Alto Pukara, the interment of a building was treated much like the interment of the mummified human buried below it (Beck 2004a). Similarly, at Chiripa, architectural interments reoccurred every twenty or so years, more or less every human generation (Bandy 2001). At Alto Pukara, such interments involved the ritual "dressing" of the buildings with bodily adornments such as gold lamina necklaces and labrets, or lip plugs (Beck 2004a), and at Chiripa, buried individuals were spiritually "fed" tubers, quinoa, and fish (K. L. M. Chávez 1988). At both centers, each shrine likely symbolized the ancestral spirit and identity of a group and served as a place to recharge collective memory in periodic ritual (Hastorf 2003). The nucleation of such complexes in Late Chiripa focused the generative ritual power and social identity of diverse communities at a few major centers, and most importantly, perhaps, at Chiripa itself.

Chiripa productive economy like its rituals and myths was tied to the lake. Settlement in any region spanned a range of microenvironments, favoring well-drained areas on the low hillslopes and summits hugging the lake and its nearby pampa floodplains. Unlike Wankarani communities, Chiripa communities emphasized farming, fishing, and hunting, rather than herding, as demonstrated by the incredibly high densities of plowing tools and bones of fish and lake fowl at many sites. Farming involved a number of locally adapted strategies focused on rain and canal-fed fields. Some argue that communities developed small-scale raised fields in marshy areas and terraces on adjacent hillslopes (Stanish 1994, 1999:123). In sheltered areas along the lakeshore, it is not beyond reason that Chiripa farmers cultivated small strains of maize (S. J. Chávez, pers. comm., 2001). Faunal and archaeobotanical analyses at Chiripa revealed that crops such as tubers and quinoa (Bruno and Whitehead 2003) and fish and aquatic birds were important (Moore, Steadman, and DeFrance 1999) for local diets and ritual feasts.

Chiripa communities thrived on a vibrant economy that transcended subsistence and kin-based distribution. Crafted items, including elaborate ceramic wares, metal adornments, and sculpted stelae and panels, bespeak well-defined artisanry. Most specialists probably enjoyed relatively high status within a community owing to their ability to transform valued natural resources into elaborate crafted items of social and ritual significance (Helms 1993). Some may have been so-called attached specialists who produced largely for political leaders, religious specialists, or others of high status. The widespread distribution of shared ceramic technologies and the appearance of common iconographic themes on stone and other objects indicate that humans, goods, and ideas traveled vigorously across the Lake Titicaca Basin following vibrant, multidirectional interaction networks (Browman 1980). Boat travel was a primary form of travel and exchange. Matt Bandy (2001) hypothesizes that, in addition, the drying of Lake Wiñaymarka in the Middle Formative facilitated the expansion of circumlacustrine llama caravan networks across the southern basin. Water and land trade linked communities and shaped far-flung identities of shared practices and ideals. Chiripa sites and material culture beyond the Titicaca Basin indicate that longer caravan routes linked Chiripa communities to more distant cultures and regions. Such long-distance networks had both economic motivations, to obtain resources such as salt, exotic minerals, coca, and valued foods, and social reasons, to foster distant alliances, clients, and friendships.

Yet each Chiripa-affiliated community maintained a distinct identity grounded in local landscape features, ancestors, and ritual practices. Local identities are evident in styles of monumental constructions, stone iconography and sculptural styles, and ceramic styles. Lee Steadman's (1995, 1997, 1999) rigorous ceramic analyses at several Chiripa sites indicate that, while many stylistic attributes were shared across the southern basin, in any region most ceramic wares were locally produced and included local stylistic twists. Chiripa wares included elaborate serving and ceremonial vessels for social gatherings, community feasts, and rituals of greater religious gravity (Figure 3.7). Of particular significance were decorated flat-bottom bowls and ceramic trumpets with stylized appliqué felines or human faces. Specific aspects of such wares varied from region to region and site to site. Around Camata in the western basin, ceramic assemblages included Qaluyu elements, a cultural complex centered further north. Overall, it appears, Chiripa consisted of interacting communities and polities that formed more encompassing, overlapping cultural identities and interaction networks.

Chiripa was not a hierarchical polity or "proto-state" as some have suggested (Portugal Ortiz 1998a). The site of Chiripa was a symbolic center of mortuary ritual and collective memory for several Middle Formative communities (Hastorf 2003). Still, lake-oriented regions supported multiple ritual centers and settlement clusters. Ritual practices emphasizing group ancestors and community ceremonies were important across the region. Considering religion essential, the Chávez's hypothesize that major Chiripa centers and their settlement clusters represent so many "temple dominions." Cross-culturally, the two-tier site-size clusters so characteristic of Late Chiripa settlement are a hallmark for emergent chiefdoms (Wright 1984). In such societies, spiritual power and sociopolitical integration go hand in hand (see Earle 1989; Sahlins 1985). With this in mind, some hypothesize that the Early-Middle Formative witnessed the emergence of interacting, moderately ranked societies, essentially competing simple chiefdoms in which high-status groups and social power focused at major centers. According to Stanish (1999, 2003), sponsored feasting and commensalism, as witnessed in elaborate serving bowls and sunken courts, were fundamental to Chiripa's rise. Bandy (2001) suggests that increasing social tensions fostered social ranking.

In this scenario, decreasing options for settlement dispersal, in the face of population growth over generations, fostered the rise of large villages, community ceremonies, and other integrative practices. By 400 BC, at Chiripa's peak, ambitious leaders had emerged who could capitalize on the new trade routes that opened up once Lake Wiñaymarka began to recede far from established centers.

Chiripa was a pan-regional cultural complex characterized by a specific range of productive adaptations, recurring practices, and worldviews. Many or all of the previously noted processes – new ceremonies and ritual centers, feasting, social tensions, shifting environment and trade routes – most likely played a hand in Chiripa's emergence, ongoing transformation, and ultimate disappearance. As essential in my view were profound changes in ritual practice that increasingly emphasized vast communities and their ritual-political centers and common ancestors. Such changes were keyed to local participation in a pan-regional religious tradition known as Yayamama. By the end of the Middle Formative, prestigious community leaders and high-status groups obtained and employed, perhaps for relatively exclusive rituals, powerful symbols and objects associated with this tradition. Beyond other characteristic elements, Chiripa was one in a range of nested and overlapping spheres of cultural affiliation, each of which corresponded with a distinct domain of social identification and ritual practice.

Qaluyu

Qaluyu was an equally influential and enduring formative cultural complex located at the opposite end of the Lake Titicaca Basin. For lack of research, however, little is known of it. The namesake site is an extensive mound severed by a modern highway. Like Chiripa, Qaluyu formed an extensive network of ritual-political centers and productive regions. Qaluyu cultural affiliation extended north to Cuzco (K. L. M. Chávez 1977; Rowe 1956:144), east into the warm *yungas* (Plourde and Stanish 2001), and south to basalt outcrops in the Puno Bay, the border zone between Qaluyu and Chiripa (Frye and Steadman 2001; Steadman 1995). Important ritual-political centers included the site of Huatacoa, which incorporated several trapezoidal sunken court complexes built sequentially and over many generations (Cohen 2008). Closer to the lake was Taraco (Kidder 1943), home of the beautiful Yaya-Mama stela and high frequencies of obsidian from Cuzco. The Azángaro Valley, located en route to Cuzco, was particularly important. Located here was the large site of Asiruni, which comprised several bounded enclosures with sunken courts and sculpted stone stelae (Chávez and Chávez 1970;

Figure 3.7 Chiripa ceramic vessels and trumpets (adapted from Bennett 1936).

Stanish 2003:111–112). Such centers were located to procure valued resources and crafted goods (Burger, Mohr-Chávez, and Chávez 2000: 311–312).

Qaluyu settlements clustered far from the lake and extended into regions beyond the basin. Such a geographical distribution indicates that productive strategies and desired resources differed from those of Chiripa communities in the south. By the Middle Formative, llama herding and caravan exchange came to play a major role in local economies and regional interaction. Items sought and exchanged included valued minerals such as basalt and obsidian, crops such as maize and tubers, and exotic lowland goods such as chili peppers (ají), coca, and medicinal herbs. Farming and lacustrine activities such as fishing and algae harvesting were critical in lake-oriented communities. Clark Erickson (1988, 1993) found that Qaluyu-affiliated settlement was dense in the extensive marshy floodplains near Huatta. Extensive agriculture and perhaps specialized farming practices were critical in this area of Qaluyu's vast web.

Qaluyu like Chiripa encompassed highly diverse material styles and local communities. Research suggests that neither namesake site was the primary center of a religious tradition or polity, even though each played a key role in shifting networks of cultural identity and interaction. Affiliated communities used elaborate items with overall affinities to broader traditions but crafted according to local canons of technical and decorative style. Chiripa and Qaluyu were not as much centers for the dissemination of cultural, religious, or political influence as their broader spheres were encompassing matrices of social interaction and cultural identity in which local polities developed.

The Yayamama Religious Tradition

Forging a broader scale of political development and religious identity in the basin was the Yayamama religious tradition. Archaeologists have acknowledged an encompassing domain of religious and cultural affiliation since 1934, when Arthur Posnansky identified a double-faced style of stone sculpture at the site of Mocachi he termed "Pa-Ajanu." Following further refinement by archaeologists (Browman 1972, 1997b; Portugal Ortiz 1998b), Sergio and Karen Mohr Chávez rechristened it "Yaya-Mama" (Father-Mother in Quechua) in 1975. Ensuing analysis of the Yayamama style led to its acceptance as an ecumenical "religious tradition" that coalesced around the Lake Titicaca Basin after 400 BC, during the later Middle Formative. Associated with both Late Chiripa and Late Qaluyu complexes, the tradition is considered to "represent the first widespread unification of diverse groups . . . who used different pottery styles" (Burger, Chávez, and Chávez 2000) and maintained distinct productive regimes. In addition to stone sculpture, Yayamama is characterized by temples with sunken courts, ritual paraphernalia such as ceramic trumpets and burners, and, depicted on such media, elaborate mythical iconography (K. L. M. Chávez 1988; S. J. Chávez 2002; Steadman 1997). Yayamama gave rise to later sculptural styles such as Pukara in the northern basin and Khonkho to the south.

The Yayamama tradition involved ritual practices and religious ideals that were to varying degrees adopted and inculcated by groups across the basin. Trapezoidal courts, usually sunk into raised platforms, emerged as a significant form of ritual space by 400 BC. Stelae and panels portraying ancestral figures and mythical images decorated the interiors and walls of the temples, affording each the sense of the sacred it was meant to conjure in key events. As in similar temples across the Andes, ceremonies conducted in sunken courts often were group or community rituals that invoked the chthonic, generative, and animistic forces of the earth. Platforms served to "mark off" such places as significant ritual sites, but the courts themselves, set into the ground, served, most likely, as human-built loci for invoking group memory and establishing mutual agency among forces and beings in the realms of society, nature, and the cosmos. Rituals of particular gravity formed segments of larger community ceremonies, which as Stanish points out involved sponsored rituals of consumption. Such events, set in view of ancestral and mythical icons and accompanied by music and dance, invoked an immediate sense of "collective effervescence" (Durkheim 1915) and what Victor Turner (1969) termed *communitas*, through which group identities were recharged and status distinctions contested, created, or reproduced.

Yet no two Middle Formative temples were alike. Details in the orientation, spatial arrangement, and sculpted icons of temples varied site to site and region to region. Communities adopted certain widespread religious ideals and practices, but interpreted them drawing on local ideas of spirituality and ritual practice that had been developing for generations. Local styles of material, iconographic, and spatial designs point to significant local religious diversity founded in the development and coexistence of distinct Yayamama cults and their syncretism.

The paraphernalia involved in Yayamama ceremonies included decorated serving wares, incense burners, and ceramic trumpets. Late Chiripa and Late Qaluyu wares, vehicles for the food and drink that accompanied ceremonies, depicted some of the animal, mythical, and human-like images found on sculpted panels and stelae. Decorated burners and trumpets are found largely in ritual contexts, indicating that they were highly valued, restricted craft items that were produced by specialized groups. Ceramic burners, we can imagine, served to prepare ritual settings by enclosing spaces in the pungent aromas of resins, herbs, or liquids that invoked the vital and generative forces of the earth. Ceramic trumpets, perhaps much like Strombus-shell trumpets found at Chavin de Huantar, Peru (Rick 2004), infused rituals with persistent and penetrating tones that intensified participants' awareness and experience through sound. Trumpets depicted important Yayamama religious images following relatively uniform stylistic canons. Taste, movement, scent, and music piqued all senses and defined spaces as potent ritual places pregnant with the forces that generated society and nature.

At the heart of the Yayamama religious complex were the sculpted stone stelae and panels that decorated temples, plazas, and other built environments in Middle Formative settlements. Surprisingly little research pertaining to such monuments has been published, and to complicate matters, the timing and context of most sculptures, many of which are now found in local and international museums, is unclear. The names Pa-Ajanu and Yayamama refer most specifically to stone stelae that depict humanlike images on opposing faces. Several of these are known from the basin (Chávez and Chávez 1975; Kolata 1993a:79–81). The Yaya-Mama stela from Taraco depicts two humanlike opposing figures, one male and the other female (Figure 3.8). They wear different styles of headdress, neck ornaments, and plantlike designs over the navel, and each stands above a gnarled root from which sprouts a tuber, vegetable, or fruit. Social and biological complementarity accompanies other expressions of symmetry. Between the figures on the narrow faces of the stela are two pairs of double-headed serpentlike creatures, one above and one below a checkered waistband that enwraps the entire sculpture. Above each serpent-creature hovers the navel design from one of the two figures, associating the creature with the male or female domain. Thus, as Kolata notes (1993a:83), "principles of organization of the social world of humans extends to the natural world of plants and animals." By the same token, dual complementarity in human society derived from a specific view of nature. The Yaya-Mama stela elegantly depicts one dimension of an entire cosmology that viewed society, nature, and their constituent elements as interpenetrating and in reciprocal relation with one another.

The Yaya-Mama stela is a unique representation of iconography in the stylistic tradition. The bewildering range of known sculpted stelae and panels attributed to the tradition portrays a diversity of themes, and local versions of themes, in relation to certain shared concepts and ideals rooted in the Middle Formative (Figure 3.9). David Browman (1972, 1978a, 1997b) distinguishes enduring thematic substyles that overlapped in space and time, the most common of which he terms "Asiruni" and "Mocachi." Asiruni, from the Aymara word for "serpent," refers to relatively naturalistic depictions of "real" or mythological animals. Images depict creatures that look like fish, snakes, toads/frogs, lizards/ salamanders, and quadrupeds such as *vizcachas* or felines. Attributes of such animals are often freely combined in creative ways. Asiruni themes decorate a variety of panels and stelae across the basin. Some of the animals represented – especially fish, toads, and serpents – either inhabit rivers and lakes or herald the rainy season. Their undulating bodies conjure meandering, flowing rivers (Kolata 1993a:81). Overall the images invoke the wet, teeming, and life-giving powers of the earth, and thus

Figure 3.8 The Taraco Yaya-Mama Stela (adapted from Chávez and Chávez 1970, redrawn by Jennifer Ohnstad).

natural and agricultural fertility. Frequently accompanying them is a navel-like icon that may well represent a cosmic center of birth or creation.

The central image in most Mocachi-style stelae and panels is a human-like figure (Figure 3.10). Only a few stelae (including Yaya-Mama) represent two opposing figures. Facial features are generic, their expressions are impassive, and they are decorated with nose, chin, and other mask adornments. Frequently crawling around the head, navel, or sides of the figures were Asiruni toads, serpents, and lizards or salamanders. Arms are crossed over the chest, usually with the right arm over the left, sometimes with the left arm over the right, and in some cases with both arms raised. Navel adornments are depicted as a ring in some, as a flowering image

Figure 3.9 Two Yayamama panels (adapted from Ponce 1970).

in others or as a face with radiating heads, and in several cases from the eastern basin, a checkered cross. If this image represented a generative cosmic center, it varied by region or local cult.

Most likely, Mocachi stelae depict the deceased or mythical ancestor(s) of a community, much as did short, plump monoliths in Early Intermediate Period Recuay (Lau 2002). The depiction of masks, crossed arms, and other elements suggests that they portrayed the mummies that, normally kept in buildings such as those on the Chiripa platform, would have been brought out, dressed up, and celebrated during special ritual occasions. The cosmic navel and Asiruni images directly link the figures to the life-giving forces of the earth and cosmos, and by extension, to the reproductive capacities and well-being of the group that claimed common ancestry.

By the end of the Middle Formative, ancestors and fertility, both natural and human, were shared themes in Yayamama iconography and ritual practice across the basin. In some regions, these themes were interwoven with the idea of primordial male-female complementarity. Yet this ideal may not have been common to all communities who participated in the religious complex. In the eastern basin, the cosmic center as checkered cross may have been of particular importance and perhaps a cult fetish. Numerous plaques here, from sites such as Titimani and Tambo Kusi, depict elaborate, isolated versions of this image (Portugal Ortiz 1998b).

Figure 3.10 The tapered stela of Santiago de Huata.

In the southern basin, from the Taraco Peninsula to Santiago de Huata, several plaques and at least one stela depict an image consisting of a face or mask with four radiating scrolls and, above and below, an extended leg and foot. Whatever the meaning of such provocative images, variability in iconographic expression and in the use of interchangeable images for powerful concepts point to diverse local cults.

The Late Formative

Ten years ago the Late Formative was a black hole in the chronology of the Lake Titicaca Basin. Most recent archaeological research reveals critical regional developments across the basin and its environs. These developments emerged out of dynamic Middle Formative cultural and environmental shifts and ultimately gave rise to the nascent Tiwanaku state. In that sense, the phase has been a critical "missing link" in the cultural history of the south-central Andes. We now know that major autonomous sociopolitical formations developed in places across the basin, including Titimani to the northeast; the Santiago de Huata Peninsula to the southeast; the Juli-Pomata region to the southwest; and the Island of the Sun in the lake itself. Yet most important for long-term history were

Pukara in the northwestern basin, and the multicommunity polities of the southeastern basin that eventually formed the Tiwanaku heartland.

Pukara and the Northern Basin

Until recently, Pukara (Klarich 2005) was the best-known Late Formative sociopolitical formation in the Lake Titicaca Basin. Pukara thrived in the northern basin between 200 BC and AD 200, or Late Formative 1 (Figure 3.11). The processes leading to the wane of Qaluyu and the emergence of Pukara, and the shift from Qaluyu to Pukara cultural practices, remain unclear. Pukara temples and houses consistently cover Qaluyu occupations, and a large Qaluyu site underlies Pukara itself (Stanish 2003). Many of the sites associated with Qaluyu maintained strong affiliations with Pukara, suggesting that it was as a realignment and expansion of older Qaluyu trade networks, productive systems, and ritual practices.

Located some 80 kilometers from the lakeshore on a meandering river, the site of Pukara developed into an extensive settlement of at least 1 square kilometer (S. J. Chávez 1992). Set in front of an imposing cliff, it incorporated a high terraced platform that contained three large sunken courts, one of which was flanked by a hemispherical enclosure of small buildings with bins and niches (Figure 3.11b). Unlike most Middle Formative sunken courts, this one consisted of masterfully carved rectangular blocks and pilasters. Some of the bins in surrounding buildings contained wrapped human interments, most likely the ancestral mummies of local kin-based groups. The four chambers fixed on each side of the court also contained wrapped human interments with elaborate offerings (S. J. Chávez 1992:78–83).

Other platforms and sunken courts surrounded the raised monumental complex. Their architectural styles and orientations varied significantly, indicating that their construction did not follow an overarching plan. Rather, different communities most likely built them sequentially, maintaining each for locally sponsored feasts and rites. One of the courts contained dozens of human mandibles and skull parts, the remains of human sacrifices or dedications (S. J. Chávez 1992; Stanish 2003:143). Around the temples were extensive residential areas inhabited by groups of differing social status. Excavations revealed one commoner compound near the riverbank (S. J. Chávez 1992:59–68) and one high status compound closer to the central complex (Klarich 2005).

Pukara production and land use involved a shift toward floodplain farming and intensified regional interaction. A significant proportion of settlement shifted from the hillslopes down to the wetlands, so it is likely that some intensive wetland farming, and possibly small-scale raised field

A

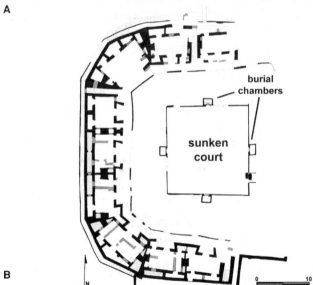

B

Figure 3.11 View (a) and map (b) of a ritual enclosure at Pukara (b, adapted from K. L. M. Chávez 1988).

agriculture, developed at this time. A shift to the pampas also points to intensified harvesting of lacustrine resources. Boosting local economies were multidirectional trade networks that extended in all directions. Some routes extended north toward Cuzco, as manifested in significant quantities of Cuzco obsidian at Pukara (Burger, Chávez, and Chávez 2000).

High quantities of such obsidian at Cotos, on the Capachica Peninsula to the south, suggest that the site was a regional center for its processing or distribution (Stanish 2003:145). Trade routes extended south toward the Puno Bay and into the southern basin, while others threaded into the humid *yungas* through passes in the Huancané and Putina valleys. Others extended into the drier coastal valleys of southern Peru and northern Chile, as manifested in Pukara-related ceramic styles in Moquegua and textile designs in Azapa (Goldstein 2000; Mujica 1985; Rivera 1991). Goods as diverse as agricultural produce, minerals, and lowland herbs traveled via llama caravan along these routes, linking diverse societies and geographical zones.

The character and complexity of Pukara are under debate. Some describe Pukara as a city (Kolata 1993a:70; Lumbreras 1981:202; Mujica 1978; Rowe 1963) and others as an agglutinated settlement (Stanish 2003:142). Some speak of Pukara's sphere as a state and others as a loosely integrated polity. Whatever its precise character, Pukara was an extensive settlement at the center of a far-flung network of political alliances, social interactions, economic exchanges, and ritual practices that had developed out of and replaced Qaluyu. Pukara may have been the first polity in the basin to focus on a primary center. Its networks included a core region in the northern Lake Titicaca Basin where Pukara leaders and religious specialists wielded significant influence and authority. Its networks linked far regions with which Pukara traders interacted and exchanged goods. Long-distance social and economic interaction became increasingly synergistic, giving rise to vigorous interregional alliances, sexual relations, kin bonds, and common identities.

Multicommunity Polities in the Southern Basin

Cultural development in the southern Lake Titicaca Basin during the Late Formative was vastly different from that in the north. No regional polity comparable to Pukara developed in the region until after AD 200, once Pukara itself began to wane in regional importance. Regions of particular importance include the Tiwanaku and Katari valleys, the Taraco Peninsula, and Machaca. What precisely occurred in these areas as Chiripa's distinctive ritual practices and sociopolitical organization began to disappear remains unclear. Overall continuity characterized certain social and material patterns, including the construction of raised platforms and trapezoidal sunken courts for community ceremonies and the use of carved stone monuments to render key mythical themes and spiritual ideas. Nevertheless, details of court construction and the iconography of religious stone sculptures changed considerably. Ceramic assemblages changed dramatically in technical and decorative style.

Serving bowls were smaller and decorated with simple red-painted rims and more elaborate ceremonial wares were limited to high status and ceremonial contexts. The widespread distribution of such elaborate wares temporarily came to an end.

Settlement and production shifted considerably. More people began to settle the pampas and major centers emerged in inland locations far from the lake and major rivers. Herding became more important in many local and regional economies (Webster and Janusek 2003). By the end of the Late Formative, local communities were most likely building and cultivating raised field segments on a relatively small scale, as one in a diverse array of farming technologies (Janusek 2001). Climatic shifts may have helped instigate these shifts in settlement and production (Abbott et al. 1997).

Political shifts also played an important role. Most of the important new centers in the southern basin were not those that had been of greatest importance in the Middle Formative. Late Formative occupations at Tiwanaku, Lukurmata, Kala Uyuni, and Khonkho Wankane all cover relatively small habitation sites that were at the peripheries of Middle Formative political communities (Bandy 2001; Janusek 2004b). Thus, cultural shift was tied to the establishment of new leaders and ritual centers on the edges of older polities, and thus arose out of shifting fields of alliance and competition. Dramatic cultural and economic shift involved both environmental change and sociopolitical volatility, and this would not be the last time such an historical conjuncture would transform the southern basin.

A number of important centers arose in the southern basin in Late Formative 1. Traditionally, we knew most about Tiwanaku based on early excavations (Bennett 1934; Kidder 1956; Ponce 1961, 1990, 1993). Carlos Ponce's excavations under the Kalasasaya exposed a primary occupation consisting of large cobble foundations, rectangular and circular structures, and offerings and burials containing elaborate Kalasasaya wares (Figure 3.12). The occupation included a terra-cotta whistle molded as an early house or shrine. The area appears to have been a residential compound that housed relatively high-status individuals and perhaps religious specialists. Adjacent to the east was a trapezoidal sunken court built early in the Late Formative (the Sunken Temple, see Chapter 4).

Tiwanaku was the center for a society that encompassed a significant part of the Tiwanaku Valley. It consisted of two adjacent residential communities: one centered on the Sunken Temple and another near what would later become the Pumapunku (Lemuz 2005). Nearby were several smaller settlements such as Kk'araña, which housed both rectangular and circular buildings. Other sites included Kallamarka (Albarracin-Jordan, Lemuz, and Paz 1993; Lemuz and Paz 2001) and Chuñuni several

Figure 3.12 Results of sub-Kalasasaya excavations: Late Formative 1 compound foundations (a–b), a Kalasasaya incision-zoned jar (c), and a terra-cotta whistle (d) (adapted from Ponce 1993).

kilometers to the east, Tilata just to the northwest (Mathews 1992), and Iwawe on the lakeshore (Burkholder 1997; Isbell and Burkholder 2002). Some of these sites incorporated ritual platforms or a sunken court. The inhabitants of such sites hunted, herded, and consumed camelids; farmed nearby fields; and at Iwawe, harvested lake resources such as fish and *totora* reed.

In the Katari Valley, Lukurmata became a major regional center (Figure 3.4). A Late Formative ritual complex remains to be found, but one most likely exists under later monumental structures perched atop the prominent hill of Wila Kollu. Marc Berman's (1994:59–96) excavations in a saddle just below the hilltop revealed a long sequence of

Figure 3.13 Excavation of a ritual chamber at Kala Uyuni.

superimposed residential occupations, each with clay living surfaces as well as garbage pits, work areas, hearths, and burials. Affiliated settlements included the Quiripujo Mound Group in the adjacent Koani Pampa (Janusek and Kolata 2003). These settlements were some of the first to occupy the floodplain, opening this flat zone – now drier than it had been for centuries – to human occupation and intensive farming. Mound inhabitants produced agricultural tools and, in turn, many were buried with them upon their death. Ritual practice was important at such settlements. The Kirawi mound housed a building of pure red clay with a clean-swept floor. Buildings such as these, we may hypothesize, served local household or other local ritual practices while monumental complexes at major sites housed periodic communal rituals and political gatherings.

The Taraco Peninsula remained an important center of cultural development in Late Formative 1; yet, it witnessed significant changes in settlement distribution. Many of the largest Middle Formative centers, including Chiripa, decreased in size and importance while some former villages emerged as large settlements with sunken courts and carved monoliths. Cultural development shifted to the peripheries of old communities as new leaders and cult centers emerged. One of the most important was Kala Uyuni, settled on the flanks of the Taraco range overlooking Lake

Wiñaymarka. Incorporating two sunken courts atop a prominent hill during the Middle Formative, the site's later settlement shifted to the lower piedmont below, where recent excavations revealed residential middens and a small ritual chamber (Figure 3.13) (Paz Soria and Fernandez 2007). Bandy and Hastorf (2007) interpret the site as the center of a multicommunity polity that encompassed most of the peninsula and thrived alongside the Tiwanaku and Lukurmata polities to the east.

In the Machaca region of the Upper Desaguadero Basin, south of the rugged Kimsachata-Chilla range, Khonkho Wankane emerged as a major regional center in Late Formative 1 (Janusek 2005a, 2008b; Janusek, Ohnstad, and Roddick 2003). Settlement shift in the Middle to Late Formative transition was as substantial here as it was elsewhere. Set on a low terrace in the pampa some 30 kilometers from the Desaguadero River, Khonkho's rise was coeval with a shift to drier conditions and new productive emphases. At around AD 1, populations covered the terrace and an early occupation with a massive rectangular mound. Overlooking a vast landscape, the mound incorporated a trapezoidal sunken court (Figure 3.14). As in Tiwanaku's court, the primary entrance into Khonkho's was in the south wall. One descended into a ritual space that expanded slightly to the north, visually aggrandizing ceremonies or monuments located at the opposite end. The walls consisted of carved or shaped pilasters alternating with sections of roughly shaped fieldstones. A unique characteristic of Khonkho's court was that its primary entrance consisted of bricks fired to vivid green, yellow, and orange hues. The superimposed floors of the court were littered with ceramic sherds and splintered bones of camelids and small mammals. Apparently, among ceremonies conducted here were lively rituals of consumption.

The sunken court at Khonkho joined places for both intimate and communal activities. On its east side was an extensive, walled residential compound containing circular dwellings (Figure 3.14). An opening in its west wall faced a small private entrance into the sunken court. Most likely, this compound, like the sub-Kalasasaya compound in Tiwanaku, housed a high-status group who tended the court and planned and choreographed its ceremonies. At least two other compounds occupied the east side of the mound, including a massive ritual-residential compound containing clusters and patio groups of circular structures. The court and the compounds opened into an extensive plaza that served communal ritual and political gatherings. Underneath it ran a massive stone-lined canal that drained the entire ritual-residential complex. Khonkho was the center for numerous villages and hamlets in the region and we can imagine that representatives from these places and more distant centers and regions periodically gathered in the main plaza for a variety of significant

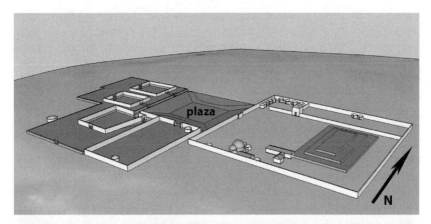

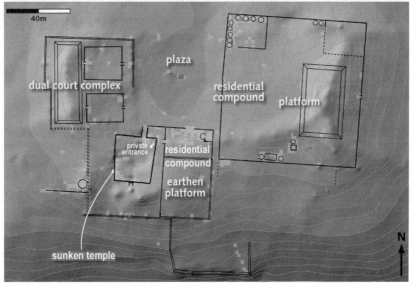

Figure 3.14 Khonkho Wankane's ceremonial complex during Late
Formative 2.

events. It is an intriguing parallel that today, on every June solstice, representatives from each *ayllu* in the region and people from more distant places gather in this same spot to conduct community rituals, feast and dance, and elect new leaders (Text Box 2.1).

By AD 200 much of the basin comprised a macroregion of what Renfrew (1986) terms "peer-polity interaction." Rather than well-defined political units or "chiefdoms" with hard-and-fast boundaries, these polities were fluid in composition, their networks of influence shifting with changing climatic, political, and socioeconomic conditions. Further, if analogies with Early Dynastic Mesopotamia or Pre-Classic Maya civilization serve as useful analogies, influential "über-leaders," heading more encompassing interregional polities, emerged for brief periods. Yet, a centralized polity on the order of Pukara arose only after AD 400.

Tiwanaku emerged from fluid networks of several multicommunity polities as a ceremonial settlement beyond parallel and, eventually, as the primary cultural, religious, and political center in the basin. Although we cannot pinpoint precisely the process behind Tiwanaku's emergence, it is clear that major changes were afoot across the basin by AD 250, or Late Formative 2. First, lake cores detect a wetter climate and rise in lake levels about this time, which may have flooded old circumlacustrine trade routes and opened opportunities for inland sites such as Tiwanaku (Abbott et al. 1997). Second, the Pukara polity "collapsed" after AD 200, possibly as part of this long-range shift in climate and interaction networks. Whatever other processes were involved with Pukara's political and cultural decline remain to be discovered, but it involved substantial settlement dispersal, a hiatus in monumental construction, and an end to Pukara's elaborate ceramic and clothing styles. The succeeding Huaña formation was a fluid sociopolitical landscape of interacting agropastoral communities and small-scale polities much as had characterized the southern basin.

Third, the southern basin witnessed important changes in settlement and material culture. Replacing elaborate Kalasasaya wares were Qeya ceremonial wares, a suite of elaborate vessels even more restricted in distribution than Kalasasaya wares (Janusek 2003a). On the Taraco Peninsula, Kala Uyuni waned and other settlements were abandoned. The Santa Rosa settlement group at the tip of the peninsula, far from Tiwanaku and Lukurmata, became more important during Late Formative 2. Iwawe came to serve as a port where inhabitants worked large andesite blocks brought by raft from quarries across Lake Wiñaymarka (Isbell and Burkholder 2002; Ponce et al. 1971). Lukurmata became a more important regional center and established closer ties with Tiwanaku (Bermann 1994). Occupations in the saddle below Wila Kollu incorporated special-purpose buildings for storing surplus crops and yielded Qeya wares in an elaborate local style closely related to precocious ceramic styles in Cochabamba, far to the southeast. In Machaca, Khonkho Wankane expanded precipitously (Janusek 2008b). A new Dual-Court complex on the site's west platform faced the massive ritual-residential compound to the east (Figure 3.14). Spatial organization followed a new east-west axis keyed to rising ideological concerns, including the sun's annual cycle.

This occurred just as Tiwanaku itself expanded into a major settlement of nearly 1 square kilometer with new residential sectors and diverse ritual environments. Whatever specific religious, economic, and political cards were at play, and tied to whatever historical vagaries, they trumped the ideals of competing centers. In Late Formative 2, an early version of the Kalasasaya was built over the residential compound next to the Sunken Temple (Ponce 1981). The site expanded precipitously as people were attracted to Tiwanaku's burgeoning opportunities and rising religious prestige and, perhaps, in fulfillment of obligations to high-status and religious groups. Tiwanaku's population most likely grew by reproduction, immigration, and conscription. By AD 500, Tiwanaku was the most extensive center in the Lake Titicaca Basin and its prestige was grounded in cultural values and religious ideals that had been developing in the region for centuries.

Myth, Ritual, and Iconography

Changes in politics and environment accompanied changes in religious themes, ritual practices, and the depiction of mythical and spiritual forces. Across the basin, such changes are apparent in ceramic iconography, stone sculpture, and ritual paraphernalia. Pukara artisanry in ceramics, textiles, and stone sculpture was unprecedented, indicating that specialists were fully dedicated to their professions. Ceremonial ceramic wares depicted a wide range of incised-and-painted iconography that, Sergio Chávez argues (2002), boils down to two principal themes: the Camelid Woman and the Feline Man (Figure 3.15). Like depictions of nativity or the "twelve stations" for Christians, vessels depicted scenes or icons associated with a fundamental Pukara mythical narrative. The Camelid Woman, found exclusively on certain burners, faces the viewer holding a staff in the right hand and a tethered camelid in the left. On either side of her personage is a flowering or dormant plant. The Feline Man, often represented on ceramic trumpets, is usually depicted in profile wearing a feather headdress and a tunic and holding a trophy head in one hand and a ceremonial knife in the other. Isolated motifs on other vessels may refer to one or the other of these master narratives. If this gendered association of motifs is accurate, then the Camelid Woman conjured generation, domestication, and authority while the Feline Man conjured battle, sacrifice, and shamanic power.

Stone sculpture depicted a range of themes that developed out of Yayamama iconography. Pukara surpassed Yayamama sculpture in size and sophistication. Sculptures now included tall stelae and monoliths, many notched, and their design included intricate low relief carving as

Figure 3.15 The Camelid Woman (a) and Feline Man (b) (redrawn from S. Chávez 1992 by Jennifer Ohnstad).

well as effigy sculptures carved in the round. Asiruni figures remained focal icons on many sculptures, often depicted in panoptic skeletal view. Some low-relief monoliths depicted series of panels containing elaborately stylized images in dual and quadripartite symmetry. The Arapa-Thunderbolt stela (S. J. Chávez 1976; Kidder 1943; Uhle 1912) depicted undulating serpent-bodied creatures, opposing terraced platforms, and converging lightning bolts, each image centered on a focal icon set in a

Figure 3.16 Detail of the Arapa-Thunderbolt stela.

diamond-shaped panel (Figure 3.16). Browman (1997b) believes mono-liths represent the culmination of Asiruni expression in depicting, in an abstracted style, the earthy and generative forces of the cosmos. In overall design the dense, byzantine images approximate the mental "entoptics" commonly induced by hallucinogenic experience, and so implicate the use of mind-altering substances in Pukara ritual.

Another sculptural tradition developed out of the Mocachi substyle, and it depicted anthropomorphic beings and ancestral images. Low-relief monoliths depicted elaborately garbed beings, perhaps deified ancestors, wearing magnificent headdresses with feathers, animal masks, and feline appendages. On most a navel-like icon of cosmic generation occupied the upper, bladelike portion of the notch. Specialists developed a style that emphasized figures carved in high relief or in the round. A number of these sculptures depicted humanlike figures with alert oval eyes, arms crossed over the chest in a variety of manners, and a face mask and short tunic over the lower torso. In some, the body was depicted in skeletal view showing ribs, suggesting that the individuals were ancestors (Kidder 1943). In others, humans with feline features hold trophy heads in gestures of intimidation and power, intimating that battle, ritual or otherwise, was a significant Pukara practice. Such images associated community ancestors with ritualized violence and trophy head capture.

Ceramic iconography in the southern basin incorporated Pukara themes but followed different stylistic and ideological canons. Kalasasaya decorated wares, found in Late Formative 1 ritual contexts, were similar in certain elements of design and iconography to Pukara decorated wares. They even shared certain stylistic traits with vessels from the Paracas cultural complex on the Peruvian south coast (Sawyer 1977). Iconographic themes included three-tiered platforms, perhaps abstract mountains or terraced platforms, and spotted felines in motion (Janusek 2003a:54–55). Felines were characteristically depicted with a profile body in a dynamic "running" position and a grimacing frontal face that confronts the viewer (Figure 3.12c). Such a face commonly stood alone on stone sculptures and on vessels and other media associated with Pukara and Paracas. The face became a figurative mask with feline-human characteristics and conjured the religious ceremonies and dances in which ritual specialists and participants transformed into mediators between natural/human and ancestral worlds as well as present and past time.

Specialists in Qeya ceremonial wares during Late Formative 2 elaborated these themes and created others. Abstract geometrical images included three-tiered steps, nested crosses, and stylized "chevron" heads. Felines remained important, but the naturalism of human-felines dropped in favor of surreal mythical beings hovering on a black background, reminiscent of Paracas textiles or contemporary Jalq'a textiles from central Bolivia (Figure 3.17). The beings often have feline or avian characteristics but always have three tentacle-like appendages capped with rings. The ideal, it appears, shifted toward representing *desconocidos*, or composite creatures unknown to this world that live in dreams, a supernatural domain, or past time. Ceremonial vessels depicting such images included incense burners crafted as effigy felines themselves, objects that would have been used in rituals designed to invoke such beings or ancestors. The relative rarity of Kalasasaya and Qeya wares

Figure 3.17 A Qeya ceremonial vessel and typical Qeya-style
mythical beings (drawings adapted from Bennett 1934).

alludes to the restriction of ritual power to specific ritual contexts, social
groups, or religious specialists.

Late Formative residential groups crafted and used paraphernalia for
storing and ingesting mind-altering substances (Bermann 1994; Janusek
2004a). Found at sites across the southern basin are bone tablets, spoons,
spatulas, stoppers, and tubes depicting pyroengraved iconography. The
substances have not yet been identified, but we can imagine that they
included mild medicinal plants such as coca and any of a vast array
of powerful hallucinogens of the genera *Ilex*, *Datura*, *Banisteriopsis*, and
Anadenanthera (Browman 1978a), all native to the nearby, subtropical
eastern *yungas* (see Chapters 2 and 6). Chewing coca may have been
a common practice with social and medicinal roles similar to those it
still has today. Ingesting hallucinogens would have profoundly enhanced
ritual experience and efficacy.

Stone sculpture in the southern basin includes two traditions; Pukara
and Khonkho. Pukara style sculptures, we may infer, dated to Late Formative 1. Some figures were carved in the round much like those in the
northern basin, and some hold a trophy head. Four intriguing sculptures
from Pokotia in the Tiwanaku Valley depict kneeling figures with skeletal
chests and visible navels (Figure 3.18; Portugal Ortiz 1998b). Each of
the figures wears a turbanlike headdress from the back of which hang
two serpentlike braids ending in profile feline heads. The zoomorphic
braids are similar to those found on sculptures from the northern basin.
Nevertheless, the overall design and pose of the figures are unique, and

Figure 3.18 The Pokotia sculptures (adapted from Posnansky 1945, Vol. 2).

suggest repose. Like most Pukara-related sculptures in the late Mocachi tradition, these may depict ancestral personages.

Some Khonkho-style monoliths date to Late Formative 2. Some of the most elaborate – several over five meters high – are from Tiwanaku and Khonkho Wankane, but others are known from sites in Taraco, Katari, and Santiago de Huata. They manifest a stylistic culmination of the Mocachi substyle and its stylized depictions of apical ancestors. Like early ancestral depictions in Yayamama style, Khonkho figures are shown with arms crossed over the chest, either right over left or left over right (Figure 3.19). The faces of the figures vary greatly. The monoliths incorporate discrete panels, each depicting an isolated scene that freezes a moment in mythical time. They include opposed ascending felines or humans, a "falling man" with skeletal ribs, and a clothed llama-human with a wing and a headdress of animal heads. Encircling each figure's waistband and slithering up and down its sides are opposed figures with serpen-tine bodies and whiskered faces. They mimic the pre-adult catfish that inhabit Lake Titicaca and the streams and marshes that surround sites

A　　　　　　　　　　　B

Figure 3.19 Khonkho's Wilakala monolith and winged llama design
(drawing by Arik Ohnstad, photo by Wolfgang Schüler).

such Khonkho Wankane. Khonkho monoliths, much like totem poles
in more recent native societies on the northwest North American coast,
appear to depict representations and stories of apical ancestors and their
respective communities. Each was decorated with mythical images representing shared religious ideals, but each also depicted a distinct range
of icons and images particular to that personage and its representative
community.

It is likely that such monoliths stood in sunken courts during the
Late Formative. Bennett (1934) found two Khonkho-style monoliths in
Tiwanaku's Sunken Temple lying next to the later Bennett Monolith.
This likelihood raises the possibility that rituals in such spaces focused
on and were conducted in panoptic view of such icons. Assuming that

the monoliths depicted ancestors with close genealogical relations to high status groups, such groups had come to hold privileged positions in society and the cosmos. Thus, sunken courts at centers such as Khonkho and Tiwanaku were microcosmic spaces in which social relations and time, remembered as genealogical ties, were telescoped and frozen in an intimate ceremonial environment.

New forms of expression and iconography mark fundamental shifts in religious ideology in the Lake Titicaca Basin. New religious values developed out of Yayamama traditions, but they took form alongside significant changes in ritual practices and social relations. Such shifts are apparent in at least three new characteristics of Late Formative sculpture and iconography. First, they now depicted figures holding trophy heads, images typically interpreted as representing intensified militarism or social hierarchy (Cook 1994; Kolata 1993a; Stanish 2003). While evoking militarism and social power, the images may refer most directly to ancestral warriors and their past victories and trophies, which were enlivened in later oral histories and military acts. Second, iconography, vessels, and ritual paraphernalia point to an increasing reliance on mind-altering and hallucinogenic substances. Altered states of consciousness helped forge a memory path into the realms of deceased ancestors and primordial beings, effectively tapping the ancient, generative, and chthonic powers of the cosmos. Third, stone sculptures emphasized the social and spiritual centrality of ancient community ancestors. They did so both in size and in design, in that Asiruni images evoking generative powers were now depicted as mythical "stills" on a central personage. Militarism, transcendence, and mythical ancestry were three social values that increasingly came to shape social and religious values just as Tiwanaku became the major center in the south-central Andes.

Conclusions

Between AD 400 and 500, Tiwanaku crashed the party as the most prestigious center in the Lake Titicaca Basin and the south-central Andes. The question, "Why Tiwanaku?" as yet yields obscure answers. Tiwanaku was one of many coexisting, competing political-ceremonial centers in the southern basin and would soon become one of the most influential centers in the Andes. The Lake Titicaca Basin was inherently productive and, as recent settlement surveys indicate, densely populated. Yet there was no preordained reason this settlement would become an unparalleled cultural, economic, and political center. Tiwanaku commanded no inherently privileged landscape or important economic resource.

Natural phenomena and historical circumstance undoubtedly played their unexpected hands in Tiwanaku's ascendance. After AD 200, increasing rainfall caused the lake to rise and its shores to expand, shifting the course of circum-Titicaca trade routes to inland locations such as the Tiwanaku Valley. Shifting political circumstances also played their part. In particular, Pukara was no longer a significant force in the basin. Regardless, no circumstance or process single-handedly determined the history of the world region as it was about to unfold. Rather a conjunction of circumstances, forces, and emerging cultural principles and human activities appear to have been at work.

Searching for the reasons behind state development in general, and Tiwanaku's rise in particular, encourages a shift in focus to their deeper historical trajectories and encompassing cultural milieu. The Lake Titicaca Basin and surrounding regions supported the development of local complex societies over the many generations of the Formative, in particular during the Late Formative. With a shift toward sedentism and an increasing reliance on domestic crops and animals came new types of social relations, regional interactions, and cosmologies. In the face of increasing settlement density, and given the natural risk and unpredictability of the environment, regional interaction and reciprocity emerged as key socioeconomic principles. Intricate interaction networks were well in place by the time Tiwanaku emerged as a regional center. Forged by trains of llamas packed with crops, salt, minerals, coca, and other valued goods, they formed both local circuits and longer cyclical treks perhaps months in duration that linked regions and trade hubs. High-status groups expanded their social networks and secured access to exotica and prestige goods such as ceremonial wares and obsidian. At the end of Late Formative 2, the Lake Titicaca Basin housed a pan-regional network of interactive local rulers who collectively identified as a distinct cosmopolitan class. Class distinction was most patently practiced in home communities, where high-status groups sought to control the flow of valued goods, dominate access to ritual spaces and activities, and situate their ancestral personages at the centers of social and religious life.

Interaction also had religious meanings and goals. People sought non-local friendships, kin ties, and alliances as well as the mind-altering means to gain otherworldly experience and religious inspiration. Cosmologies emphasizing representations of mythical ancestors, prominent landscape features, and ultimately trophy heads, became increasingly widespread and prestigious. Vibrant regional interaction fostered and was shaped by shared religious ideologies and ritual practices. Thus, Tiwanaku emerged as an encompassing political community in a regional setting already characterized by far-reaching political, economic, and spiritual interaction and cultural affiliation.

Throughout the Formative, multiple centers rose, coexisted, and eventually waned. Even in the naturally productive Lake Titicaca Basin, no single center controlled or unilaterally influenced other lakeside regions. Within and beyond the basin, the drive to find single primary centers has failed. At any time, the south-central Andes incorporated multiple political-ritual centers, diverse groups, and overlapping economic and religious networks. Sites once considered primary centers were not the only influential settlements or even the most influential centers. Internalizing and interpreting common themes, each region and to some extent each center cultivated a distinctive brand of ritual practice and ideology, as witnessed for example in local twists on sculptural style in the Yayamama tradition. Multiple centers developed, interacted, and competed, and out of this climate Yayamama emerged as a diversified, syncretic interaction network rather than a uniform religion. Pukara became a complex polity in Late Formative 1, but only in dynamic interaction with other communities, polities, and religious traditions. Analogous to pan-regional formations in other world areas, including the Olmec horizon, the Chaco phenomenon, and the Uruk world system, south-central Andean communities forged far-reaching social identities and cultural affiliations.

The question is not simply why Tiwanaku rose to power or how it came to influence vast regions and peoples but, rather, in what manners did the south-central Andes as a socially and environmentally diversified region foster state coalescence. To be sure, a particularly astute or charismatic group of leaders and religious specialists, perhaps even an embryonic dynasty, had gained power at the right place and time in Tiwanaku during the fifth century. Yet a more important question is: How did diverse local societies and the emerging "global" situation foster Tiwanaku's far-reaching prestige and influence? The early cultural patterns outlined in this chapter go some way toward addressing such questions; yet, they raise far more questions than they provide answers. The next three chapters, which deal, respectively, with the Tiwanaku city, its geographical heartland, and its geopolitical relations, outline the expansionist formation that emerged out of these critical phases of cultural development in the Lake Titicaca Basin.

4   The City of Tiwanaku

Cities are compelling. They are also extraordinarily complex. Consider New York, arguably *the* cultural center of the United States and a major socioeconomic and ideological center in the current global order. Now, articulate a definitive perspective of New York's significance. Not so easy, is it? We all know quite a bit about New York. We may understand the symbolic importance of the Statue of Liberty, appreciate the cultural appeal (and malcontents) of Central Park, and admit the economic power of Wall Street. We intuitively know these places but cannot fully articulate their overall meaning and roles in our lives. Cities like New York are incredibly complex and ever-changing phenomena. We cannot completely wrap them up in a singular definition or "wrap our heads" around their manifold significance.

Archaeologists likewise struggle to understand ancient cities. Ancient cities are places where populations came together for various reasons. Many were cultural, political, or economic centers. The Australian archaeologist V. Gordon Childe considered "urban revolution" the main force driving the rise of civilizations. For Childe, ancient cities had both divisive and integrative institutions. In early cities, a tiny ruling class siphoned surplus production from farmers, herders, and other low-class populations (Childe 1950:16). Yet diversified occupations ultimately integrated urban groups and the ancient city became a social community *sui generis*. According to Childe, in successful ancient cities there was "no room for skeptics and sectaries."

Traditional approaches to urbanism underemphasize the protean and experiential character of many ancient cities. Past cities changed significantly along with shifting ecological conditions, sociopolitical systems, and religious ideologies. Like major cities today, cities in the past were constantly under construction. Some landmarks remained for generations, such as Rome's Hut of Romulus, Constantinople's Hagia Sofia, and Chicago's Water Tower. In such cases, the monument endured while its significance transformed over time. In addition, if past central cities were concrete symbols for a vast community they were also supremely fascinating to experience. Cities such as Rome in Europe, Teotihuacan in Mesoamerica, and Uruk in Mesopotamia were meant to evoke. They were built and continually enhanced to inspire awe among elites, citizens, diplomats, and pilgrims.

Further, many ancient cities were cosmopolitan. They incorporated people of varied status and ethnicity and appealed to the varied activities and ideals of commoners and elites alike. Archaeology testifies that many ancient cities incorporated significant social diversity. People living in the same city and participating in the same state culture in Rome and Teotihuacan also differed in status, occupation, ethnicity, kinship, ancestry, and other expressions of social identity. Ethnic segments, craft specialists, barrio communities, political factions, descent groups, age grades, and gender-based sodalities were vibrant domains of activity, identity, and power for those who also considered themselves Roman or Teotihuacano.

Tiwanaku is one of the most evocative and curious ancient sites in South America. For many travelers and early archaeologists, it was an empty ceremonial center situated in a forbidding landscape. For Bolivian nationalists and others, it was the urban capital of an expansive military empire. Most recently, Tiwanaku is interpreted as the political-ritual center of a noncentralized federation of *ayllus*, ethnicities, and polities. Each perspective brings something useful to the table, but none adequately captures Tiwanaku in its historical and social intricacy. The extremes of each position seek to find in Tiwanaku a fundamental determining essence. A more nuanced perspective demands greater attention to its dramatic transformations, religious significance, and cosmopolitan character.

In Chapter 3, I described the formative regional setting in which Tiwanaku emerged, and the importance of specific environmental, sociopolitical, and ideological changes in Tiwanaku's rise to power and prominence. This chapter sharpens the focus spatially to delineate the later urban history of the settlement. It concentrates first on Tiwanaku's impressive temples, monuments, and material culture, moves on to Tiwanaku's role as a center of elite power, and then shifts to the significance of its constituent non-elite poplations. It benefits from a wealth of recent research into Tiwanaku's monumental complexes, elite activity zones, and vast residential and craft-production sectors (Figure 4.1). I ask: How did Tiwanaku change through time? What was the role of religious symbolism and experience in the center? Was their room for "skeptics and sectaries" in its massive temples and vast residential barrios?

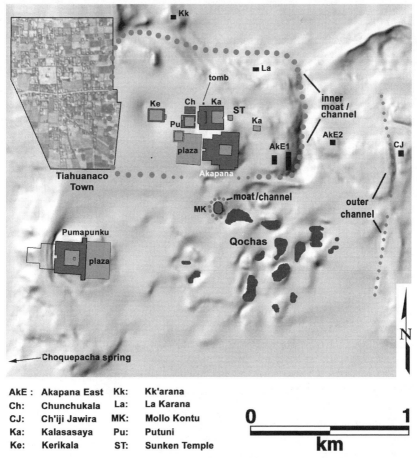

Figure 4.1 Principle features and excavated areas of Tiwanaku (base map by Arik Ohnstad).

AkE :	Akapana East	Kk:	Kk'arana
Ch:	Chunchukala	La:	La Karana
CJ:	Ch'iji Jawira	MK:	Mollo Kontu
Ka:	Kalasasaya	Pu:	Putuni
Ke:	Kerikala	ST:	Sunken Temple

Tiwanaku as Cosmic Symbol and Religious Experience

Monumental Architecture and Ceremonial Space

Tiwanaku incorporated several monumental complexes and numerous stone monoliths and portals. Visually dominating the ruins today are two groups of monuments, one to the northeast and one to the southwest. Structures in these complexes were built at different times in Tiwanaku's history and most were continually refurbished, rebuilt, or transformed. The most prominent structures of the northeast group include the Sunken Temple and Kalasasaya platform, first built in the Late Formative, and the Akapana platform, begun either near the end of this period or early in Tiwanaku 1. The Pumapunku platform, on which construction was begun in Tiwanaku 1, lies to the southwest. Although no formative structures are currently visible here, high frequencies of formative artifacts around the complex may indicate that the Pumapunku covers them (Lemuz 2005).

Tiwanaku's monuments were built to evoke awe among local and non-local populations alike by emphasizing solidity, mass, and permanence (Figure 4.2). William Conklin (1991:20) observes that, grounded in "an obsession with the horizon," Tiwanaku monumental "building intended to convey religious imagery and to impress." Each major complex was linked to others via paths that guided people into and through the urban core. Each structure drew subjects up onto raised platforms, through portals and passages, and then down into smaller inner temples and courts that were the setting for powerful rituals and dramatic performances. Tiwanaku was meant to be experienced up close.

Sunken Temple. Monumental architecture first appeared in Tiwanaku during the Late Formative. The first known structure was the Sunken Temple, a relatively small rectangular subterranean court with a single staircase that directed people into it from the south (Figure 4.3a). Sunken courts of various shapes and dimensions had become common around the Lake Titicaca Basin during the Early-Middle Formative. Tiwanaku's court comprised walls of sandstone pilasters alternating with segments of smaller ashlar and fieldstone masonry. The walls were fitted with tenoned effigy heads, many of them carved out of pink-hued stones (Figure 4.3b). Some depict deity-like beings with impassive faces and elaborate headdresses, others appear to represent skulls with desiccated skin and sunken eye sockets, and still others appear to be wailing phantasms like the banshees of Irish lore. Many depict beings with culturally modified heads. The images may represent ancestors of the various groups that formed the Tiwanaku ritual-political community at this time (Couture 2002; Kolata 1993a). They all faced one or more large Khonkho-style monoliths that stood in the courtyard. These monoliths depicted what were most likely the more ancient and powerful mythical ancestors of the collective community. Differentiated social groups and powerful supernatural forces were concatenated to form a comprehensive community united by place and ritual kinship.

The Sunken Temple was a built icon that physically mirrored an idealized social and cosmic order. Its south entrance framed the peak of Mount

Figure 4.2 Aerial view of Tiwanaku's main monumental core (photo
courtesy of Marilyn Bridges).

Kimsachata to the south and may have been positioned to mark the rise of
important constellations in the nighttime sky (Benitez 2005, 2006). The
iconicity of the temple was breathed life in the rituals that periodically
took place within its confines. These rituals were most likely dedicated as
much to the chthonic forces of the earth that the structure inhabited, as to
the animistic power of mountains in the surrounding landscape and the
predictable cycles of celestial bodies and constellations over the horizon.

Kalasasaya. West of and facing the Sunken Temple, the Kalasasaya platform was initiated in Late Formative 2 and embellished over time (Figure 4.4). The platform covered an early residential complex with elaborate
tombs, rich offerings, and finely crafted prestige objects (see Chapter 3).
In building the Kalasasaya over this residence, which may have been home
to some of Tiwanaku's high-status founders, those in charge sought to
position themselves as legitimate inheritors of Tiwanaku's early ritual
prestige (Couture 2002:314–315). This was among the first of many
monumental constructions to follow an east-west axis, a new spatial
practice that established novel visual and proxemic pathways to major

Figure 4.3 The Sunken Temple and its tenoned heads.

Figure 4.4 The Kalasasaya (photo by Wolfgang Schüler).

terrestrial features and celestial bodies. A shallow sunken court occupied the eastern bulk of the platform, which was framed by megalithic revetment walls. Like the walls of the Sunken Temple, these alternated monolithic pilasters – but now, massive sandstone blocks – with sections of ashlar and fieldstone masonry. Terraces and hallways with painted murals abutted sections of the platform. The plan of the complex, with its outer platform and sunken inner sanctum, and its east-west orientation, established a prototype for later monumental construction and was a key element of Tiwanaku's developing cosmology (see "Portals and Ritual Movement," below).

Early in Tiwanaku 1, a balcony supported by massive and superbly wrought andesite pilasters was added to the west side of Kalasasaya. This served as an observatory for calendar-keeping priests (see Box 4.1; Benitez 2005), and the famous Sun Portal that stands nearby may have served as an accompanying almanac.

Akapana. Early Tiwanaku 1, a dynamic phase across the basin, witnessed intensification and dramatic innovations in the planning and construction of monumental complexes at Tiwanaku. Perhaps most impressive was the Akapana (Figure 4.5). Following a directional orientation slightly different from that of Kalasasaya, the Akapana consisted of seven superimposed terraces that culminated in a high platform (Manzanilla 1992).

Box 4.1 Sun Portal as Solar Almanac

Calendrical knowledge is critical in agropastoral societies. People must learn and pass on to their children accumulated knowledge regarding celestial-seasonal cycles and recurring climatic shifts that dictate cycles of life and regeneration for humans, crops, and animals. Specialized knowledge of natural cycles is implicated in the rise of many prehistoric states, including Tiwanaku. The emergence of intricate knowledge regarding celestial cycles allowed certain people to accurately predict seasonal changes as well as unusual events such as eclipses, and to effectively orchestrate a recurring round of calendrical rituals and feasts throughout the year. This objectification of time, as the domain of ritual specialists and perhaps their associated leaders, was doubtless a key reason for Tiwanaku's rise to power.

In the southern Titicaca Basin, a spike in the importance of keeping accurate and intricate calendrical knowledge occurred sometime during the fourth or fifth century, in Late Formative 2. It is manifested in spatial organization as a shift at some major centers from sunken courts to architectural complexes aligned along an east-west orientation. The entrances of early sunken courts at Khonkho Wankane and Tiwanaku faced south, forming visual pathways with important local peaks (Sajama at Khonkho, Kimsachata at Tiwanaku) and celestial constellations (Benitez 2005). The construction of the Dual-Court complex at Khonkho and the Kalasasaya at Tiwanaku materialized a new orientation that approximated the daily path of the sun. In their orientation, these monuments harnessed the sun's symbolic power. They directed people through portals and ritual places according to paths of movement that replicated the sun's ancient and enduring daily journey. Further, they facilitated the observance and prediction of more esoteric, recurring annual events.

The Sun Portal has long been considered a kind of almanac for tracking and predicting calendrical cycles and events (Figure 4.18). The rayed headdress of the principal figure conjures the sun's visual brilliance. Some have noted that the number of repeated figures approximates important numbers in the Gregorian calendar (Kolata 1993a; Posnansky 1945). The thirty profile attendants approximate the number of days in a month. The total number of frontal rayed faces, adding that of the main figure to the eleven frontal faces entwined in the undulating band at the bottom of the frieze, marks the number of months in the year. Yet the last interpretation is somewhat forced in that it imposes Western timekeeping practices on a monument produced in a very different cultural setting.

The key to understanding the Sun Portal, argues Leonardo Benitez (2005), lies in the western balcony wall nearby. For years, Bolivian archaeologist Cesar Kalisaya considered this architectural extension, which Ponce (1981) interpreted as a Tiwanaku 1 "embellishment," a kind of solar observatory. The wall is supported by eleven massive and impeccably crafted andesite pillars, some of the largest in Tiwanaku. Facing the wall within the Kalasasaya some thirty meters to the east are the eroded remains of a central platform. Combining firsthand observations with computerized models, Benitez finds that, for an observer on the platform in Tiwanaku times, the outer two pillars would have visually demarcate the setting sun on the two solar solstices: the north pillar indicated austral winter (June 21) and the south pillar austral summer (December 21). Every second pillar between them (the second, fourth, sixth, eighth, and tenth from each end) marked a thirty-day countdown of setting suns from one to the next, and the central pillar, or sixth from either end, marked the setting sun on the equinoxes (March and September 21).

The pillars between the latter (the third, fifth, seventh, and ninth from each end) do something truly extraordinary: beginning with the third pillar, they integrate a more complex cycle of lunar observations (Benitez 2006). By linking solar and lunar calendars, the observatory provided the visual basis for a precisely synchronized annual calendar; one that ensured that seasonal changes remained "in synch" with the solar calendar over the years. The discovery of elaborate offerings to the east of the Kalasasaya, in alignment with key solar events, indicates that important rituals accompanied major turning points in the calendar.

The Sun Portal's iconography mirrored the visual sequence of Kalasasaya's new observatory. The eleven rayed faces of the Sun Portal's lower band depict not successive months in a Gregorian calendar, but the eleven recurring setting places of the sun marked by Kalasasaya's solar pillars. The Inca had similar pillars that they termed *sucanca*. In quintessential Andean fashion, the faces represented "places" as much as times, visual pathways as much as conceptual abstractions, and ritual moments as much as everyday material concerns. It seems likely that the portal once stood on the nearby platform, as a portal into the observatory and as a ready guide for the ritual specialists who effectively kept time in Tiwanaku.

Accurate timekeeping to mark oncoming seasonal changes, coordinate major ritual events, and perhaps to predict longer-term environmental shifts, were critical to Tiwanaku's rise to power sometime between AD 400 and 600. This weighed heavily in Tiwanaku's
trumping the authority of major Late Formative centers such as
Khonkho and its emergence as the rising star of the south-central
Andes.

The main staircase scaled its west side. Surrounding its landing stood
massive andesite pedestals that supported intimidating *chachapuma*
images – grimacing human-feline figures holding trophy heads – sculpted
in stone. The high platform it led to may have surrounded a deep sunken
court (Escalante 1997). Akapana's plan has been likened to half of an
"Andean cross," a symbol found on many Yayamama stelae and a key
icon on many Tiwanaku stone sculptures. Its form and "overengineered"
drainage systems lead Kolata (1993a) to interpret Akapana as a human-
wrought sacred mountain and icon of abundance. He suggests that rituals
conducted there were dedicated to the ancestral peaks in charge of natural
and social reproduction.

The Akapana was first built in Early Tiwanaku 1 and may have been
refurbished at around AD 800 (Janusek 2004a). As in earlier structures
at Tiwanaku, each terrace consisted of an outer revetment composed of
large pilasters and intermittent ashlar segments. In Akapana, the architectural "ante" was raised in that many blocks consisted of durable gray
andesite that were uniquely beveled and impeccably fitted (Figure 4.6).
Supporting each outer wall was an intricate buttress system consisting of
an interior retaining wall with recycled and (in many sections) roughly
fitted ashlars (Vranich 2001). Between the interior and outer walls were
small walled chambers filled with earth, adobes, and fieldstones. The base
of many of the chambers contained the residues of major dedication rituals, human dedications, and feasting events. Some chambers included
hundreds of smashed ceremonial vessels, most of them highly elaborate
and filled with food and drink (Alconini 1995; Wright, Hastorf, and
Lennstrom 2003).

Akapana's intricate engineering must have been developed over many
generations. It seems that following partial collapse of its upper terraces,
the Akapana was refurbished with its intricate buttress system at around
AD 800. This would explain the use of recycled ashlars in the retaining
walls (Vranich 2001); they came from collapsed sections of the earlier
structure. Both the construction and refurbishing of the Akapana, each
of which may have occurred upon the ascendance of a new ruling lineage,

A

B

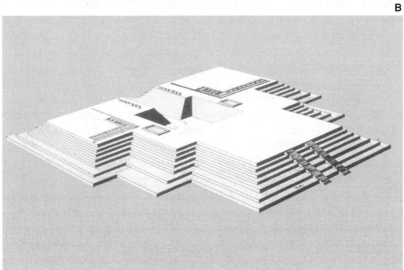

Figure 4.5 The Akapana (b, adapted from Manzanilla 1992).

was a significant bid for power and glory. Like Akapana's initial construction, its rehabilitation effectively helped legitimize the position of a new ruling group by firmly rooting it in the sanctity and devout work of its predecessors.

An important element of these construction projects were major ceremonies, feasts, and offerings dedicated to the structure and the animistic forces it sought to embody. Complex offerings accompanied construction, reconstruction, and perhaps other significant events (Figure 4.6b) (Alconini 1995; Kolata 1993a; Manzanilla and Woodard 1990). These included dozens of partially disarticulated llamas and humans offered as ritual dedications in front and on top of the well-preserved foundation terrace. Many of the human remains reveal no evidence of violence, suggesting that they were deposited as partially articulated mummy bundles. Yet many reveal evidence of violent cutting, skull bashing, and other traumas (Blom 1999; Blom and Janusek 2004; Danilo Villamor pers. comm. 2006). Chemical analysis of some bones with evidence for trauma indicates that these people were not from Tiwanaku; they were foreigners (Knudson et al. 2004). This may indicate that dramatic Akapana ritual offerings involved both ancestral bundles and sacrificed captives taken in battle.

Akapana invoked fertility and abundance and it commemorated Tiwanaku's power over nonlocal people and lands (Blom and Janusek 2004; Kolata 1993a; Manzanilla 1992). It formed a sacred and social *axis mundi*. Akapana's conjoined social and animistic significance was revitalized again and again in rituals and dedications and in periodic reconstruction projects coordinated by its elite patrons, whose power and deeds were in turn made manifest and celebrated.

Pumapunku. Located several hundred meters southwest of Akapana, the Pumapunku formed an independent ritual complex (Figure 4.7). Its initial construction dates to Early Tiwanaku 1, making it at least partly contemporaneous with the Akapana. Construction continued over at least three major phases, as represented in elaborate superimposed floors for ceremonies and theatrical performances, the earliest consisting of vivid green plaster (Vranich 1999). Elaborate stone-lined drains, here joined by bronze cramps that were poured and formed in situ (Lechtman 2003), emphasize the significance of water in local rituals.

Though considered by some to be "Akapana's twin" (Kolata 1993a; Ponce et al. 1971), the Pumapunku differed significantly in form, spatial configuration, and the character of ritual activities conducted therein. The main platform was extensive, measuring over a half-kilometer east-west and consisting of superimposed terraces that were roughly T-shape in plan. Its primary entrance scaled the west side, as did that of the Akapana. Pumapunku's stairway rose over a natural escarpment sculpted into a massive esplanade that visually aggrandized the structure. In light

Figure 4.6 Akapana stonework (a) and foundation offerings (b).

of this and its position at the west edge of the settlement, Vranich considers Pumapunku Tiwanaku's "Ellis Island" (Morell 2002), welcoming diplomats and indoctrinating pilgrims into Tiwanaku's prestigious culture and esoteric religious symbols and beliefs. One moved up the stairway

Figure 4.7 The Pumapunku from the air (a) and in reconstruction
(a, courtesy of Johann Reinhard; b, courtesy of Alexei Vranich).

Figure 4.8 Pumapunku *totora* lintel (a) and paved courtyard patio (b)
(a, photo by Wolfgang Schüler).

through stone portals, some covered with lintels carved as *totora* reed
bundles (Figure 4.8a), and into a narrow, walled passage. This led to
an inner courtyard containing a sunken paved patio (Figure 4.8b).
Bordering Pumapunku to the east, and located between the platform and

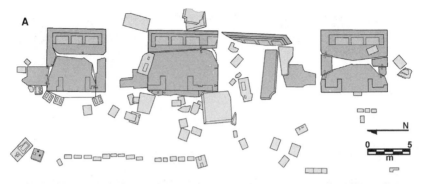

Figure 4.9 Plan (a) and view (b) of Pumapunku's collapsed East
portico (a, redrawn from Posnansky 1945, Vol. 2).

an extensive plaza, was a portico of carved stone portals set on megalithic
sandstone slabs (Figure 4.9; Cobo 1990[1653]:100–103; Protzen and
Nair 2000, 2002). Weighing tons, these slabs are among the largest
employed in New World monuments.

Construction in Pumapunku as in Akapana was an ongoing process. In fact, the south side of the complex, facing away from the city
core, was never finished (Figure 4.10). Vranich (1999:232) notes, "The
Pumapunku complex remains ... a monumental contradiction: overengineered yet unfinished, monumental in appearance, yet façadelike in
reality." Ongoing construction continually transformed the significance
of the complex. Particularly significant were construction projects in the

Figure 4.10 Unfinished south wall of Pumapunku (note unsmoothed stone surfaces).

eighth or ninth centuries, and possibly coeval with reconstruction in Akapana. The green floor was swept clean and ritually interred under a platform that supported a raised surface of red clay. Meanwhile, the walled passage from the main stairway to the inner court was filled (Vranich 1999:231–232). The courtyard remained central for ritual activity: in fact, its west edge was fitted with an elegant stairway that facilitated entry from the now higher platform. However, access to the court was more restricted and perhaps more closely monitored by priests or elites who served as privileged "interlocutors with the divine" (Kolata 1993a:164). It is plausible that increasing spatial exclusivity after AD 800 facilitated, and was shaped by, increasing social exclusivity.

Just southwest of Pumapunku was the Choquepacha spring (Figure 4.11a), emphasizing the temple's ritual association with water. The spring is located at the west edge of a low rise that extends across the valley from Kimsachata, carrying with it a rich subterranean aquifer. Carved stone conduits currently scattered around the spring are the remains of an elaborate construction that was still relatively intact by the time of Max Uhle's visit in 1895 (Bruno 2000). The waters feed a vast *bofedal* of marshy grasses, sedges, and rushes suitable for grazing. It appears likely that in Tiwanaku times the spring was a sacred shrine for rituals and

Figure 4.11 View of Choquepacha (a) and Posnansky's (1945, Vol. 2) drawing of the subterranean tomb north of Kalasasaya (b).

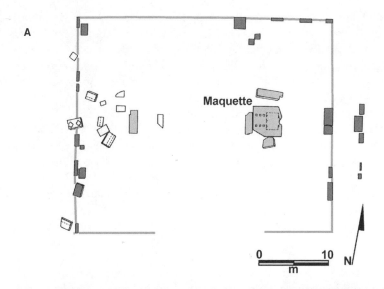

Figure 4.12 Plan of the Kantatayita (a) and view of its andesite
maquette (b) (a, redrawn from Escalante 1997).

offerings dedicated to water and to Kimsachata's regenerative power,
while it fed pastoral fields located west of the city.

Other Ceremonial Structures and Features. Tiwanaku's ceremonial core
incorporated many other monumental structures. Of note is the Kantatayita (Figure 4.12). Located 100 meters northeast of the Akapana, it

consisted of a moderately sized rectangular temple precinct (Escalante 1997:245). The precinct enclosed a large andesite maquette of a sunken temple and platform structure, and an impeccably carved, if heavily damaged architrave (see figure 4.17). Complete with stairway entrances, the effigy stone is usually interpreted as an architectural model. Yet, would Tiwanaku stonemasons expend such effort when more malleable materials cast at a smaller scale would have sufficed (Protzen and Nair 2002:220)? It is more likely that the stone served as an altar for rituals conducted in the precinct and as a stage for planning and orchestrating complex dances that occurred in nearby courts and plazas.

Plazas were central architectural features of Tiwanaku's ceremonial landscape. A massive plaza was associated with each of Tiwanaku's primary Middle Horizon constructions, Pumapunku and Akapana. The little studied Pumapunku plaza occupied the area east of the megalithic portico. Akapana's extensive plaza occupied the west side of the platform and was surrounded on its other sides by elaborate courtyards. Consisting of a cobble pavement that was resurfaced multiple times (Yates and Augustine 2006), it could have held hundreds of people during major ceremonies. Excavations underneath it revealed a series of parallel, elaborately built subterranean canals that drained waste produced during ceremonial events and runoff during the rainy season.

Although intact elite tombs have not been located so far (Korpisaari 2006), the architecture of one likely subterranean elite tomb is still visible several meters north of the Kalasasaya (Figure 4.11b). Like so many other Tiwanaku remains, this one was ransacked within the last hundred years (Posnansky 1945, Vol. 2:114). Posnansky mistakenly identified it as a cramped subterranean dwelling: "without any doubt," he was convinced, "the ancient man of America lived under the ground in artificial caves" (ibid.:116–117). Rather, the structure is very similar to the intact elite tombs recently excavated at the sites of Wari and Conchopata in Peru (Chapter 7). The tomb consisted of impeccably carved andesite ashlars sealed with lime, which rendered it waterproof to protect its sacred contents. The tomb facilitated periodic access to and communication with the interred remains. An ashlar stairway covered by an aboveground portico, as in Wari elite tombs, facilitated entry into the burial chamber, perhaps to periodically remove the interred mummy for rituals and to refresh grave offerings. Also, a small perforation in the ceiling slabs, precisely like the *ttoco* of Wari tombs (see Figure 7.6b), served as a psychoduct that facilitated spiritual communication between the living and the deceased ancestor. Thus, the tomb emphasizes the continuing significance of ancestral remains among Tiwanaku's living elite inhabitants.

Figure 4.13 The monumental east stairway of the Kalasasaya (photo by Wolfgang Schüler).

Ancestors likely anchored the social identities of elite groups and afforded those elites political legitimacy and spiritual well-being much as they did Wari elites and later Inca *panacas*.

Portals and Ritual Movement. Unlike many "restricted-access" complexes and cities in the coastal Andes (Moseley 2001), access to each of Tiwanaku's main temples was provided via a large, monumental stairway that led directly onto the platform and into an inner temple. In the Pumapunku and Kalasasaya, these stairways are monumental and show heavy wear, suggesting long-term use by relatively large numbers of people (Figure 4.13). Yet just who was allowed into their innermost sancta is under debate and may well have changed over time.

Attesting the importance of movement through Tiwanaku's built landscape is an obsession with portals. Numerous megalithic portals such as the well-known Sun Portal are known from the site, though most are now shattered and *ex situ* (Stübel and Uhle 1892). Several portals stood on Pumapunku's eastern portico (Figure 4.14; Protzen and Nair 2002). In each, the doorway had a double jamb in front, a nested step molding around the door crown, and inset niches in back. Architectural analysis indicates that most such portals opened into narrow chambers, instilling a sense of mystery, disorientation, and esoteric power as a person entered

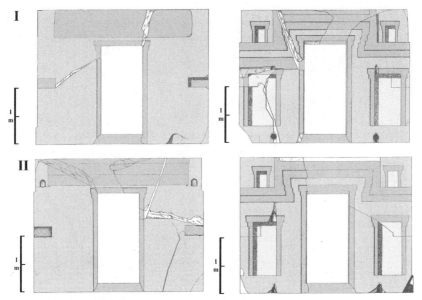

Figure 4.14 Reconstructed portals of Pumapunku's East Portico (redrawn from Protzen and Nair 2002).

increasingly sanctified and intimate spaces. Portals are commonly represented as icons on the stone sculptures that decorated ceremonial architecture. Images of portals included open and "blind" miniatures and are often depicted in repetition (Figure 4.15).

Portals had profound experiential and symbolic significance in Tiwanaku religion. As standing megaliths they were practical means of facilitating movement between mundane and sacred spaces. They also had more abstract symbolic significance. The nested plans of the Akapana and Pumapunku approximated the nested double-jamb and step-molding designs of characteristic portals. Like doorways that provided movement into and through ceremonial spaces on a horizontal plane, the inner sancta of Tiwanaku's principal monuments formed the symbolic portals that facilitated movement between different realms of the cosmos on a vertically aligned plane. Tiwanaku monumental complexes were symbolic portals that facilitated communication between humans and animistic forces.

Monoliths. Ancestral personages facilitating proximity to the sacred were sculpted onto massive sandstone and andesite monoliths. Archaeologists

Figure 4.15 Blind Portals as sculpted decoration on andesite architectural elements (photo by Wolfgang Schüler).

have recovered two intact monoliths in context: Bennett and Ponce (Figure 4.16). The Bennett monolith, hewn of sandstone, was placed in the Sunken Temple beside the earlier Khonkho-style monoliths. Crafted of andesite, the Ponce Monolith was placed in Kalasasaya's inner court. The monoliths depict either the mythical ancestors of living elite groups or elite rulers decked out as such personages (Janusek 2006). Their placement in the innermost sancta of Tiwanaku's most ancient temples indicates that religious experience was mediated by their ancient spiritual power. The potency of rituals conducted in view of them was perhaps attributed to their elite descendent group.

Erecting monoliths in Tiwanaku's early sacred temples by later generations were politico-religious coups. Through such acts emergent elite factions boldly sought to embed their authority and prestige in the ancient places created by their predecessors, thereby appropriating such places to their own political and ritual ends. Such places thereby accrued new meaning and transformed significance. The Sunken Temple incorporated monoliths and icons of different styles and eras. Under a new ruling regime, the ancient Sunken Temple may have come to embody Tiwanaku historical and cultural patrimony, ironically similar to the importance that a replica of the temple in La Paz has for the Bolivian nation today.

Monumental Meaning and Diversity. Tiwanaku temples were constructed to observe and track timeless celestial cycles and to evoke the animistic power of significant natural features. The shift in ceremonial space and human ritual movement to an axial east-west orientation occurred in the Late Formative, and it facilitated esoteric observations of the sun's bi-annual solstice settings and other celestial events (Benitez 2005). Accompanied by massive ceremonies, solstice celebrations included human sacrificial victims (Verano, Vranich, and Gardella 2006). Effective calendar-keeping was a significant innovation during this time, when Tiwanaku was competing with Khonkho Wankane and other centers. Close tracking of annual celestial cycles served to objectify time and to create a reliable calendar for scheduling ritual events and coordinating diverse productive activities, including fishing, herding, and raised field agriculture (see Chapter 5). To be sure, the leaders and specialists who coordinated the calendar had some purchase "over the ritual production of cosmic space-time" (Turner 1993). In providing religious specialists and emergent elites a *raison d'etre*, accurate calendar keeping was instrumental in Tiwanaku's rise to power just before the early Middle Horizon.

The east-west orientation of Tiwanaku temples approximated the clearly observable daily path of the sun, which rises over the rugged Eastern and sets behind the older Western Cordillera. At auspicious times, it afforded dramatic visual paths with the most important peaks in those ranges from different points in the ceremonial landscape. For someone scaling Kalasasaya's eastern staircase, it afforded a dramatic view of Ccapia to the west. For someone scaling the Pumapunku western staircase, it afforded a dramatic view of Illimani. In fact, for someone approaching Tiwanaku from the west, Illimani disappears from view as one approaches Pumapunku's massive esplanade. "Only when you climb the very last stair and reach the temple's flat summit," notes Morell (2002:127), "does the mountain reappear, blue and white shining."

Figure 4.16 The Bennett (a) and Ponce (b) monoliths (a, photo by Clare Sammels).

Variation in the orientations and sightlines of Tiwanaku's temples indicates that each had a particular place and complementary role in Tiwanaku's ritual round and ceremonial landscape.

If religious specialists and elites were gathering power, religious experience in Tiwanaku was neither solely academic nor completely appropriated by elites. It did not reside solely in the heads of high priests as did the intricate ritual calendars of the Classic Maya. Sacred geography afforded direct experience of the animistic powers that Tiwanaku was built to evoke and that were immanent in its design.

The importance of personal experience in Tiwanaku is apparent in the sense of intimacy built into ceremonial space and the importance of esoteric experience in ritual and iconography. Extensive spaces for public ceremony were prominent in Tiwanaku 1, as manifested in the large plazas adjacent to Akapana and Pumapunku. Yet the focal ritual place in each monumental complex was a relatively small space that afforded close proximity with sanctified objects and images (Moore 1996). As Goldstein has pointed out (1993a), monumental architecture guided priests, pilgrims, and ritual participants sequentially up staircases, through portals, and with great anticipation, toward increasingly smaller, enclosed inner sancta. It is here that the most potent rituals culminated and where at least some of Tiwanaku's (or a specific ruling group's) most potent icons – such as monolithic effigy ancestors – stood. Pilgrimage involved long sequences of offerings, dedications, and feasts that formed entire processions or sacred journeys. For a pilgrim en route to a temple, it was in close proximity to its sculpted portals, sacred objects, and monoliths that its exquisite craftsmanship was apprehended and its intricate religious meanings were learned. Attention to intimacy was not as much about creating exclusive ritual environments as it was about transferring the intimacy inherent in Tiwanaku's adobe dwellings and family life to communal social and ritual domains.

Monumental architecture incorporated symbolic elements derived from quotidian places. The andesite *totora* lintels that covered portals in the Pumapunku, for example, represented reed bundles typically used to thatch house roofs. Enclosure, proximity, and the quotidian, all were elements of a metaphorical transposition of domestic to more public ceremonial domains. This transposition rendered meaningful and spiritually powerful the places of worship that fed Tiwanaku elite authority and religious prestige, but also facilitated the shared experiences and forged the communal identity that ultimately made Tiwanaku possible, successful, and ultimately, millennial.

Tiwanaku monumentality manifested a tension of order and heterogeneity. Tiwanaku was conceived as an "an icon of . . . rule and a cosmogram that displayed symbolically, in the spatial arrangement of public architecture and sculpture, the structure that framed the natural and social orders" (Kolata and Ponce 1992:318). Kolata notes (following Posnansky 1945, Vol. 2:121) that an artificial channel or moat surrounded most of Tiwanaku's monumental complex, forming an ontological barrier that physically isolated the "sacred essence of the city" from the sprawling peripheries (Figure 4.1). I hypothesize that this channel was first constructed during the Late Formative (Janusek 2004a, 2006). By the end of Tiwanaku 1, it emphasized a conceptual "concentric cline" of elite residence and religious power that diminished toward the urban periphery, dividing the space and time of the sacred from "the space and time of ordinary life" (Kolata and Ponce 1992:318). An outer channel, most likely built long after the first, defined Tiwanaku's eastern urban edge. Tiwanaku simultaneously was divided on an east-west axis according to the daily solar path and on a north-south axis following a sociopolitical division that centered on Tiwanaku's two monumental groups.

Yet each monumental complex was different from all others in architectural form, spatial organization, and religious meaning. Although the structures coexisted throughout the Tiwanaku period, each followed a slightly different orientation. The Sunken Temple harkened Tiwanaku's primordial origins. Ceremonies conducted there invoked ancestral chthonic and celestial forces to ensure social and natural reproduction. While the Akapana dominated the urban core in height, the Pumapunku emphasized the horizon and ritual passage. The Pumapunku itself disrupts the idea of a centripetal focus of sacred power, for it lies far southwest of the main monumental area.

Tiwanaku monumentality harbored an ingenious balance of singular order and local design. Its emergent concentric and axial designs sought to approximate a grand order by integrating profound ritual and social differences. Each monumental complex was a key component of Tiwanaku's emerging cosmic vision yet each also was a place of worship for a particular social group or faction. Monumentality itself was an ongoing practice in which Tiwanaku religious power and cultural identity were created and reproduced. It was in building events and in cyclical rituals that Tiwanaku's encompassing politico-religious identity was breathed life. Social empowerment in such potent moments was manifold rather than exclusive. In them, the identity and legitimacy of both the emerging state and its leaders and various participating groups were affirmed.

Religious Art and Iconography

Accompanying Tiwanaku's rise was a remarkable explosion in religious expression that drew on early iconographic traditions such as Yayamama, Pukara, and Khonkho. Stone sculpture and architecture were among the most significant media for depicting key religious themes. The particular type of stone, whether sandstone, andesite, or basalt, invoked a distinctive natural or animistic essence (Text Box 4.2). Given the significance of portals in Tiwanaku ceremonial space and religion, it is not surprising that many architraves depict elaborate iconography. Many lintels depict humanlike deities placed head-to-head on their undersides (hence their name, "anticephaloid lintels") that peer down on those passing through a portal. The friezes of others depict elaborate mythical themes and ritual scenes. The "Calle Linares" lintel, which Posnansky found in La Paz,

Box 4.2   Sandstone and Andesite

The Tiwanaku employed stone to emphasize mass, permanence, and antiquity in their principal icons and monumental constructions. Particular types of stone had powerful spiritual meaning for the Tiwanaku. Most significant for raising temples, building elite residences, and crafting monolithic icons were sandstone and andesite. Sedimentary sandstone employed in Tiwanaku is a brilliant red hue and derives from quarries in the Kimsachata-Chilla range just south of Tiwanaku. Mountain quarries yield "preform" monoliths, or roughly carved blocks that had never been hauled to Tiwanaku for fine sculpting. Volcanic andesite is a bluish-gray mineral that was quarried in more distant outcrops at the foot of Mount Ccapia, one of the most important peaks or *malkus* in the altiplano, offshore of Lake Titicaca. Blocks were sailed on large rafts to ports such as Iwawe, where roughly carved blocks remain scattered over the shore today.

The origin, color, and use of these two stones offer clues to their meaning. Quarried in local mountain outcrops, sandstone may have invoked Tiwanaku's origin myths and ancestral deities. The color red is especially significant. Red is the ground color of Tiwanaku ceremonial vessels, key material symbols of Tiwanaku culture, and today it invokes blood, or *wila*, the primary life-ensuring element of humans and llamas alike. In keeping with the "humanization" of significant buildings that predated Tiwanaku, red sandstone afforded spiritual life to the sacred buildings and icons it constituted. These constructions conjured the memory of ancient deeds and beings, and so joined the persons who built and employed them with the ancient times to which Tiwanaku people made reference in guiding their daily and spiritual lives.

If red sandstone invoked the ancient bedrock of nearby mountains, bluish-gray andesite invoked the life-giving principles of more distant sacred peaks and Lake Titicaca. Titicaca in Aymara means "gray-haired puma." Bluish-gray indexes the color of the lake and the felines that traditionally inhabited altiplano peaks, and it was a rare ceramic color employed to depict felines on Tiwanaku drinking vessels. Just as the materiality of sandstone invoked the bedrock of local mountains, andesite indexed more distant sacred peaks venerated by numerous altiplano communities, while symbolizing the complementary life-principle of water in Lake Titicaca.

By the Tiwanaku period, Tiwanaku incorporated sandstone and andesite constructions and monuments. Central to Tiwanaku's proselytizing religion, sandstone and andesite invoked complementary religious, ecological, and imperial domains (Janusek 2006). Sandstone derived from local mountain quarries and andesite from more distant lakeside sources. Furthermore, sandstone had been employed during the Late Formative at many centers, while andesite, a much more durable mineral that is difficult to sculpt with stone tools, was crafted on a major scale only during the Tiwanaku period, and largely at Tiwanaku itself. It was during the Tiwanaku period that leaders began to incorporate the more distant lands that hugged the lake shore and provided access to andesite outcrops. It was now also that lakeshore pampas became increasingly important as human-wrought landscapes dedicated to intensive raised-field farming (Chapter 5). In andesite, Tiwanaku's success was propagandized in an advanced technology dedicated to the production of icons and temples that, in their materiality, conjured places and landscapes newly incorporated into its realm.

Sandstone now invoked Tiwanaku's locality and re-fashioned historical consciousness, while andesite gave material expression to its geographical and imperial destiny. Jointly employed to form Tiwanaku's monument's, they presented complex sociopolitical relations and dynamic historical moments as inseperable material and spiritual values.

depicts a central front-facing deity (or a deity impersonator) clutching two staffs and flanked by flying figures with unusual bird-like "beaks" (Figure 4.17a). Yet the Kantatayita architrave and Sun Portal are particularly noteworthy for their iconography.

Kantatayita Architrave. The face of the Kantatayita architrave has a beautiful, elliptically sculpted backside that as Protzen and Nair point out (2002:205), "would tax any stonemason's skills today" (Figure 4.17). The arch-shaped frieze depicts two opposing groups of figures with elaborate headdresses and beaks similar to those on the Calle Linares lintel. The figures fly toward one another clutching weapons or staffs in their hands. Their floating or flying position is reminiscent of the "falling man" depicted on Late Formative monoliths from Khonkho Wankane. Metallurgists pressed gold sheets over the frieze and the resulting inlay was held in place by regularly placed pins. The gold panels have long since been removed, but the pins are still visible as deeply drilled holes around the image (Conklin 1991:283). Posnansky (1945) found traces of gold in the pin holes of other Tiwanaku sculptures. For Inca and other later Andean cultures, gold materialized the sun's transcendent powers. Leaves of gold

Figure 4.17 Rendering of the Calle Linares lintel (a) and view (b) and detail (c) of the Kantatayita architrave (a, adapted from Conklin 1991 by Jennifer Ohnstad).

covered the Kantatayita and other friezes so that they shimmered spectacularly when facing the rising or setting sun that they both represented and, in reflecting its rays, celebrated.

Sun Portal. The andesite Sun Portal displays a frieze that concisely and elegantly summarizes key elements of Tiwanaku's emergent religious ideology (Figure 4.18). Surrounding the impeccably incised central frieze, which was "conceived as a whole," were outer panels carved by a later, less experienced hand using coarser tools and techniques (Protzen and Nair 2002:198; also Conklin 1991; Stübel and Uhle 1892). Configured as a "textile that is draped across stone" (Stone-Miller 2002:133), the frieze presents a prominent central deity or deity impersonator who wears a

Figure 4.18 The central frieze of the Sun Portal.

rayed headdress. The figure faces the viewer at the center of three rows of genuflecting profile "attendants" who face it on either side. The central personage stands on a three-tiered platform and holds an arrow bundle (left hand) and a spear thrower (right hand). Two rows of profile attendants – top and bottom – depict forward-facing anthropomorphic figures while the middle row depicts upward-looking condor-headed figures; they hold either an arrow bundle or a staff. Exemplary of Tiwanaku iconography, abstracted elements of key animals, especially bird, feline, and fish heads, and significant objects, such as conch shells and tail feathers, adorn the weapons, headdresses, wings, faces, and clothing of the central and peripheral figures. Below the profile attendants, a serpentine band weaves together eleven frontal faces that replicate that of the central deity. On either side of it stands a diminutive profile figure who raises a sacrificial blade and carries a severed trophy head.

Various iconographic elements of the frieze give visual form to natural features and forces. The rayed face conjures the sun, the terraced platform depicts a mountain or temple and the weapons may allude to lightning bolts (Demarest 1981; Kolata 1993a:148). The central figure may depict an ancient Tunupa-like protagonist, the Aymara mythical hero deity who, after journeying southward along the Desaguadero River, ascended a mountain to become the principal deity of storms, warfare, and fertility. The frieze also presents calendrical knowledge and calculations relating to solar and other celestial cycles (Text Box 4.1; Benitez 2005; Kolata 1993a; Posnansky 1945). This raises the intriguing possibility that the portal once stood in the center of Kalasasaya's west balcony on a place for viewing those events on the distant horizon.

Other elements of the portal codify aspects of Tiwanaku sociopolitical organization. The attendants form a decimal system and are structured as three rows of ten figures each (five on a side), all focused on the central figure. This system anticipated the system devised by the Inca in accounting their labor tax (*mit'a*) wherein incorporated societies regularly paid the state revenues in kind. In this sense, the profile attendants may represent in stylized form the various societies or regions incorporated into the Tiwanaku polity.

The entire image communicates order, symmetry, and hierarchy (Cook 1994). It is strikingly reminiscent of the *Deesis* in an Orthodox church, an icon in which Christ is flanked by John the Baptist on his left, the Virgin Mary on his right, and various saints beyond them. Like the portal the frieze adorns, the *Deesis* of Byzantine temples occupied a prominent position in an *iconostasis*, a threshold of icons – or "window to heaven" – that simultaneously divided and facilitated communication between humans and the divine. I suggest that the Sun Portal was a representation of the cosmos, one specific to its particular artisans and the elites who commissioned it, in which – more comprehensively than in a *Deesis* – social, natural, and supernatural phenomena were linked and together subjected to a hierarchical order. Key elements in this cosmic vision drew on earlier themes, such as fertility, militarism, and ancestry. New themes of solar power and conspicuous hierarchy paralleled shifts in architectural orientation and religious experience in Tiwanaku. They collectively manifested a profound shift in religious values.

Stone Monoliths. Effigy monoliths carved in the round, including the Bennett and Ponce monoliths, formed another class of stone architecture that depicted key elements of Tiwanaku religious ideology. Tiwanaku monoliths had their origins in the stelae of Formative societies, and as in those societies, stone iconography became more complex over time. By the Tiwanaku period, monolithic icons depicted either deified ancestors or deity impersonators such as priests or rulers (Stone-Miller 2002:130–132).

The Bennett and Ponce monoliths, found in situ, both depict elegantly dressed, crowned, and masked figures standing erect and impassive, clutching in their hands a *kero*, or drinking chalice, in the left hand and a snuff tablet in the right (Figure 4.16; Torres 2001). The substances alluded to, fermented beverages and psychotropic substances, facilitated memory of and perhaps contact with ancestral beings and forces (Abercrombie 1998; Saignes 1993). The clothing and bodies of both figures are carved in low relief, and while they depict common icons and themes, the overall symbolism varies markedly between them. The Bennett personage (Figure 4.19a), Kolata demonstrates (1993a:135–141), incorporates

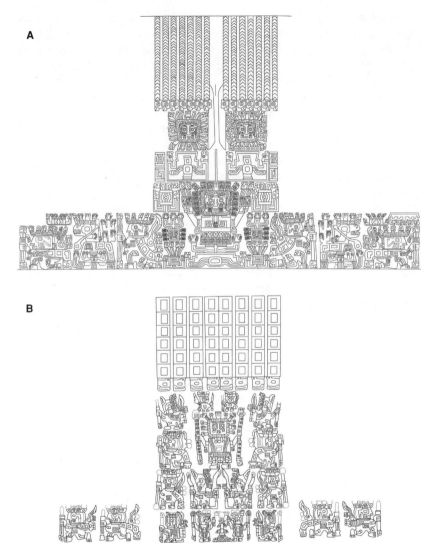

Figure 4.19 Rendered iconographic details from the backs and sides of the Bennett (a) and Ponce (b) monoliths (drawings by Jennifer Ohnstad; a, adapted from Posnansky 1945).

depictions of flowering plants and dressed llamas, and thus advertises farming and husbandry as interlinked foundations of its ancestral power. Mescaline-bearing San Pedro cacti sprout from the rayed faces that decorate the figures' waists. Adorning the main figure's facial ornament and braids are profile condor faces.

The Ponce figure, by contrast, depicts braids terminating in faces with upturned mouths that have been identified as fish (Figure 4.19b; Posnansky 1945). The Ponce figure was more squarely associated with lake and river resources, a critical productive enterprise in the altiplano that by post-Tiwanaku times was the domain of a distinct ethniclike group (see Chapter 5). Another sandstone monolith, the so-called Fraile, or Monk Monolith, in the southwest corner of the Kalasasaya, also depicts a figure associated with water and lake-focused pursuits (Portugal Ortiz 1998b:181–182; Posnansky 1945). Like others the figure holds a *kero* and what may be a snuff tray (though the icon is eroded), but in this case, a fish head adorns the mask ornament and a series of crustaceans decorate the sash.

All monoliths share common iconographic elements (an impassive face, an elaborate crown and tunic, a *kero*, and a snuff tray) and yet they differ in important iconic details. Each represented a unique Tiwanaku mythical ancestor – or perhaps a unique interpretation of a distant ancestral deity – and perhaps the distant patron ancestor of an emergent elite group. The distinctive themes of each monolith may allude to the particular symbols, socioeconomic characteristics, or productive concerns of a group or community. Placing a monolith in a sanctified place such as the ancient Sunken Temple or Kalasasaya afforded it a new stratum of meaning pertinent to the group and leaders that the icon represented.

Textiles. Woven clothing was among the most significant media for depicting religious symbols and marking social identity in Tiwanaku. In the Inca Empire and other Andean societies, it was an important domain of female production and artistry. Unfortunately, the relatively wet climate and intense rainy season of the altiplano prevent buried textiles from preserving very long. Yet textile clothing was doubtless of utmost social, political, and spiritual importance in Tiwanaku. The layout of lintel friezes such as that on the Sun Portal, and the elaborate clothing worn by monolithic effigy ancestors, all allude to textiles as templates for religious themes and media for personal and group identity. As in many past and present cultures worldwide, bodily decoration in Tiwanaku was a potent domain of ideological expression and identity negotiation.

Textile fragments from sites on the Pacific coast and in dry caves nestled in the eastern Andean valleys provide some sense of the thematic content and organization of woven Tiwanaku iconography (Conklin 1983; Frame 1990; Oakland 1986; Wassén 1972). Analysis reveals a tapestry style using mostly camelid fibers – in particular alpaca – and composed of woven mantles, tunics, hangings, and hats that were produced in many different workshops. Religious iconography spun and dyed onto known textile fragments is strikingly similar to that carved on stone at Tiwanaku. Textiles tend to depict crowned and dressed feline or bird-headed (or masked) figures that stand, genuflect, or fly while holding staffs, weapons, or trophy heads. Figures similar to the profile attendants and sacrificers of stone portals are common and are often framed in repeating, symmetrically arranged blocks. Textiles adorned bodies and buildings and provided templates for many key Tiwanaku symbols and religious themes.

Ceramic Vessels. Ceramic vessels formed an important class of portable prestige goods that advertised key elements of Tiwanaku religion and state culture. Tiwanaku vessels depicted a wide variety of iconographic themes, some reminiscent of Tiwanaku stonework and weaving and others quite distinct. Their appearance at around AD 500 marked the appearance of new religious iconography that developed out of formative themes but was strikingly different in execution and meaning. Abstract geometrical images included step motifs representing platforms and mountains, continuous volutes representing water or *chicha*, and, less commonly, the Andean cross as cosmic center (Janusek 2003a). Replacing the surreal Qeya *desconocidos* were stylized but discernible animal figures, most commonly felines, birds, camelids, and serpents (Figure 4.20). In many cases, the figures incorporate humanlike characteristics or represent religious specialists, warriors, or rulers dressed in ritual masks and attire. By AD 700 it was common to represent animals as disembodied design elements (heads, wings, canines, legs, etc.) that were combined to create composite abstractions. The images challenge Picasso's cubism in aesthetic sophistication.

For the first time many vessels depicted humans and humanlike ancestors and deities. Their depictions emphasized the ideology of integrated diversity that characterized Tiwanaku religion. Profile human heads with variable facial features and painting or tattoos decorated the bulging torus of many *keros* (Janusek 2003a: Figure 3.38). Some wore a split-eye mask. Frequently depicted as repeating elements on the Bennett, Ponce, and Kochamama monoliths, the split-eye motif represented an important cosmic symbol with unknown meaning. The heads are thought to represent stylized trophy heads (Burkholder 1997; Kolata 1993a:126; Manzanilla and Woodard 1990:145), or, perhaps, profile ancestor and deity faces. The images indicate that heads and faces (or masks) – human, ancestral, and divine – were considered central loci of religious power and social identity.

Vessels depicting the crowned frontal face of the Sun Portal personage were common. The impassive face or mask was similar from one vessel to the next, but like profile heads, each incorporated idiosyncratic facial

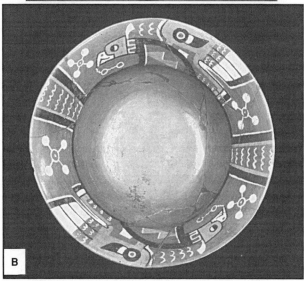

Figure 4.20 Ceremonial drinking *kero* (a) and *escudilla* bowl (b) depicting animal imagery (photos by Wolfgang Schüler).

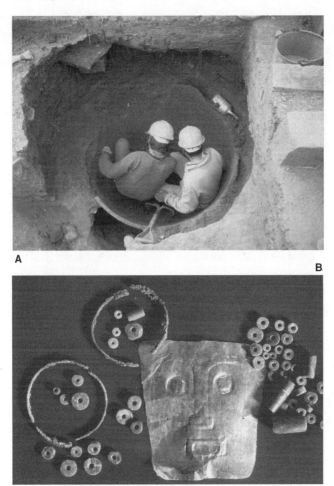

Figure 4.21 Excavation of a massive mortuary urn (a) and some of the elaborate adornments found in Putuni's mortuary complex (b) (a, courtesy of Alan Kolata; b, photo by Wolfgang Schüler).

designs such as tattoos, painting, or masks. Further, the stylized crown, or headdress, varied from one *kero* to the next (Bennett 1934; Goldstein 1989). Like the Sunken Temple's tenoned heads, the faces may depict the mythical progenitors of Tiwanaku's constituent social groups. Iconographic commonalities in the ceramic imagery suggest that the beings shared the divine essence of a more ancestral Tiwanaku supreme deity. The Sun Portal's attendant figures, thus, may represent the recent (or proximal) ancestors of a more ancestral deity of an encompassing community. In this scenario, the portal portrayed an inclusive state ideology that subsumed Tiwanaku's diverse groups and ancestors within a single hegemonic system.

Tiwanaku as Center of Elite Power

Archaeologists have recently explored the homes of the elites who are portrayed on Tiwanaku's elaborate monuments. High status groups occupied discrete segments of Tiwanaku's urban core. In particular, the area west of the Kalasasaya and Akapana housed vibrant elite residence and activity (Figures 4.1 and 4.2). It incorporated extensive walled compounds, each presumably occupied by a core elite group or lineage along with their specialists and retainers. One such compound was the Kerikala, which measured some 50 meters north-south by 75 meters east-west (Escalante 1997:244). Many narrow rooms and corridors surrounded an extensive open courtyard. Adjacent to it and built somewhat later was the Putuni complex.

Elite Ritual Space and Residence in Putuni

In Tiwanaku 1, two residential compounds occupied the area later covered by the Putuni complex (Couture 2002; Couture and Sampeck 2003; Janusek 2004a). The north compound incorporated several dwellings and a kitchen for communal food preparation. The kitchen contained subfloor hearths, storage pits, and garbage pits. Several meters north of the kitchen archaeologists located two unusual tombs (Figure 4.21a). Each of the individuals had been buried in a massive ceramic urn – one of them decorated with vertical red stripes – that had been set into a specially prepared pit lined with pure sand.

High-status groups dwelled near their deceased relatives and ancestors to affirm their own privileged ancestry and position. The south compound incorporated a burial complex for high-status persons (Couture and Sampeck 2003:240). Though archaeologists recovered no human remains, this may indicate that the burials had contained venerated ancestral mummy bundles that were later moved elsewhere. The tombs themselves yielded elaborate sumptuary offerings depicting Tiwanaku religious icons and themes (Figure 4.21b). Some were filled with smashed ceramic vessels, including massive ceremonial burners, elegantly flared bowls (*escudillas*), and large *chicha* fermentation jars (Couture 2002; Janusek 2003a). These were the material remains of ceremonies that accompanied elite funerals. The smashed vessels were poured into a grave as a ritual finale after the wrapped remains were buried.

Distinguishing the high-status district of the urban core from other residential areas was a spectacular subterranean drainage network. Stone basins set into floors of the Kerikala and Putuni compounds fed runoff and waste into cobble and ashlar-lined subterranean drainage canals. These canals fed into massive north-trending canals lined with carved sandstone ashlars, each of which followed the same alignment as above-ground monumental complexes. Measuring nearly a meter to the side and sealed with clay, each descended gently at a shallow gradient northward toward the Tiwanaku River (Janusek and Earnest 1990; Ponce 1961:22). Muck-filled "manholes" provided access to the canals for periodic cleaning and maintenance.

At around the turn of the ninth century, both early compounds were razed to prepare the construction of the elaborate residential-ceremonial Putuni complex. The event was accompanied by ritual offerings of camelids, humans, and their body parts. Human remains included both males and females and adults and children; apparently, human offerings were not strictly delimited by gender or age. The offerings closely parallel those recovered at the base of the Akapana, pointing to a shared pattern of ritual behavior in Tiwanaku that accompanied major episodes of architectural transformation and renewal (Blom and Janusek 2004; Couture and Sampeck 2003). These episodes were symbolic rites of passage that represented the "death" and subsequent "rebirth" of a place. Whether ancestors, relatives, or captive sacrifices, the offerings "humanized" such a place and identified it with a particular community. Built places such as Akapana and Putuni came to embody and express the social power of Tiwanaku elite groups.

Putuni consisted of an extensive architectural ensemble (Figures 4.2 and 4.22) centered on a platform and courtyard structure (Couture 2002; Kolata 1993a). The main structure measured approximately 50 meters north-south by 70 meters east-west. An elaborate multicolored staircase led into the courtyard from the east and several smaller staircases led up onto the platform. Each staircase connected the Putuni with paved corridors and small rooms that surrounded the platform, including a series of rooms to the north that restricted access to the complex.

Surrounding Putuni's inner courtyard were several paneled niches with covered openings. These may have housed the mummified remains of local ancestors and other ritual paraphernalia. Nicole Couture (2002) speculates that the elite group that commissioned Putuni transferred mummy bundles previously interred in the tombs mentioned above, to these more elaborate tombs. To be sure, celebrating ties to ancestors was more than ever a critical means of building power and privilege among Tiwanaku elites. With "mummy houses" surrounding an open court,

Figure 4.22 Detail of the Putuni's impeccably constructed east
platform wall.

the overall plan of Putuni mimicked the placement of tenoned ancestral
heads around the Sunken Temple's courtyard. Further, it mimicked in
monumental terms the typical arrangement of a residential patio group,
with its household structures surrounding an open patio for everyday
activities and periodic feasts. In this sense, Putuni symbolically captured
and aggrandized the social and spiritual parameters of ancient ritual and
intimate domestic spaces.

The west side of the Putuni accommodated an elite residential complex consisting of two elaborate structures on a paved plaza (Figure 4.23).
The plaza was covered with smashed ceremonial serving wares and high
quantities of large jars for brewing and consuming *chicha*. The East Palace
was an elaborate edifice built into the Putuni platform. Resting on carved
andesite ashlars, its adobe walls were painted in brilliant hues of red, yellow, orange, green, and blue (Créqui Monfort 1904; Kolata 1993a:153–
154; Posnansky 1945). Its floors were drained by stone basins that carried
water and waste into a massive subterranean drainage canal, sediment
inside of which included gold lamina and obsidian flakes. Palace residents used well-crafted ceramic wares such as flaring bowls. Domestic
goods included obsidian arrow points, sodalite necklaces, copper pins,

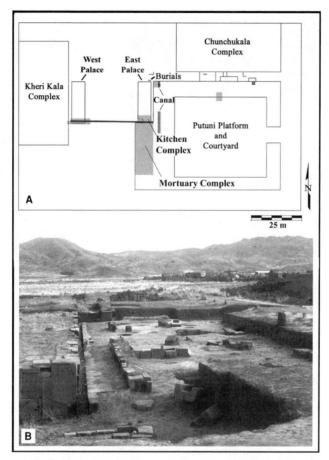

Figure 4.23 The Putuni elite residential complex: plan (a), and view (b) of the excavated East Palace ruins (a, adapted from Couture and Sampeck 2003).

carved marine shell, and a silver tube. A human offering under the palace contained a lead flask and a gold pectoral hammered into a deity mask.

Thus, at approximately AD 800 increasing status and wealth in Putuni produced new architectural forms, material culture, ritual practices, and ideas about sanitation. These aspects of social distinction mark the crystallization of an emergent elite class in which privilege and power were supported by unique origin myths and intermarriage. The inhabitants of Putuni were very possibly among Tiwanaku's leaders and may have formed an ascendant dynasty.

Elite Residence on the Akapana

Elite groups of distinct lineages and with different roles in Tiwanaku society resided in the urban core. One group occupied the uppermost platform of the Akapana after its reconstruction (Alconini 1995:115–142; Kolata 1993a:114–118; Manzanilla 1992:54–70). A series of interconnected rooms surrounded a paved patio that, much like the Putuni plaza, was covered with high quantities of smashed *chicha* fermentation jars (Figure 4.24). Six individuals were buried under the patio. Their tombs were organized so that five of them were aligned east-west behind and facing the principal individual. The principal burial included a bone snuff spoon and the individual held in his/her lap a shattered feline effigy ritual burner, or *incensario*. Such a vessel, oddly enough, was uncommon at Tiwanaku and far more popular as a grave offering at Lukurmata in the Katari Valley. The location of the burials atop Tiwanaku's highest monument and their associated objects suggest that at least the key person was a ritual specialist, and perhaps among Tiwanaku's high priests. It appears likely that the ascendance of an elite class by AD 800 involved different castelike groups with specialized occupations including rulers, bureaucrats, and ritual specialists.

Elite Residence and Ceremony in Akapana East

In Tiwanaku 2, elite groups extended their direct presence across the urban landscape. About the same time that the Akapana was reconstructed and the Putuni complex built, much of the city outside of the immediate urban core was refabricated to facilitate elite ends. Excavations in the "near east side" or Akapana East 1 (see Figure 4.1), on the inner edge of the moat, revealed a remarkable transformation in which one neighborhood of residential compounds was completely refashioned as an urban sector dedicated to elite-sponsored ceremony and feasting (Janusek 2003b, 2004a). Two adjacent compounds were built directly over earlier, Tiwanaku I occupations. The south compound included several small structures around an extensive outdoor patio, a large communal kitchen, and a burial complex (Figure 4.25). The structures were "shoddy" and decidedly unlike those of higher-status residential complexes. For instance, foundations here supported walls of organic sod rather than adobe. The kitchen included several hearths littered with thousands of cooking vessels sherds, including a unique type of roasting bowl, as well as splintered and butchered camelid, guinea pig, and bird bones. The patio revealed high quantities of jars used for storing and fermenting *chicha*.

Figure 4.24 The late occupation atop the Akapana (a) with a *chicha* fermentation jar smashed in situ (b) (photos courtesy of Alan Kolata).

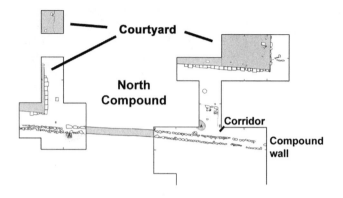

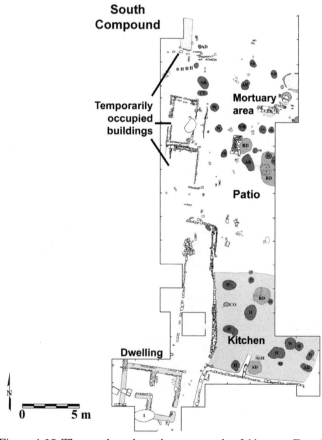

Figure 4.25 The north and south compounds of Akapana East 1.

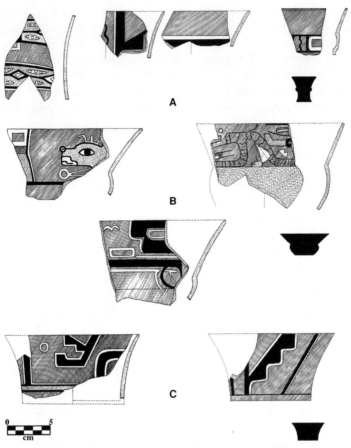

Figure 4.26 Fragments of typical Tiwanaku ceremonial wares:
drinking *keros* (a), elaborate *escudilla* bowls (b), and more common
tazon bowls (c) (drawings by Sonia Alconini).

Fewer areas in Tiwanaku were as different from the south compound as
the adjacent north compound. The north compound enclosed an extensive edifice that incorporated one or more sunken courtyards. Reminiscent of Putuni, construction techniques and materials contrasted sharply
with those in the south compound. Walls consisted of clean, finely selected
clay standing on ashlar foundations, and the sunken floors inside were
prepared with a gravel aggregate base. Artifacts included high proportions of exotic and sumptuary goods, including a variety of nonlocal
vessel sherds, copper ornaments, and a tripod bowl exquisitely carved
of volcanic basalt (Janusek 2004a:Figure 7.5). Yet they also included

consumption residues similar to those found in nearby residential areas, including butchered camelid bones and sherds of cooking and ceremonial wares. A corridor located between the wall dividing the compounds and this edifice was employed to prepare food and drink.

I believe the south compound was dedicated to the production of feasts enacted in courtyards of the north compound, which were loci for ceremonial activities sponsored by an elite group or groups. Excavations around the north compound indicate that it and its courtyard edifices were surrounded by compounds dedicated to the specialized production of food and drink for elite-sponsored rituals of consumption. Such a scenario explains local archaeobotanical patterns. In the south compound, quinoa and maize were present in high proportions and in addition, maize kernel-to-cob ratios were far higher here than in any other excavated area (Wright, Hastorf, and Lennstrom 2003). Grown in warm valleys far from Tiwanaku, maize entered the compound as already-shelled kernels and was possibly provisioned by high-status groups who sponsored local feasts. Grains were roasted to make fermented *chicha* in the unique roasting bowls of the kitchen. Thus, in a massive project of urban renewal, Akapana East 1 was converted into an extensive sector dedicated to elite-sponsored feasting and drinking, a cultural practice that was becoming more significant across the city and region in Tiwanaku 2.

Ritual Feasting and Social Inequality

Commensalism and ritual consumption were critical elements of Tiwanaku "state culture." By state culture, I mean a suite of technologies, styles, practices, and ideals that was internalized and idealized by elites and commoners alike. Tiwanaku ceramic assemblages appeared with a bang at around AD 500 and remained fundamental to Tiwanaku state culture for several hundred years (Figures 4.20 and 4.26). In sharp contrast to Late Formative ceremonial wares, finely crafted Tiwanaku wares were ubiquitous; all groups had access to some forms and styles. They also were stylistically conservative. Tiwanaku serving wares comprised an entire intricate technology of everyday and ritualized consumption. Their popularity and widespread distribution was an innovative populist measure that helped foster a sense of community and mutual participation among diverse populations. More than likely, such wares often were given in reciprocal compensation for work devoted to specific elites projects. By Tiwanaku 2, Tiwanaku style vessels were being mass-produced for popular consumption. Increasingly through time, Tiwanaku vessels were the vehicles that made Tiwanaku power relations tick (Janusek 2002, 2004a).

Major feasts were organized cyclically according to a master calendar that afforded Tiwanaku a distinct urban rhythm. In this sense, Tiwanaku was a mega-*marka*. As a place of social and ceremonial convergence, its population rose and fell in pulsating waves according to major calendrical and "life-cycle" events. The ubiquity of polychrome ceremonial serving wares indicates that commensalism was as much a part of daily consumption, local social gatherings, and life-cycle rituals as it was a part of elite-sponsored events conducted in the plazas and courtyards of Putuni and Akapana East. As in the Andes today, major feasts involved ritually charged moments for jockeying, asserting, redefining, and obfuscating identity in vibrant social settings emphasizing intimacy, sharing, and, again to quote Durkheim (1915), "collective effervescence."

In Tiwanaku 2, the city housed powerful elite groups that headed increasingly large factions centered in the urban core. In this sense, Tiwanaku was analogous to the later Andean cities of Chan Chan and Cuzco (Conrad 1981, Zuidema 1990). Each of these cities incorporated increasing numbers of competing elite kin-focused groups that claimed descent from a mummified, deceased ruler. In each, the sequential construction of palaces, temples, and estates mapped in built form the history of royalty in the polity. The residential districts of Tiwanaku's urban core appear to have been analogous, and feasting provided moments for competitive display among elite-focused factions. At least as important, it was critical for maintaining an ideal of reciprocity in elite-nonelite relations and for building factions with grassroots constituents. This became especially critical as class distinctions crystallized and state hegemony intensified in Tiwanaku 2, precisely when spaces devoted to commensalism came to dominate the urban landscape and its recurring practice urban social interactions. Gestures of reciprocity enacted in rituals of consumption helped legitimate increasing inequality just as state strategies were seriously straining the etiquette of accepted social relations.

Tiwanaku as Cosmopolitan City and Place of Local Power

Yet Tiwanaku was far more than a center of monumental architecture, elite power, and elite-sponsored rituals of consumption. In Tiwanaku 1, it expanded precipitously over the nearby landscape as the scope of ritual and elite activity expanded and as social groups of diverse regions and livelihoods occupied the settlement. New residential neighborhoods were built around the formative core at a rate that may well have seemed alarming at the time. Important excavated non-elite residential sectors include (see Figure 4.1): Akapana East 1 on Tiwanaku's near east side and within the old moat-bounded core; Akapana East 2 just outside of the moat-bounded core; Ch'iji Jawira at the far eastern edge of the site; and Mollo Kontu, an extensive area beyond the moat and south of the northeast monumental group.

Urban Growth and Spatial Order

Tiwanaku's moat had physically defined the boundary of Tiwanaku in the Late Formative. In this sense, its symbolic significance may have been similar to that of the *pomerium* around early Rome, which legend tells us bounded and protected the early town built by Romulus. By AD 700, the moat acquired new symbolic meaning. It now served to physically reinforce a "concentric cline" of status and sacred power that, as Kolata puts it (1993a), dissipated with distance from the now-ancient monumental core. It came to focus social power and ideological legitimacy on that old core, its increasingly monumental temples, and its emergent elite lineages.

By AD 700, Tiwanaku was a bustling center of between 4 and 6 square kilometers that housed perhaps ten to twenty thousand people. It stretched over a vibrant urban landscape that incorporated diverse types of built and modified natural environments, specialized activities, and social groups. A fascinating and rarely noted characteristic of Tiwanaku is its incorporation of complex waterways and extensive *qochas* or sunken basins (Figure 4.1). The east side of the moat, for example, connected with another perpendicular channel that extended further out into the urban periphery. Even farther east, near the east edge of the city at its greatest extent, was a smaller modified channel that followed the orientation of all other urban architecture. This channel may have served to replicate the original significance of the primary moat in forming the far boundary of the expanding city.

The southeast segment of the city, an area known as Mollo Kontu, incorporated an interconnected cluster of *qochas*. As discussed in Chapter 5, studies of *qochas* indicate that they served any of several overlapping roles – to support nearby gardens or fields, as grazing areas, and as reservoirs – and would have been particularly useful during the dry season when water tables dropped. Thus, it seems likely that at least this segment of the city supported some farming and possibly herds of llamas and alpacas. Ongoing research here promises to shed light on these possibilities (Couture and Blom 2004).

A striking characteristic of Tiwanaku was a common orientation and spatial order that characterized all urban architecture excavated to date. First apparent in Late Formative 1, this order uniformly guided the construction of new residential compounds and ritual complexes over local cycles of construction and renewal. The orientation physically manifested an idealized spatial cosmology, a master plan that meshed the built and the social with the natural and the spiritual. Like core monumental architecture, it linked Tiwanaku space and society to timeless celestial rhythms, especially the daily and annual paths of the sun, and created

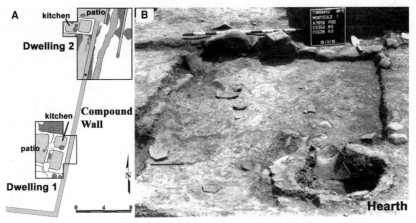

Figure 4.27 Excavated dwellings in (a) an Akapana East 1
compound, and (b) a close-up of the kitchen in Dwelling 1.

visual pathways to sacred mountains such as Kimsachata and Illimani.
It approximated the inviolable cycles and forms of sacred features and
mythical protagonists. The linkage was not simply abstractly conceived by
urban planners but instilled locally in experience and perception, for people lived and traversed the city every day. Recurring experience over life-
times and generations in the built landscape – just as in Chicago, London,
or any modern city– instilled a sense of spatial order that surpassed the
knowledge, life, and power of any particular group or living person.

Residential Patterns

The city grew in great part through the planned construction of enclosed
and uniformly aligned residential compounds (Janusek 2002, 2003b,
2004a). Each compound was bounded by a large wall and in some cases
by open channels, and many clustered together to form larger urban
communities, or barrios. Between compounds, unpaved streets provided
arteries of movement and convenient places to throw out ash and refuse.
Reminiscent of modern Andean pueblos and pre-Industrial European
cities, open drains capped by stone basins within compounds funneled
waste and runoff through the streets and toward open channels. Clearly,
part of the rich sensory experience of Tiwanaku's busy back streets was
a festival of curious and pungent aromas.

Each compound incorporated one or more households (Escalante
2003, Janusek 2004a: Figure 4.27). Each household had its own kitchen,
patio, wells, refuse pits, storage bins, animal pens, and refuse dumps (Figure 4.27). Many of the activities conducted within compounds involved

domestic reproduction, including food preparation, cooking, making stone and bone tools, weaving clothing and tapestries, eating, and drinking. Yet compounds incorporated a range of activities not typically considered "domestic" by today's Western middle-class standards, such as human burial, ritual offerings, llama butchering, and, in some cases, craft production.

Enclosed compounds and encompassing barrios formed salient loci of social difference and group identity in the city. Residential activities, dietary habits, styles of valued goods, domestic rituals, and the organization of space differed remarkably among them. I have interpreted each compound or neighborhood as the locus for a kin-based group analogous and perhaps historically antecedent to the micro-*ayllus* that characterized sociopolitical organization in the later Andean highlands. Yet not all of those residing in a compound were necessarily biologically related to the others, for it is likely that fictive kin (godparents, close friends, etc.), as well as hired servants or apprentices, periodically resided in the same walled enclosures.

Intriguing evidence that local compounds were dedicated to ceremony and feasting as well as domestic activity comes from the Tiwanaku 2 feast production complex in Akapana East 1. Although the south compound incorporated at least one dwelling, each of the rest of the excavated structures lacked a full range of domestic features and activities (Figure 4.25). Further, the buildings had very lightly trampled floors, indicating that they were only temporarily occupied. The same pattern characterized at least one other compound near the elaborate courtyard complex just to the north. In modern pueblos, residents often construct special rooms or buildings to house relatives, guests, and hired servants during major feasts, when each compound – and especially that of a feast sponsor – becomes a place of bustling activity. It is plausible that the Akapana East 1 buildings served such a role. Further, the structures appeared once Tiwanaku's political economy was increasingly becoming a "feasting economy" and when entire urban sectors were dedicated to commensalism. Akapana East and much of the city may have witnessed periodic influxes of relatives, friends, servants, and pilgrims from elsewhere to help produce and participate in elite-sponsored and local festivals.

Status Differences in the City

Kolata notes (1993a; Kolata and Ponce 1992) that Tiwanaku was ordered according to a concentric gradient of social status that diminished with distance from the urban core. Such a social order differs markedly from a suburban view of urbanism in modern North American cities, in which the inner city is considered by many to be dirty, dangerous, and best avoided. By late Tiwanaku 1, the moat in Tiwanaku came to emphasize physically this concentric order in the urban landscape. Residenital architecture and spatial organization also came to distinguish nonelites from elites. Compounds in Akapana East 1 and 2, Ch'iji Jawira, and Mollo Kontu incorporated vernacular architecture with cut sod walls and cobble foundations rather than finely crafted adobes on ashlars, and people inhabited relatively small and, in some cases, somewhat cramped living spaces rather than spacious halls with paved plazas. Valued goods used for social gatherings and feasts further distinguished groups. Residents in areas outside of the core tended to obtain and employ less finely made ceremonial serving wares, with far fewer (if any) of the most elaborate forms found in the Putuni and Akapana. Sanitation also distinguish social classes, as manifested both in the relatively dirty and ash-ridden spaces of local streets and compounds and the use of the far less effective drainage systems than characterized the urban core.

Tiwanaku social hierarchy and cultural identity were also defined in terms of generational history and relative "foreignness." Living near Tiwanaku's increasingly ancient core temples was a status statement in itself, strengthened by the social appropriation of the temples (by elaborating them and placing monoliths in them) and claims to ancestry with those buried in and under them. Barrios beyond the moat such as Akapana East 2 and Ch'iji Jawira were those most recently occupied and thus of greatest distance in generation and community memory to the great founders and ancestors. In addition, some of these groups maintained enduring ties with communities and regions outside of the city and even beyond the altiplano, which in cases such as Ch'iji Jawira may well have been their original homelands.

Urban Diversity and Social Identity

Tiwanaku was a cosmopolitan city composed of social groups and communities differentiated in status and many other mutually interwoven manners. Each group occupied a discrete place in the urban landscape. Each also maintained a distinct identity that transcended status differences and involved social and economic ties to groups in other parts of the city, other settlements in the region, and distant regions. Each compound group obtained and employed a variety of ceramics to serve food and liquor, and each group's "china" was distinct from that of most others. Many groups used substantial quantities of vessels associated with polities in distant regions such as the eastern valleys and the southern altiplano (Janusek 2003a, 2004a; Rivera 2003). The role of style became significant in ceremonial feasts and other gatherings when it communicated something about the position or identity that a group wished to convey (as well as those things it did not wish to convey).

Urban groups also maintained distinct dietary habits. Painstaking botanical analysis of carbonized root and seed remains indicates that proportions of tubers and grains such as quinoa and maize varied significantly among compounds, neighborhoods, and site sectors (Wright, Hastorf, and Lennstrom 2003). Maize in particular varied significantly among residential areas. Maize was a highly valued grain (in great part because of its social and ritual significance as fermented *chicha*) that grows well only in lower, warmer regions such as the eastern Andean valleys. While we expected to find high measures of maize in elite contexts such as Putuni, it was most common in residential areas of the urban periphery such as Akapana East 2 and Ch'iji Jawira. These areas housed people who also used substantial proportions of exotic serving wares from the warmer valleys. Rather than following a concentric cline of status centered on the city core, relative maize consumption followed another sociospatial logic grounded in local ties to distant regions. Status alone did not completely determine access to valued foods and goods. Locally managed social and economic networks also contributed, and perhaps in tension with increasingly intensified status differences.

Evidence supporting the coexistence of enduring ethniclike identities in Tiwanaku comes from Deborah Blom's recent bioarchaeological investigation of past human body modification (Blom 2005). Most telling are patterns of cranial modification (Figure 4.28). A number of techniques – including boards and turbanlike bandages – were employed to shape a child's skull to a desired shape. Historical documentation indicates that cranial modification marked ethnic identity in the Andes and that specific techniques expressed a group's ideals of health and beauty and emulated the form of their sacred peaks. Persons buried in Tiwanaku had one of three different head shapes: natural and unmodified, elongated ("cone-shaped") or flattened. No shape correlated with a particular status, sex, or even place in the city. However, the two modified head styles corresponded with those of different incorporated regions. Katari Valley people "wore" mostly cone-shaped heads and those in the distant Moquegua Valley to the west (see Chapter 6), entirely flattened heads. Remains of both conical and square (four-cornered) woven hats from dry coastal regions (Frame 1990) suggest that hat type accentuated head shape in public settings.

Blom's study concludes that bodily modification marked groups with far-reaching ethniclike ties, and that diverse groups co-resided and co-mingled in Tiwanaku. The fact that burials in some compounds included persons representing different head shapes may indicate that different ethnic groups intermarried. Urbanism undoubtedly created new social

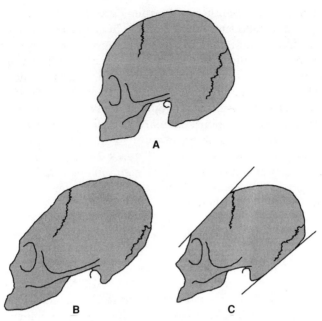

Figure 4.28 Unmodified (a), annular or elongated (b), and flattened (c) Tiwanaku head shapes (drawing by Deborah Blom).

relations, alliances, and communities. Tiwanaku was a center of ceremonial *and* social convergence and the place where powerful new identities, including that of the overarching Tiwanaku community, were formed.

Urban Economy

In light of its cosmopolitan character, economic life in Tiwanaku must have been vibrant. The relative insignificance of market-based trade at the time of European contact has stimulated interpretations of the distant past in which economic interaction is considered fully embedded in sociopolitical relations. Following John Murra's (1972) models of verticality, economic interaction in the highlands occurred mostly *within* communities via transhumance, colonization, and redistribution. Kolata concludes that "Tiwanaku's raison d'être had little to do with commercial, or mercantile activities. The social map of Tiwanaku was not a riotous mosaic of many peoples anonymously and independently pursuing their livelihoods" (Kolata 1993a:173–174).

Carlos Ponce (1981, 1991) and David Browman (1978a, 1981), however, interpret Tiwanaku as an economic hub. They hypothesize that Tiwanaku and other major altiplano settlements were dynamic centers of economic production in which groups specialized in creating a wide variety of valued and sumptuary goods. The presence of courtyards and plazas in and around the urban core suggests that barter, trade, and perhaps even periodic fairs were recurring activities in Tiwanaku. The role of the city as a cosmopolitan hub for llama caravan trade makes this especially likely (Chapter 5; Nuñez and Dillehay 1995). Goods of various stripes and flavors moved into and out of the city in increasing volume and intensity. The extent, depth, and ubiquity of refuse pits and sheet middens indicate that the volume of things acquired and consumed everyday and in periodic feasts was phenomenal (Janusek 2007b). As living transport vehicles facilitating movement of such goods in bulk, camelids were most likely quartered at (or near) Tiwanaku on a rotating basis. Trade and exchange most likely followed the temporal rhythms of vibrant public rituals and feasts. Economic activity intensified for these lively occasions, when people and herds from various regions converged on the center.

Tiwanaku also was a center for the production and distribution of goods. On the basis of stone artifact analysis, Martin Giesso (2000, 2003) suggests that the acquisition of certain exotic raw materials and the production of certain tools were directed by and for elite interests. First, high-quality basalt from Querimita in southern Oruro and obsidian from the Colca Valley, Peru, were most common in around the urban core. The acquisition of such valued goods most likely came to be controlled by elite groups and made possibly by commissioning specialized herders and quarry workers. Second, the production of chert, quartzite, and obsidian projectile points, some of the most finely crafted and standardized of Tiwanaku tools, was an activity conducted by specific households or compounds (Figure 4.29). Giesso hypothesizes that households produced projectile points as a tax that funded hunting, ritual, and warfare.

Yet most forms of specialized production and distribution were locally controlled (Rivera 2003). Residents of Ch'iji Jawira, with nonlocal ethnic affinities at the east edge of Tiwanaku, also specialized in making certain types of ceramic wares. These included large jars, flared bowls, and mold-made keros with effigy feline, condor, and llama heads. Production here was relatively informal. Firing took place in expedient pit-kilns on a knoll that maximized the force of predominant winds. A potentially toxic or at least bothersome productive activity, firing here was optimally located downwind of other residential sectors. Thus, multiple forms of productive organization coexisted in the city. The production of many valued goods, including ceramic wares, was embedded in the sociospatial fabric of local residential life in the urban periphery (Janusek 1999).

Figure 4.29 Tiwanaku arrow points were typically small, and most had stems.

Local Religious Life and Ritual Diversity

Many local ritual practices attest the coherence and endurance of local identities. As they did in monumental complexes, ritual dedications in residential compounds punctuated construction cycles and afforded a sense of spiritual continuity and well-being in the life cycle of the associated group. When building houses, people buried fetal llamas under house floors and walls and when repaving floors they smashed vessels on older surfaces. Small bone (and occasionally stone) tubes, spoons, and trays for ingesting mind-altering substances formed an important part of local ritual practice. Substances included resins that were masticated with coca to release its potent enzymes and a number of powdered hallucinogenic pods and cactus native to the eastern valleys and Amazonian lowlands (Figure 4.30). Pyroengraved iconography on bone tube containers used to store psychotropic substances depicted llama-masked decapitator figures or simply rows of decapitated trophy heads. In household, compound, and neighborhood rituals, masticating coca and ingesting hallucinogenic

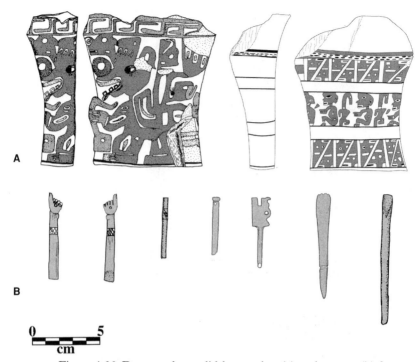

A

B

0 _____ 5
cm

Figure 4.30 Decorated camelid-bone tubes (a) and spoons (b) for
storing and ingesting psychotropic substances.

snuff helped establish a memory path with mythical and supernatural
beings through the intercession of ancestors and other spirits.

Some deceased relatives and ancestors were buried in tombs and clustered in discrete mortuary complexes under living spaces within residential compounds (Figures 4.25 and 4.31). Keeping the bodies of dead
ancestors close to home – in some cases right under house floors – contrasts sharply with contemporary Western attitudes about the dead and
where they are to be interred. For centuries in the West it has been cus-
tomary to relegate the dead to discrete cemeteries far from home, putting
in practice an obsession to render a sharp division between realms of life
and death. In Tiwanaku and other Andean societies, keeping the deceased
under or near living spaces afforded each group a direct link to its unique
past and tied it to a particular place. In Akapana East 2, a stone marked
the place of a burial with three individuals – an adult and three children –
who were interred under the floor of a household's outdoor patio. It
was common to bury deceased relatives as already-decomposed bundles
wrapped in colorful woven mantles.

Figure 4.31 A middle-aged woman buried under a patio in an Akapana East compound.

These practices outline a form of local ancestor veneration in which communities periodically conducted rites and bestowed offerings on deceased individuals claimed to be household or "*ayllu*" progenitors. Yet that both adults and children, and women and men, were buried in compounds indicate that ritual commemoration included a wide range of deceased kin (in spirit or blood). Commemorating deceased ancestors and kin, considered alive in spirit and effective in the workings of "living" society and nature, clearly played an important role in reanimating group identity, forging local memory and historical continuity, and negotiating and legitimating position and status in the city and in Tiwanaku society.

Furthermore, local neighborhoods maintained discrete built ritual places, indicating that suprahousehold rituals were not restricted to the urban core. In Akapana East 1, an early complex of adobe buildings dating from Late Formative 2 to Tiwanaku 1 was dedicated to local esoteric rituals (Figure 4.32a; Blom and Janusek 2004; Janusek 2004a). Many characteristics of the complex distinguished it from surrounding residential places. Floors were kept impeccably clean and consisted of specially selected and finely prepared soils differing in color and texture. Floors

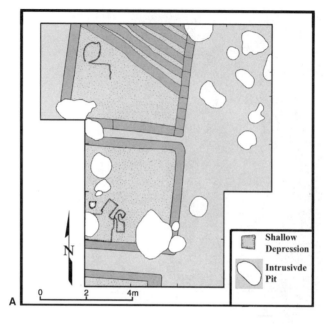

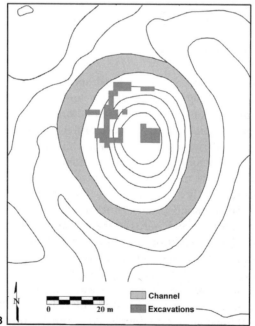

Figure 4.32 Local urban ritual places in Tiwanaku: a ritual chamber in Akapana East (a) and a platform complex in Mollo Kontu (b, redrawn from Couture 2003).

inside of the buildings contained shallow depressions in well-defined geometric shapes, perhaps to support monoliths and other icons long since removed. More striking was evidence for the unusual treatment of human remains. The outside patio contained shallow pits lined with pulverized and discolored bone. Further, three carefully curated human bundles were interred in the mound that covered the complex, two of which had been defleshed. Defleshing and pulverizing the bones of deceased relatives were practices associated with cannibalizing deceased relatives in some recent western Amazonian societies (Conklin 2001). Whatever the precise nature of the rituals, they were fastidious, intimate, and involved the veneration and perhaps "compassionate cannibalism" of deceased relatives or ancestors.

Late in Tiwanaku 1, a ritual complex was built in Mollo Kontu. The Mollo Kontu Mound was a small terraced platform built along the north-south visual path between Akapana and Mount Kimsachata (Figures 4.1 and 4.32b; Couture 2003). Bounded by an outer revetment and with a uniquely scalloped northern edge, the platform included high quantities of quartz and obsidian fragments that may have been intentionally placed in the fill to accentuate the monument's sacred status as a miniature icon of a mountain. A channel surrounded the platform. This was most likely the source of the platform's construction fill, and as a micro-analogue of Tiwanaku's moat, emphasized its symbolic importance.

Thus, local ritual complexes punctuated the urban landscape that surrounded the most sacred and prestigious part of the city. Ritual environments like those in Akapana East 1 and Mollo Kontu were surrounded by residential spaces, suggesting that they were tended by local residential groups. Like core monumental complexes, each was the focus of a specific cult and urban community. Each formed a complementary segment of Tiwanaku's emerging master cosmology, but each was also the focus of a separate ritual group or faction. Diverse cults thrived as constituent segments of Tiwanaku's emerging dominant ideology.

In the city, religion remained incorporative and syncretic. Groups of diverse backgrounds and social networks affiliated with an emerging Tiwanaku identity, accepting and internalizing key elements of its predominant mythical narratives and religious practices. Yet each group forged and strategically re-formulated its own nested and overlapping affiliations, in part by building local ritual places and conducting characteristic ritual practices at Tiwanaku. Both cosmopolitan city and ritual-political center, Tiwanaku comprised multiple religious groups and their specific collective memories, ancestral rites, and mythical narratives.

The importance of local ritual encourages us to reconsider the full role and significance of core temples such as Kalasasaya, Akapana, and Pumapunku. If these were icons of elite power and ideology, then the ideals and identities of nonelites, those who actually built them, worshiped in them, and served as attendants in them, also were enmeshed with them. As Tim Pauketat (2000:117) notes of native Mississippian period monuments in the U.S. Midwest, "Unless we assume that [the masses] were duped, were consciously coerced, or were without dispositions, then we must admit the possibility that their dispositions in some ways shaped monumental constructions."

Hollywood myths and fantasies have (mis)shaped our imagination of the role of nonelites in past monuments and their construction. In Cecil B. Demille's *Ten Commandments*, we see whip-driven slaves building the great Egyptian pyramids, and Charlton Heston's Moses offering succor for an unfortunate soul trapped between massive blocks (for, "blood makes poor mortar"). Yet research in many past civilizations indicates that in many cases, including pharaonic Egypt (Mendelssohn 1971), nonelites voluntarily (if grudgingly) gave their labor – and their blood – to build and tend such monuments in reciprocal obligation to a ruler or ruling group, in great part motivated not by the whip but by a sense of responsibility, identity, and immediate benefits or future redemption. So it was in Tiwanaku.

Discussion: Local Power and the Production of Tiwanaku

Especially before AD 800 in Tiwanaku, there was neither the technology and infrastructure nor the hegemonic productive, political, or ideological conditions that would facilitate coercive interactions with or full elite "power over" social groups. To the extent that leadership was consensual and leaders represented groups with unique interests and identities, people would have failed to cooperate in the creation of things openly divergent from traditional and accepted values and representations. Communal construction events mark significant periodic events in which groups gathered to recreate or enlarge significant built places. Such moments of interaction and their sponsored ceremonies and feasts involved the periodic affirmation of inclusive social identities. Ritual renewal in local temples such as those in Akapana East and Mollo Kontu fostered local community identities and bonds while successive stages of construction in elite-sponsored monuments such as Akapana and Pumapunku fostered an encompassing politico-religious community identity. Probably not clearly foreseen by leaders and commoners alike, the construction of such ritual places served, at various scales, to forge the emerging Tiwanaku polity in all of its developing complexity and inequality.

The monuments and monoliths that punctuated Tiwanaku's ceremonial landscape had to "make sense" to be meaningful and ritually potent. They aggrandized shared values even as they paradoxically (especially after AD 800) aggrandized the leaders who planned and coordinated their construction. In their spatial organization and iconography we see the local and the vernacular built into monumental design: a consistent emphasis on intimacy, the patio-focused design of courtyards, and the meticulously carved *totora* reeds on lintels covering Pumapunku's gates. Most telling is the ritual gesture assumed by the iconic figures of the Bennett, Ponce, and other monoliths. On the one hand, the great ancestral deities of Tiwanaku and its emergent elites stand erect and impassive. They evoke power, cold aloofness, and serious business. On the other hand, they each hold objects that, in the very "human" elements they contained – drink and drugs – linked elites and nonelites as well as ancestors and the living in gestures of social and cosmic reciprocity. As monuments still standing today, they may still evoke in us a sense of Tiwanaku's humanity, bridging distant times and cultures with similar passions for intimacy, conviviality, consumption, and power.

Tiwanaku was forged on a covenant in which a place in the hierarchy and a role in the system were (at least in spirit) reciprocated in material goods, economic opportunities, an elegant cosmic vision, ritual conviviality, and religious redemption. Monuments were bids for elite power; yet, they also inspired an ethos of spirituality and a sense of community for all. The covenant worked for centuries. Yet it rested on shaky foundations, especially as elite factions increased in influence, power, and disrespect for shared Tiwanaku values. Ultimately, as potent symbols of elite power and ancestry, monuments provoked disillusionment and vengeance (Chapter 8).

Conclusions

Tiwanaku was designed as a cosmogram, or an ideal representation of the world, and during the Tiwanaku Period, it became a place of elite residence and activity. Tiwanaku also was highly dynamic, pulsating in population and activity according to calendrical and periodic rituals and shifting with changing sociopolitical and pan-regional conditions (see Chapters 6 and 7). Major rites and feasts were times of social encounter when hundreds, perhaps thousands of pilgrims and extensive trains of llama caravans, packed to the brim, descended on the city. For days, the elite hosted massive feasts, priests were busy choreographing ceremonies, and traders hawked their wares. Over centuries, prominent monuments endured, but their forms continually acquired new meanings. The moat and the Sunken Temple are clear examples, and as in any modern city, major temples such as Pumapunku were always under construction. Construction was likely a key element of many major ritual events. Tiwanaku's significance as a symbolic and ceremonial place of convergence was constantly in flux.

Tiwanaku was important not just as a cognitive model in the minds of ruling elites and high priests but as it was experienced. Spatially aligned with celestial cycles and ancient peaks and ritually attuned to repeating seasonal cycles, Tiwanaku's rise was due in part to its objectification of natural and spiritual forces. It was a ceremonial urban center, broadly similar to the contemporaneous coastal city of Pachacamac (Chapter 7), and it remained a spiritually potent place of pilgrimage and worship. The sanctified hearts of massive temples were intimate places, and religious iconography was esoteric and best appreciated up close. Facilitated by paths of movement into the ceremonial core and through its mysterious and carnivalesque ritual complexes, worship at Tiwanaku was as direct and immediate as it was abstract and transcendent. This was, in great part, the spiritual power of Tiwanaku religion.

Tiwanaku was as much a cosmopolitan center as it was a royal city. Social stratification followed a roughly concentric order that corresponded broadly with proximity to the most sacred places and icons. Yet the diversity of ritual places and social practices across the urban landscape highlights a tension between the dominant cosmology and multiple local religious views and ideologies. Tiwanaku housed diverse bounded groups, each with distinct social relations, economic concerns, remembered histories and identities. As a dense sociospatial landscape Tiwanaku facilitated a play of multiple forces, including a dynamic tension among several elite factions and multiple nodes of local power. From the Late Formative, Tiwanaku was a syncretic conjunction of religious ideas and rituals, and throughout the Tiwanaku Period, it remained a nexus of diverse ideological views and cults. Indeed, Tiwanaku had plenty of space for skeptics and sectaries, as well as divergent, even counterhegemonic views.

The conservative and conformist character of Tiwanaku style – in ceremonial wares and religious icons, for example – strategically responded to this diversity. It afforded a common language, history, and identity among highly diverse societies: an encompassing political, economic, and religious community. Through learning and internalization, Tiwanaku style in everyday actions and materials served to forge a common state culture. Relations grounded in an ideal of intimacy and in "sectarian" interests formed the matrix out of which this common language, its institutions, and its elite strata were built. As discussed in Chapter 8, they can also be counted among the forces that ultimately brought Tiwanaku down.

Tiwanaku was not an isolated city but a sociospatial phenomenon physically and symbolically tied to the high landscapes of the southern Lake Titicaca Basin where it emerged and thrived. The next chapter once again broadens the geographical focus by treating human-landscape relations in Tiwanaku's immediate hinterland.

5   The Hinterland

Popular venues promote the seductively glamorous notion that archaeologists routinely fly off to exotic places to discover spectacular monuments such as the Egyptian pyramids or royal Inca estates such as Machu Picchu. While discovery is at the foundation of archaeology and the reason many of us got into this field of study, over the past fifty years, archaeologists have become more interested in understanding past social processes. Excavating a temple or discovering a deity-faced gold pendant is exciting and important, but most archaeologists are now more interested in what motivated their production and their roles and meanings in past societies. Sprawling cities and towering monuments were as dazzling in the past as they are today, but they were integrally linked to the hinterlands they punctuated and the local populations that afforded their impact and meaning.

A shift toward regional approaches in archaeology helped steer archaeologists away from city and monument-centered investigations and paved the way to an understanding of past interrelations of society and environment and city and hinterland. Gordon Willey's (1953) study of settlement systems in the Virú Valley, Peru, was seminal in laying the groundwork for such studies. It was followed by highly influential research in other world regions, including Mexico's Central Basin (Parsons 1976) and Oaxaca regions (Flannery 1976) and Iran's Susiana Plain (Wright and Johnson 1975). Regional settlement studies depend largely on the recognition of ancient sites and site networks on present landscapes. They work on the premise that visible characteristics of sites, including presence of monumental architecture, valuable goods or administrative artifacts (such as Mesopotamian cylinder seals), position on the landscape relative to other sites, and site size correlated with their specific role in a past settlement system and the sociopolitical complexity of past societies.

Although traditional settlement studies are highly informative, they are somewhat limited. They tend to assume that a site's size and monumentality directly correlate with its population and importance. Because environments are always shifting, many sites in a region have been buried, "deflated" (blown away), eroded, or completely obliterated by later natural and human processes. Thus, just about any settlement survey, in which archaeologist locate sites in a given landscape, will to some degree return skewed results. Further, past human settlement should be considered not as systems abstracted from the places they inhabit (for example, many early studies drew on Medieval German market-focused networks to understand past "settlement systems" around the world) but as integrally interwoven with local environment, landscape, and production. The Andes in general and the altiplano in particular, and even specific regions of the high plateau, brought unique conditions to bear on human settlement and social organization.

Also important are the relations that link humans with each other and with their distinct productive regimes and landscapes. In light of the multiethnicity of the altiplano upon European contact and social diversity in the past city of Tiwanaku, there is every reason to believe that Tiwanaku's immediate hinterland was also pluriethnic and multilingual. Alan Kolata (1993a) speculates that Tiwanaku's core hinterland included at least three ethniclike groups, each of which maintained a primary association with a specific range of ecological niches and a particular productive regime. Kolata turns to ethnohistorical and ethnographic analogy to identity the groups. He speculates that Aymara tended herds of llamas and alpacas and cultivated tubers, the Pukina were the wetland farmers *par excellence* who developed raised-field systems, and the Uru, at the base of the regional sociopolitical hierarchy, specialized in fishing and foraging aquatic resources. In this view, political authority emerged out of ethnic alliances and interactions, which afforded consensual relations between local communities and the emerging state. A cohesive state structure, Kolata suggests, coalesced as Aymara and Pukina elites, the dominant groups at the time, intermarried among their dynasties.

Although it is unlikely that these ethnic identities had endured as such for hundreds of years, the idea provides an opportunity to investigate the relation between human society and environment in a new key. It opens a perspective of the altiplano as diversified rather than homogeneous and provides a conceptual foundation for understanding the dynamic mutual interpenetration of human settlement and landscape. A key theoretical point of this chapter is that inhabited physical environments such as the altiplano were not strictly "natural"; they were anthropogenic cultural spaces. Space in this view is not simply a passive cipher that is acted upon, transformed, and imbued with cultural meaning, but rather, through production, ritual activity, and *dwelling*, configures settlement patterns and social organization; space becomes place, and place conditions culture (see Ashmore and Knapp 1999; Barrett 1994; Smith 2003).

Built Tiwanaku monuments celebrated natural features such as mountains, water, and *totora* reeds, while the entire city embodied the power of ancient peaks and the rhythms of timeless celestial cycles. Entire floodplains such as Katari were "landscaped" to support raised-field farming, which in turn configured movement, production, and settlement in the past just as it continues to affect livelihoods in the present. Even more subtle engagements with the environment through fishing, *totora* farming, and herding had cumulative affects on the landscape and human settlement systems (Browman 1987; Erickson 2000). Worldwide, human-environment relations and the transfiguration of landscapes, understood as sociocultural spaces, are implicated in long-term shifts that gave rise to increasingly complex and influential if often destructive human societies.

Investigating past societies and settlement networks in relation to local production and land use highlights the natural diversity of the altiplano and its inhabitants. Today fishers, farmers, and herders in the altiplano employ a range of social and productive strategies to make an effective and secure living at more than 3,800 meters. In such an intractable and sometimes unpredictable environment, making a living is frequently not as much about maximizing profit, the ideological cornerstone of capitalist enterprise, as it is about minimizing risk. Fishers, farmers, and herders must be flexible and pragmatic and must often forego big instant returns to ensure successful livelihoods in the long run. Families and communities past and present emphasize diversification in socioeconomic interaction, in locations of fields, fisheries, and grazing lands, and in productive systems and practices. Leaders in past polities did the same by maintaining far-flung networks and diverse productive regimes, while leaving most production in the hands of the local families and communities who knew them best. While Tiwanaku leaders and engineers developed and expanded one ingenious and well-adapted productive regime – irrigated, raised-field farming systems – at an unprecedented scale, they did so within a broadly diversified productive panorama that included fishing/foraging, herding, and other farming systems to minimize disaster in periods of drought.

In this chapter, I focus on Tiwanaku's hinterland, defined as three broad subbasins and their intramural hills and mountains: the Tiwanaku, Katari, and Desaguadero valleys and the Taraco Peninsula. I first examine relations of settlement and landscape and then discuss the distinct productive regimes of fishing, farming, and herding and their different social and spatial conditions. I trace patterns from the Formative through the Tiwanaku periods to emphasize long-term changes and continuities.

Settlement, Society, and Landscape
in the Tiwanaku Hinterland

During the Early-Middle Formative, no clear "capital" or ritual-political center existed but rather many relatively small ceremonial centers. A "one center, one polity" model fails to apply to areas of greatest incipient social complexity. Rather, social dynamics were complex and, it appears, volatile. Bandy (2001, 2004) finds evidence for "settlement fissioning" by the end of the Early Formative, in which increasing social tensions in a community reached a critical threshold once population approached two hundred people. By the Middle Formative, however, settlement options were decreasing such that kin-groups with political differences continued to reside in or near their home settlements. Along with new trade routes and an increasingly vibrant ceremonial life after 450 BC, many sites experienced unprecedented growth as the distribution of resources and prestige became concentrated in the hands of the most successful groups. True social ranking and the formation of regional polities had begun.

Regional settlement patterns and social networks shifted dramatically after 200 BC. Settlement and society became more complex and much habitation shifted down into now marshier, low-lying pampas. Such changes may be linked to another rise in lake levels and a shift in trade networks southward across the Tiwanaku and Desaguadero valleys (Bandy 2001). New centers emerged at the peripheries of Middle Formative settlement clusters. Many, including Khonkho Wankane and Tiwanaku, were located farther inland and distant from the aquatic axis. In tandem with new material culture and the rise of Pukara to the north, the settlement shift indicates that a tectonic productive, sociopolitical, and cultural shift was transforming the entire basin at this time. The basin now supported a plethora of fluid, interacting multicommunity polities and their cadres of new elites.

Tiwanaku emerged in this dynamic geopolitical setting as the primary center in the basin after AD 400. This occurred as two growing communities – one focused around the Kalasasaya and one around the later Pumapunku – formed a single urban center. Habitation continued to concentrate in the pampa and its adjacent low piedmont zones throughout the Tiwanaku Period. Former autonomous centers in the southern basin, such as Lukurmata and Khonkho Wankane, formed affiliated ritual-political centers. By the seventh century, settlement networks formed four-tier settlement hierarchies distributed across local landscapes (Figure 5.1). From the beginning, Lukurmata was Tiwanaku's most important local center and was something akin to a dual center (see Chapter 6).

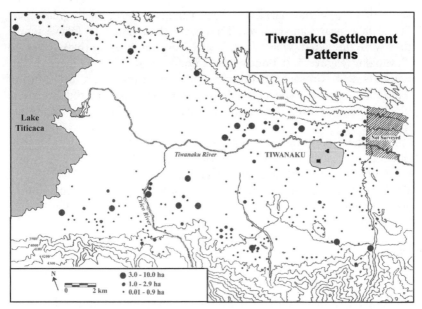

Figure 5.1 Tiwanaku-period settlement patterns in the Tiwanaku Valley (adapted from Albarracín-Jordan 1996a).

Smaller sites included settlements that we can categorize as towns (10–20 hectares), villages (3–10 hectares), and hamlets (under 3 hectares). Many towns had monumental structures and platforms, including Kallamarka in the Tiwanaku Valley (Portugal and Portugal 1975), Qeyakuntu in Katari (Janusek and Kolata 2003), Chiripa on the Taraco Peninsula (Hastorf 1999), and Tumatumani in Juli-Pomata (Stanish and Steadman 1994). Major formative centers now served as local ritual-political centers. Tiwanaku hegemony involved the refurbishing of old monumental structures and ceremonial spaces to follow the new styles and ideals that characterized Tiwanaku ritual environments. The size and population of many centers increased substantially, while others waned.

In the Tiwanaku Period, we see clear evidence for site-based occupational specialization and craft production. In the Tiwanaku Valley, inhabitants of the small site of Obsidiana crafted obsidian tools (Albarracin-Jordan 1996a), and much of TMV-332 may have been dedicated to breeding guinea pigs as a tasty delicacy for human consumption (Webster 1993). On the lakeshore, Iwawe served as a port and as a center for finishing andesite blocks (Isbell and Burkholder 2002). Destined for Tiwanaku's emerging monuments, these blocks had been quarried and roughly cut and shaped at quarries below Mount Ccapia on the western shore of Lake Wiñaymarka and near Yunguyu, Peru, on the main part of the lake near Copacabana. They were then rafted to Iwawe where they were unloaded, worked, and carted overland, using thick ropes, to Tiwanaku (Figure 5.2; Bandy 2001; Ponce et al. 1971). Likewise, settlements near Kimsachata, the most prominent mountain due south of Tiwanaku, may have specialized in quarrying and finishing red sandstone blocks. Roughly carved monoliths remain in situ in nearby mountain quarries.

Hinterland communities took on or intensified the acquisition, production, or distribution of some critical resource, and entire sites and residential precincts became bustling ceramic, stone, or metal workshops. Producing the Tiwanaku polity required intensification in occupational specialization and the production and consumption of crafted utilitarian and prestige goods.

Tiwanaku settlement locations were very similar to those of the Late Formative. Most settlements continued to be inhabited though people used new styles of material culture and organized their lives according to new practices and ideals. Among the most dramatic transformations in the hinterland was the widespread use of Tiwanaku serving and feasting wares as well as large jars for fermenting and storing *chicha*. At most sites, these were less common and more expediently crafted than they were in Tiwanaku's urban core, but nevertheless, they were ubiquitous. Also notable was the continued use of the hallucinogenic complex. In the hinterland as in the city, feasting, drinking, and ingesting mind-altering psychotropic substances, practices at the heart of Tiwanaku culture, and ritual activities so powerfully depicted on Tiwanaku's monoliths, were important in familial and community lives.

Tiwanaku's expansion, unlike that of some cities, did not create a rural vacuum. Rather it corresponded with a surge in population and settlement density across much of the hinterland. In many areas, this trend continued through Tiwanaku 2. Combined survey revealed over 450 sites in those segments of the Tiwanaku-Taraco-Katari region investigated to date. In most areas of the hinterland, sites formed clear clusters that focused on one or several large settlements, and they housed extended households and other kin-based coresidential groups. With the aid of quantitative analysis, archaeologists have defined several macroclusters in the Tiwanaku Valley (McAndrews, Albarracin-Jordan, and Bermann 1997), each of which may represent a proto-*ayllu* community. Settlement distribution in the Katari Valley was different due to regional physical characteristics and productive concerns, which since the Late Formative had focused on the marshy pampa. Settlement distribution lined the low piedmont that bordered the pampa, affording settlement a roughly linear character.

Figure 5.2 A large andesite block on the lakeshore near the site of Iwawe (photo courtesy of Kenneth Garrett).

Natural features such as rivers and mountain ranges formed boundaries that linked and divided sociopolitical communities. Mountain ranges were temporarily populated, important "wild" places that divided the hinterland into valleys inhabited by different ethnic groups (or macro-*ayllus*). Through the floodplain of each valley flowed a river that divided it into two physical and social zones that, in a general sense, mirrored one another. The Tiwanaku valley may have comprised two complementary moieties, each composed of three or more settlement macroclusters (Albarracin-Jordan 1996b). We can hypothesize that a similar dual arrangement formed part of the physical, social, and conceptual organization of the Katari and Desaguadero valleys. The Katari River was artificially straightened and fixed with a levy to prevent regular flooding and, perhaps in addition, to form an ideal symbolic boundary between two macrocommunities. The Desaguadero River, both a path of commerce and a cultural boundary, most likely served a similar physical-symbolic role.

The hinterland was home to communities integrally tied to particular places, routes, and productive activities. Groupings ranged in scale from homesteads and kin-focused groups to moieties and ethniclike communities. Punctuating local landscapes were the sacred places that pertained to specific groups. Communities were physically linked via paths and roads that joined settlements, households, and ritual places. While only segments remain, some of the most important roads traversed the lower piedmont that joined mountains and pampas on either side of each valley. Each moiety, in this scenario, may have guarded and maintained its own roadway. These are not only the most passable routes in the valleys but precisely the location of rural roads in Bolivia today. Numerous pathways traversed both pampas, which linked local communities, and mountain ranges, which linked vast regions. Of particular significance are pathways that still cut over the Taraco range, linking Tiwanaku and Lukurmata, and much longer, steeper paths that wind up and across Kimsachata, linking Tiwanaku with Khonkho Wankane.

Settlements and kin groups formed larger imagined communities by virtue of timeless natural features. The primary aquatic axis of the lake and the Desaguadero River provided boat travel and interaction across regions, crosscutting land-based routes and boundaries. Rivers joined moieties to form ethnicities, while mountain ranges joined ethnicities to form larger networks of interaction. At the heights and joining earth and sky, the rugged snow-capped peaks of Illimani, Illampu, Ccapia, and Sajama surrounded and quartered the hinterland. They peered over local ranges as one walked, emerging as fully visible peaks at the summits of mountain passes, places that today punctuate a traveler's journey with a brief rest and libation. The four peaks approximate Tiwanaku's orientation to the cardinal directions. Through processions and pilgrimages, dedications and sacrifices, the ancient peaks were remembered and their powers ritually tapped to forge an encompassing identity. Settlement, landscape, and the Tiwanaku polity, as an emerging macrocommunity, were inseparable.

Next I map the location of settlements and social groups in relation to the primary productive regimes that characterized the prehispanic altiplano at the time of Tiwanaku hegemony: fishing/foraging, farming, and herding. Doing so emphasizes that the altiplano was a dynamic and diverse environment that shaped and was transfigured by human activity through a variety of productive enterprises.

Fishing, Foraging, and Hunting

The archaeology of fishing communities in the high Andes is just beginning. Throughout prehispanic history many populations fished, harvested lake plants such as *totora*, and hunted various species of birds. Settlement dispositions indicate that lacustrine pursuits were an important part of life in the northern altiplano beginning with the first sedentary communities in the Late Archaic. A predisposition for lake and

Figure 5.3 Flamingos on Lake Titicaca (photo by Alan Kolata).

river-oriented settlements suggests that the earliest sedentary communities focused primarily on fishing, foraging, and hunting, and recent research confirms this idea. Throughout the Early-Middle Formative, fish and lake birds made up a disproportionate portion of the diet on the Taraco Peninsula (Figure 5.3; Moore Steadman, and DeFrance 1999). In Chiripa, fish constituted two-thirds of the total consumed biomass (up to 97 percent of total diet), thoroughly eclipsing agricultural and camelid portions of the diet. Inhabitants of Iruhito on the Desaguadero River maintained similar livelihoods (Perez 2005). Yet at both Middle Formative sites, lake-oriented populations combined fishing, foraging, and hunting with some rain-fed farming (Graffam 1990; Hastorf 1999).

Shifts in settlement choices during the Late Formative marked an important shift in sociopolitical relations, productive concerns, and cultural identity. By Late Formative 2, many of the most important centers were at inland locations. The aquatic axis no longer determined settlement choices, the location of major centers, or human livelihoods as thoroughly as it had during the Early-Middle Formative. This shift was part of a profound sociopolitical transformation in which new social groups and settlement networks gained increasing prestige and social power. Excavations indicate that their livelihoods focused on farming and herding rather than on fishing and foraging (Browman 1978a, 1981; Janusek 2001; Janusek and Kolata 2003; Webster 2003).

Yet many settlements continued to thrive on the shores of the lake and its rivers, forming a broad aquatic swath that included Lukurmata, Iwawe, and Iruhito. Those who relied on wild resources, traditional technologies, and old livelihoods in the basin may have come to be identified as "backward," perhaps supported by their inhabitation of visible Middle Formative ruins. Gradually, perhaps over centuries, fishers and foragers came to assume a regional identity and low status position as ancient, less civilized "fossils" of an earlier time, even as people at inland settlements avidly exchanged for and consumed their products. Interaction and trade among shoreline communities may have been at times more vibrant and important than it was between shoreline and inland communities, creating and reproducing a pan-regional "aquatic identity" that crosscut others. The distinction of fishers/foragers and farmers/herders, later manifested as a distinction of Aymara and Uru, perhaps had its origins in this early transformation.

Fishing, foraging, and hunting remained disproportionately important at some sites under Tiwanaku hegemony; for example, at Lukurmata, the primary center of the Katari Valley and Tiwanaku's second city. While located on the lakeshore, excavations in most residential compounds revealed proportions of faunal remains very similar to those at Tiwanaku. It is at the north tip of the site where full- or part-time fishers resided (Janusek 2004a:259; Wise 1993), if largely during phases of intense lacustrine activity. Elsewhere in Katari, fishing was the domain of small rural sites. Middens from small pampa sites such as the Quiripujo mound group yielded high proportions of fish bone (Janusek and Kolata 2003). Yet local residents were not exclusively fishers; they also farmed the pampa and may have owned small herds. Further south, Iruhito has yielded some of the highest quantities of fish bone of any Tiwanaku site (Perez 2005). Evidence to date suggests that resident groups in multiple sectors of the site remained primarily dedicated to fishing, hunting, and foraging.

Some of the best evidence to date for long-term shifts in the role of lacustrine pursuits comes from Iwawe, on the south shore of the Taraco Peninsula. Fish remains as well as bird bones and egg shells were extremely abundant in middens that dated from Late Formative 1 through the Tiwanaku period (Capriles 2005; Isbell and Burkholder 2002). Most common among fish was *carachi* (*Orestias luteus*), which still thrives in shallow waters such as those of Iwawe's shores (Orlove 2002). Comparing remains of fish and other fauna through time yields the following results: In Late Formative 1, fish provided the most important food source, complemented in Late Formative 2 by an increasing reliance on camelids;

under Tiwanaku hegemony, fish and camelids remained roughly equally important (42 and 58 percent of biomass, respectively), but by the end of Tiwanaku 2, fish had become most important once again. This preliminary case study points to the rise of a "regionally integrated economy" founded on fishing at the end of the Late Formative (Isbell and Burkholder 2002:230), as the region came to form the core of a regional state. A concommitent decrease in the average size of fish consumed and an increasing concentration on a single fish species suggest to Jose Capriles (2005) that fishing was increasingly standardized and most likely intensified – quite possibly even overexploited – under Tiwanaku hegemony.

In the Tiwanaku Period, aquatic productive strategies were probably similar to those of recent altiplano fishers, before trout was introduced into the lake and traditional implements were relegated to museums and exhibits. Like later populations, prehispanic fishers rarely used hooks. Working alone or together, and most often working on moonless nights, they employed a number of techniques using different types of nets made of grass, reed, or camelid wool, the only remaining evidence for which would be the stone weights used to hold large seines below the surface. Tools might have included the small dip net attached to a long wooden pole; a variety of scoop nets and drag nets; the larger trawl net; and the basket trap, which employs intricately twined and lashed grass stems (La Barre 1947; Orlove 2002; Tschopik 1946). Although it remains to find hard evidence, past fishers may have used harpoons in shallow water. A particularly productive technique would have been "fence fishing," whereby fish are scooped up in quantity by submerging a woven screen of *totora* at an angle from a dense reed bed.

With multiple tools and flexible techniques, ancient fishers procured numerous fish species, most importantly pupfish of the genus *Orestias* that included, *carachi* and the larger, now extinct *umantu*. With basket traps, fishers caught high quantities of *ispi*, a silvery minnowlike fish that looks like a tiny sardine. Another important fish flock included catfish of the genus *Trichomychterus*, more recently captured with harpoons (Orlove 2002:126–127). Residents of shoreline communities harvested aquatic plants such as *totora* reeds as well as submerged anaerobic species (Figure 5.4), which provided food, basketry, roofing, and crafting the world-renowned reed boats, or *balsas*, that are now iconic of native Andean (and specifically Uru) identity (Figure 2.4). Furthermore, they hunted and gathered eggs from numerous bird species that were drawn to the lake margins, including "ducks, geese, gulls, coots, grebes, herons, ibises, and flamingos" (Bermann 1994:46; also Moore, Steadman, and DeFrance 1999; Perez 2005).

Figure 5.4 Harvesting submerged plants on Lake Titicaca.

Fish and water were celebrated as sources of social and cosmic regeneration in the iconography of religious art in the altiplano, highlighting their central role in social and spiritual realms. Asiruni images on Yayamama, Pukara, and Khonkho sculptures include stylized catfish and serpentlike beings. It is possible that the serpent creatures represent mythical lake creatures such as the *katari*, or sea serpent, a dangerous being that fishermen fear (Orlove 2002). By the Tiwanaku Period, stylized profile fish heads with upturned mouths, representing the popular *Oresitas*, commonly adorned monolithic stone sculptures (Figure 5.5) and, less commonly, polychrome serving wares (Couture 2002; Janusek 2003a). Stylized fish heads dangle from the tresses of the Ponce Monoliths' ancestral personage and they radiate from the Sun Portal's central deity and its peripheral attendants. These compositions positioned aquatic resources among the primary elements comprising Tiwanaku's social and spiritual realms.

The groups who emerged as specialized fisher folk during the Late Formative and Tiwanaku periods engaged in other productive activities. Their location along altiplano waterways and their status as master seafarers gave such groups a strategic advantage in trade and in acquiring and moving goods. The lake formed a complex landscape in itself, marked off by invisible but very real boundaries between communities

Figure 5.5 An *Orestias* fish (a) and *Orestias* iconography (b) trailing from an avian-masked attendant of the Sun Portal (a, from Posnansky 1945).

and crisscrossed by entrenched routes of travel and trade (Orlove 1991). Lake- and river-oriented groups controlled not just fish but the movement of goods that elites sought in order to build monumental centers. As a key element in the fortification of a pan-regional aquatic identity, the movement of andesite, in particular, was very likely in their hands. It is they, master raft builders and sailors, who assured that valued building materials reached the shore, where specific communities such as Iruhito and Iwawe did the finer cutting.

The aquatic axis held great economic and ritual potency. Those who made it their livelihood had substantial economic wealth and effective power. During the Tiwanaku period, those who inhabited the lake and specialized in its resources formed a far-flung community of practice with a potent regional identity. Thus, an enduring view of such communities as primitive fossils, ironically much like modern Western notions of Aymara and other agropastoral societies as "primitive," is seen for the ethnocentric ideology it was. It was perhaps not Uru incivility that caused Aymara communities and their sometime allies, the Spanish, to decimate their waning populations in the Colonial Period. More likely, it was their resilient identity and productive power (Choque 2003; Wachtel 2001).

Farming

Of the broad productive concerns that tied altiplano populations to their landscapes and subsidized Tiwanaku's rise to power, we know most about farming practices. In part, this is because they left indelible impressions on the landscape. Yet it is also because we tend to conceptualize past civilizations as agrarian states grounded most fundamentally in intensified, irrigation-fed agricultural production. Such thinking is at the foundations of Western civilization, as configured and reproduced in Classical Greek philosophy, Imperial Roman politics, Medieval European religion, and Victorian anthropology. Hunters, fishers, and herders were usually considered nomadic and primordial "savages" who eventually settled down to cultivate as "barbarians." They in turn eventually smartened-up and discovered factory lines, tariff laws, and the market's invisible hand. Western urbanites still romanticize peasants; they are envisioned as our close "cultural ancestors." It is not surprising that many past urban civilizations, including Mesopotamia and Egypt, also came to consider subsistence careers such as hunting, fishing, and herding as less civilized. Tiwanaku promoted a similar ideology in which farming, and in particular state-coordinated raised-field agriculture, was glorified and held in high regard in relation to other, "pre-Tiwanaku" livelihoods and productive technologies.

Altiplano communities developed complex agrarian practices that effectively tapped the landscape's productive potential. During the Tiwanaku Period, in particular, state leaders played a heavy hand in the development, coordination, and maintenance of complex productive systems (Kolata 1986, 1991; Kolata and Ortloff 1996a). Supplementing local rain-fed farming, these included sunken basins (*qochas*), hill slope terraces, and raised fields. Not surprisingly, such productive systems were multifunctional and simultaneously enhanced fishing and herding.

Qocha *Systems*

Qochas were artificial (or modified) reservoirs or ponds that collected and stored rainwater in landscapes with a low water table. In general, they were circular or oblong in plan, though Jorge Flores Ochoa (1987) records rectangular *qochas* near present-day Puno, Peru. *Qochas* continue to be built and cultivated today, and their construction and morphology are intricate. Their extent and depth varies greatly, but they tend to have a flat bottom, gently sloping sides, and series' of concentric, radiating, or zigzag furrows. These features aid in managing water intake, retention, and drainage, while hindering erosion. They can serve any or all of three interrelated productive roles. As artificial ponds, they create miniature aquatic environments that seasonally support fish flocks and migrating bird species. Tubers and grains can be grown on their sloping sides and such crops are rotated to maximize productive longevity. Especially in times of fallow, after four or five years of cultivation, *qochas* serve as grazing locales for camelid herds. Thus, they are not strictly "farming systems," but in characteristic Andean fashion mesh cultivation with aquatic and pastoral regimes.

Qochas were especially important in relatively high and dry areas of the altiplano, and they remain so in some such areas today (Flores Ochoa and Paz Flores 1983; Flores Ochoa 1987). Fossil *qochas* are still apparent across the Lake Titicaca Basin, though detecting them is hindered because they resemble natural ponds and small lakes (Figure 5.6). As exemplified in the Mollo Kontu sector of Tiwanaku, groups of *qochas* were linked together to form regional or microregional systems via channels that facilitated water management and drainage. They clustered in several discrete, relatively dry valley bottoms of the hinterland: at the eastern edge of the lower Katari Valley, just east of Mount Katavi; in the southern section of the Tiwanaku Valley, southwest of Tiwanaku; and in inland zones of the Desaguadero Valley. Because they have not been directly investigated, their timing remains uncertain. Nevertheless, surface artifacts suggest that communities were building them as early as the Late Formative (Flores Ochoa 1987).

Envisioning Tiwanaku production as founded principally on raised-field cultivation, Binford and Kolata (1996:49) consider *qocha* systems post-Tiwanaku adaptations that primarily supported camelid herds in drought conditions. Yet fossil *qochas* are located in high areas of valley bottoms where raised fields never were viable, and some yield surface artifacts dating to Formative and Tiwanaku periods (Albarracin-Jordan 1996b; Flores Ochoa 1987). Further, stone hoes on the surfaces of *qochas* in the Tiwanaku Valley point to their roles in cultivation. We can hypothesize that *qochas* were developed early on as a multifunctional productive regime well-adapted to dry zones and in complement to other productive systems, such as raised fields. Further, *qocha* production was the domain of specific communities. Most *qochas* in the Tiwanaku Valley cluster among settlements located in its mid-southern section, the inhabitants of which may have excelled in this form of agropastoralism. Such groups and their *qocha* systems, even if they provided relatively limited planting areas and return rates (Ortloff and Kolata 1993), played an important role in the state's broader, diversified political economy.

Hillslope Terracing

A less well understood form of land use and intensive farming during Formative and Tiwanaku periods was hillslope terracing, which consisted of modifying the piedmont to form steplike platforms. Terracing opened up relatively steep areas of the landscape to production by forming level surface areas that simultaneously slowed erosion, reduced risk of frost, and provided effective water management by diverting water from high springs to field beds via intricate canal networks (Denevan 1987; Donkin 1979; Guillet 1987). Terraces are present throughout the Tiwanaku hinterland and in particular at lakeshore piedmont sites. Nevertheless, most date to later periods. Inca leaders expanded terrace systems on an unprecedented scale throughout the highland Andes, opening up thousands of square kilometers of mountainous terrain to tuber and grain cultivation. While most remnant terrace systems in the Andes were built under Inca rule, they had been widely employed during the Middle Horizon (Albarracin-Jordan 1996a, 1996b; Isbell 1977; Schreiber 2001) and possibly even earlier (Lemuz 2001; Stanish 2003).

Albarracin-Jordan (1996b) argues that local populations developed extensive terrace systems in the southern part of the Tiwanaku Valley during the Tiwanaku Period. The most significant were broad, shallow "apron terraces" situated on erosional fans adjacent to the pampa. The platforms were extensive, averaging 60–65 meters in breadth, and they were faced with short walls of cobbles and irregularly cut sandstone

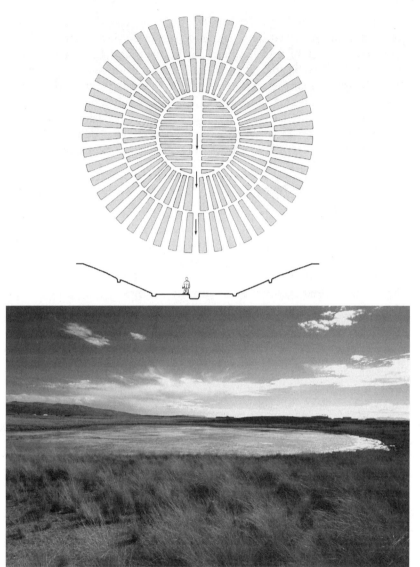

Figure 5.6 Plan of a modern *qocha* near Puno, Peru (a), and view of an ancient *qocha* in Mollo Kontu, Tiwanaku (a, adapted from Flores Ochoa 1987).

blocks. Canals guided water onto and through the terraces, and from there downward toward raised-field segments further out in the pampa. While dating terraces can be tricky, Albarracin-Jordan found Tiwanaku ceramic sherds in the clay fill that formed their beds and on several associated sites. He argues that they represent one of Tiwanaku's many diversified productive strategies (cf. Kolata 1991, 1996a). While the true extent and chronology of pre-Inca terracing in the Lake Titicaca basin remains to be refined, it is plausible that, like *qochas*, they formed a productive strategy well adapted to specific microzones of the Tiwanaku hinterland.

Raised-Field Systems

Most striking in the landscape of the Lake Titicaca Basin, and to date most thoroughly investigated, are relict raised fields (Figure 5.7). While raised fields are not unique in the Andes – similar farming regimes are known from South America's Pacific coast, Central America, and parts of North America – they proved a highly effective technology of agrarian production in low, marshy zones of the altiplano (Denevan and Turner 1974). They are particularly dense and extend continuously over many square kilometers near Huatta and Juli-Pomata, Peru, the upper Desaguadero Basin of Peru and Bolivia, and the Katari Valley, Bolivia (Erickson 1988, 1993; Janusek and Kolata 2004; Kolata 1986, 1991; Seddon 1994; Smith, Denevan, and Hamilton 1968; Stanish 1994, 2003). Fields consisted of elongated, elevated planting beds separated by alternating water-filled canals, or swales. The planting beds ranged greatly in size, from 1.5 to 10 meters in width and up to 200 meters in length. In ideal conditions they provided well-drained topsoil in which plant roots were kept moist through capillary action. Swales derived their water from natural springs, valley streams and hill *quebradas*, and most importantly, percolating groundwater. Some raised fields included intricate hydraulic systems that involved a sophisticated coordination of groundwater inputs (Ortloff 1996:153). Hydraulic systems such as canalized streams, aqueducts, canals, river shunts, and dikes enhanced and regulated water flow to and from raised-field systems (Kolata 1991; Ortloff and Kolata 1989).

Rehabilitation projects in Peru and Bolivia illustrate some of the ways in which raised-field systems enhanced productivity in the altiplano. Swales were rapidly colonized by nutrient-trapping aquatic macrophytes which, through periodic skimming and dredging, provided a natural fertilizer for what were normally nitrogen-poor soils (Biesboer, Binford, and Kolata 1999; Binford, Brenner, and Leyden 1996; Carney et al. 1993; Kolata 1991). Water-filled swales effectively absorbed and conserved heat from

Figure 5.7 The Koani Pampa of the Katari Valley.

solar radiation during the day, forming a "heat envelope" that effectively protected growing plants from frost damage at night (Erickson 1985; Kolata 1991; Kolata et al. 1996; Sanchez de Lozada 1996). Further, a perennial water supply shortened the duration of a crop cycle, making it possible to double-crop or to devote time to other productive concerns. By supporting fish and waterfowl, raised fields also formed anthropogenic water-rich environments that effectively expanded productive possibilities by combining agrarian and lacustrine pursuits.

Raised-Field Systems: Local or State-Run Enterprises? Despite overall consensus regarding the productivity of raised-field farming, its social organization is fiercely debated. Basic points of contention revolve around the questions of who built and maintained raised fields, whether local communities or state authorities, and when raised fields were first cultivated, whether before, during, or after Tiwanaku hegemony. Based on extensive research in the Huatta Pampa, Clark Erickson (1988, 1993) argues that raised-field technology developed during the Middle Formative out of the knowledge and skills of kin-based communities. While such groups suffered wave after wave of subjugation by Andean states such as Tiwanaku, state rulers, in Erickson's view, never "tampered with" raised-field systems (Erickson 1988:315). Interpreting surface relations of relict fields and settlements in Juli-Pomata, Chip Stanish (1994, 2003) agrees

that raised-field farming formed perhaps one-third of the regional political economy in the Middle Formative; however, he believes that it was
intensified in subsequent Late Formative and Tiwanaku societies under
the authority of emergent elites. Kolata and others (1986, 1991; also
Binford and Kolata 1996; Seddon 1994), working in the southern basin,
have argued that raised fields were first developed and cultivated most
intensively under Tiwanaku state leaders. By AD 500, much of the
Tiwanaku hinterland, it is argued, was "a constructed landscape of
state production" (Kolata and Ortloff 1996a:150). Finally, Gray Graffam
(1990, 1992) hypothesizes that raised fields were designed and managed
by kin-based *ayllus* largely after Tiwanaku collapse.

Disagreement about the organization of altiplano raised-fields focuses
in part on different interpretations of their surface features. Erickson
points to the variability in design of relic fields. He notes that fields in any
pampa tend to be segmented into discrete blocks that vary greatly in size
and form, suggesting that they were built incrementally by local communities. In this view, the boundaries between segments may have marked
the plots of specific groups (Lennon 1983; Smith, Denevan, and Hamilton 1968), as they did in the *chinampa* systems of Aztec period Central
Mexico. Kolata and colleagues, by contrast, emphasize the regional features linking diverse raised-field segments in parts of the Tiwanaku and
Katari valleys (Kolata and Ortloff 1996a; Ortloff and Kolata 1989). For
them, fields varied in design following local ecological and groundwater conditions. Sophisticated hydrological features, they argue, included
extensive canals that alternatively served to divert water toward or away
from fields, depending on the season or circumstance. Further, much of
the Katari River was canalized and straightened, a massive reclamation
project that permitted some control over groundwater levels and periodic
flooding.

Debate also revolves around the problem of timing. In interpreting
the chronology of raised-field use, archaeologists typically rely on the
proximity of inhabited sites to surface field beds. Yet dating raised-field
production according to site proximity is problematic for two reasons.
First, proximity does not necessarily reflect contemporaneity, and second,
farmers did not have to live right next to the fields they cultivated. Today
in the altiplano, families ideally maintain numerous fields in a mosaic
of distinct microenvironments, some nearby and others several hours or
even days from their primary residences. There is no reason to assume that
people living in piedmont zones several kilometers from raised fields were
not the same people who cultivated them. In fact, absence of settlement
in the largest pampas may suggest that they were cleared for particularly
intensive cultivation.

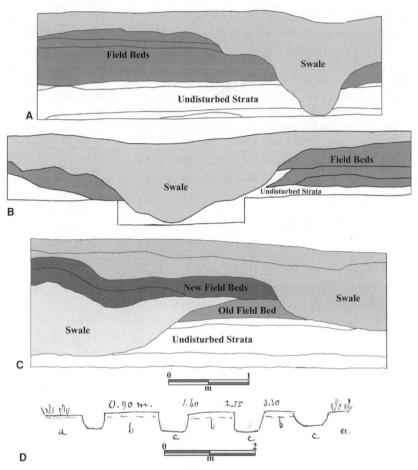

Figure 5.8 Raised-field profiles, including excavated raised fields
in the Katari Valley (a–c, adapted from Seddon 1994, note
superimposed fields in c; and Max Uhle's 1895 diagram of
cultivation plots at Iruhito (d).

Rural Archaeology: Changes in Production and Land Use. Until recently,
absolute dates for raised-field construction and use were lacking. A large-
scale project of rural archaeology that I helped direct in the Koani Pampa
produced some of the most reliable radiocarbon measurements to date
for raised fields construction and use (Janusek and Kolata 2003, 2004;
Kolata and Ortloff 1996a; Seddon 1994). Results of this research support Kolata's overall interpretation but challenge and refine its details
(Figure 5.8a–5.8c). Combined with research elsewhere in the Tiwanaku

hinterland, they indicate that, during much of the Middle Horizon, Koani Pampa and other raised field landscapes came to be constructed landscapes of state production.

Shifts in settlement and landscape incrementally facilitated agricultural intensification in the hinterland. Settlements first occupied the Koani Pampa in the Late Formative, when Lukurmata was intensively occupied. People living in small sites in the Tiwanaku and Katari valleys, such as the Quiripujo Mound Group, crafted stone hoes of basalt, quartzite, or slate. Mound inhabitants on the Koani Pampa may have used them to cultivate proto–raised fields on a small scale. The role of farming for such small communities contrasted sharply with its role in formative major centers such as Tiwanaku, Lukurmata, and Khonkho Wankane (Giesso 2003). Hoes were uncommon in these centers, indicating that most residents pursued other livelihoods tending temples, crafting goods, or herding. Such centers were to a great degree divorced from agrarian production even though their residents consumed cultivated crops. Consumable goods were provided to such centers via tribute or exchange, whether in return for goods and religious services, through feasts and ceremonies, or via networks of kin and *caceras* (reprat customers).

Major changes accompanied agricultural intensification in Tiwanaku 1. Settlement expanded and population increased across the hinterland. Low marshy areas were reclaimed for raised-field farming. Somewhat paradoxically, stone hoes declined in importance at most settlements. Raised-field farming, which involves dredging dense, clay-rich altiplano soils, may have required more durable farming tools. It is possible that large wooden foot plows of the sort recently employed among highland Andean communities now became important (Bandy 2001; Janusek and Kolata 2003). These would have been crafted primarily of hardwoods obtained from warmer valley regions, leaving only subtle traces in the archaeological record.

The human landscape of raised field production in Tiwanaku 1 comprised a marshy pampa of cultivated beds punctuated by guardian mounds, crisscrossed with canals and causeways, and ringed by settlements in the adjacent foothills. A series of raised causeways linked specific settlements in the piedmont with sites and field segments in the Koani Pampa. Longer trans-pampa causeways linked major centers to guardian mounds, hydraulic features, and large field segments. Each community maintained a specific network of causeways and fields that their members guarded and cultivated. Each thus managed a specific segment of the Koani Pampa. While coordinated by and perhaps largely geared toward central authorities, inhabitants of local communities directly managed productive activities.

Social organization of raised-field production varied in the hinterland according to variable social and natural conditions. The hinterland differed significantly in elevation, soil, drainage and groundwater conditions and thus demanded a range of productive configurations. For example, the Tiwanaku Valley has hydrological characteristics very different from those in Katari. Here, a seasonal wetland environment necessary for raised fields occurs largely in the north side of the valley, around the Tiwanaku River and near the Taraco hills (Kolata and Ortloff 1996a). While raised-field complexes show relatively continuous distributions in the Katari and Huatta pampas, in the Tiwanaku pampa, they cluster along the north side of the valley and form discontinuous pockets around major Tiwanaku settlements. In the south part of the valley, qochas, hillslope terraces, and most likely rain-fed fields were cultivated alongside raised-field segments. The distinctive landscape and productive requirements of the Tiwanaku Valley fostered a settlement configuration very different from that in Katari during Late Formative and Tiwanaku periods. Settlements clustered in the pampas as well as the lower piedmont and in many cases near discrete raised-field and qocha systems. Perhaps more patently than in Katari, such systems were directly worked and managed by local communities.

Critical for understanding the social production of landscape in the Tiwanaku hinterland are major changes that occurred in the Tiwanaku Period. Though state leaders may have stimulated raised-field construction in Tiwanaku 1, each community managed local field segments by drawing on the labor of constituent household units. The short production cycle and perennial water supply of raised fields allowed communities to maintain diversified local productive economies (Bandy 2001). Communities working raised fields most likely also maintained rain-fed fields, qochas, and herds. By rotating labor, state and community leaders staggered productive concerns enough to reduce labor bottlenecks over the agricultural year and minimize conflict between state and local interests. Overall, state strategies sought accommodation with local groups and productive regimes.

Production and settlement shifted dramatically in Tiwanaku 2. Increasing state power and human population in the hinterland placed great demands on local farming systems (Mathews 1992, 2003) and encouraged overexploitation in land use, material resources, and human labor. In Katari, the city of Lukurmata was all but abandoned and its monumental complex left to deteriorate (Bermann 1994; Janusek 2004a). These changes had deep roots and profound consequences. Lukurmata had enjoyed a long pre-Tiwanaku history, a coherent community identity, and a well-tested role in Tiwanaku's political economy. At the far edge of the Koani Pampa and hugging the lakeshore, Lukurmata was strategically positioned to oversee and benefit from a state productive economy that balanced lake trade, fishing, and agriculture.

However, in Tiwanaku 2 the balance of production shifted decisively toward agricultural intensification. The Katari Valley was completely transfigured as a landscape dedicated to state production. Old settlement networks were transformed, and community identities were altered and fragmented. Lukurmata and other major settlements in Katari were all but abandoned as a new settlement network emerged to coordinate raised-field production. Small pampa sites served as field stations for guardians who, living in tentlike structures on a rotating basis, guarded community crops against theft, predation, hail, and frost (Kolata 1991; Winterhalder and Thomas 1978). The Lillimani Valley emerged as a direct transportation route between the Tiwanaku and Katari Valleys, and Lakaya, at its mouth, served as a local entrepôt for intervalley traffic (Janusek and Kolata 2003, 2004). At this time, Tiwanaku leaders built ingenious hydrological features to join discrete field segments and facilitate production. A long trans-pampa causeway linked the Lillimani route and Lakaya to the Quiripujo Mound Group, an important cluster of field guardian mounds in the Koani Pampa. To meet labor demands, farmers may have been conscripted from other regions. These changes had profound consequences on Tiwanaku's historical trajectory.

At Tiwanaku's apogee, raised-field farming became the signature productive regime of the Lake Titicaca Basin. Its technology and coordination became primary state concerns. Specialists and communities involved in raised-field farming enjoyed special status and wealth in the scheme of productive enterprises. Herding, fishing, and rain-fed farming occupied lower rungs in the socioeconomic hierarchy. Yet the reasons motivating raised-field expansion under Tiwanaku appear unorthodox in the scheme of Western economic principles. No evidence indicates that produce was redistributed in bulk to communities (as a form of "staple finance"). Rather huge portions of the harvest funded the ritual consumption that was intensifying precipitously after AD 800. In classic Andean spirit, it fueled recurring bouts of feasting and drinking that were increasingly central to Tiwanaku's political economy. Raised-field farming subsidized the ritualized tournaments in which people negotiated statuses and identities, community representatives distributed obligations, and leaders forged state power.

Who farmed raised fields? Evidence for their cultivation in the Formative indicates that Tiwanaku leaders did not invent the technology but rather appropriated and aggrandized it to serve state interests. It points to a far-flung network of communities around the basin that specialized in its initial development and stood to gain from its subsequent expansion under Tiwanaku. Indeed, production shaped identity in the Andes (Janusek 1999). Shared daily concerns and circum-Titicaca interaction configured a shared community of practice and pan-regional identity among altiplano marsh dwellers. These microenvironments closely overlapped with those of fishers and hunters. In fact, raised fields created anthropogenic environments that effectively expanded those "wild" domains. It is reasonable to hypothesize that such communities were either ancestral to later Uru or closely tied with them, as were the Pukina. It is intriguing that Max Uhle (1895) documented the Iruhito Uru, and Alfred Metraux (1945) the Chipaya Uru, cultivating tubers and quinoa in intricate raised-field systems (Figure 5.8d).

Such communities had much to gain as raised-field farmers. In the Katari Valley, they formed coherent identities within Tiwanaku's very sociopolitical core (Janusek 2002, 2004a). Their power over production may help explain settlement transformation, including Lukurmata's decline, in the face of increasing state control over raised-field farming. This was arguably a strategic move on the part of a new ruling regime or dynasty that was designed to weaken vibrant identities with entrenched attachments to the landscape, and to break their hold over the wealth that subsidized local elite power. Though speculative, it is tempting to see here the disappearance of a coherent proto-Pukina language and identity and the dawn of a millennial interethnic struggle that culminated in the near-decimation of the Uru several centuries later.

Herding

In the excitement of investigating raised fields and discovering their key role in Tiwanaku's rise and consolidation, archaeologists have tended to put camelid herding on the backburner of research agendas. While Kolata and others interpret Tiwanaku "as having developed primarily from a surplus-producing agricultural economy centered [in] Lake Titicaca" (Dillehay and Nuñez 1988:610), others point out that domesticated camelids and llama caravan trade played at least as important a role (Browman 1978a, 1981, 1990; Lynch 1983; Nuñez and Dillehay 1995). These archaeologists envision a central role for economic production and exchange within major settlements such as Tiwanaku, and for intensive llama caravan movement and trade among quasi-independent settlements and largely autonomous polities. Raised-field farming, despite its socioeconomic status, was but one glorified part of a diversified macropolitical economy that also rested on herding and llama-based transport and trade.

Postmortem Roles of Camelids

Camelids served important postmortem roles that spanned consumption, domestic production, and local and elite-sponsored ritual. Ann Webster's (1993) analysis of faunal remains in the Tiwanaku Valley refines what anyone who has excavated there soon discovers: Camelids formed a critical food resource throughout the Late Formative and Tiwanaku periods. Consuming llama and alpaca meat played a relatively minor role during the Early-Middle Formative. This resource pattern began to change during the Late Formative, in line with a shift in settlement to inland locations and the rise of regional polities. Camelid meat began to predominate in local diets, and llamas were far more commonly consumed than alpacas. Dental analysis revealed that young animals (60 percent of most samples) of 1 to 1.5 years were most commonly consumed. This pattern contrasts with recent herding patterns in which animals for wool and transport were consumed only late in their lives. Perhaps along with or anticipating fishing and farming practices, herding was intensifying.

In the Tiwanaku period, young llamas (up to 70 percent of local faunal samples) bred specifically for consumption became the most important meat source in Tiwanaku diets. The animals were butchered and divided up into meat packets, salted and dried to form *charqui*, and their bones were fragmented to extract fat and marrow. Consuming young camelids or "carnivorous pastoralism" (Browman 1978a, 1981) was fundamental to the cultural transformations that characterized emergent social complexity in the altiplano. The relative infrequency of older or "prime age" camelids in residential homes indicates that many strains were bred specifically for wool, transport, and sacrifice.

Camelid bodies served many other critical domestic and ritual roles. Their fat provided ritual offerings and may have fueled the ceramic burners (*sahumadors*) that kept domestic chambers lighted and warm (Janusek 2003a). Since trees and shrubs have been scarce in the altiplano for centuries, camelid dung served as a handy and hot-burning fuel for the fires that provided cooking, warmth, and ritual dedications. Worked hides served as mats, bed warmers, clothing, and container covers. Camelid bones provided a ready and durable material with which to craft myriad tools and ritual objects. These included weaving tools such as awls and needles, domestic implements such as knives and spatulas, and bodily adornments such as beads, buttons, and rings. They were crafted into a variety of musical instruments, including whistles, flutes, and panpipes, as well as snuff trays and spoons for rituals requiring the consumption of psychotropic substances (Bermann 1994; Webster and Janusek 2003). Camelids occupied a central place in Tiwanaku's mundane and spiritual realms.

A

B

Figure 5.9 Camelid offerings at Tiwanaku: llama fetus buried under the floor of the large kitchen structure in Akapana East 1 (a), and adult llama bones buried under the paved floor of Chunchukala in the monumental core (b, photo courtesy of Alan Kolata).

Camelids were important for the ritual reproduction of Tiwanaku society and cosmos. In particular, they were critical for ritual dedications conducted in domestic and more public ceremonial settings (Figure 5.9). The current native practice of burying a fetal or juvenile llama under the corners of a new house in order to "root" it to the earth and its chthonic forces (Arnold 1992) originated centuries ago (Bermann 1994; Janusek 2004a). In Late Formative and Tiwanaku settlements, families buried fetal llamas under the corners and floors of residential structures, most likely with perishable items no longer discernible such as coca, *thola* aromatic herbs, and fat.

Dramatic llama sacrifices took place in the ceremonial structures of Tiwanaku's urban core. The dedications that accompanied construction, renewal, and closing rituals in the Akapana remain among the most spectacular residues of Tiwanaku ritual discovered to date (Chapter 4) (Kolata 1993a; Manzanilla 1992; Webster 1993). The animals would have been unblemished individuals specially bred and culled from specific herds. Pockets of articulated body parts and disarticulated bones of sacrificed llamas were buried in front of the Akapana's foundation terrace alongside human remains. Centuries later, the disarticulated bones of some forty individuals were strewn over the ruins of an elite residential complex atop the structure, possibly as part of a dedication that accompanied the monument's ritual closing. The ceremonies that these dedications accompanied involved conspicuous ritualized consumption on a grand scale. They punctuated critical moments in the life history of the monument and in the ritual community and political factions that it represented. Sacrificed camelids, like human dedications, transferred the sacred life force of a critical Tiwanaku resource to that monument and its community as a prayer to facilitate safe passage from one moment to the next. By sacrificing sanctified animals, ritual sponsors also positioned themselves at the nexus of social, ancestral, and animistic forces of the cosmos.

Premortem Roles of Camelids

More critical were the premortem roles of camelids in providing wool and facilitating transport and trade. Herds of alpacas were grazed in marshy areas to provide wool, while herds of llamas served as transport animals. Llama caravans managed by specialized herders facilitated the movement of goods and the maintenance of social networks across regions. Agriculture was a risky enterprise in the altiplano, with serious limiting factors that included "frost, drought, nutrient-deficient soils, and periodic . . . hail and torrential seasonal rainfall" (Binford and Kolata 1996:54). Overlapping caravan circuits offered flexibility, security, and alternative

Figure 5.10 Llama herders from Machaca bring salt to the Tiwanaku and Katari valleys in exchange for staple goods.

sources of goods and wealth for communities throughout the altiplano (Browman 1987, 1990).

Caravan circuits facilitated networks of friendship and alliance among far-flung settlements, communities, and polities (Figure 5.10). Axel Nielson (2001:167) notes that "pastoral society was flexible, pragmatic, and closely related to a vast social and territorial domain." It makes sense that under Tiwanaku hegemony, herding increased just as agriculture intensified. In the face of social and natural unpredictability, Tiwanaku's increasingly intricate political economy was increasingly at risk. Camelid herding intensified along with agriculture to promote productive diversity and interregional social networks while reducing short-term environmental risks.

Like shoreline fishing and raised-field agriculture, herding forged a community of practice that joined far-flung settlement networks, trade routes, and sociopolitical groups. Settlements far from the lake, in inland locations and in the central and southern altiplano, of necessity remained focused on pastoral regimes.

During the Early-Middle Formative, major settlements in the south-central Andes emerged as caravan trade hubs, or what Nuñez and Dillehay (1995) term "axis settlements" (Dillehay and Nuñez 1988:612). These were farming, fishing, or craft-focused settlements that also defined the routes and end points of well-trodden caravan circuits. During the Late Formative, major settlements in the southern Lake Titicaca Basin such as Khonkho Wankane and Tiwanaku emerged in part because of their critical positions in such networks of trade and interaction. This helped determine their rising sociopolitical careers and delineated their mutual interaction and competition. If intensive farming afforded Tiwanaku its "cutting edge" after the sixth century AD, social and economic interaction facilitated by herders and their extensive caravans remained central to its increasingly complex political economy. Llama herds were temporarily put up at Tiwanaku among the *qochas* of Mollo Kontu and elsewhere. They linked Tiwanaku inhabitants to exotic people, regions, and resources. They facilitated interaction among the diverse populations influenced by or incorporated into Tiwanaku's hegemonic sphere. They also secured access to the nonlocal crops and crafted goods – salt, maize, coca, peppers, and ceramic wares – that supported Tiwanaku's increasingly consumptive political economy.

Punctuating transport routes between axis settlements were campsites for rest, territorial boundaries, and ritual offerings (Aschero 2000; Nielson 2001; Nuñez 1976, 1985; Paz Flores 1988, 2000). Many such places had rock art depicting llama caravans, ceremonies, and humanlike figures. One such site is Jaqui Kayu ("human feet") in the southern Tiwanaku Valley (Albarracin-Jordan 1996a; Portugal Zamora 1980), which is located at a key point of entry into the valley from Machaca. Glyphic scenes etched into a red sandstone outcrop depict human footprints, mythical human and animal-like figures, individual camelids, and llama caravans. Most likely beginning in the Late Formative, the site defined an important physical and symbolic passage between regions, and one that led to the prestigious center of Tiwanaku.

With Tiwanaku's rise to power, long routes and pan-regional identities converged on this political, religious, and cultural center. Although dependent on agriculture, it was also a major trade entrepôt and a mega-axis settlement. Even if markets in the sense we know them were sub-dominant or absent, Tiwanaku was still a bustling nexus of trade and social interaction. As noted in Chapter 4, Tiwanaku was a ceremonial city and a center of periodic social and ceremonial convergence. Major rituals and feasts served as periodic fairs before and during which extensive llama caravans converged on Tiwanaku with exotic goods and highly desired produce from distant regions. They left the center, no doubt, burdened with valuable wares and trinkets crafted by Tiwanaku specialists, abundant produce grown in nearby raised fields, and fish, birds, and eggs from lakeshore fisheries. While caravans entered and left on a regular basis throughout the year, traffic increased precipitously during major feasts and ceremonies when Tiwanaku temporarily became a cosmopolitan center that served commensalism, lively socializing, catching up on news and gossip, and vibrant trade. Makeshift kiosks most likely emerged for a week or two in Tiwanaku's extensive plazas and courtyards, where returning customers bargained and traded with kin, friends, acquaintances, and *caceras*. In this critical sense, the socioeconomic and religious domains of life in Tiwanaku were inseparable.

Conclusions

Unique and internally diversified, the altiplano conditioned the local productive relations that characterized cultural and political development in the southern Lake Titicaca Basin. Kolata's model for the relationship of particular groups and productive regimes resonates with recent evidence, especially if we consider such relationships as interwoven and in flux. Perhaps it was primarily ancestors of the contemporary Uru who fished and foraged, of the Uru or Pukina who cultivated raised fields, or of the Aymara who herded and tended *qochas*. Yet the diversity of the landscape and its productive resources encourage a complex portrait of such relations. Natural and cultural features such as mountains, rivers, and roads divided the region into discrete inhabitable landscapes and drainage basins that corresponded in some cases with discrete ethniclike groups. The landscapes worked and inhabited by fishers/foragers, raised-field cultivators, and herders cross-cut such divisions. Each gave rise to a relatively discrete community of practice: fishers/foragers worked the shorelines, raised-field farmers worked the adjacent extensive marshy areas, and herders occupied inland and drier locations.

Nevertheless, such groups and their resource domains were interdependent. Past fishers/foragers were closely tied to raised-field farmers and may have shared a common identity, just as past herders and *qocha* cultivators may have been closely interlinked and in some cases one and the same. Production and place were critical in defining a family's identity, yet interaction, alliance, and intermarriage among groups simultaneously blurred and wove together such identities, giving rise to broader community identities and religious traditions.

Focusing on the hinterland, Tiwanaku can be viewed as a grand project of productive diversification and social unification. In Tiwanaku 1, Tiwanaku leaders promoted intensification in multiple productive regimes, and raised-field farming was appropriated as the symbol par excellence of state production and civility and quite possibly a dynasty's signature productive enterprise. They promoted incorporative strategies in which productive enterprise was by and large left in the hands of, or delegated to local communities and sociopolitical groups. Leaders did this following an enduring Andean etiquette of reciprocity but also out of necessity, for they had not the technology, knowledge, resources, or power to completely appropriate resources or transform predominant sociopolitical relations. If amalgamated and to some extent centrally coordinated, the diverse productive regimes, land-use strategies, and resources that formed Tiwanaku political economy remained grounded in local labor and knowledge and divided among discrete groups and geopolitical entities.

A balance of local and state power began to shift in Tiwanaku 2, in what appears to have been a tectonic regime change in Tiwanaku. Maximization became a more prominent theme in Tiwanaku ideology, especially in regard to raised-field farming and productive integration in regions such as Katari. This change turned on increasingly transformative strategies of productive and regional appropriation, which severely shifted the balance of diversity toward unity, autonomy toward dependence, and minimizing risk toward maximizing surplus. These shifts had powerful consequences in the face of environmental unpredictability and deeply entrenched local ideologies and identities, a theme to which we return in Chapter 8.

Political economy in Tiwanaku turned on religious ideology and periodic ceremony as well as entrenched social ideals. Raised-field production and caravan trade supported local populations and economies. Yet they did not simply serve all-out redistribution to local populations and commoners. Raised-field production, in particular, served Tiwanaku's increasingly top-heavy feasting economy, which provided the tournaments in which elite factions vied for power and reciprocal obligations were enacted with and distributed among factions and potential nonelite supporters. It also served the temples and their discrete religious cults, which kept pilgrims and diplomats coming to Tiwanaku and spread Tiwanaku's religious messages and prestige across the Andes.

Festival and ceremony were among the direct reasons for Tiwanaku's productive intensification. Such events had supreme social value due to entrenched, shared ideals regarding politics, wealth, and power relations. Once such ideals were severely breached, and in the face of major environmental shift after AD 1000, Tiwanaku faced a severe crisis.

6   Tiwanaku Geopolitics

Many political systems seek to expand. Indeed, geographical extension and social encompassment are among a state's most fundamental characteristics. Studying how past states influenced or incorporated multiple societies is fundamental to understanding their character. Surveys of ancient world civilizations reveal multiple forms of state influence and control (e.g., Alcock et al. 2003; Feinman and Marcus 1998). These range from Imperial Roman autocracy to Classical Athenian "democracy" and from Shang Chinese theocracy to Uruk Mesopotamian "econocracy." Military conquest and direct control of far territories were common fare in many past regimes. From written histories, we know that many Roman, Shang, and Uruk leaders were not loath to employ force in establishing state control or exacting labor and tribute.

Yet in depth archaeological study into the regions incorporated into past imperial realms often presents an alternative perspective. In many cases, local polities and societies remained largely autonomous and intact within imperial domains. Many societies were ruled indirectly by some form of hegemony in which local sociopolitical relations and economies, to varying degrees, continued to thrive. Local change occurred, but it was often more complex and usually more subtle than many written histories lead us to expect.

To take one example, if Rome had depended solely on militarism to build a pan-Mediterranean empire it never would have enjoyed a long history. Along with coercion went a compelling and seductive state culture that provided ample opportunity for local wealth and position. Rome represented civilization. Citizenship, Latin language, huge jugs of wine, and a flexible pantheon of deities were prestigious elements of a state culture that many local populations vigorously accepted, internalized, and consumed. And who but the most cynical failed to seek out the nearest amphitheater to watch the gladiatorial games?!

The various intellectual lineages that treat Tiwanaku geopolitics take different perspectives on the motivations and character of its influence and expansion, as noted in Chapter 1. In the ceremonial center model,

Tiwanaku influence was primarily due to its spiritually potent symbols and rituals that were transported around the Andes via traders, pilgrims, and zealots. The centralized state model has various ramifications: For some, Tiwanaku was a predatorial empire that expanded through military conquest; for others, Tiwanaku colonized warmer zones to gain direct access to desired resources while maintaining a heavy hand over interregional trade. According to local autonomy models, Tiwanaku influence was a product of far-reaching economic networks and the increasing popularity of a prestigious religious complex. Tiwanaku was a convergence of social influences, political forces, and religious ideals that an astute group of elites in the southern Lake Titicaca Basin capitalized on and integrated. In this view, colonization in many regions was the ongoing project of local kin groups and ethnic "communities in motion" (Goldstein 2005) rather than the product of state-directed expansion.

In this chapter, I evaluate these ideas and discuss evidence for state influence, incorporation, and colonization in the south-central Andes. I categorize Tiwanaku's sphere of influence somewhat arbitrarily as roughly concentric rings that included: an inner and greater heartland or *core*, more distant or environmentally distinct *near peripheries*, a constellation of *far enclaves or peripheries*, and a *frontier*. These are heuristic divisions rather than interpretive categories; they do not necessarily coincide with degree of influence or state control. Within any broad zone, and even in the heartland, Tiwanaku simultaneously involved multiple strategies of regional control and its influence in most societies was interactive and reciprocal. Further, in many regions the scale and degree of local control or influence changed significantly at around AD 800 due to shifting sociopolitical and geopolitical conditions.

I employ the complementary terms *incorporative* and *transformative* to distinguish modes of state influence and power over local affairs. Incorporative state strategies were low in impact and involved relatively minimal changes, whereas transformative strategies involved intensive, high-impact shifts in local sociopolitical, productive, and ideological conditions. In many places, state power was incorporative, or configured according to preexisting local conditions, and in others, it was direct and transformative, involving significant reconfiguration in local landscapes and sociopolitical systems. In some regions, state power shifted from incorporative to transformative over Tiwanaku's long career.

If not Rome in scale, Tiwanaku forged multiple incorporative strategies that for sheer ingenuity and intricacy give the ancient Mediterranean empire a run for its *Caesar*-centric money. These strategies ensured Tiwanaku's early success and subsequent longevity. They included populist measures such as the widespread distribution of elaborate

Tiwanaku-style goods with ceremonial importance or spiritual significance; the rise of lively feasting practices and their attendant technologies and economies; and an overarching hegemonic system that left much
craft and subsistence production in the hands of the local communities
of practice that had developed and perfected them.

Key domains of state hegemony transcended overt political relations and consciously-devised geopolitical strategies. Following a practice approach, we also consider the multiplex loci of human agency and
the more subtle, seductive, and emotive influences that forged and reproduced state power. In this chapter, we find that Tiwanaku did not simply
expand out from the southern basin like a tumorous growth over the
altiplano and into the valleys. As noted in Chapter 3, a vast landscape
of interacting formative societies had already laid the pan-regional foundation for state emergence and expansion, facilitated by local ingenu-
ities, technologies, and desires. Like Rome, Tiwanaku was not simply a
political system. It was a compelling and, in this case, profoundly spiritual state culture. Tiwanaku transformed significantly over time in scale
and impact, but it was never the rigidly bordered "nation" that dominates
our own practical consciousness of political systems. Studying Tiwanaku
encourages us to reconsider our ideas regarding past and present empires.
It sheds new light on the highly distinctive and increasingly volatile world
of competing nation-states and transnational empires that we inhabit
today.

Inner Core: Lukurmata and the Katari Valley

Throughout the Tiwanaku Period, the Katari Valley remained the most
important heartland region outside of the Tiwanaku Valley. Together,
the two valleys formed the inner state core (Figure 3.4). The Katari
Valley was particularly lucrative with its lacustrine resources, including
extensive *totora* beds and abundant lake fowl, and its low marshy pampa
that supported extensive raised-field systems. Most Late Formative settlements continued to be occupied under Tiwanaku hegemony, which
correlated with population growth, increase in the size of many, and new
styles of material culture. Settlement choices and productive conditions
developed more or less continuously out of Late Formative choices and
conditions.

In Tiwanaku 1, Katari housed a well-defined scalar (though not strictly
social) settlement hierarchy that favored the edges of the pampa. The
tasks of building, maintaining, and managing fields, *totora* beds, and fisheries were not completely centralized but rather distributed among the
inhabitants of such settlements. If production was at all subsidized and

coordinated by state rulers, it was most directly administered by a network of communities that distributed tasks and labor among constituent groups and their leaders. Until AD 800, state authority depended on local leaders and groups, who, in the process of state developmont, gained considerable wealth and prestige. Co-optation and management of local production was delegated and incorporative.

Social groups and communities in Katari shared a vibrant regional identity that was expressed in styles of ceremonial ceramic wares, ritual practices, bodily modification, periodic regional ceremony, and regional leadership. Assemblages of ceramic vessels for consuming food and drink differed in style from those at Tiwanaku and other settlements in the Tiwanaku Valley. Vessels in a distinctive Lukurmata style included modeled feline and llama-effigy *incensarios* and tanwares, or serving vessels that displayed a highly polished, decorated beige surface rather than the usual Tiwanaku red or orange slip (Figure 6.1a; Bermann 1994; Janusek 1999, 2003a, 2004a). Decoration emphasized certain iconographic motifs over others, especially interlinked volutes that represented liquids such as water and *chicha* (Figure 6.1b). Further, ceramic paste recipes at Lukurmata were derived from local clay sources, indicating that the region supported local centers of ceramic production. Prominent in residential contexts at Lukurmata are high quantities of foreign wares associated with societies in warmer valleys east and southeast of the altiplano (Figure 6.1c). Members of urban neighborhoods apparently maintained relations with societies in distant warmer regions.

Ritual practices also distinguish Lukurmata and the Katari Valley from Tiwanaku (Bermann 1994; Janusek 2002, 2004a). Offering contexts associated with the principal monumental complex at Lukurmata included deep pits containing effigy *incensarios* or other elaborate vessels with burned organic matter. As at Tiwanaku, in Katari Valley settlements mortuary rituals were an important part of domestic life, and many burials consisted of subterranean cists excavated under or near living spaces. Important burial clusters or mini-cemeteries have been located in two sectors of Lukurmata (Figure 6.2). Many burials in these clusters included effigy *incensarios* as grave offerings, indicating that these distinctive wares played important roles as incense burners and lamps in mortuary rituals. In the Ridgetop sector, two burials had a unique two-chamber arrangement in which an effigy burner rested in an upper offering chamber over the interred human (see Bermann 1994: Figure 6.3). Two-chamber burials with elaborate Lukurmata-style wares also were common in the K'atupata sector below the ridge, though here, offering chambers were placed next to rather than above the main chamber. Similar offering chambers are unknown in the Tiwanaku Valley,

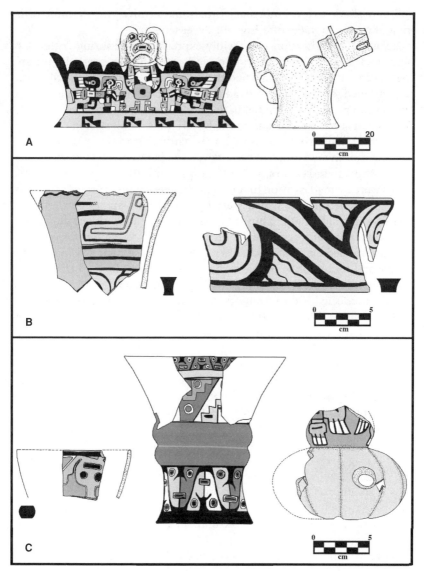

Figure 6.1 Local Lukurmata-style ceremonial wares: (a) an *incensario*, (b) tanware vessels with volutes, and (c) foreign-influenced vessels.

and they allude to local mortuary rituals that involved the periodic revisiting of graves to make offerings for deceased kin.

Regional identification was vividly expressed in enduring patterns of body modification and decoration, and in particular head shapes and the woven hat types that adorned them (Blom 1999, 2005). While natural, flattened, and elongated head shapes were relatively well distributed among compounds at Tiwanaku, the elongated or cone-shaped style predominated at Lukurmata and in the Katari Valley (composing 89 percent of analyzed skulls from local burials). Accentuating an elongated head was a conical hat shaped much like the woven ear-flapped *chullus* worn by men in the altiplano today (Frame 1990; Janusek and Blom 2006). Elongated heads were formed early on in life by intricately wound, turbanlike bands, unlike flattened heads, which were fashioned by tying a contraption of boards to a child's skull. Thus, in addition to particular head shapes and their associated attire, elaborate turbans and board contraptions on the children carried on women's backs would have been highly visible in day-to-day and more public political-ritual events. They formed elements of a distinctive way of doing things and a regional community of practice that distinguished Katari from other communities in the Tiwanaku core.

Between AD 400 and 500, Lukurmata expanded into an urban center of perhaps 1 square kilometer and the primary political-ritual center for the southern Katari Valley (Figure 6.2). It was surrounded by several smaller settlements. As at Tiwanaku, a water-filled channel, in places reinforced with stone, formed an arc that extended in from the lake edge, effectively isolating the urban core from the rest of the city and its satellite settlements (Kolata 1993a). Beyond its symbolic-social role in defining a ritual core, the channel may have served as a port that facilitated movement into the site for reed boats.

Towering over the settlement and set on a high ridge that juts into the marshy lake edge was the Willa Kollu monumental complex (Figures 6.2b and 6.3). An entire portion of the natural ridge was modified to form a massive pyramidal platform consisting of superimposed cobble and earth-faced terraces (Rivera Sundt 1989). The platform supported two contiguous structures (Bennett 1936). The higher structure had an outer revetment of massive cut andesite blocks, and like the Kalasasaya at Tiwanaku, it incorporated a smaller paved inner temple. Three stairways provided access up onto the structure and into its inner sanctum. Built into the lower structure was a small sunken temple with an interior wall faced with cut andesite blocks. Many have pointed out similarities between Wila Kollu and the Kalasasaya-Sunken Temple complex at Tiwanaku, and some consider Wila Kollu a smaller version of the latter. To be sure, the use of andesite characterizes later Tiwanaku monumental

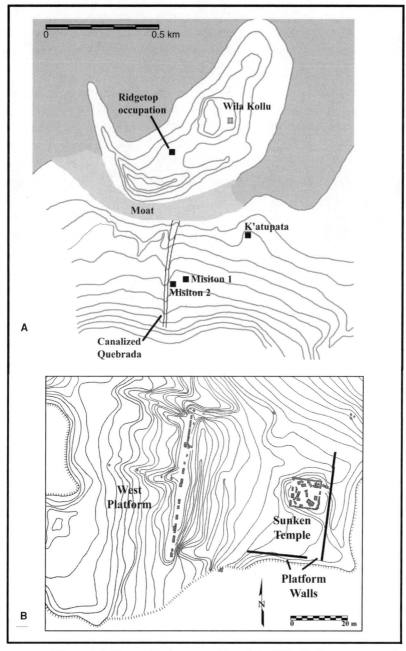

Figure 6.2 Maps of Lukurmata (a) and the Wila Kollu monumental prominence (b).

Figure 6.3 The Wila Kollu towers over the marshy lake edge.

construction, as does the orientation of the complex a few degrees askew of north. Wila Kollu materialized in architectural form important elements of Tiwanaku cosmology.

Yet a platform-and-sunken court template for monumental construction had appeared long before Tiwanaku hegemony. Further, the form, configuration, and construction of the Wila Kollu platform were distinctive. The structures capped a naturally modified hill, the sunken court was faced with andesite, it was square rather than trapezoidal, and entry into it was through a narrow portal nestled into its southwest corner. Further, local offerings included buried *incensarios*. Overall, Wila Kollu was a unique complex that combined enduring local ideological traditions with emergent architectural elements and cosmic ideals attendant on Tiwanaku hegemony. It creatively emulated Tiwanaku monumentality while embodying a distinct local style. It was the ideal monumental icon and place for periodic political and ritual activity for a city and a region with a marked community identity in Tiwanaku's hegemonic sphere.

Like Tiwanaku, Lukurmata incorporated a variety of local ritual places. While periodic regional and community ceremony focused on Wila Kollu, ritual places associated with local groups and neighborhoods dotted the urban landscape. At the west edge of Lukurmata, and near the satellite community of Ch'iarkala, was the small platform of Wila Waranka. Set into the marshy base of an intermittent hillside stream, or *quebrada*, it like the Mollo Kontu mound was a local shrine isolated and sanctified by

Figure 6.4 View of an excavated Misiton compound (a) and a detail showing a cache of flutes *in situ* (b).

water. Southeast of Wila Kollu was an extensive earthen ritual platform known as K'atupata that had been constructed during the Late Formative. Capping the platform was a prepared floor of cobbles packed in plaster, which supported buildings built of finely selected yellow adobe (Janusek 2004a: Figure 4.5). Although the significance of the platform is unclear, it was kept entirely free of debris until it was ritually interred, much like the early ritual complex of Akapana East 1 at Tiwanaku (see Chapter 4).

Lukurmata incorporated numerous neighborhoods, many of which were home to important activities and crafts. Excavations in a saddle just below Wila Kollu exposed a residential precinct that had been inhabited since Late Formative 1 (Bermann 1994, 1997). By Late Tiwanaku 1, this Ridgetop area consisted of a terrace compound that enclosed several domestic patio groups. Inhabitants engaged in generalized domestic activities, including the crafting of llama mandible tools (though their function remains unclear). Further out in the periphery, and outside of the water-bounded core, residents in the Misiton neighborhood crafted camelid bone panpipes (Figure 6.4; Text Box 6.1; Janusek 1999). A compound at the edge of the neighborhood incorporated a circular dwelling, a rare domestic form in Tiwanaku sites that may have pertained to an urban comunity with distinctive cultural affiliations (Janusek 2004a: Figure 6.6).

Lukurmata remained the most important heartland regional center in the Tiwanaku polity until AD 800. The two centers had interacted intensively since Late Formative 1. For centuries, each community had been the primary political-ritual center of a regional landscape and settlement network with an enduring identity and collective memory. Yet, their histories and identities were intimately interwoven. Indeed, it is not entirely accurate to focus on Tiwanaku as the center of early state development. Rather, state development involved the rise of multiple centers and their sustaining regions, but most significantly, Tiwanaku and Lukurmata and, respectively, the Tiwanaku and Katari valleys. It is reasonable to suggest that the inner core, and thus Tiwanaku's fundamental political structures, productive regimes, and religious ideologies, were conceived as an asymmetrical dual organization of complementary societies and landscapes grounded in the Tiwanaku-Katari unification (Janusek 2004a). Evidence for distinctive bodily forms and nonlocal interaction networks in each region suggests that a dual conceptualization, if it existed, had interregional geopolitical dimensions that extended into the warm valleys beyond and below the altiplano (Blom 2005). The division may have anticipated the later politico-ecological boundary of Urkosuyu and Umasuyu that crossed right through this part of the southern basin (see chapters 2 and 8)

Box 6.1 Making Music in the Tiwanaku Heartland

Calendrical festivals and life-cycle ceremonies were important aspects of life in Tiwanaku. Much like today in the Andes, music was critical for inducing a festive or solemn atmosphere, depending on the occasion. We know that later Andean music also induced dance and narrated stories of past events and current conditions. Music and song accompanied the annual Inca ritual opening of the earth, or *hailli*, as well as outpourings of grief during mourning rites after an individual's death. Of the many instruments played, among the most significant were panpipes (*ayarichiq* in Quechua, *siku* in Aymara).

Musical instruments have been found at Tiwanaku and at other sites in the heartland. Research in coastal regions demonstrates that many instruments were crafted of reed or cane, materials that do not preserve in the altiplano. All that remain in the highlands are instruments of stone or bone. Early excavations in Late Formative contexts under the Kalasasaya revealed a stone whistle effigy of a small house or shrine. Excavations in Tiwanaku residences produced a variety of whistles and flutes made of llama long bones. Those with air holes are reminiscent of contemporary *quenaquenas*, and those without holes are much like today's *pinkillus*. One of the most unique artifacts I found was an ocarina crafted from a guinea pig (*cuy*) skull!

Excavations in Lukurmata exposed an entire neighborhood dedicated to making musical instruments, and specifically panpipes (Janusek 1999). These instruments were made of llama long bones. The raw material itself was most likely significant, for the sound panpipes make is today likened to that of a llama's cry. Caches of panpipes of various lengths were left in place half-finished. Their sounds emphasized specific tones, which translate in western notation as E, A, B, and C-sharp. A variety of simple tools accompanied the flutes, offering clues to their production. Sharp quartzite flakes served as expedient knives, llama pelves made handy "cutting boards," and river pebbles served to polish the "raw" bone ends. (Martha Stewart, eat your heart out.)

Production marks and by-products offer clues about the process of making panpipes. Cut marks were common on semifinished flutes and severed long bone ends, especially near their severed ends. Also common were short segments of bone severed at bone ends. These patterns are easily explained as the consequences of creating specific desired tones through trial and error. That is, the craftsmen were tuning the instruments. Now, it is likely that well-seasoned specialists did not create these patterns. Lave and Wenger (1991) argue that in communities of practice, learning is an ongoing process of increasing legitimate participation in a specialized activity. These patterns implicate the participation of relative novices, perhaps children or young "journeymen" who were directly involved in production. While some were most likely members of the families who occupied the neighborhood, others may have hailed from elsewhere.

Archaeological studies of craft production generally focus on its economic aims and emphasize its role in fostering a division of labor and sociopolitical complexity in past civilizations. The production of panpipes in Lukurmata highlights the local nature of production and its persistent learning curve, and alludes to the significance of music and ritual in Tiwanaku.

In Tiwanaku 2, traditional relations that had long held between the Tiwanaku center and this part of the heartland were breached. Just as the Koani Pampa was appropriated and its sustaining settlement networks transformed to support ruling activities and interests, much of Lukurmata was abandoned. An intricate storage complex was built in Misiton at the endpoint of a road that links Lukurmata and Tiwanaku (see Janusek 2004a:Figure 8.1). It most likely served as a local depot for collecting and distributing goods en route to and from Tiwanaku. The location of the complex explains why it was one of the few areas of Lukurmata to be reoccupied in Tiwanaku 2, just when other areas of the settlement were being abandoned and the valley was being converted into a centrally managed productive estate. A neighborhood of musicians was being transfigured to serve the demands of a more tightly centralized political economy by collecting and distributing a variety of goods to support state interests and activities. Such profound changes ruptured traditional alliances, transfigured enduring ideologies, and initiated a new era of transformative state power.

Greater Core

Hegemony in the greater core (Figure 6.5), which encompassed the shores and islands of Lake Wiñaymarka (the southern portion of Lake Titicaca), including the Taraco Peninsula and Pariti Island (Text Box 6.2, Figure 6.6), and the Machaca region of the Upper Desaguadero Valley, promoted the strategic incorporation of some Late Formative settlements and a shift in productive emphases. Centers and landscapes amenable to lacustrine pursuits or raised-field production waxed in importance. In relation to this shift, the waning of other Late Formative centers and landscapes attest the rise of new interests, ideals, and practices, including

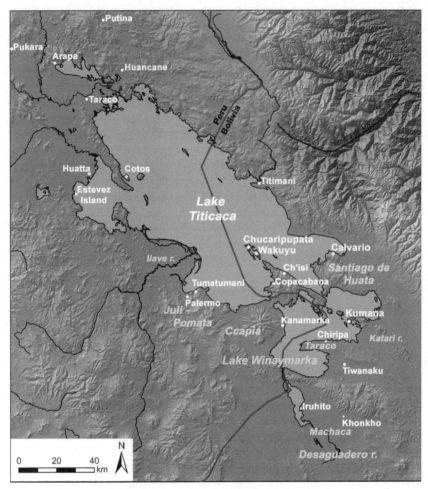

Figure 6.5 Map of the Lake Titicaca Basin showing key sites and geographical features (base map by Steve Wernke).

a political economy grounded in water-oriented environs and a political strategy bent on circumventing or breaking up old local allegiances.

On the rocky Kumana Peninsula northwest of Katari, a platform temple faced with cut sandstone and andesite blocks (and with a west entryway like those in Akapana and Pumapunku) was built at the Late Formative center of Pajchiri (Bennett 1936:456–467). Pajchiri was a moderately sized Tiwanaku settlement with a monumental platform temple complex. An important role for its inhabitants was managing aqueducts that guided water down Kumana's steep slopes and away from raised fields in

Box 6.2   The Pariti Island Ceramic Offerings

In 2003, an Aymara community and a Finnish-Bolivian archaeology team discovered and later excavated one of the most spectacular sets of Tiwanaku ritual offerings known to date. Located on the Island of Pariti in the southern portion of Lake Titicaca, the offerings consisted of several cylindrical pits dug into the earth, two of which the team systematically excavated. In them, the team recovered, among *chachapuma* figurines, sodalite necklace beads, and butchered camelid bones, thousands of sherds pertaining to nearly 500 smashed vessels. Led by Antti Korpisaari, Martti Pärssinen, and Jedú Sagárnaga, archaeologists reconstructed some of the most unusual Tiwanaku ceramic vessels ever found (see Korpisaari 2007; Korpisaari and Pärssinen 2005; Korpisaari and Sagarnaga 2007). These included oversized drinking goblets or *keros*, modeled "foot beakers" reminiscent of some Wari ceremonial vessels, *keros* depicting the crowned face of the Sun Portal deity, *keros* crawling with snarling mythical beings or with painted images of dragonlike creatures devouring humans, and effigy jars depicting ducks, serpents, and monkeys. Many painted scenes include the color pink, a rare hue previously known only on a few sherds from Tiwanaku. Radiocarbon measurements date the offerings to Tiwanaku 2.

Arguably the most striking vessels are the forty or so modeled human portrait and effigy vessels that had been included among these smashed and "ritually killed" vessels. Remarkably, many were made and offered in pairs, attesting a deep value on dual symmetry and mirrored identity in the ideology infusing the offerings. The effigies include strikingly naturalistic portraits of males wearing ear plugs much like the later Inka, lower lip plugs much like the effigy human on this book's cover, as well as a variety of elaborate headdresses, including wrapped turbans and a diadem-crowned helmet. Other effigies include full-bodied jars representing male and female figures (Figure 6.6). Male effigies include characters with side burns and upper lip plugs as well as the now-famous "Señor de los Patos" ("Man of the Ducks," Korpisaari and Parssinen 2005:Plate 7). Protruding from their backs are long, phallic spouts. Female effigies more uniformly depict women with faces framed by paired braids (or long mantillas) and wearing decorated shawls. Some carry on their backs effigy storage jars that served as wide vessel spouts.

The Pariti offerings are significant for what they communicate regarding the varied gender roles and other dimensions of identity, perhaps including ethnicity, depicted on the figures. Surprisingly, ceramic paste analysis indicates that a single group made most of these vessels, despite the varied identities expressed in bodily features and adornments (Korpisaari 2007). In light of their naturalism and ornamentation, Korpisaari interprets the representations as existing individuals or archetypes of high status groups, and the offerings in total as an expression of the particular social worldview of that community, whether they lived on Pariti or hailed from elsewhere. To be sure, these finds are important in helping us give some of the Tiwanaku the faces, bodies, and indeed the lived and embodied realities that they had.

the northwest sector of the Koani Pampa, to hinder erosion and seasonal flooding (Ortloff and Kolata 1989).

Settlement and production on the Taraco Peninsula continued Late Formative patterns, perhaps because, like Kumana, much of the landscape was unsuitable for intensive farming. Settlement patterns and productive strategies, which combined fishing, rain-fed hillslope farming, and herding remained much as they had developed early on. Yet specific centers witnessed important changes. The temple complex at Chiripa remained an important ritual locus that was reformulated to follow Tiwanaku canons (Bennett 1936; Browman 1978b, 1998). The Late Formative 2 Santa Rosa site group on the peninsular tip waned in importance, suggesting that its leadership had been circumvented. As with other areas that came under Tiwanaku hegemony, the creation and popular distribution of elaborate ceremonial wares, which local leaders could not monopolize, was at least one astute strategy to this effect (Bandy 2001: 233).

Transformations in Machaca manifested new productive priorities and political conditions. Settlement in the immediate hinterland of Khonkho Wankane, in the high pampa far from the Desaguadero River, changed relatively nondramatically during the Tiwanaku Period (Janusek 2005a, 2008b). Yet large sectors of the ritual-political center itself, including most of the Late Formative monumental complex, were abandoned and left to collapse. Only one of two courts in the dual-court complex may have remained intact under Tiwanaku, and the Tatakala monolith was eventually left to deteriorate and slump over in the center of the main plaza where it still lies today.

Yet Khonkho's leaders had big plans on the eve of its decline. Four massive sandstone blocks from quarries near the peak of the Kimsachata range had been left in place in the process of being hauled to the site. In 2006, our team discovered several monolith "preforms" left unfinished at these quarries, located twelve kilometers away from and 800 meters above the site. Some displayed elements of a novel style that never was

Figure 6.6 Male (a) and female (b) effigy jars from offerings on the Island of Pariti (photos courtesy of Antti Korpisaari).

to materialize, and one, the largest known intact monolith in the Lake Titicaca basin, would have stood nearly nine meters tall!

Just as Khonkho declined, primary interest in the region began to center on the wetter zones of the Desaguadero River. The river here is wide and forms broad marshes that ebb and flow with periodic lake-level cycles. Preliminary research indicates that a long line of river-oriented sites, first occupied as early as the Early-Middle Formative, was reoccupied on a large scale during the Tiwanaku Period (A. Perez 2004; M. Perez 2005). One of these was Iruhito, which housed at least one platform complex. Excavations in the complex revealed diminutive feline-masked sacrificers, or *chachapumas*, carved in characteristic Tiwanaku style (Figure 6.7). Each figure stands erect with fangs bared, and holds a sacrificial knife on one side and a decapitated trophy head on the other. From the early Colonial Period until today, inhabitants of Iruhito and nearby communities have identified as Uru, and (as discussed in Chapter 5) there are reasons to believe that their ancestors identified with a similar macro-identity. These communities experienced substantial population growth and increasing prestige and wealth under Tiwanaku hegemony. Ongoing investigation may reveal whether transformative state policies such as those that

Figure 6.7 Small andesite *chachapuma* ("were-feline") sacrificer from Iruhito.

transfigured Katari in Tiwanaku 2 also affected the river-oriented societies and landscapes of Machaca.

The greater Tiwanaku core had given rise to multiple multicommunity polities and their ritual-political centers during the Late Formative. Each center and its constituent communities occupied distinct areas of the altiplano's diverse landscape and thus emphasized a particular array of productive strategies. Not surprisingly, Tiwanaku hegemony crystallized as multiple strategies of incorporation, which varied according to location on trade routes, prior political conditions, and feasibility of intensive farming. The careers and importance of previously autonomous (or quasi-autonomous) centers shifted as they became regional centers of state power.

Near Peripheries

The Lake Titicaca Basin

Tiwanaku influence across the Lake Titicaca Basin was a kaleidoscope of historical continuity and radical change. Settlement and production changed very subtly in many areas. The presence of abundant camps above 4,000 meters indicates that seasonal and year-round herding remained important for many local populations (Stanish 2003). Further, most Tiwanaku regional centers across the basin had been important ritual-political centers during the Late Formative. In Juli-Pomata, monumental complexes in early centers such as Palermo and Tumatumani underwent rehabilitation and expansion under Tiwanaku (Stanish et al. 1997). Continuity in settlement in Juli-Pomata and many other areas of the basin suggests that prior political structures and productive systems were merely co-opted by state leaders (Stanish 2002). Many local political and economic systems with long histories remained intact over many generations of Tiwanaku hegemony.

Some areas remained the domain of autonomous polities. There is an intriguing absence of Tiwanaku style material culture and monumentality in the northern basin. Homeland of the Late Formative Pukara polity, this area remained an autonomous polity or cultural complex throughout the Tiwanaku Period. Stanish (2002, 2003) terms this complex Late Huaña. Settlement patterns and material culture (e.g., ceramic styles) are more or less continuous with prior occupations. Locally made Tiwanaku style artifacts appear in relatively small quantities at sites such as the terraced hillside settlement of Unacollo. Groups in the region apparently interacted with Tiwanaku but by all accounts interaction was based on communication and trade rather than direct political or economic control.

Other areas of the basin were moderately transformed. Santiago de Huata and the Island of the Sun are two examples. Both regions have mountainous terrains unsuitable for farming in waterlogged pampas. In both regions, populations now concentrated in a smaller number of large centers and many sites now clustered near hillsides, possibly indicating that hillslope terracing intensified under Tiwanaku (Bauer and Stanish 2001; Lemuz 2001; Stanish 2003). If some centers had been important during the Late Formative, new centers such as Calvario in Santiago de Huata point to significant shifts in local sociopolitical conditions (Lemuz 2001). The Island of the Sun became an important ritual location under Tiwanaku, beginning a tradition that the Inca would revitalize many centuries later (Seddon 1998; Stanish 2003). Two centers emerged in the Tiwanaku Period: Chucaripupata at the north end of the island and Wakuyu to the south. While Wakuyu became the island's political center, Chucaripupata became a major center of ritual for populations around the basin.

Tiwanaku hegemony on the Island of the Sun changed significantly at around AD 800, in synch with changes occurring elsewhere (Seddon 1998). At Chucaripupata, a monumental temple complex was built over early occupations. Underwater research on a submerged reef just off the island indicates that people now dropped elaborate Tiwanaku gold objects and ritual burners into the lake as offerings (Ponce et al. 1992; Reinhard 1992). Meanwhile, a new route linked the religious center to Wakuyu and the south side of the island (Bauer and Stanish 2001; Stanish 2003). This route may have facilitated religious pilgrimage to Chucaripupata from the mainland, much as a similar route did for the Inca some four hundred years later. Water-bounded islands were central to Tiwanaku religious ideology, and the Island of the Sun may have become the primary ritual center outside of the central city itself. Quite possibly, this local center was reinterpreted as a place of mythical origins for the regime that came to power at the beginning of Tiwanaku 2.

Other areas in the basin transformed profoundly. The Puno Bay experienced substantial transformation under Tiwanaku (Stanish 2003). The reason most likely resides in the Huatta Pampa on its north edge, a vast low floodplain that was converted into the largest contiguous landscape of raised fields and hydraulic support systems in the basin (Erickson 1988, 1993). Tiwanaku sites encircled the pampa. The site of Pancha, strategically located amid the raised fields, was probably the ritual-political center for raised-field cultivators and managers (Erickson 1988:344–345). It incorporated a limestone-faced platform like that of other Late Formative and Tiwanaku ceremonial centers. As in Katari during Tiwanaku 2, the locus of settlement in Huatta was on the edges of the raised-field landscape, perhaps suggesting that many people came to work fields temporarily during agricultural crunch times such as planting and harvest (cf. Erickson 1988, 1993).

Tiwanaku settlement networks were particularly dense on the bay just south of Huatta (Stanish 2003:186–188). Here, numerous hamlets and villages surrounded large regional centers with monumental platforms. In addition to farming, fishing, and lake foraging, some hilltop settlements specialized in metal extraction. Inhabitants of Punanave on the route toward Moquegua specialized in making stone tools. Yet true to Tiwanaku religious principles, the primary ritual-political center in the Puno Bay was Isla Estevez, a water-enclosed island close to the shore. A luxury hotel currently covers the massive platform structure that once occupied the natural hill and towered over extensive residential sectors below (Nuñez and Paredes 1978; Stanish 2003:187). Amid other co-opted local polities, the Puno Bay became one of the most important local state-controlled Tiwanaku provinces in the Lake Titicaca Basin.

Tiwanaku hegemony in the Lake Titicaca Basin was flexible, diversified, and highly strategic. It ranged from direct provincial control over the Puno bay, to co-option of local polities such as those in Juli-Pomata, to interaction and trade with autonomous communities and polities such as those of Late Huaña. Parallel with its geopolitical variability, Tiwanaku-style material culture ranged from local emulation in incorporated regions to elite-sponsored production in more directly controlled provinces. In most regions, material culture was not imported from the core but rather emulated Tiwanaku style while drawing on ancient regional traditions. Crafted objects from co-opted regions were mostly local interpretations of Tiwanaku style. In Juli-Pomata, for example, Tiwanaku ceramic wares were restricted to *keros, tazons* or flaring bowls, and *sahumadors,* and decoration was restricted; polychrome decoration and many "classic" Tiwanaku motifs such as condors and felines were rare. Tiwanaku-style material culture in the Puno Bay was far more common, elaborate, and diverse (Stanish 2003:200).

Ancient canons of monumental construction, manifested in platforms, sunken courts, and plazas, were common at regional centers and major settlements. Strikingly, however, the ancient tradition of stone sculpting was now largely restricted to the Tiwanaku inner heartland, and massive monoliths were restricted to Tiwanaku itself. This indicates that they were now largely iconic of ruling lineages. Monoliths came to literally embody the elite ancestors, deities, and ideologies on which state power was centered.

Far Peripheries

The Central and Southern Altiplano

Communities surrounding the Lake Titicaca Basin, in the regions I term the far peripheries, provided important resources for the Tiwanaku core. In turn, many sought to participate in Tiwanaku's vibrant interregional political economy. The descendants of the ancient Wankarani culture in the central altiplano facilitated trade with Lake Titicaca in valued items such as basalt, salt, *chuño,* and *charqui.* Many local settlements grew in size and internal complexity during the Tiwanaku period. Christine Beaule (2002; also Bermann and Estevez 1993) found that the site of Jachakala expanded in poplation and was divided into bounded sectors that housed groups differentiated in status and wealth. Yet inequality at Jachakala was not new; social differences had already existed during the Formative. Formative social differences centered on wealth in herds and in access to the most valued portions of camelid beef. In the Middle Horizon, the inhabitants who for generations had procured basalt from Querim-ita came to enjoy privileged access to nonlocal goods such as obsidian, copper, marine shell, and Tiwanaku vessels. This is not surprising given their newfound place in pan-regional trade circuits.

Figure 6.8 Martin Giesso stands amid abundant basalt debitage in Querimita (photo courtesy of Martin Giesso).

Thus, interaction with Tiwanaku did not create but merely intensified socioeconomic differentiation at Jachakala. Pre-existing social arrangements configured participation in the interregional networks that developed after Tiwanaku's rise. Nor were inhabitants of sites such as Jachakala passive recipients of Tiwanaku goods and ideas. Local inhabitants established relations with Tiwanaku and other communities on their own terms, if to variable degrees, and they adapted new goods and ideas to traditional local values and practices.

Fine-grained basalt from Querimita on the southwestern shores of Lake Poopó was one of the most important materials produced in the central altiplano (Ponce and Mogrovejo 1970). Even today, sharp knives of Querimita basalt are used to (quickly and efficiently) castrate llamas (Giesso 2000). In the past, basalt nodules were quarried in tunnels dug deep into metamorphic outcrops. Their preparation as cores for blades and arrow points left massive piles of debris still visible today (Figure 6.8). Basalt proto-forms and tools were then shipped to the Lake Titicaca basin and elsewhere, and almost exclusively to regional centers such as

Tiwanaku and San Pedro de Atacama (Giesso 2003). An exotic raw material, basalt was a fairly "expensive" nonlocal commodity. High proportions of pottery near Querimita suggest that local groups specialized in basalt procurement and distribution, a labor that may have been commissioned by elite Tiwanaku lineages.

Tiwanaku influence in the southern altiplano was indirect and based largely on the long-distance movement of exotic and valued goods. Santiago de Huari, near the eastern shores of Lake Poopó, was an important trade hub that may have housed Tiwanaku-affiliated households (M. Michel, pers. comm., August 2006). It was strategically located on a nexus of routes that linked Tiwanaku, Cochabamba, and San Pedro de Atacama. It was also located near critical mineral resources, including extensive salt pans left by ancient lakes and extensive silver veins in nearby mountains. It was a trade hub most important for securing access to minerals rather than cultivated resources. The recent discovery of a nearby burial of massacred traders confirms the importance of Santiago de Huari and the Tiwanaku–San Pedro de Atacama connection that it facilitated (Text Box 6.3).

Eastern Yungas

Interaction between the altiplano and adjacent upper eastern valleys, or *yungas,* followed a similar pattern of mutual interaction, strategic negotiation, and differential participation. Some yungas communities provided agricultural products to the altiplano. The site of Pasto Grande was located in the Chuquiapu Valley at 1,100–1,800 meters above sea level (Estevez 1988). Stretched over a steep mountain, the site was consolidated with steep cobble-faced terraces that facilitated the cultivation of lowland products such as coca and maize. The presence of Tiwanaku pottery at the site confirms interaction with the altiplano. Whether the site was a colonial enclave or a local center, and whether it was inhabited by highlanders, local groups, or both remain to be investigated. Yet evidence to date, including an absence of large sites in the region, supports the idea that it was native communities who cultivated lowland crops at Pasto Grande, and in part for highland consumption.

The eastern yungas also provided direct access to delicacies such as chili peppers and tropical fruits as well as psychotropic substances and medicinal herbs such as coca. Ingesting psychotropic snuff had been important in the Tiwanaku heartland during the Formative period, as witnessed in abundant spoons, tablets, and tubes of the so-called hallucinogenic complex. A carved snuff spoon from Middle Horizon occupations in Akapana

Box 6.3 The Juch'uypampa Caravaners

The southern Bolivian altiplano has been home to llama caravan traders for millennia. The recent discovery of five persons interred in a cave near Uyuni, a salt and silver-rich region of Potosí, sheds light on Middle Horizon traders and trading networks. The cave, discovered by a local teacher in the 1990s, contained the interred remains of three adult men and two children. Its aridity facilitated the preservation of remarkable textile, wooden, and basketry offerings.

One young man – apparently a principal, high-ranking person – wore an elaborately woven, polychrome Tiwanaku-style tunic depicting a stylized profile attendant reminiscent of those on the Sun Portal and other stone sculptures. On the tunic, each figure wields a human by the hair in one hand and a sacrificial axe in the other. The man's head had been modified into the elongated shape popular in the Titicaca Basin. An older male next to him wore elaborately woven braids reminiscent of the long tresses that descend from the heads of ancestral figures depicted on Tiwanaku monoliths. Placed beside him was a well-worn wooden bow and a quiver of point-tipped arrows, suggesting that he was a warrior. He and one of the children each wore a striking red-dyed tunic (Agüero 2001). The second child wore a thick garment appropriate for the austral winter. Each of the adults had suffered the kind of physical violence, including severe head trauma, that likely caused their deaths.

Accompanying them was an offering cache of stunning material goods in styles characteristic of both Tiwanaku and San Pedro de Atacama. It included four woven hats, two in the square or "four-corner" Tiwanaku style; two plumed headdresses; several basketry containers in the form of *keros* and *tazons*; a variety of metal adornments; and several wooden and bone implements for preparing and ingesting snuff, including a snuff tray with a pyroengraved sacrificer.

It is likely that this remarkable cave burial contained the remains of traders who drove llama caravans laden with elaborate goods between Tiwanaku and San Pedro. Such a living, which involved crossing political boundaries and enemy territories, was risky business. Piracy and interethnic strife were constant concerns for such people. If the principal man was a high-status caravan driver, the "warrior" may have served as a marksman who protected the group en route.

Some have speculated that these people were killed en route from Tiwanaku, and others suggest that they hailed from San Pedro. Yet chemical isotope analyses of the adult teeth and bones indicate that the individuals grew up on a diet typical of the Juch'uypampa area where they were buried and that at least two of the adults were born there (Knudson et al. 2005). Thus, they were locals.

The cave burial offers intriguing evidence that Middle Horizon trade was not completely monopolized by Tiwanaku or its elite trading partners. Rather local communities facilitated much of the vibrant trade that linked diverse ethnicities and communities. The transethnic interaction and socioeconomic integration that characterized Tiwanaku was initiated to a significant degree in regions far from Tiwanaku, and over generations of caravan-based trade, travel, and communication. Much of it was masterfully orchestrated by local traders such as the unfortunate massacred individuals buried in a lonely cave in Juch'uypampa.

East, Tiwanaku, depicted a clenched first with an extended thumb (Figure 4.31b), a symbolic gesture still carved on Kallawaya amulets to ward off illness or fright and to induce prosperity.

Direct evidence for local interaction with Tiwanaku through ritual-medical specialists comes from early cave tomb sites in valleys east of Lake Titicaca, home of the more recent Kallawaya (see Chapter 2). When Spaniards arrived, Kallawaya deceased relatives were mummified and buried in mountain cists and caves. During planting and harvest rites these tombs were visited and the mummies carried out to agricultural fields (Bastien 1978). Kallawaya curers and diviners considered their own spiritual power to derive from such ancestral graves. In the early Colonial period, missionary zealots forcibly removed many mummy bundles from these tombs and burned them. Nevertheless, intact cave burials at the sites of Niño Korín and Amaguaya contained ritual bundles of paraphernalia used by past ritual-medical specialists.

At Niño Korin (Rydén 1957; Wassén 1972), bundled objects included bone and reed tubes for storing and inhaling snuff, baskets, hunting implements such as arrows and *bolas*, woven bags – one with a clump of medicinal *Ilex* leaves – wooden snuff tablets, and a surgically perforated or "trepanned" cranium. Snuff tablet handles depicted Tiwanaku iconography, which included an upward-facing, beaked profile attendant, similar to the attendants on the Sun Portal; a winged condor; and a clenched fist reminiscent of the spoon handle in Akapana East (Figure 6.9).

A ritual bundle from Amaguaya included a woven Tiwanaku-style bag with a number of wrapped ritual items and a large, remarkably crafted

Figure 6.9 Wooden snuff tablets from the site of Niño Korín (adapted from Wassén 1972).

snuff tablet (Capriles and Flores 2000; Rendón 2000). Among the wrapped items was a quartz crystal, several miniature llama amulets (*illas*) for ensuring camelid reproduction and health, mica flakes, and an arrow point. The handle of the tablet depicted a "sacrificer" gripping a scepter in one hand and the braids of a trophy head in the other. The figure faced upward, with a long nose or bill similar to those of the flying figures on the Calle Linares lintel from Tiwanaku (Rendón 2000). The tablet incorporated exotic items and semiprecious stones, including Spondylus shell from the Pacific coast, sodalite, malachite, turquoise, and bronze.

To conclude, valley communities east of Lake Titicaca came to form polities or semiautonomous federations of communities that provided critical agricultural goods, delicacies, psychotropic substances, and ritual paraphernalia for Tiwanaku highlanders. In return, they gained clients, affiliations, and Tiwanaku-style goods. These communities also may have mediated Tiwanaku's access to rare exotic goods from distant Amazonian lowlands, such as feathers, pelts, and jaguar canines for necklaces, such as the one found in Akapana East (Chapter 4).

Peripheral Enclaves

Formative Developments

If there is one thing clear about Tiwanaku geopolitics in the south-central Andes, it is that the Lake Titicaca Basin had no geographical monopoly on increasing complexity. Complex sociopolitical institutions and far-reaching interaction networks had been developing across the south-central Andes during the Formative period, and the Tiwanaku state emerged out of this dynamic and mutually interactive macroregional matrix.

Of particular importance were Formative cultural developments in the fertile valleys of Cochabamba and Moquegua (Figure 2.1). Early cultural development in Cochabamba involved at least two emergent traditions, one focused in the immense Cochabamba Valley and the other in the subtropical Mizque Valley to the southeast (Anderson, Paz, and Sanzetenea 1998; Brockington et al. 1995; Céspedes 2000; Gabelmann 2001; Higueras-Hare 1996, 2001; Pereira, Sanzetenea, and Brockington 2001). As early as Late Formative 1, settlements in both societies occupied low hills and terraces over the valley floors, where people farmed, hunted, herded, and conducted ritual activities. Inhabitants of Cochabamba interacted intensively with altiplano peoples such as Wankarani, while inhabitants of Mizque formed gateway communities that facilitated the movement of goods, information, and ideas between highland valleys and tropical eastern lowlands. In Late Formative 2, material culture diversified as each region experienced an economic boom. Diverse styles of polychrome ceramic serving and ceremonial wares (e.g., Sauces, Tupuraya, and Mojocoya) became common, emphasizing a range of diagnostic forms that included tripod bowls and the first known *keros* in the Andes (Céspedes 2000).

Meanwhile, in the coastal Moquegua Valley, Peru, the Huaracane culture complex emerged during the Formative. A society of farming villages with no central political or ritual center (Goldstein 2000), it occupied a small but verdant midvalley plain and interacted with coastal Paracas-Nasca communities further north and highland Pukara sites in the Titicaca basin. Some Huaracane families maintained far-ranging relations with distant regions. Elegant textiles and pottery from both Paracas-Nasca and Pukara appear in some local residential and mortuary contexts. High-status Huaracane families buried their deceased in elaborate "boot tombs," which in some ways mimicked Paracas communal tombs. The person interred in one such tomb was clothed in garments woven in Nasca, Pukara, and local Huaracane styles.

Paul Goldstein attributes these patterns to the crystallization of several competing high-status factions, the members of which desired access to such elaborate exotica. Elaborate adornments and exotic items gave material expression to the long-distance relations and transcultural identities they forged in order to bolster their status and identity back home.

Cochabamba and Its Environs

During the Middle Horizon, Tiwanaku leaders sought to take advantage of Cochabamba's and Moquegua's natural productivity. At an average of 2,600 meters above sea level, the temperate central Cochabamba valley was ideal for cultivating maize and a host of other lowland products. Under Inca hegemony, it was transformed into a maize-producing *mitmaq* colony for the ruler Wayna Capac's *panaca* (Wachtel 1982). Maize cultivation was of primary interest to Tiwanaku as well (Bennett 1936; Browman 1981; Kolata 1993a; Ponce 1981; Walter 1966). Recent research at mound sites such as Sierra Mokho, Piñami, and Quillacollo reveal two local phases (Illatoco and Piñami) of Tiwanaku influence that correspond respectively with Tiwanaku 1 and 2 (Anderson 1999; Céspedes 2000; Céspedes, Muñoz, and Sanzetenea 1998).

Tiwanaku material culture suddenly became common in Cochabamba after AD 500. Ceramic vessels imported from the Lake Titicaca Basin were used alongside locally made vessels that combined Tiwanaku and local styles. By AD 800 a full-fledged local "Cochabamba Tiwanaku"–style appeared just as many preexisting local styles disappeared. Distinguishing features included tapering kerolike *challadors* and small rounded bowls (Bennett 1936; Céspedes 2000; Ibarra Grasso, and Querejazu Lewis 1986; Rydén 1959). In producing Cochabamba Tiwanaku wares, local specialists adopted some of the advanced firing techniques that had developed in the Lake Titicaca Basin (Anderson 1999). To facilitate increasing commensalism, local populations now also produced high-volume cooking *ollas* and storage *tinajas* similar to those in the highlands. Pyroengraved bone spoons and tubes in Cochabamba sites attest the adoption (or perhaps continued importance) of the medicinal-psychotropic drug cult. This may have been facilitated by direct interaction with ritual specialists from the Kallawaya region which lies between Cochabamba and the altiplano.

Cochabamba was a thriving Tiwanaku enclave in which highland cultural influence and political hegemony intensified over time. Highland groups most likely resided among native populations, though whether Cochabamba formed a colony or diaspora settled en masse by highland

and other nonlocal groups, as did the later Inca colony, is subject to chemical analysis of local human remains. Regardless, social identities no doubt often interwove and transformed through co-residence and intermarriage.

Reciprocally, Cochabamba influenced Tiwanaku. Like Katari and other regions, Cochabamba influenced Tiwanaku style (e.g., the *kero*) and developed a creative local stylistic tradition that became popular throughout the south-central Andes. Local groups even colonized the altiplano. The occupants of Tiwanaku's Ch'iji Jawira neighborhood may have originally hailed from Cochabamba. The metal accoutrements of a high-status individual's tomb from the site of San Sebastian (Money 1991) depict Tiwanaku-like motifs but in a very distinct style, emphasizing the local foundations of Cochabamba elite culture (Figure 6.10). Evidence suggests that Cochabamba formed a semiautonomous polity or federation of communities with local populations and leaders who claimed political allegiance to Tiwanaku and consolidated their allegiance through alliances, trade agreements, and intermarriage.

Cochabamba's transformation gave rise to a cluster of prestigious trade hubs. Local leaders and entrepreneurs had much to gain from their favorable geopolitical location on east-west caravan routes linking highlands, tropics, and valleys. They maintained mutual interactions and influences with other polities and communities in the central altiplano (Beaule 2002), the tropical lowlands (Pereira, Sanzetenea, and Brockington 2001; Prümers et al. 2002), and other valleys to the south (Anderson, Céspedes, and Sanzetenea 1998; Janusek and Blom 2006). At some sites, the appearance of Tiwanaku wares corresponded with an explosion of exotic goods from other distant regions. Middens at Quillacollo, for example, revealed birds, marsupials, and fish from the deep tropics to the east.

Tiwanaku influence in Mizque was more interactive and economic than it was political. Settlement choices and productive practices changed minimally between the Late Formative and Middle Horizon (Higueras-Hare 1996). During the Late Formative, settlement networks concentrated around three major settlements, a pattern that continued in the Middle Horizon. Yet local culture and economy boomed during the Middle Horizon, and the ubiquitous Tiwanaku drug cult gained popularity here as it did elsewhere. Middle Horizon ceramic styles burgeoned in diversity to include a number of styles, including Cochabamba Tiwanaku, Mojocoya, and the Omereque homeland style (Anderson 1999; Céspedes 2000; Higueras-Hare 1996). Tiwanaku style was but one among many. Vessels in local styles were distributed across the valleys, through the altiplano, and into Tiwanaku core cities, indicating that local groups were involved in interregional networks that extended across the south-central Andes. If Tiwanaku leaders in the altiplano and in Cochabamba took advantage of Mizque's long history of trading expertise, groups in the

Figure 6.10 The precious metal accoutrements of a high-status
person in Cochabamba (adapted from Money 1991).

Mizque Valley came to form an autonomous polity (or group of polities)
that took advantage of the new trade networks and opportunities attendant on Tiwanaku expansion.

Moquegua and Its Environs

On the opposite side of the altiplano as well, Tiwanaku interaction with
societies in western valley zones ranged from direct colonization and control to mutual interaction and influence.

Figure 6.11 View of the Moquegua Valley (a) and the now-deserted site of Chen Chen (b).

Moquegua. The clearest evidence for Tiwanaku colonization comes from the middle Moquegua Valley in the Osmore Drainage of southern Peru, some 300 km (a 10–12-day walk) from the Tiwanaku heartland. It is a relatively small but fertile valley that ranges from 900 to 2,000 meters above sea level (Figures 6.11 and 6.12a). The valley is a visually striking narrow green strip that traverses one of the driest deserts in the world. Interdisciplinary research under the auspices of Programa Cuntisuyu, initiated by Michael Moseley, provides an in-depth view of highland-lowland interaction and environmental shift over the long term.

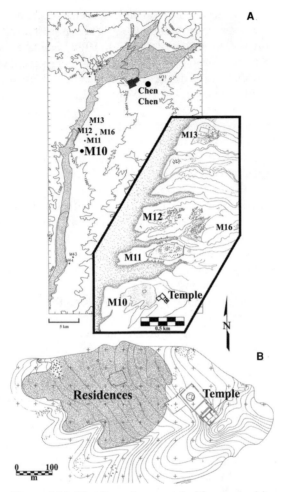

Figure 6.12 The Omo site group in Moquegua (a) and the site of
Omo M10 (b), showing its ceremonial complex (adapted from
Goldstein 1993a).

Interaction between Moquegua and the altiplano intensified significantly in Tiwanaku 1, the local Omo phase (Pari 1987). Sites appeared
on bluffs overlooking the middle Moquegua Valley and on upper valley
slopes en route to the southern Lake Titicaca Basin. The largest settlement in the middle valley was Omo M12, which housed "inns" for making
and consuming *chicha* (Goldstein 1993a, 1993b, 2003). Paul Goldstein
argues that middle valley sites formed an enclave dedicated to cultivating
the fertile valley floor. Their inhabitants used Tiwanaku-style ceramic

wares almost exclusively. Archaeological and bioarchaeological evidence concur that the new sites were inhabited by a diaspora native to the Tiwanaku heartland (Blom 1999; Blom et al. 1998; Goldstein 2005). They brought with them Tiwanaku material culture, craft technologies, and expertise in farming. Presumably, the Huaracane had left the valley or had become completely assimilated before or shortly after the initial occupation.

Tiwanaku interaction intensified after AD 800, initiating the Chen Chen phase that corresponds with Tiwanaku 2. Chen Chen settlement and material culture extended well beyond the area inhabited by Omo sites. Moquegua was being transfigured as an integrated Tiwanaku provincial landscape (Goldstein 2005; Goldstein and Owen 2001) parallel with contemporaneous reorganizations in Katari, the Island of the Sun, Cochabamba, and Tiwanaku. Settlement focused around four major site complexes at the edges of the Moquegua valley floor: Omo, Rio Muerto, Cerro Echenique, and Chen Chen. Each complex was located near an extensive irrigated pampa, indicating that now more than ever cultivation was a primary concern (Williams 1997:90). The expansion of intricate farming systems on vast horizontal plains overlooking the valley bottom is consistent with a parallel emphasis on pampa-focused farming in the altiplano. One major canal network at the massive site of Chen Chen irrigated at least 90 hectare of preserved fields. This site and most likely others in the valley were largely dedicated to farming and processing lowland crops.

Chen Chen incorporated vast residential sectors, including seasonal dwellings at the site's flanks that housed temporary laborers during agricultural "crunch" times (Figures 6.11b and 6.12a). Residential areas yielded abundant hoes and hundreds of grinding stones for processing grains. The site also had massive storage sectors. These included 7,500–11,000 standardized and neatly arranged subterranean storage cists for storing cultivated grains (Bandy et al. 1996; Goldstein 2003:156). Dental and chemical analyses of hundreds of individuals from Chen Chen's twenty-eight cemeteries indicate what other evidence indirectly suggest: local populations cultivated, processed, and consumed high quantities of maize (Blom 1999; Tomczak 2001). Moquegua quite possibly had become the most important maize-producing province of the Tiwanaku state.

Much of Moquegua's maize was destined for the altiplano, perhaps in large part to subsidize the elite-sponsored feasts that were becoming increasingly important for Tiwanaku's expansive political economy. Maize ultimately made it, in some cases already "shelled" and processed, to places such as Putuni and Akapana East 1 in Tiwanaku, where it was fermented and brewed as *chicha* to support elite-sponsored rituals of consumption. Llama caravans and specialized herders played an important role in this commensal economy. They hauled processed maize from Moquegua to the state heartland, and in turn brought stone tools, salt, and other goods from the heartland to Moquegua. In the hills above Chen Chen, massive geoglyphs depict llamas en route to and from the valley (Goldstein 2003).

Ceremonial complexes in Moquegua synthesized Tiwanaku and local architectural styles. In the Omo phase, temples were relatively small structures. Examples include walled enclosures with offering pits and Omo pottery at the foot of Cerro Baúl in the upper valley (Goldstein and Owen 2001; Owen 1998). Yet Omo M10 was chosen as the principal ceremonial center for the Moquegua enclave (Figure 6.12b). The site incorporated monumental walled enclosures that funneled priests and worshipers into a plaza, through a large courtyard, and up and into a smaller court (Goldstein 1993a). On the one hand, many elements of the complex were quintessentially "altiplano": movement through open spaces toward more intimate inner sancta, foundations of andesite masonry, a central sunken court, and Tiwanaku ritual vessels such as *sahumadors* and effigy *incensarios*. On the other hand, the overall design of the complex was local. Distinctive elements included a circular structure in the center of the plaza and an offering pit with miniature ceramic jars. For centuries, circular courts had been key elements of ceremonial architecture on the coast. Like other local ceremonial complexes affiliated with Tiwanaku, the Omo cultural complex synthesized Tiwanaku with local architectural and religious traditions.

Local styles of material culture and body modification indicate that Moquegua inhabitants formed a distinct society within Tiwanaku's broad geopolitical sphere (Goldstein and Owen 2001). They included highly polished blackware *keros*, "Coca-Cola" glass *keros*, and specific ceramic design motifs, including reticulated patterns and waterfowl (Figure 6.13a–13d). Confirming Moquegua regional affiliation was a single form of cranial modification. All Moquegua people practiced a tabular or flattened style of head shape that, if common in Tiwanaku, was rare in Katari (Blom 1999, 2005). Excellent local preservation in woven items suggests that the flattened head shape corresponded with a distinctive, square, or four-corner, hat.

Successive waves of people colonized Moquegua, giving rise to mutually differentiated diaspora communities over the long term (Goldstein 2005; Owen 2005). Early immigrants continued to produce and consume Omo-style material culture even as new groups arrived after AD 800. These later groups, in turn, tended to produce and employ a more

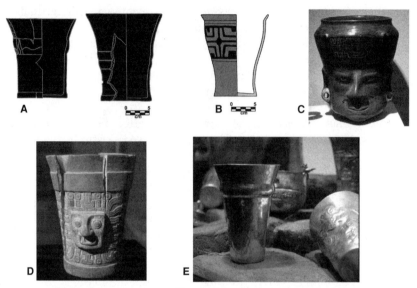

Figure 6.13 A pageant of kero styles from the coastal region: blackware (a), "Coca-Cola glass" (b), portrait (c), and wooden *keros* (d) from Moquegua, and gold keros from San Pedro de Atacama (e).

standardized (or "orthodox" as Tiwanaku goes) Chen Chen style. Thus, this Tiwanaku enclave incorporated distinct communities of people who most likely hailed from different regions of the altiplano.

Chiribaya and Azapa. Like Puno Bay and Cochabamba, the Moquegua enclave was surrounded by polities and societies that maintained distinct cultural identities and variable degrees of interaction with the Lake Titicaca Basin. Significant in this regard were the Chiribaya polities of coastal Osmore, downriver from Moquegua, and Azapa in nearby northern Chile. Both have been considered Tiwanaku enclaves. Chiribaya emerged out of prior coastal cultures during the Chen Chen phase (Lozada 1998; Lozada and Buikstra 2002; Reycraft 2005). Its rise was predicated on economic opportunities and sociopolitical conditions that followed increasing highland influence in western valleys such as Moquegua. Tiwanaku-style objects appear as grave offerings in Chiribaya sites. Nevertheless, Chiribaya material culture, cranial modification, and human genetic traits reflect closer affiliation with other coastal societies than with Tiwanaku-affiliated populations. Overall, then, Tiwanaku's strategy in Osmore involved direct control over maize production in the Moquegua midvalley and indirect access to marine resources via trade with autonomous coastal communities such as constituted Chiribaya.

Coastal valleys south of Osmore such as Locumba and Azapa are thought to have been profoundly influenced or colonized by the highland polities of Pukara and Tiwanaku (Berenguer, Castro, and Silva 1980; Berenguer and Dauelsberg 1989; Mujica 1985; Muñoz 1995–96; Rivera 1991, 2002). A Late Formative polity had developed in the Azapa Valley during the local Alto Ramirez phase (Berenguer 2004; Goldstein 1995–1996). Local communities prepared their dead as bundles and then buried them at marked locations in cemetery mounds, some of which grew to monumental proportions over generations. The mounds came to serve as loci for rites dedicated to community ancestors. Pukara-related textiles and ceramics were placed in some burials (Rivera 1991, 2002) alongside local and exotic goods, indicating that some local groups forged relations with formative societies in the Lake Titicaca Basin.

Interaction with the altiplano during the Middle Horizon, the local Cabuza phase, intensified. As in Moquegua, communities with strong relations to Tiwanaku concentrated midvalley near natural springs. While some suggest that Tiwanaku established a colonial enclave in Azapa based on evidence from cemeteries, recent research indicates that Tiwanaku influence was more subtle, diplomatic, and indirect (Berenguer 2004; Goldstein 1995–1996). Tiwanaku-style offerings were placed in some burials. They included ceramic wares, woven clothing, and wooden objects (including snuff implements). As in Moquegua, ceramic wares now included blackware *keros*, which identifies them as part of a pan-regional Western Valley tradition. Local practices and material culture experienced other stylistic innovations. These included fetal-position burials, four-cornered caps, loom weaving, and wooden implements (Berenguer and Dauelsberg 1989; Goldstein 1995–1996; Rivera 2002).

If altiplano immigrants lived among the Cabuza, they were a minority. Habitation sites with evidence for Tiwanaku occupation are uncommon. Only three small settlements have been located to date, and none of them have monumental architecture. The proportion of Tiwanaku-affiliated burials was small, and human bone chemistry analysis to date indicates that no foreign groups occupied the valley (Sutter 2000). Burials with Tiwanaku offerings also tended to have the most elaborate Cabuza items, and in some cases, these were located at the centers of local cemeteries. Several such "Tiwanaku" burials were placed in ancient, visually impressive Alto Ramirez burial mounds (Muñoz 1987). Through such practices, communities claimed both the local past and cultural affiliation with the distant altiplano, and in the process reinterpreted ancient sites and built landscapes according to new ideals and ends.

In summary, hegemonic variability was shaped by preexisting local sociopolitical conditions. If Cochabamba and Moquegua were colonized, Mizque and Azapa were incorporated. In all cases, highland-lowland interaction was mutual, interactive, and in great part driven by local communities. It revolved around Tiwanaku's interest in lowland agricultural, mineral, and marine resources as well as lowland interest in establishing cosmopolitan connections and acquiring Tiwanaku-crafted items and ritual knowledge. At stake in dynamic negotiations of state and local interests were Tiwanaku material culture, technologies, ritual practices, and ideals. Communities in Mizque and Azapa interacted with Tiwanaku leaders and nearby polities, capitalizing on trade and communication networks that were expanding in multiple directions during the Middle Horizon. By AD 800, powerful autonomous polities came to thrive in such places, at the edges of colonial enclaves such as Cochabamba and Moquegua.

Civilizations on the Frontiers

During the Middle Horizon, the south-central Andes transformed in the face of emerging state networks and shifting local conditions. Some regions were colonized and directly controlled, some were incorporated as semiautonomous polities and regions, and others maintained informal social alliances and trade relations with the Tiwanaku core. It is safe to assume that no society remained unchanged over the course of Tiwanaku hegemony. Yet most local changes were instigated by macroregional transformations that emanated from multiplex sources and so transcended state conniving and control.

The "multiethnic aggregation known to us today as Tiwanaku" (Llagostera 1995:75) was a complex, fluid, and variable phenomenon. It is not felicitous to assume that Tiwanaku monopolized religious experience, economic exchange, social interaction, and political hegemony in the south-central Andes during the Middle Horizon. New evidence opens our eyes to the multidirectional interactions and multiple affiliations that any society juggled with Tiwanaku and with other communities and polities. In coming to some understanding of Tiwanaku hegemony, it encourages a shift in focus from Tiwanaku-centric explanations to explanations that foreground the dynamic roles of local societies and their reasons for participating in the Tiwanaku phenomenon.

Ideal places to examine local trajectories of cultural and political development are the distant frontiers, Tiwanaku's "far" (Kolata 1993b) or "ultra" peripheries (Berenguer and Dauelsberg 1989). Here, interaction among people of diverse identities was predicated on llama caravan trade. Tiwanaku and other elites patronized some caravan circuits, but independent caravan companies thrived on "commissions" and reciprocal services (see Browman 1990). Local booms emerged out of economic opportunities and interaction networks that expanded at the dawn of

Figure 6.14 View of San Pedro de Atacama showing the edge of the oasis (photo by Tom Dillehay).

the Middle Horizon. If in part instigated by state emergence, emergent cultural developments in San Pedro de Atacama and Chuquisaca created their own interaction networks and sociopolitical contexts. Many a local center became a bustling entrepôt for trade, socializing, and cultural exchange (Nuñez and Dillehay 1995), and some became cosmopolitan political centers of frontier polities.

San Pedro de Atacama, Chile

The nature and intensity of Tiwanaku influence in San Pedro, located in the Atacama Desert of northern Chile at 2,430 meters and some 800 kilometers south of Tiwanaku, is under debate (Figure 6.14). While some have argued that San Pedro housed substantial colonies from the Tiwanaku heartland (Kolata 1993b; Oakland Rodman 1992), recent research may indicate otherwise (Berenguer 2004; Llagostera 1995; Torres and Conklin 1995; Torres-Rouf 2002). One problem is that past research in San Pedro de Atacama focused almost exclusively on human burials. Between 1955 and 1980, the Jesuit priest Gustavo Le Paige (1961, 1965) excavated more than three thousand tombs in cemeteries distributed among San Pedro's thirteen agricultural oases. Many burials were remarkably rich, yielding elaborate offerings of textiles, snuff implements, musical instruments, and vessels of wood, ceramic, and gold. On the basis of such work, we know that the local Middle Horizon consisted of two phases – Quitor, AD 400–800, and Coyo, AD 800–1000 – that correspond roughly with Tiwanaku 1 and 2. Local polished black ceramic wares (*negro pulido*) predominated in both phases, but as in Azapa, during the second phase, local potters adopted and adapted the *kero* form to local technical and decorative styles (Goldstein 2003:153). Some burials included *keros* hewn of hammered gold, a sumptuary local adaptation of a popular Tiwanaku form that was used by high-status individuals and leaders (Figure 6.13e). Across northern Chile, ritual consumption, and especially drinking *chicha*, became particularly significant in local social arenas.

Tiwanaku-style objects were included in burials alongside local style ceramics, textiles, and other crafted items. In the Coyo cemetery as in Azapa, tombs with Tiwanaku-style grave goods were spatially segregated from those with local or other exotic goods (Oakland Rodman 1992). Yet Tiwanaku goods formed a very small proportion of burial offerings overall (Torres and Conklin 1995). Collectively, they include some thirty woven textiles, several pyroengraved bone tubes, snuff implements, and a handful of ceramic vessels (Le Paige 1961; Nuñez 1964; Tárrago 1989; Torres 1987, 2001). Further, in most tombs, Tiwanaku items accompanied objects in other exotic styles, including La Aguada in northwestern Argentina, Chicha and Tarija in southern Bolivia, Mojocoya in central Bolivia, and Ica in southern Peru, among others (Llagostera 1995; Stovel 2002; Torres and Conklin 1995). It is telling that in tombs, an individual's head shape did not correspond with the presence of Tiwanaku offerings, and that head-shape styles changed only minimally at the onset of Tiwanaku hegemony (Torres-Rouf 2002).

Carved snuff tablets depicting Tiwanaku iconography form the largest category of Tiwanaku-style objects from San Pedro burials; yet, they make up less then 10 percent of the 614 total snuffing kits recorded so far (Figure 6.15; Torres and Conklin 1995:81). They depict frontal staff deities, profile sacrificers, camelids, and other symbols that approximated motifs found on monoliths housed in Tiwanaku's heartland temples (Berenguer 1998; Torres 1987, 2001); one depicted the Kallawaya clenched-fist motif found at Niño Korin and Tiwanaku (Torres and Conklin 1995:84). Only in one known case did a snuffing kit accompany an individual shrouded in Tiwanaku textiles. The total inventory of snuffing kits included undecorated implements and implements decorated in other styles. Further, an early date for one snuffing kit and the appearance of a few Yayamama motifs indicate that the ritual-medicinal drug cult and some of its associated "Tiwanaku" iconography had appeared long before Tiwanaku hegemony. Indeed, portable snuff tablets and woven clothing

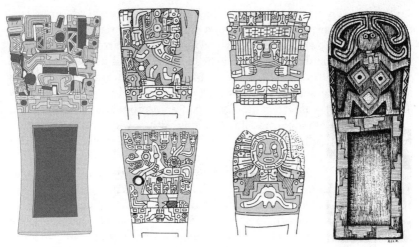

Figure 6.15 Wooden snuff tablets from San Pedro de Atacama.
Those with relatively orthodox Tiwanaku iconography are on the
left and those with locally-based iconography are on the right
(redrawn by author and Jennifer Ohnstad from Llagostera 1995
and Young-Sanchez 2004).

may have predated and inspired the carved iconography of Tiwanaku's
stone monoliths (see the beautiful, radiocarbon-dated Late Formative
textiles in Young-Sanchez 2004).

Overall, evidence from San Pedro adds a new perspective to the
south-central Andean ritual-medicinal drug cult. Rather than a uniquely
Tiwanaku phenomenon, it was part of an ancient and widely shared set
of ritual practices that became more popular and more widely distributed
under Tiwanaku hegemony. Tiwanaku – affiliated groups adopted, popularized, and perhaps proselytized particular views on bodily health and
the cosmos (that even then may have been the specialized "sciences"
of proto-Kallawaya ritualists), but they had no monopoly over them. I
suggest, in fact, that carved wooden snuffing kits were fashioned in San
Pedro de Atacama and perhaps other regions where trees abound and
then brought to the Tiwanaku heartland by San Pedro traders in exchange
for other Tiwanaku crafted goods. In that light they were material com-
ponents of an early pan-regional tradition of ritual practices that were
adapted to local views and traditions in various regions, including the
Tiwanaku core.

San Pedro de Atacama was the core of a distinct sociopolitical formation that housed high status groups and specialized caravan traders who
forged and maintained relations across the southern and south-central

Andes. No Tiwanaku settlement has been found in the desert oasis. Rather than a far periphery, it was an autonomous frontier polity or federation with its own "cultural focus whose primary art was not stationary and monumental... but was instead intimate and portable" (Torres and Conklin 1995:79). In fact, wealth and influence among its elites increased as interaction with Tiwanaku intensified. Living in a relatively isolated desert oasis, Atacameños forged a cosmopolitan mortuary tradition through alliances and interactions with a wide range of distant communities, polities, and regions. Cosmopolitan relations in San Pedro peaked during the Coyo phase, contemporary with Tiwanaku 2 in the Lake Titicaca Basin. The relation between San Pedro and Tiwanaku, as well as other distant polities such as La Aguada in Argentina (Gonzales 1998), was based on reciprocal exchange in goods and ideas.

Tiwanaku was a favorite trading hub for local high-status groups. Long caravans laden with minerals, copper, salt, and crafted goods such as snuff implements frequently embarked on the long trek to the Lake Titicaca Basin for major Tiwanaku feasts, rituals, and other events (Text Box 6.3). Traders stopped at major hubs along the way, such as Santiago de Huari near Lake Poopó, to exchange goods with friends and established trading partners. Relations between local and distant groups were most likely personal, and often cast as fictive kin and forged on clientage as they are today (Browman 1990; Kolata 1992, 1993b; Nielson 2001). It is likely that social and trade relations were frequently cemented via marriage, and that Tiwanaku elites did as much to secure trustworthy and reliable sources of valued raw materials and goods.

Chuquisaca, Bolivia

Multidirectional interaction and a cosmopolitan focus were emerging trends in many regions of the south-central Andes during the Middle Horizon. Ongoing research demonstrates as much in the central and southern altiplano (Beaule 2002; Lecoq 1987, 1999; Marcos Michel, pers. comm., 2005) and eastern Andean valleys of Cochabamba, Potosi, and Chuquisaca (Angelo 2003; Lima 2000). These regions are home to numerous archaeological styles, each of which was traditionally considered to represent a single ethnic group or polity (Ibarra and Querejazo 1986; Walter 1966). It was conventionally thought that such groups represented archipelago-like colonies that were established by highland polities such as Tiwanaku. As it turns out, most valley regions were home to autonomous local polities, federations, and communities that acquired, produced, and used a bewildering variety of material cultural styles.

Exemplary in this regard were political communities in Icla, which emerged during the Middle Horizon in the dry valleys of Chuquisaca

(Janusek 2000, 2008a). Sociopolitical development here hinged on location along trade routes that followed major rivers such as the Pilcomayo. These routes were punctuated here as they were elsewhere in the south-central Andes by ritual locations with painted petroglyphs. Throughout the Middle Horizon, groups in the region maintained remarkably diverse ceramic wares. Some (such as Yampara) were "home" styles, while some show influence from the altiplano, others from the tropical lowlands, and still others (such as Tupuraya, Mojocoya, and Omereque) from valleys to the north such as Mizque and Cochabamba. In some cases, several vessels in distinct styles were placed as offerings in a single tomb. The only "pure" Tiwanaku vessel was found at a petroglyph site, emphasizing the role such sites maintained in caravan rituals. All others were of the Cochabamba Tiwanaku style more directly characteristic of Cochabamba.

Thus, relations with Tiwanaku were indirect, tenuous, and mediated by trade and interaction with southern altiplano polities and Cochabamba-Mizque. Groups in Icla maintained cosmopolitan ideals tied to livelihoods that privileged llama herding and caravan exchange with distant regions. Local goods earmarked for export included semitropical fruits, chili peppers, maize, and psychotropic/medicinal plants. Inhabitants of two settlements crafted elegant necklaces from the red-lipped shells of large snails that are native to nearby tropical lowlands. These ornaments were traded across the south-central Andes and even reached Tiwanaku. Thus, while parts of the eastern valleys were indeed colonized by highland communities and polities, much of the Andean fringe supported emergent, autonomous polities. These polities took advantage of expanding trade routes that transformed and linked together distant regions and communities of the south-central Andes during the Middle Horizon.

A Desire for Raw Stone

Many of the raw materials that altiplano groups desired and obtained were located in regions inhabited by well-entrenched societies and complex polities that had been procuring such resources for trade long before state emergence. An excellent case is the Querimita basalt quarry near Lake Poopó. Here, during formative periods native groups had been quarrying and trading tools and partially worked "preforms" with far regions. The presence of Tiwanaku artifacts at sites near the quarry, and the fact that the distribution of Querimita tools was restricted in the Tiwanaku heartland – in fact, limited to Tiwanaku itself – suggests that during the Middle Horizon Tiwanaku high status groups came to play a strong hand in securing its supply (Giesso 2000, 2003).

Tiwanaku populations also sought obsidian. Obsidian was highly valued because of the sharp edges that a knapping virtuoso can achieve to make effective arrow points and cutting tools. Obsidian sources have distinctive mineral signatures, so trace element analyses of artifacts can determine their origin. Obsidian flakes and points were common in the Tiwanaku heartland, and particularly at the central city. Researchers submitted eighty-seven samples for instrumental neutron activation analysis at University of Missouri's research reactor (Brooks, Glascock, and Giesso 1997; Giesso 2000). Countering expectations, analysis revealed that Tiwanaku obtained its obsidian from at least ten different, distant sources. These included Quispisisa, some 600 kilometer northwest of Tiwanaku; Sora Sora, about 200 kilometer south of Tiwanaku; and Cerro Zapaleri, on the "tri-country" border of Bolivia, Chile, and Argentina some 625 kilometers to the southeast. Clearly, obsidian traveled great distances.

Yet Tiwanaku obsidian was most commonly procured from Chivay (90 percent of the samples), located in the Arequipa region of southern Peru just north of Moquegua and about 300 kilometers northwest of Tiwanaku. Chivay obsidian was well-distributed throughout the heartland, and it was the only obsidian type found in elite and ceremonial contexts of Tiwanaku's urban core (Giesso 2003). Other obsidian types were most common in other contexts, in some cases along with Chivay obsidian. For Giesso, this suggests that Tiwanaku elites monopolized Chivay obsidian through centrally administered trade or elite-sponsored patron-client relations, while local groups maintained varying trade connections with other regional sources. This is in keeping with the distribution of other valued resources and goods in Tiwanaku, which together emphasize Tiwanaku's socioeconomic diversity alongside elite-sponsored production and interaction. Tiwanaku elites may have controlled Chivay obsidian because it was the only type in the heartland that was transparent, as opposed to common dark varieties. As it did for the Inca, transparency may have conjured water and ancestors (Giesso 2003), two elements at the core of Tiwanaku religious values. Controlling the distribution a highly valued exotic item with powerful spiritual allusions was of great concern for Tiwanaku rulers. It is plausible that obsidian nodules were distributed to local specialists who then, as part of a labor tax, transformed them into working weapons of hunt and battle.

Consumers in Tiwanaku desired Chivay obsidian as much as consumers in the United States desire oil, a not-so-transparent valued commodity. Like the world's great oil reserves, the Chivay source remained firmly in the hands of local polities. Tiwanaku sites were common in the southern portion of Arequipa (Chapter 7; Cardona 2002). In the spirit of Tiwanaku, they were located on high ground near flat pampas and natural water sources, facilitating surveillance over cultivated fields and visual pathways with local peaks such as the active volcano Misti. A large expanse of cultivated fields near the Tiwanaku site of Sonqonata, now covered with ash from Huaynaputina's devastating eruption in 1600, covered as much as 20 kilometers. Yet survey near the Chivay source itself yielded "no evidence for imperial administration by Wari or Tiwanaku" (Wernke 2003:167). Thus, it appears that Tiwanaku elites obtained obsidian by negotiating trade relations with the local groups who controlled the quarries, facilitated by Tiwanaku-affiliated groups living in southern Arequipa.

Tiwanaku elites and local inhabitants in Arequipa had another serious concern: controlling the border zone between Tiwanaku and Wari (Chapter 7). After AD 600, Wari emerged as Tiwanaku's "peer-state" and major rival in southern Peru. It is not clear precisely when Tiwanaku and Wari colonized or influenced Arequipa, but Tiwanaku's strikingly high site locations and its apparent concern with surveillance suggests that Wari was of concern for Tiwanaku and most likely vice versa.

Tiwanaku Geopolitics: A Synthesis

Tiwanaku influence in the south-central Andes was flexible, strategic, and dynamic. It ranged from direct to indirect influence, and in many cases shifted from incorporative to more profoundly transformative strategies of integration. The conventional model of an expansive, managerial, patrimonial state resonates with Tiwanaku control over certain regions in the heartland, hinterlands, and periphery. Yet the overall portrait that emerges from recent archaeological research is far more complex. Increasing awareness of cultural and political diversity within and among Tiwanaku's hinterlands and enclaves encourages a more holistic interpretation of the south-central Andes during the Middle Horizon. Direct vertical complementarity via the establishment of colonies in distant regions was one of many strategies Tiwanaku employed to gain access to nonlocal lands, labor, resources, and goods. Yet while Tiwanaku elites came to dominate the south-central Andes politically and culturally, interactions, influences, and exchanges were to a significant degree mutual, multilocal, and interpenetrating.

During the Formative period, this world region had been the setting for multiple trajectories of local cultural development and interwoven, overlapping interaction circuits. A centralized state gradually emerged out of this diversified environmental and cultural matrix, but it never fully controlled the region. Rather the south-central Andes comprised multiple centers and polities linked by veritable highways of movement along which people, llamas, goods, and ideas traveled; not simply in one direction, from Tiwanaku outward, but reciprocally and in multiple directions. The region formed a discontinuous mosaic of Tiwanaku influence and control.

Taking a long-term and spatially broad geopolitical focus encourages us to consider the dynamic roles of Tiwanaku's prior and contemporary cultural developments. Complementing intensive farming systems in its heartland and enclaves, the many socioeconomic networks that converged on Tiwanaku remained at the foundation of state power. Such a convergence was the activity of elites, entrepreneurs, and nonelites both in local communities and polities as well as in the Tiwanaku heartland. Overall, and especially in the early Middle Horizon, Tiwanaku was an incorporative more than it was a transformative polity in which leaders simultaneously implemented multiple strategies of regional control and influence. Tiwanaku was not a contiguous block of imperial control as it is sometimes portrayed, and in most places it was more about local emulation and reciprocal interaction than it was about conquest.

Modes of state incorporation and influence were conditioned as much by local physical and sociopolitical conditions as they were by the specific resources Tiwanaku elites, traders, and consumers sought to acquire or control. We can define four board types of regions that correspond with different forms of interaction with Tiwanaku: directly controlled regions, peripheral enclaves (however incorporated or colonized), incorporated polities, and autonomous regions. Katari and the Puno Bay, with their waterlogged pampas and adjacent lake shores, were perhaps the most important directly controlled regions. Moquegua and Cochabamba are the largest known Tiwanaku enclaves, and along with Katari and Puno Bay, they share a common denominator: potential for intensive farming. In Katari and Puno Bay, farming involved high-altitude grains and tubers in extensive raised-field systems, and in Moquegua and Cochabamba, it centered on maize cultivation in vast irrigated pampas. It is not terribly surprising that Tiwanaku's key concern was food production, given the central role of food and drink in its political practices and state culture. In particular, maize would have been critical for elite-sponsored commensalism involving *chicha*. Nor is it surprising that Tiwanaku intensified production and regional control in these regions after AD 800, just as the roles of mass consumption and feasting intensified. Smaller enclaves such as Santiago de Huari and Querimita in the altiplano procured salt and desired raw mineral resources.

Incorporated semiautonomous polities and autonomous regions surrounded Tiwanaku's heartland and its strategic enclaves. Adjacent to the Tiwanaku heartland were the warmer *yungas*, south of Puno Bay were the

Juli-Pomata polities, southeast of Moquegua was Mizque, and south of Moquegua was Azapa. These regions were incorporated into or heavily influenced by Tiwanaku, and most appear to have been colonized by small groups from the core, but all retained some degree of political autonomy and regional identity in Tiwanaku's encompassing ambit. Autonomous regions and polities characterized areas such as the old Pukara heartland and the diverse polities on Tiwanaku's frontiers. Frontier polities such as Chiribaya, San Pedro de Atacama, and Icla increased in influence, wealth, and political power based in part on interaction with the Tiwanaku heartland and its dependencies and on their expanding roles as interaction nodes for multiple regions and polities.

As Browman and Kolata note, Tiwanaku elites likely administered some interaction with distant regions by patronizing or contracting particular caravan "companies" as well as establishing their own. Secure interaction was established by creating trustworthy kin (via marriage or proxy) and loyal kinlike relations with trading partners. Relations between Tiwanaku and its enclaves, incorporated polities, and frontier regions were reciprocal, as were interaction networks between those societies and more distant polities. Conducted via caravan highways, this interaction demanded a significant degree of "international security" across the south-central Andes and harmony among its constituent societies (Nuñez and Dillehay 1995). To be sure, warfare and piracy periodically occurred, as witnessed in the Juch'uypampa cave burials. Yet the long-term success of trade indicates that a *pax tiwanakota* characterized much of the Middle Horizon. This was critical to Tiwanaku's popularity, success, and longevity.

Rather than consider Tiwanaku a "weak" state with limited means, as has been done, such a fascinating case of past sociopolitical development should make us question our own presumptions about past states as uniformly agrarian, nationlike entities with singular goals, rigid boundaries, and uniform power over subjects or citizens. It encourages us to become aware that our own ideas are steeped in a nation-focused ideology. As we know living day to day in any country, nations are hardly as singular in aim, rigidly bounded, or culturally homogeneous as they are often characterized in conservative and populist rhetoric. Further, power relations are established as much through local internalization of and affective attachment to new or dominant ideals and moralities as they are through coercion. Consider the cultural "work ethic" that emerged in conjunction with capital-focused, industrial societies in eighteenth-century Europe (Weber 1930), and that continues to thrive in a transmogrified form today. Regularly going to work or school is to some degree coercive. Yet what truly supports postindustrial polities (along with their wealthy CEOs and high-paid university chancellors) is a potent sense of responsibility, return (financial or educational), and hope of long-term success. Beyond habit, it is this that drives us to get to the office or class-room every day. Power relations in Tiwanaku, especially early on in the Middle Horizon, were fostered less by elite heavy-handedness than they were by negotiated local acceptance, fostered by a prestigious state cul-ture, a compelling worldview, and a chance at worldly success or spiritual redemption.

As a pan-regional phenomenon, Tiwanaku was culturally diverse and ideologically syncretic; yet, it comprised a range of shared values and practices that defined a common state culture and political community. Across the south-central Andes, Tiwanaku material culture and ideolo-gies were transfigured and selectively adapted to enduring local identi-ties and ideologies. Just as no two Tiwanaku temples were alike, ritual practices and ceramic assemblages varied substantially among the vari-ous regions that formed the Tiwanaku state. Yet certain goods and typ-ical practices were shared among groups affiliated with or influenced by Tiwanaku. These included the increasing popularity of a psychotropic and medicinal cult that hinged on access to plants in warm valley zones, ritual specialists from the eastern *yungas* and elsewhere, and the produc-tion and distribution of "snuffing kits." While often considered distinctly Tiwanaku, ingesting mind-altering and curative substances were popular practices during the Late Formative and perhaps earlier in some regions. It was adapted and popularized, perhaps even proselytized, as part of Tiwanaku cultural influence. Often glossed as a "hallucinogenic cult," the drug cult also was about curative medicine. Thus, it involved a new and popular worldview regarding health and the human body and may well have centered on the notion of a healthy body as an ideal cycling of vital elements: most importantly blood, the material element of human life, and fat, the material element of human energy. Such a view is at the heart of a more recent Kallawaya worldview regarding the body and the mountain landscape they inhabit.

As central to Tiwanaku state culture was consumption and commen-salism, which hinged on a specific range of vessels for eating and drinking in quotidian and ceremonial settings. These appear across the Andes in a vast range of styles and designs, and in various ways adapted to local material culture and assemblages. At the center of such assemblages were drinking goblets, or *keros*. It was the *kero* that was most frequently emu-lated in local assemblages. Also, interestingly, it was the *kero* that differed so visibly and profoundly among peripheral Tiwanaku regions: consider the tanware *keros* of Lukurmata, narrow-base *challadors* of Cochabamba, the reduced blackware and "Coca-Cola glass" *keros* of Moquegua, and the gold *keros* of San Pedro de Atacama. Variable forms of the characteristic Tiwanaku drinking vessel were inextricably tied to regional and community identities.

*Kero*s facilitated the consumption of drinks that were essential to Tiwanaku culture and politics. Commensalism was a fundamental strategy for currying favor and drawing on labor, for building prestige and wealth, and for competing with rival individuals and groups. While conducted at multiple social scales across the south-central Andes, it was most intensive at Tiwanaku itself, especially during major events and calendrical feasts when people and caravans from far regions converged on the city. Quite literally, Tiwanaku was built on food and drink.

Like snuff tablets, *keros* facilitated consumption that induced an altered state of consciousness. Paring a snuff tablet and a *kero* in the hands of Tiwanaku's iconic ancestor-deities indicates that both were central to Tiwanaku culture and religion. Like ingesting herbal medicine, drinking *chicha* may have been promoted as an act that helped circulate vital bodily fluids, a notion held at the time of European contact (Gose 1996:8; Randall 1993). Drinking also was a highly spiritual act that forged a "memory path" to one's deceased relatives and ancestors, who were claimed to be descended from or linked to the great primordial and elite ancestors (Abercrombie 1998; Salazar-Soler 1993; Saignes 1993). Drinking thus fostered good health and social memory in moments of collective effervescence, thereby engendering a powerful, affective sense of community. State power was strengthened in such subtle but ultimately profound symbolic and spiritual domains.

Woven clothing and textiles were as central to Tiwanaku state culture. It is unfortunate that woven cloth fails to preserve in the altiplano, for as it is today in the Andes, woven clothing was most likely the single most effective and meaningful media for expressing personhood, social identity, and cultural affiliation in the Tiwanaku realm. Weaving technologies advanced considerably in the south-central Andes as Tiwanaku's power and influence increased. The great ancestors hewn in stone are decked out in elaborate woven clothing decorated with religious icons and calendrical notation. Like food and drink, woven cloth was central to Tiwanaku politics as a valuable emblem of status and affiliation that was given as a gift in return for loyalty to Tiwanaku's leaders and active participation in state activities such as farming, building, trading, or quarrying. Textiles had multiple symbolic connotations and political ends. Like cranial modification, wearing elaborately woven and decorated clothing was a manner of identifying and "beautifying" bodies. For feasts and ceremonies, women and men were decked out in colorful skirts or tunics that depicted Tiwanaku emblems and icons.

A fascinating avenue of inquiry is whether textile production was the domain of women, as it was for the Inca. The Inca established an institution centered on *aclla,* or specially selected women drawn from local populations who lived communally in *acllahuasi* in major imperial centers (Rowe 1946). *Aclla* tended the major shrines, they wove the most elaborate clothing for elites, and they cooked the food and brewed the beer that fueled the most important public feasts. Elite *aclla* were sometimes taken as secondary wives by the emperor, while others were gifted as wives to cement relations with local leaders and elites. *Aclla* offered women a complex network of roles and statuses in a state institution that simultaneously directed women's sexuality, reproduction, and labor toward state interests (Silverblatt 1987). Fascinating avenues of inquiry are whether women were the primary weavers and brewers in Tiwanaku, and how state-promoted gender relations and roles compared with those of the later Inca.

Identification with Tiwanaku and its global ideologies and moral codes was clearly compelling. Consumption was at the core of Tiwanaku state culture in knappable, comestible, potable, ingestible, wearable, and other goods. As important as elite-devised strategies and patronized interactions was consensual participation in Tiwanaku socioeconomic interactions and ceremonial practices and affective attachment to its predominant worldview and ideals. Elites and commoners alike in Tiwanaku and local centers forged and reproduced state-focused power relations. *To the extent that people inculcated and creatively transformed Tiwanaku practices, internalized and transfigured Tiwanaku ideals, and voluntarily or grudgingly worked for state projects, they were consuming the state.* The notable ubiquity of Tiwanaku valued goods and practices and the widespread participation of diverse societies in the state political economy indicate that Tiwanaku state culture was promoted not just by Tiwanaku leaders but by vast communities throughout the south-central Andes. Perhaps more than a "state" in a classical political sense, Tiwanaku was a prestigious and profoundly spiritual macrocommunity, and participation in its religious, economic, social, and political spheres fortified local wealth and standing. As a potentially volatile dynamic, state power resided in the widespread internalization of Tiwanaku state culture, which in turn emboldened local identity and power.

Throughout the Middle Horizon, sociopolitical conditions across the Andes were in flux. In particular, at the turn of the ninth century state culture and local conditions changed significantly in many regions. This shift is coincident with major changes in the Tiwanaku core that may be linked to the rise to power of a new regime or dynasty. It also appears coincident with a fundamental change in the broader geopolitical relations of

Tiwanaku and the state of Wari to the north. Quite likely, a major series of confrontations along contested areas of the Tiwanaku-Wari border played an important hand in the emergence of new conditions in the late Middle Horizon. Many regions, settlements, and productive systems witnessed an intensification of state activity, influence, and control. Elements of material culture such as feasting vessels were increasingly mass-produced as the intensity of feasting and drinking, and in particular elite-sponsored commensalism, magnified to meet intensified state production and control. Tiwanaku lords began to assert greater control over key resources and socioeconomic networks by developing transformative strategies of administration and intensifying resource appropriation. Mounting evidence points to the creation of a more tightly integrated and centralized political economy.

The trajectory of Tiwanaku's transformation indicates that change was not masterminded by elites. Though incited by historical circumstances, this shift emerged out of cumulative social interactions and cultural values and practices that had developed over many generations. The human agentive power behind this macrochange resided with nonelites as well as elites and with local as well as state leaders, even as conditions slowly began to favor the latter and as enduring etiquettes of social interaction and leadership were breached. Ultimately, the new sociopolitical conditions proved unstable.

7   Wari and Tiwanaku

Tiwanaku was one of many complex polities that thrived in the Andes during the Middle Horizon. Other centers of great religious influence or political hegemony that rose and fell during Tiwanaku's long history include Pachacamac on Peru's central coast, Pampa Grande on Peru's north coast, and Marcahuamachuco in the northern Peruvian highlands. Yet most significant for Andean cultural and political development and Tiwanaku's long history was Wari, centered in the Ayacucho Basin of south-central Peru.

Wari and Tiwanaku headed two autonomous states (Figure 7.1). Though the character of their relationship has been veiled in mystery, ongoing research in borderland regions such as Moquegua is now shedding light on their dynamic long-term interaction and mutual development. This research invites us to consider the dynamics of "peer-polity" interaction. Globally, cities and states often developed in dynamic interaction. Peer-polity interaction, meaning dynamic long-term relations of exchange, influence, alliance, and conflict among polities of similar organization and complexity, fostered state formation in many cases around the world. Tiwanaku and Wari affected each other's trajectory of political development and shaped each other's distinct cultural expressions, ideologies, and hegemonic strategies. Much as in nation-states today, but through very different processes, cultural identities and ideologies in Tiwanaku and Wari crystallized in relation to one another.

Interpreting Tiwanaku and Wari as autonomous polities was a long time in coming. On the basis of his research at Tiwanaku and Pachacamac, Max Uhle (1903) first defined a widespread pre-Inca Andean "style" that would later be termed the Middle Horizon. For many later archaeologists, this "Tiahuanaoicoid" style derived, whether by religious diffusion or conquest, from Tiwanaku. Only by the 1940s–1950s did archaeologists such as John Rowe (1956) and Rafael Larco Hoyle (1948) begin to consider Tiwanaku and Wari as separate phenomena, and Wari as the source of a distinct cultural style prevalent throughout Peru. Later archaeologists began to debate their interaction, and some

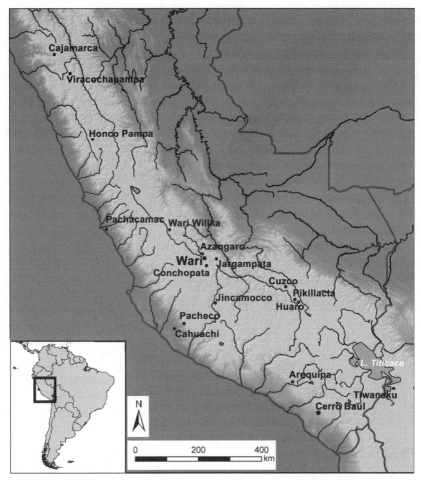

Figure 7.1 Map of the Central Andes showing important Wari sites
(base map by Steve Wernke).

interpretations, not surprisingly, followed national interests and research
agendas. Dorothy Menzel (1964, 1977), who first analyzed Wari ceramic
styles and defined a Wari chronology, considered Wari an expansive state
inspired by Tiwanaku's religious iconography and ideology. Peruvian
archaeologist Luis Lumbreras (1974, 2000) took this idea further. He
suggested that Wari pilgrims to Tiwanaku became zealot warriors, who
then proceeded to establish a despotic empire throughout the central
Andes by military force, "destroying any way of life different from theirs"
(Lumbreras 1974:165).

This interpretation inspired strong reactions among Bolivian archaeologists, who bristled at considering Tiwanaku a benign pilgrimage site and Wari a military empire. Carlos Ponce Sanginés (1981:84–85), in particular, countered that it was Tiwanaku that had expanded by military force and, in fact, had ultimately conquered Wari, which was then converted into an "architecturally inferior" regional center.

Hard-boiled nationalist rhetoric aside, by the end of the twentieth century, most Andeanists considered Tiwanaku and Wari distinct phenomena with concrete political agendas. Current interpretations of Wari vary widely and, much like interpretations of Tiwanaku, follow three broad intellectual lineages. Some consider religious ideology of fundamental importance to Wari expansion. Drawing an analogy with ancient Greece, Dan Shea (1969) argues that the Peruvian Middle Horizon was characterized not by imperial hegemony or religious expansion, but by a confederation of ceremonial centers centered at Pachacamac. Out of this confederation, he suggests, an overstretched and short-lived empire may have emerged. More recently, archaeologists have come to consider a cosmology focused on calendar cycles, water sources, sacred peaks, and ancestral forces fundamental to Wari state expansion (Anders 1986, 1991; Glowacki and Malpass 2003; T. L. Topic 1991). The dominant idea among Wari scholars is that Wari was a politically centralized, imperial state "that established political and economic sovereignty over vast regions and large populations" in what is today Peru (Schreiber 2001:92; also Isbell 1987; Isbell and McEwan 1991; Isbell and Schreiber 1978; Lumbreras 1974, 1981; McEwan 1991, 1996; Schreiber 1992). Others critically question evidence for political unity, and suggest that Wari was either a confederation of ethnic groups (J. R. Topic 1991; Topic and Topic 1992) or a network of autonomous centers connected by trade (Shady 1981, 1989; Shady and Ruiz 1979).

In this chapter, I examine Wari and Wari-Tiwanaku interaction in light of such divergent interpretations and perspectives. I describe Wari's political and cultural center in the Ayacucho Basin, followed by a brief discussion of characteristic Wari art and iconography. Next, I examine Wari state expansion, which remarkably like that of Tiwanaku, developed over two major phases and had inextricably interwoven political, economic, and ideological dimensions. Then I briefly examine the relation of Pachacamac and Wari, followed by a discussion of Wari and Tiwanaku interaction in the borderlands, and in particular Moquegua, southern Peru.

The City of Wari

Wari emerged in the Ayacucho basin of Peru, some 700 kilometers or a three-to-four-week trek (shorter if by lake) from Tiwanaku (Figure 7.2a).

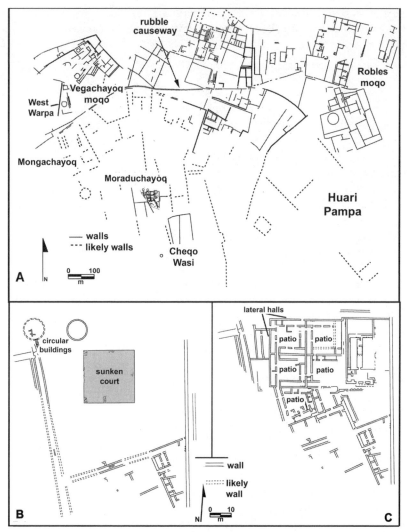

Figure 7.2 Maps of (a) the Wari site and the Moraduchayoq sector during (b) Wari 1 and (c) Wari 2 (adapted from Isbell, Brewster-Wray, and Spickard 1991).

Like that of Tiwanaku, Wari's rise to power and fame is not predictable from its location. Wari covered some 3–5 square kilometers of a vast sloping ridge in the Peruvian sierra between two small tertiary tributaries of the Mantaro River, ranging in altitude from 2,500 to 3,000 meters. It was situated near the boundary of the Huamanga and Huanta drainage basins, which may have afforded a politically strategic edge in the coalescence of the early polity (Isbell, Brewster-Wray, and Spickard 1991:20).

Early Wari Urbanism

Wari urban expansion remains little studied, in part because Ayacucho was home to the Shining Path insurgence during the 1980s and 1990s, and because the site has been ravaged for centuries by farmers and looters. The area had been inhabited since the Early Horizon, contemporary with the Lake Titicaca Basin's Middle Formative, and occupation intensified during the subsequent Early Intermediate Period, when several modest communities occupied the ridge (Isbell 1997b). We still know little of Warpa, the cultural complex that occupied the region preceding Wari. Warpa settlement networks, much like Late Formative networks in the Lake Titicaca Basin, were nonnucleated and focused on several political-ritual centers (Leoni 2004; Lumbreras 1974, 1981; Ochatoma and Cabrera 2002). They formed multiple interconnected communities or polities that shared similar styles of material culture and activities. In AD 400–600, the settlement of West Warpa became the most important on the ridge. Its architecture included unusual circular structures and rectangular enclosures built in a style that foreshadowed characteristic Wari patterns, including high, thick walls of fieldstone set in deep trenches dug into bedrock. Ceramic style suggests that Warpa communities interacted with the coastal Nasca region to the southwest and possibly the Lake Titicaca Basin to the southeast (Ochatoma and Cabrera 2002:244).

Sometime after AD 600, the settlement of Wari emerged out of this cultural matrix. In a sector known as Moraduchayoq, a stone-faced sunken court may have been first built long before this time (Figure 7.2b; Brewster-Wray 1990; Isbell 1997b). The walls of the temple consisted of well-carved blocks of beige volcanic tuff that, judging from trace pigment, had been painted red. The stones had been finely selected, for they contained "none of the harder and darker particles that are visible in most of the bedrock exposures" near the site (Isbell, Brewster-Wray, and Spickard 1991:29). The courtyard was periodically renovated and eventually capped with an elaborate floor of irregularly shaped tuff blocks. Channels built into walls and floors drained rainwater and perhaps other liquids during communal gatherings and ceremonies. The court appears similar to sunken temples in the Lake Titicaca Basin, yet is distinctive in construction and in form. For example, at 24.11 meters to a side it formed a perfect square. Ultimately, it was enclosed in an extensive compound. Overall spatial organization bespeaks a profound interest in efficiency, regularity, and enclosure in space and society.

Located nearer the old West Warpa community was the temple complex of Veqachayoq Moqo (Bragayrac 1991; Gonzales et al. 1996). By AD 400, it housed a westward-facing U-shaped complex of terraced platforms surrounding a central courtyard. This was an ancient form for ceremonial complexes of the central Andean region (Schreiber 2001:81). The complex was transformed after AD 600, once it was incorporated into the expanding urban center. A north-facing D-shaped structure with a fine plaster floor was built in the courtyard and smaller D-shaped structures were built on the platforms (Bragayrac 1991). Such structures characterized Wari architecture at many other sites, and at Conchopata, a D-shaped room yielded associated offerings and human trophy heads, suggesting that they served as intimate spaces for ritual sacrifice (Cook 2001; Tung and Cook 2006). The main Vegachayoq Moqo structure may have housed bench-like seating for observers to witness the bloody rituals conducted therein (Tiffiny Tung pers. comm., March 2007). During the ninth or tenth century, the entire ceremonial complex was enclosed in a compound with two doorways. Fitted into the wall were slab-covered niches, reminiscent of the niches built into the Putuni platform at Tiwanaku. These later housed multiple human burials, but their original purpose is unclear. Between the doorways, in the street that passed outside of the precinct, was a small multicolored building that received offerings dedicated to the temple inside (Bragayrac 1991:71).

Two precincts in Wari yielded evidence for mortuary rituals involving elite subterranean masonry burials. While reminiscent of the masonry burial chamber in Tiwanaku (Figure 4.11b), those in Wari formed elaborate multistoried complexes. Each precinct yielded stone effigy sculptures that apparently served as spirit burial guardians (Benevides 1991:63; Bragayrac 1991:80; Cook 2001; Tung and Cook 2006). Southeast of Moraduchayoq was Cheqo Wasi, an architectural complex that included a rectangular and a D-shaped structure, both of which housed several subterranean tombs (Benevides 1991). One especially well-crafted tomb in the D-shaped structure incorporated an elaborate niche and may have housed the remains of one or more elite individuals. Now completely looted, the tombs were completely lined with impeccably carved and fitted stones of volcanic tuff much like the walls of the sunken temple in Moraduchayoq.

Subterranean tombs in Mongachayoq, south of the temple of Vegachayoq Moqo, were even more elaborate and may have housed the remains of a later elite group (Figure 7.3; Perez 2000). Long subterranean galleries supported by massive cut stone lintels led toward a central, multistoried mausoleum that reached more than 20 meters below the current surface. A four-chamber upper level provided access to a deeper second level that contained twenty-one stone-lined chambers. Vertical shafts provided access to the deeper third level, the plan of which, remarkably, portrayed a profile llama, and more specifically the abstract, geometrical llamas characteristic of Wari textiles (Perez 2000; Stone-Miller 2002:140).

If the two mausoleums held the remains of elite lineages, each layer may correspond with a specific generation of ancestors. Remnant prestige items from Cheqo Wasi and Mongachayoq included obsidian, turquoise, copper jewelry, elaborate figurines, and worked Spondylus shell from the coast. The deepest tombs in each case were sealed circular cists that may have housed a lineage founder. The ceiling slabs of the chambers were perforated (and in Cheqo Wasi connected to interior channels) to facilitate ancestor veneration and mortuary rites, through practices such as periodic removal of bundled remains, vocal orations and prayers, or offering libations (Cook 2001).

Late Wari Urbanism

Late in the eighth century the Moraduchayoq sunken court was ritually interred and covered with several contiguous patio groups in a major moment of urban renewal (Figure 7.2c). This so-called Moraduchayoq compound was not built at once but in stages, as manifested in the differing orientations of the patio groups. If D-shaped structures characterized Wari ceremonial space, patio groups consisting of a central court surrounded by lateral halls characterized high-status Wari residential space. Patios were sites of communal activities such as consumption and feasting (Brewster-Wray 1990:393–395; Cook and Glowacki 2003). The lateral halls served as domestic spaces and to prepare food, ferment *chicha*, and store serving wares and other items. Many halls were multistoried, and upper stories were supported by beams lashed to stone corbels (Brewster-Wray 1990; Isbell, Brewster-Wray, and Spickard 1991). Slab and clay-lined cists were sealed under the floors of patios and galleries. Cached artifacts included prestige items such as carved Spondylus shell, turquoise beads, and human remains, including long bones and curated skulls from secondary interments or mortuary bundles. It is unclear whether the cists were buried offerings or "deposit boxes" for safekeeping valued jewelry and ancestral fetish remains.

Changes in spatial organization and architectural priorities at Wari and other Wari affiliated sites around the 8th to 9th century AD (Isbell and Cook 2002; Isbell, Brewster-Wray, and Spickard 1991; Tung 2003; Williams 2001) reflect profound changes in the polity as a whole. The early sunken court and open spaces reminiscent of Lake Titicaca Basin monumental architecture were covered to make way for an expanding

Figure 7.3 The Mongachayoq mortuary complex and the llama-shaped plan of its galleries (photo courtesy of Danielle Kurin, inset adapted from Pérez 2000).

urban grid composed of enclosed, repeating, modular compounds with repetitive patio groups ("orthogonal cellular architecture," Isbell and McEwan 1991) and D-shaped temples. Unlike Tiwanaku, walls were high (up to 12 meters) to support multiple stories, and they consisted of readily available fieldstones set in clay mortar on thick, rubble-filled foundations. Compounds were lined with narrow streets and served by elaborate stone-lined subterranean drainage networks.

Although modular organization also characterized Tiwanaku, Wari ceremonial space and monumental structures were tightly enclosed. Access to any compound was restricted to a few strategically placed entryways. Further, spatial orientations at Wari varied considerably, in sharp distinction to the uniform order that characterized Tiwanaku over centuries of construction. As Isbell and colleagues note (1991:49), "[Wari] developed opportunistically," and much of the variability arose as new structures were accommodated to extant built landscapes. Thus, it seems that Wari cultural values and religious ideology were now very distinct from those of Tiwanaku. This is punctuated at Wari by the near-absence of monolithic personages (though see Lumbreras 1974:164), ceremonial portals, and stairways ascending monuments. Tiwanaku facilitated pilgrimage, popular religious experience, and movement through ritual spaces in a way that Wari decidedly did not (Conklin 1991; Schreiber 1992:280, 2001).

By AD 800, few cities could be as different as were Tiwanaku and Wari. If Tiwanaku drew people in, Wari now sought to keep many out.

Wari Art and Iconography

Despite differences in urban architecture and spatial form, Wari and Tiwanaku shared certain iconographic and stylistic elements on ceramic vessels and woven textiles. It was based largely on smashed vessels from Wari-affiliated offering deposits at Pacheco in the Nasca Valley, and Conchopata in the Wari heartland of Ayacucho, that archaeologists considered Wari a Tiwanaku-inspired phenomenon (Lumbreras 1974; Menzel 1964). Recent archaeological research at Conchopata supports the influence of Tiwanaku religious ideology but presents an alternative view regarding its character and timing (Isbell and Cook 2002; Ochatoma and Cabrera 2002). Overall, Wari ceramic style was distinctive and drew heavily on preexisting Warpa and Nasca styles (Menzel 1964). Vessels included a variety of bowls, drinking "tumblers," cups, bottlelike jars, face-neck jars, and storage and fermentation *tinajas* that, though similar to specific Tiwanaku serving and storage forms in some cases, formed a distinctive stylistic assemblage for ritual consumption. Polychrome decoration was characteristically outlined in black, often floral or curvilinear, and rendered in broad strokes that afford a "cartoonlike" quality to iconographic motifs (Cook 1994). Iconography included abstract and naturalistic motifs not found or emphasized on Tiwanaku pottery, including nested chevrons, symmetrical rayed designs, a "fleur-de-lis," as well as sprouting crops (maize, tubers, and quinoa), camelids, and humans in a variety of roles (herders, warriors, ritualists, and leaders). Wari motifs included abstract images of the hallucinogenic plant *vilca* (*Anadenanthera colubrina*), which also appears in Tiwanaku iconography (Knobloch 2000). Many large Wari jars and urns from early offering deposits depict Nasca-derived iconography, including lush edible vegetation in Pacheco and mythical sacrificers in Conchopata (Cook 2001; Isbell 1977:49; Isbell and Cook 2002). Pots depicting crops at Pacheco also depict circular storage structures where the crops were presumably stored. At Conchopata, Anita Cook (2001) has identified images of Nasca-like ritual sacrificers associated with icons of Wari D-shaped buildings, which in practice were spaces for animal and ceramic offerings and, quite possibly, human sacrifice (Tung and Cook 2006).

If early Wari serving vessels maintained a "visual affinity" with Nasca pottery (Stone-Miller 2002:151), many vessels from later offering deposits at Conchopata depicted motifs and themes reminiscent of Tiwanaku. The deposits included elaborate vessels intentionally smashed and then either buried in pits or strewn across the floor of a structure upon its

A   B

Figure 7.4 Massive Wari ceramic feasting vessels: (a) "face-neck"
jar depicting abstract local designs and (b) an urn depicting avian
imagery (a, adapted from Isbell and Cook 2002; b, photo courtesy of
Jose Ochatoma).

ritual interment (Isbell and Cook 2002). As at Tiwanaku, buildings were
conceived as powerful "living" entities that partook of the spirit of their
affiliated individuals or communities. Most common in the deposits were
two types of massive vessels; human effigy jars and open basins, or "urns"
(Figure 7.4). Iconography reminiscent of that common in the Lake Titicaca basin was most commonly and dramatically rendered on these "oversize" vessels (Cook 1994; Isbell and Cook 2002). Icons included depictions of a frontal deity with rayed headdress, in some cases with a full
body holding staffs. On one effigy jar excavated in 1977, profile attendants reminiscent of those adorning the Sun Portal at Tiwanaku flank
the figure. Profile attendants also appeared in a variety of manifestations:
genuflecting or flying as they did in Tiwanaku, floating with back feathers
as they did in Pachacamac, and on the 1977 jar, sporting a unique, triangular head. An array of icons in these depictions – feathers, staffs, trophy
heads, feline and avian heads – closely emulated Titicaca Basin iconography. In that these massive vessels served communal rites and feasts,
Tiwanaku-inspired myths were invoked in such contexts and perhaps
again in their ritualized destruction. Yet their distinct stylistic rendering, their association with Wari motifs, and of course their depiction on
unique Wari feasting vessels emphasize their adaptation to Wari mythical
themes, ideals, and social-ritual practices.

Further, many vessels from such contexts depict Wari rather than
Tiwanaku-affiliated iconography (Isbell and Cook 2002). Known offering

deposits predating AD 700 consist almost entirely of vessels with local designs and iconography. These include basins depicting a succession of decorated elite heads or a procession of warriors kneeling in reed boats that sail across either Lake Titicaca, the Pacific coast, or a mythical sea. Tiwanaku-related iconography seems to have appeared later, after AD 700, and it was largely restricted to specific elite-oriented ceremonial contexts (Williams 2001). Thus, just as Wari was emerging as an expansive state, local elites and their attached specialists, in a bid to promote their own legitimacy, began to adapt mythical imagery and religious ideals with a long history of development in the Lake Titicaca basin to an extant state culture.

As in Tiwanaku, Wari weavers – most likely women – excelled in producing incredibly elaborate and symbolically rich loom-made garments and tapestries of cotton and wool. As William Conklin points out, it is difficult to distinguish Wari and Tiwanaku textiles (2004b). In both, polychrome iconography is formatted as discrete self-contained blocks (yet Tiwanaku textiles downplayed the blocky design to emphasize iconographic themes and icons that often alternate in red and blue). The Wari "Fire Tapestry" from the south coast of Peru depicts a repeating mythical scene in which two humans make fire surrounded by winged flying attendants and repeating images of the head of the frontal staff deity (Figure 7.5). Its themes and overall configuration approximate Tiwanaku weaving style. Many fine Wari textiles tend toward profound abstraction and striking modular repetition, with icons ordered according to a rigid geometric structure (Stone-Miller 2002:144). Pastoral concerns are favored themes on large tapestries, on which camelids are frequently depicted as pregnant or giving birth. On tunics, Tiwanaku-related themes such as winged attendants and staff deities were common, but weavers transformed and abstracted the images to the point that they are nearly illegible to all but those "in the know." Winged attendants on the well-known Lima Tunic, for example, are so brilliantly abstracted that one catches but glimpses of a wing or a split eye. Much like high Modernist art at the end of the twentieth century, Wari elite textiles embodied exclusive knowledge and esoteric aesthetics.

Turquoise figurines of dressed individuals buried in offering caches at Pikillacta indicate that clothing expressed social identity, role, and status (Cook 1992; McEwan 1991, 1996). Dressed images wrought in hammered gold and silver indicate that woven tunics aggrandized their high-status wearers, affording the human body a grand, blocky shape that appears to have been a powerful Wari ideal. Idiosyncratic elements in many cases ruptured the repetition of an otherwise repetitive tunic, such as an abstract face hidden among dozens of step motifs, or the singular use a specific color for a repeating motif (Stone-Miller 2002; Stone-Miller

Figure 7.5 Fine Wari tapestry in a detail of the Fire Textile (adapted from Conklin 2004b).

and McEwan 1990/1991). These anomalies likely served as creative "signatures" that identified specific weavers (or weaving groups) and expressed a subdominant message of authorship and uniqueness in an otherwise modular and rigorously ordered design.

Remarkably, the Wari appear to have employed *quipus*, or string recording and accounting devices (Conklin 1982). In the Inca empire, *quipus* were "read" by highly regarded specialists known as *quipucamayoq*. They consisted of a primary chord from which series' of pendant chords were hung, along which sequences of dyed colors and knots encoded intricate quantitative and other information (Ascher and Ascher 1981; Urton 2003). The "wrapped *quipus*" considered to derive from Wari-affiliated burial contexts are small and different in detail from later *quipus* (Conklin 1982). Yet several examples from one secure Wari context in the Nasca region suggests that this unique and quintessentially Andean alternative to writing had a history that predated Inca hegemony by more than a half-millennium.

Expansion in Wari 1

One thing certain about Wari expansion and interregional influence is that it was different from that of Tiwanaku in scope and in strategy. Wari imperialism, like that of Tiwanaku, was diversified and dynamic. It included cultural influence, hegemonic authority, and direct political control in discrete geographical pockets (Schreiber 1992). As in Tiwanaku, Wari expansion was as motivated by a new, integrative cosmological vision as it was concerned with controlling or integrating local productive landscapes, valued natural resources, and regional trade networks (Anders 1986; Glowacki and Malpass 2003). Wari statecraft like that of Tiwanaku involved new and widely poplar ritual practices, including human sacrifice, offerings of conspicuous ritual consumption, elaborate mortuary rites (Cook 2001; Isbell 1997b; Ochatoma and Cabrera 2002; Tung and Cook 2006; Tung 2007), communal consumption, and elite-sponsored feasting (Goldstein and Quispe 2004; Jennings 2004; Nash 2002; Nash and Williams 2004). Yet Wari influence was geographically vaster than that of Tiwanaku (Isbell 2004a; Schreiber 1992, 2001). It extended as far north as Cajamarca some 800 kilometers from Ayacucho, beyond the Lucre Basin to the southeast, and to the Moquegua region further southwest. By AD 800, an arc stretching from Moquegua through southern Arequipa to the La Raya pass of the Vilcanota range defined the border zone between the two states.

In many respects, Wari's style of statecraft was also distinct from that of Tiwanaku. It emphasized great visibility in and surveillance over local regions in the establishment of regional centers. Many such centers were very different from Tiwanaku regional centers in that they formed coherently planned, rigidly organized, and uniformly imposed settlements or "enclosures."

Wari regional settlement in the Ayacucho heartland yields intersecting patterns of continuity and change. Wari populations respected prior Warpa ritual traditions. Warpa ritual-political centers maintained plazas and circular structures for ceremonies and offerings (Isbell, Brewster-Wray, and Spickard 1991; Leoni 2004). At the Warpa center of Ñawimpukyo, a ceremonial plaza perched atop a hill remained virtually unaltered as nearby residential sectors were covered and renovated following Wari reorganization. Urban expansion involved nucleation at Wari and at several other settlements just as many smaller sites disappeared. This "vacuum effect" contrasted sharply with the Tiwanaku core, where settlement density intensified across the heartland – in hamlets, villages, towns, and cities – as settlement and society stratified. No conspicuous settlement hierarchy developed in Ayacucho, where the number of secondary towns was greater than that of smaller villages and hamlets (Isbell and Schreiber 1978).

The local centers of Ñawimpukyo, Aqo Wayqo (Ochatoma and Cabrera 2001), Tunasniyuq (Lumbreras 1974:162), and Muyu Urqo yield diagnostic evidence for everyday activities and local ritual practices. These

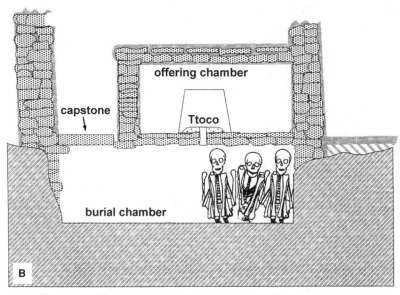

Figure 7.6 Key structures at Conchopata: (a) D-shaped structure and (b) rendering of an elaborate tomb (a, courtesy of Tiffiny Tung; b, adapted from Isbell and Cook 2002).

settlements comprised densely packed and agglutinated residential complexes, and important centers such as Ñawimpukyio incorporated D-shaped buildings and open ceremonial plazas. Mortuary chambers and cist burials for ancestor veneration and ritual offerings (of cached vessels, smashed pottery, camelids or guinea pigs (*cuyes*), and exotic objects such as Spondylus shell and turquoise) point to characteristic Wari practices in rural residential life.

The most important settlement in Ayacucho after Wari, and located some 12 kilometers from Wari in the Huamanga basin, was Conchopata. At its apogee, Conchopata covered 30–40 hectares and housed a community of pottery specialists (Lumbreras 1974; Pozzi-Escot 1991). The center incorporated at least two patio groups associated with elite activities and communal consumption, surrounded by agglutinated structures for residence and storage (Blacker 2001; Isbell and Cook 2002; Ketteman 2002). As noted, D-shaped and other buildings were sites for dramatic offerings of "ritually killed" oversized urns and human effigy jars (Figure 7.6a). The scale of such offerings at Conchopata marked the site as a distinct and particularly important Wari regional center. Some of the vessels depicted human decapitation and sacrifice (Cook 2001), practices that likely took place in the same ceremonial buildings. On the floor of one circular and one D-shaped building, human trophy heads were smashed and burned (Text Box 7.1; Tung 2003). The crania were perforated on the apex to be hung as macabre ornaments of conquest and sacrifice. Nearly one-fourth of the heads represented children between three to six years old (Tung 2007). Cut marks on the crania and mandibles indicate that at least some of the trophy head individuals had been defleshed while still fresh (Tung 2003).

Some of Conchopata's potters came to form a cadre of local Wari elite who adopted and appropriated state culture to local ends (Tung and Cook 2006). Associated with residential structures were elaborate burial vaults and cist tombs with perforated ceilings that emulated Wari's multistoried, stone-lined mausoleums (Figure 7.6b; Isbell 2000, 2004a; Isbell and Cook 2002). The burial chambers included elaborate offerings: blackware human effigy jars, copper *tupu* pins for securing woven mantles, and Spondylus and turquoise jewelry. Significantly, most of the interred adult individuals were women (Tung 2003). In some cases, a single vault held multiple female individuals that perhaps had been interred sequentially, each upon her death. Based on this data, Tiffiny Tung (2003) suggests that males may have died while away on military or administrative campaigns, while William Isbell suggests that it reflects royal polygyny (2004b). In light of the settlement's distinctive economic status and ritual practices, it may also be that women enjoyed particularly high status in Conchopata and were buried together as kin (Tung and Cook 2006). Quite possibly, some women were master ceramicists in the Wari heartland and so were afforded special treatment in local mortuary rituals.

Box 7.1 Trophy Heads and a Local Wari Cult

Few aspects of Andean culture are more intriguing than the ancient, deeply rooted "trophy head cult." The term refers to the special treatment and cultural manipulation of human heads, whether they represented ancestral relics, "coups" hunted in raids, or body parts of captives taken in ritual battle. Art depicting trophy heads was an enduring tradition in many Andean cultures, and special curation of disembodied heads is known as early as 1300–1100 BC from the Peruvian coast. In artistic depiction and ritual practice, it was a key element of Andean culture for some communities during the Middle Horizon.

The depiction of trophy heads is a common iconographic theme on Tiwanaku and Wari stone, ceramic, and woven media. Staff deities, their human impersonators, and their profile attendants are frequently portrayed holding a trophy head by the hair or a cord in one hand and an axe or a staff in the other. In Tiwanaku, trophy heads are not yet known, at least in the strict sense of skulls that were defleshed, drilled, and dangled for display after a person's decapitation. However, one offering on the Akapana at Tiwanaku alludes to a practice involving the ritual manipulation of disembodied heads. Here, archaeologists located a group of skulls that had been separated from their bodies after death and placed together on the structure's basal terrace (Manzanilla and Woodard 1990).

Obtaining, displaying, and destroying human heads were significant aspects of ongoing ritual practice at the Wari site of Conchopata (Ochatoma and Cabrera 2002; Tung and Cook 2006). Recent excavations in a circular ceremonial structure (EA143) revealed at least twenty-one trophy heads and excavations in a D-shaped structure (EA 72) revealed at least ten (Tung 2003, 2007). Tiffiny Tung's bioarchaeological research offers intriguing results. In both contexts, the heads had been smashed, burned, and left as clusters on the floors of the structures. Most derived from adult males, but nearly a quarter of the skulls represented children. Their intricate and standardized preparation points to the existence of ritual specialists who transformed the heads into sacred objects. In most cases, the top of the skull had been perforated so the skull could be hung with the face forward, in anatomical position. In some cases, constituent bones such as the occipital (back of the skull) and the mandible (lower jaw) were perforated to be worn or handled as isolated trophies of their own. The iconography of a massive urn, one of several smashed on the floor of the D-shaped structure, indicates that leaders or warriors wore the objects as macabre pectoral ornaments (Ochatoma and Cabrera 2002).

Tung's findings raise intriguing questions: Where did the individuals come from? Strontium isotope analyses indicate that at least three-fifths of the adult skulls were from nonlocal individuals, who possibly had been taken as captives (Tung and Knudson 2006). Do the skulls of children represent the ritual sacrifice of kids from the local community? Perhaps, yet it is likely that if Conchopata warriors were raiding other towns or regions, women *and* children could also have served as trophies of conquest, symbolizing the subjugation of that community.

Taking, producing, and displaying trophy heads was a recurring aspect of Andean culture during the Middle Horizon, but not at all times and places. No trophy heads are yet known from the cities of Wari or Tiwanaku. In the Wari heartland, the ritualized production and "interment" of trophy heads appears, to date, specific to the site of Conchopata. It was a local ritual practice that thrived alongside many others during the Middle Horizon, and one that may have been specific to particular communities.

Wari imperial expansion involved the intensification of sierra farming in the rugged central Andean mountains (Hyslop 1984; Schreiber 1992, 2001). Irrigated hillslope terracing became a signature Wari productive enterprise just as raised-field farming did for Tiwanaku (Figure 7.7). Because the Andean sierra varies more widely in environmental range and altitude than the altiplano, more diverse crops can be cultivated, including tubers, *quinoa, tarwi,* and, at lower altitudes, maize. Terracing in many Wari-occupied regions was designed to facilitate intensive maize cultivation (Schreiber 1992). In the sierra, where slopes are steeper in general than those in the altiplano, stone retaining walls absorb and retain more solar energy than soil, and more effectively so the steeper are the terraces (Donkin 1979; Schreiber 1992:131). Thus, analogous to raised fields, they form an artificial environment that increases average temperatures, thereby increasing crop growth rates while reducing risk of frost. Notably, many regions with Wari provincial centers were located precisely near the natural altitudinal boundary between maize and tuber cultivation (~3,000 meters). Wari terrace systems here essentially raised the upper limit of maize cultivation from ~2,900 to perhaps 3,300 meters, and possibly higher (Schreiber 1992:149).

Because the Inca appropriated this ancient productive technique and extended it across the Andes during the fourteenth and fifteenth centuries, the precise scale and character of Wari terracing still remains unclear. In lower valleys (1,000–3,000 meters) to the southwest such as Beringa and Moquegua, Wari settlements and farming systems facilitated

Figure 7.7 Terraced mountain slopes in the Central Andes.

intensification in other plant foods, including peanuts, manioc, semitropical fruits such as pacay and lúcuma, squash, beans, and, crucially, *molle* berries (Goldstein and Quispe 2004; Tung 2003). Both maize and *molle* were fermented to make *chicha* for social events at Wari settlements. In addition, coca and psychotropic substances such as *vilca* were obtained from hot valley zones.

Along with the establishment of a centralized interaction network and intensified farming systems went road networks linking strategic settlements and regions. As historical documentation indicates, to integrate Tawantinsuyu, Inca leaders largely extended and integrated roads that had been built during the Middle Horizon and perhaps earlier. In fact, archaeologists have discovered many Wari sites by retracing "Inca" roads (Schreiber 2001:82). In some cases, Wari roads clearly facilitated effective movement of people and goods between settlements and intensive farming systems (Schreiber 1992). Road networks promoted state integration and coordinated production, and as an unforeseen consequence, vibrant "extra-imperial" interaction and trade among local Andean communities.

In Wari 1, many societies in the central Andes either were heavily influenced by Wari or came under its hegemony. Of critical strategic importance was the Lucre Basin southeast of Cuzco, a core area of the later Inca state that lies en route to Lake Titicaca. Up through the early Middle Horizon, local inhabitants established vibrant trade relations with societies in the Titicaca Basin (McEwan, Chatfield, and Gibaja 2002:292). Sites yield incised ritual burners with affinities to Pukara, Tiwanaku-related ceramic wares (Bauer and Jones 2003; K. L. M. Chávez 1985), and obsidian flakes and arrow points from the Alca source to the southwest (Burger, Chávez, and Chávez 2000). These relations ended abruptly at about AD 650 just as interaction with Ayacucho intensified dramatically. For example, most local obsidian now derived from typical Wari rather than Tiwanaku sources. By all accounts, Lucre was now under Wari regional hegemony.

During this phase, the massive site of Huaro served as the primary Wari provincial center in the region (Glowacki 2002). The site incorporated elaborate ceremonial complexes and extensive residential sectors that meshed Wari and local architectural styles. Qoripata served as Huaro's elite residence and administrative center. Its architecture was orthogonal and densely packed like that of Wari and Conchopata, with plastered walls and slate floors of thick fieldstone masonry. Local elites received visitors and hosted feasts in its central patio group. The precinct also incorporated a canalized water fountain reminiscent of those found in later Inca royal estates around Cuzco, and thus may represent the beginning of an enduring "royal" tradition. Two high-status individuals were buried under the complex near an offering of snuff implements, each with elaborate vessels, copper *tupu* pins, and carved weaving tools, and each an adult women (Glowacki 2002:275). Coupled with evidence from Conchopata, these patterns reinforce the critical role of women in Wari society and suggest that, much like later Inca *aclla*, some women may have achieved high status and great wealth through state-exalted activities of weaving, brewing, and cooking.

Toward the end of the seventh century, Wari architects initiated work on the massive enclosure of Pikillacta (3,250 meters) some 17 kilometers to the northwest (Figure 7.8). Wari sites occupied each of the five primary passes into the basin and road networks linked local Wari sites to one another, to local terrace systems, and to major highways leading out of the basin (McEwan 1991). Pikillacta was one of several regional Wari centers in the Andean highlands that took the idea of a highly-ordered, modular, imposed built environment to unprecedented limits. The entire complex was planned and built as "a piece" over rugged sierra landscape, its walls rising and falling with local topography and stone outcrops (Figure 7.9a). Flanking a central rectangular compound of fieldstone masonry were two open, segmented compounds that may have served as massive corrals for camelid herds (McEwan 1996). The central

Figure 7.8 The Lucre Basin: Pikillacta is on the low plateau in the center of the photograph (photo by Nicole Couture).

compound consisted of four conjoined sectors, at least two of which, much like Tiwanaku monumental constructions, were never finished. The north sector consisted of relatively large, repetitive open enclosures that may have stored crops. The west sector contained over five hundred cramped rooms that apparently housed temporary laborers or troops (McEwan 1991). The unfinished south sector incorporated a massive plaza that may have served monumental state-sponsored ceremonies and feasts (Stone-Miller 2002). Yet the earliest sector, in the center, formed the ritual and political heart of the settlement. It incorporated two intricate patio groups for activities such as feasting, each attached to large multistoried niched halls with rounded corners (Figure 7.9b; McEwan and Couture 2005). Niched halls were finished with a bright, pinkish-white gypsum plaster, and sealed in symmetrically-aligned pits under their floors were offerings of turquoise effigy figurines, Spondylus adornments, human and faunal remains (*cuy* and llama), and copper *tupu* pins (McEwan 1996). The large niches in these halls, Gordon McEwan suspects (1998), may have provided periodic ritual access to the bundled remains of deceased individuals.

Remarkably, a single, easily policed, labyrinthine corridor provided entry into the massive compound. A second long corridor, to the west, led directly toward the large plaza. Interior spaces were regularly cleaned and the refuse dumped in extensive middens just outside of the main entrance (McEwan 1996). Such regular activities emphasize the coordinated and controlled character of everyday practices, just as the spatial order of Pikillacta, despite internal variability (Stone-Miller 2002), communicated exclusion, modular repetition, and order. Other settlements in the region maintained local characteristics of spatial organization and material culture. A built landscape of highly ordered spaces and practices, Pikillacta most likely temporarily housed local populations from those settlements – for farming, herding, food processing, and perhaps war – as a rotating corveé similar to the later Inca *mit'a* system (Rowe 1946). In return for local service, temporary workers may have periodically gathered for lively state-choreographed feasts, theaters, and ceremonies in the southern plaza.

As strategic for Wari expansion and regional influence were routes leading southwest toward warmer valleys and coastal regions. A strategic region en route to these valleys, and most notably the Nasca region, was the rugged Sondondo Valley (at 3,350 meters), where the small enclosure of Jincomocco was first built at the end of the eighth century (Schreiber 1987, 1992). Helaine Silverman notes that "Wari either conquered or strongly influenced the Nasca people of the south coast of Peru" (Silverman and Proulx 2002:272). In Wari 1, intensive highland-coastal interaction gave rise to new Wari-like mortuary and ritual practices. Many cemeteries now included multiple interments, and their looted surfaces are scattered with Wari-style or Wari-Nasca "hybrid" vessels (Silverman and Proulx 2002:276). In the lower Ica Valley, Anita Cook (1992:357) located cemeteries with mummy bundles wrapped in Wari textiles and capped with effigy heads and face masks. Local ceremonial buildings were now ritually interred and associated offerings now incorporated smashed vessels. At the Nasca regional center of Cahuachi, an early temple was carefully covered with sherds of smashed vessels (Silverman and Proulx 2002:269).

More dramatic were massive offerings of smashed Wari-style pottery at Pacheco, 7 kilometers away. In 1927, Julio Tello recovered nearly 3 tons of broken vessels here, including twenty-three oversize jars and urns. As at Conchopata, some vessels combined Nasca and Tiwanaku with Wari-style iconography, but uncharacteristic of Tiwanaku iconography, many vessels from Pacheco depicted highland crop plants (Menzel 1964). The pottery-making center of Maymi to the north also yielded offering pits filled with deliberately smashed vessels (Anders 1990; Anders et al. 1998). Attesting the creative fusion of highland-coastal material culture and ideologies, vessels here included exquisite, innovative local hybrid styles.

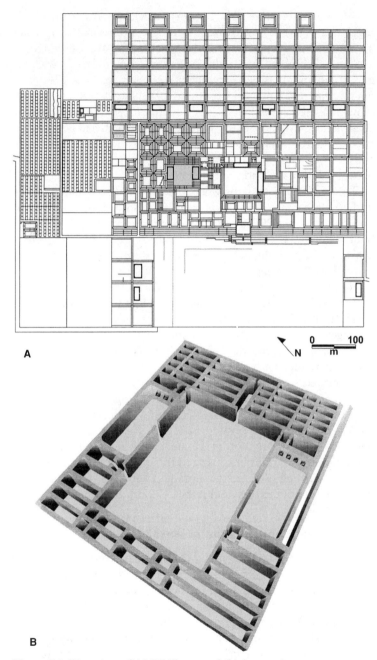

Figure 7.9 Plan view of (a) Pikillacta and (b) isometric
reconstruction of a patio with niched halls (a, adapted from
McEwan and Couture 2005; b, adapted from McEwan 1998).

Wari influence reached as far north as Cajamarca in the north-central highlands. Two sites with large orthogonal enclosures, El Palacio and Yamobamaba, may have been constructed by Wari architects (Hyslop 1984:61; Schreiber 1992, 2001). Yet evidence for early Wari hegemony in the highlands between Ayacucho and Cajamarca, if suggestive in Apurímac, Junin, and Ancash (Grossman 1983; Isbell 1989; Schreiber 1992), remains scarce. A distinct lack of evidence for Wari influence on the north coast of Peru (Mackey 1982; Wilson 1988), which had been dominated by Moche polities in the Early Intermediate Period, suggests that relations consisted of elite patronage and trade, perhaps similar to the relation between Tiwanaku and many frontier zones.

One of the largest early Wari enclosures, Viracochapampa, was built in the Huamachuco highlands over 700 km north of Wari (Figure 7.10a; Topic and Topic 2000). Like Wari enclosures elsewhere, the site was built just above 3,000 meters amid local settlements such as the massive center of Marcahuamachuco, which continued to thrive over the generations of Wari hegemony. Like other Wari sites, Viracochapampa was trapezoidal in plan and incorporated elaborate patio groups with high, multistory halls. Unique to Viracochapampa were numerous elaborately finished niched halls built in a style characteristic of local settlements in the region. A large plaza, presumably for state-organized gatherings and ceremonies, occupied the topographical center of the site. Comparing Viracochapampa with other Wari enclosures demonstrates that, while all incorporated similar architectural elements and served similar administrative roles, no two were alike. In constructing administrative enclosures such as Viracochapampa, planners and architects in coordination with local people drew on existing local styles and traditions. In fact, early dates for Wari occupation in Huamachuco may indicate that northern Andean cultural traditions inspired the imminent spatial reorganizations that transformed Wari settlements and societies, including the capital, during the ninth century (Schreiber 1992; J. R. Topic 1991).

State Consolidation in Wari 2

Around AD 800, the Wari polity endured a profound reorganization that involved intensified hegemony in some regions and decreased influence in others. The Huamachuco region, for one, no longer hosted Wari-affiliated sites, suggesting that any influence further north, such as in Cajamarca, also waned. Viracochapampa was abandoned long before it was completed, and though inhabitants took pains to block doorways and seal valuable goods in cists under room floors, they never returned (Topic and Topic 2000). Several sites dating to Wari 2 appeared in the central

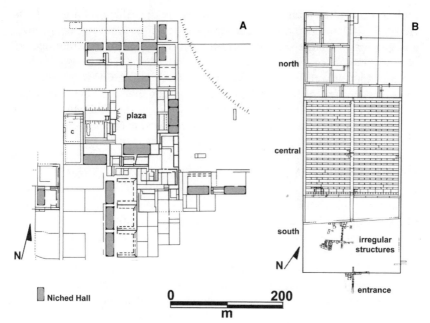

Figure 7.10 Plan views of (a) Viracochapampa and (b) Azángaro
(a, adapted from J. R. Topic 1991; b, adapted from Anders 1991).

highlands between Ayacucho and Huamachuco (Isbell 1989; Schreiber
1992:99–100). In Ancash, Honco Pampa was strategically located near
several natural trade-travel routes and incorporated two typical Wari
architectural forms, a circular or D-shaped ritual building and several
patio groups. Wari influence intensified in the coastal Nasca region, where
archaeologists recently identified two small Wari enclosures (Schreiber
1999, 2001; Silverman and Proulx 2002:273–274).

Intensive farming and elite-sponsored commensalism intensified enor-
mously and at a pan-regional imperial scale in Wari 2 (Cook and Glowacki
2003; Schreiber 2001). We see this in the intensification of hillslope terracing, establishment or intensification of Wari presence in especially
productive regions, and the increasing importance of patio groups and
associated feasting activities at Wari sites. Some settlements served to
expand local production. Located across the high *puna* east of Wari,
the small site of Jargampata facilitated the collection of crops cultivated
along the San Miguel River and elite-sponsored feasting for local leaders
and laborers (Isbell 1977). Further from Wari to the west, Wari leaders
intensified hegemony and production in the Sondondo Valley (Schreiber
1999, 2001). Wari builders expanded the enclosure of Jincomocco and

built three smaller, strategically located sites in the valley and linked them via roads. Jincomocco now incorporated numerous large storage rooms, a large plaza for large-scale events, and several adjacent, interconnected patios. Jincomocco was not only on a strategic route to the coast, but like Pikillacta it was well-located to intensify maize cultivation via terrace systems on surrounding hillsides. On a smaller scale than Pikillacta, it served as a work station and/or military garrison for rotating local laborers who were periodically treated to lively state-sponsored events.

Most remarkable was the construction of Azangáro, a highly ordered enclosure built on a plain at 2,400 meters above sea level in the warm Huanta Valley just 15 kilometers downriver from Wari (Figure 7.10b). Huanta is Ayacucho's breadbasket, and under Wari, it provided diverse products (maize, fruits, chili peppers, and coca) that growing urban populations ambitiously sought (Anders 1991:166). Huanta also yielded pigments for pottery and cotton for textiles and was en route to a major source of Wari obsidian (Burger and Asaro 1977). Azangáro served some of Wari's primary imperial interests: intensive farming, feasting, and exalting a sacred landscape. A single south entrance provided access to the enclosure and led people through the complex via long corridors. Martha Anders (1986, 1991) identified three distinct precincts in the enclosure: a north sector of large rooms, a central sector of small rooms, and a south sector containing "irregular" residences and patios built in a local style. The conjoined rooms of the central sector contained raised floors for ventilating stored produce (Schreiber 1992:91) and may have temporarily housed people (Anders 1986, 1991). Yet most of the "action" at Azángaro occurred in and around the structures in the south sector. Residences here yielded numerous broken vessels for communal consumption, as well as valued exotic objects such as Spondylus shell and turquoise for bodily adornment and offerings. Near the entrance to the single doorway of the central sector, provincial Wari elite periodically sponsored feasts for local leaders and laborers.

Now more than ever, Wari urban spaces emphasized modular organization focused on walled compounds and repeating patio groups (Figure 7.2c). Wari's own urban transformations, noted above, reflected changes occurring across the empire. Perhaps a new dynasty or elite faction came to power, which may have occurred in Tiwanaku at roughly the same time. An ideology of order, repetition, and efficiency in spatial organization became a hallmark of Wari state culture. The severe organization of orthogonal architecture in general and massive provincial enclosures in particular emphasize that Wari centers were ideological statements as much as they were functioning places – an idea emphasized by the fact that even the largest enclosures, including Pikillacta and

Viracochapampa, had been minimally occupied and remained incomplete before they were abandoned. In the minds of Wari urban planners, Wari centers were as good to see, experience, and remember as much as, and most likely more than they were good to tortuously navigate and inhabit. As novel symbols and experiences, Wari's peripheral enclosures clearly stood out from local settlements. Perhaps as important, they were also very different from Tiwanaku centers. Their predominant spatial order, which coincided with the political and cultural peak of the empire, was intentionally devised to distinguish Wari presence from that of local societies. Further, I suggest, it served to distinguish Wari cosmology and urbanism from that of Tiwanaku, even as Wari elites adopted and adapted many of Tiwanaku's characteristic icons and ideals.

Wari Imperialism and Religious Ideology

Wari profoundly influenced far-flung regions of the central Andean highlands and coast during the Middle Horizon. In Ayacucho, Cuzco, Huanta, and Huamachuco, Wari rulers established some form of direct political or economic control. In regions where Wari cultural markers are less common or absent, Wari most likely had a more incorporative or indirect influence (Schreiber 1992, 2001). In such regions, changes in mortuary practices are particularly telling of Wari's influence. On the south coast, multiple burials became more common as did the preparation of mummy bundles with elaborate false heads (Silverman and Proulx 2002); on the north coast, where evidence for direct Wari influence is negligible, flexed burial positions appeared (Donnan and Mackey 1978; Mackey 1982); and in Ancash, mortuary rituals now focused on above-ground burial chambers, or *chullpas*, dedicated to interred ancestors (Lau 2002). Ideas regarding life and death were changing throughout the central Andes. New ceramic assemblages facilitated new ritual practices, in particular vessels dedicated to commensalism. Thus, like Inca rulers, Wari leaders directly controlled some regions, established hegemonic influence in others, and dealt diplomatically with still others (Schreiber 2001). Wari leaders balanced multiple incorporative and transformative imperial strategies, their respective implementation conditioned by preexisting local conditions (geographical and sociopolitical) and ruling interests and means.

Though many archaeologists characterize Wari imperial power as absolute and bureaucratic, its state culture disseminating from a single source, many patterns suggest otherwise. New ritual practices and material culture in the central Andes differed from region to region, indicating that trajectories of change largely followed local traditions. Wari ideals were adapted to enduring local practices and differently so for each local ethnic group or polity. Wari integrated travel routes and forged new configurations of interregional interaction; yet, the Middle Horizon witnessed the rise of numerous "extra-imperial" interaction networks. For instance, groups in the north and south coast independently exchanged goods and ideas (Silverman and Proulx 2002), while Pachacamac, on the central coast, developed a quasi-autonomous sphere of influence (Menzel 1964; Shea 1969; Shimada 1991). It is significant that Wari provincial enclosures were built near major local centers or dense settlement networks that continued to thrive during the Middle Horizon. This is as true for Pikillacta and Viracochapampa as it is for Azángaro, situated in the territory of the autonomous Huanta Valley polity (Schreiber 1992:166). This strategy is very reminiscent of later Inca "imposed settlements" such as Huánuco Pampa, which were built amidst local polities and settlements (Morris and Thompson 1985). As Inca imposed settlements did, Wari enclosures appear to have provided workstations for temporary local laborers and administrators, storage facilities for their produce and crafted goods, and places for state-sponsored compensatory feasts and ceremonies. Many societies were conquered and colonized, but in the long run, their settlements were not replaced or their networks dramatically reorganized – a common European and Asian strategy – as much as they were incorporated into a centralized sociopolitical system and reconfigured landscape, whether by force, intimidation, diplomacy, or consent.

The striking monumentality and severe order of Wari's provincial enclosures belie the interactive and relatively fragile relations on which state power rested, just as its remarkable woven tunics aggrandized the bodies of Wari elites who were ultimately mortal. Each enclosure incorporated architectural elements characteristic of the local culture, emphasizing the important roles played by local people in their planning, construction, and quite possibly, administration (Anders 1986, 1991; McEwan 1996; J. R. Topic 1991). It is notable that the most common vessels for food and drink were either local wares or locally made Wari-local hybrids. In this vein, it is significant, as it is for Tiwanaku, that commensalism played such a critical role in Wari statecraft. In ceremonies and feasts hosted in the patio groups and plazas of provincial Wari enclosures and other settlements, state power and legitimacy were invigorated just as elite factions competed with one another for prestige and position. As in Tiwanaku, Wari state power was never implicitly legitimate or secure. Rather in each local region it was continually crafted, contested, negotiated, and refabricated – and on a major scale after AD 800.

Recurring patio groups and plazas facilitating a cult of commensalism, subtle but persistent local influences in enclosures, and signature anomalies in woven tunics together expose what Michael Dietler (2003:271–272) calls the "nasty little secret of history." That is, "states and empires" such as Wari "are very fragile, volatile, and transitory – far more so than their buildings and monuments. They are fluid processes rather than durable things, and they depend on constant hard work in micro-political struggles of negotiation and legitimation to survive and operate." In this light, Wari was the hardest-working operation in town.

If traditional interpretations of Tiwanaku downplayed its unique brand of imperialism, conventional thought about Wari de-emphasized its distinct religious ideology. Two assumptions have helped impede consideration of Wari religion: first, the old idea that Wari religion simply refracted Tiwanaku ideology and, second, the imperial scope and "bureaucratic" look of its far-flung centers. Wari specialists, as cultural *bricoleurs*, adapted a striking corpus of Tiwanaku iconography to textile and pottery designs, thereby meshing elements of Tiwanaku religion to Wari cosmology. It is likely that the site of Tiwanaku was not the sole source of Wari's "Tiahuanacoid" elements. On the one hand, Tiwanaku-style iconography preceded the Tiwanaku state by centuries,[1] and by the seventh century it comprised a rich variety of local expressions throughout the south-central Andes. On the other hand, by the time it appeared in Wari, it indexed what was by then a widely adopted, entrenched, and prestigious Tiwanaku culture. Some Wari elites adopted key Tiwanaku symbols to bolster their political legitimacy and perhaps foster religious inspiration in the rituals and feasts they hosted. Overall, Wari adapted specific themes to a very distinct iconographic repertoire and imperial ideology, as reflected in full material assemblages and a unique vision of urban form and sacred landscape (Anders 1986; Glowacki and Malpass 2003, Schreiber 2001).

Religious ideology focused on the veneration of ancestors and sacred natural features was a fundamental component of Wari state expansion (Glowacki and Malpass 2003; Williams and Nash 2006). Mountains, whose peaks (*apus*) today embody the great ancestors, and water, in ritually significant wells, lakes, and springs, figure prominently in areas of direct Wari control (Williams and Nash 2006). In Lucre, Huaro and Pikillacta were built near substantial mountain lakes that were later considered *pacarinas*, or the primordial origin places of local ethnic groups (Gose 1993). The complexes were also close to and visually connected with Wiracochan, an *apu* later considered the spiritual source

---

[1] In fact, some tapestry tunics in "Classic" Tiwanaku style have been radiocarbon dated to AD 200–400, or Late Tiwanaku 2 (see Young-Sánchez 2004).

of water. Similarly, Azángaro was built in the shadow of snow-capped Rasuwillka, an *apu* whose eight lakes fed irrigation systems in the Huanta Valley (Anders 1991:167).

The sacred center of Cerro Amaru may partly explain Wari interest in Huamachuco and Viracochapamapa's location (J. R. Topic 1991; Topic and Topic 1992). Cerro Amaru incorporated three wells to which Spondylus shell, turquoise, and other precious minerals were offered. The site also housed a large mausoleum that held the deceased ancestors of a local elite lineage. John and Theresa Topic (1992) interpret Cerro Amaru as a powerful local water shrine that Wari individuals visited, venerated, and at least for a time, incorporated into their realm. Hegemony over this and other regions was not only about political control and economic production. It was also about "cosmological control" of water and production "through ancestor worship" (Glowacki and Malpass 2003:439). Beyond agropastoral intensification and obtaining valued resources such as Spondylus and turquoise, Wari leaders' great interests included coopting and controlling sacred landscapes and religious centers.

Pan-regional drought in the sixth century may have precipitated Wari's practical and spiritual quest for water, farmlands, and pasture outside of Ayacucho (Glowacki and Malpass 2003; Moseley 2001). Yet if a drought did occur, it would have most effectively facilitated Wari's first wave of expansion just as the drought ended. In this scenario, Wari leaders opportunistically linked new productive techniques and a prestigious religious ideology with a return to prosperity, thereby facilitating state legitimacy in the hearts and minds of local leaders and groups. A place that figured prominently in Wari's political legitimacy and in its power to bring water was the cult center of Pachacamac.

Wari and Pachacamac

Located at the mouth of the Lurín Valley on the central Peruvian coast, Pachacamac became a third major political and ceremonial center during the Middle Horizon. Pachacamac had been settled during the Early Intermediate Period, but it gained interregional influence and fame after AD 600 (Shimada 1991). The badly damaged Pachacamac Temple, excavated by Max Uhle in 1896, was the primary temple and oracle in the city. Perhaps much like the Saint James Cathedral in Compostela, Spain, during the European Middle Ages, the ornate monument came to be a place of worship and pilgrimage for people throughout the Andes. According to one chronicler, polychrome frescoes depicted animals, plants, and waves, and the portal of the inner sanctum was encrusted with "coral, turquoises, crystals and other stones" (Estete

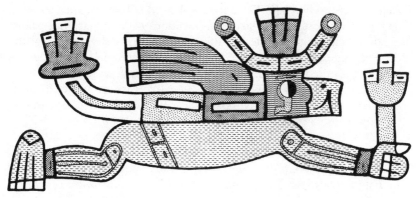

Figure 7.11 The Pachacamac Griffin (adapted from Menzel 1964).

1891[1534], in Uhle 1991[1903]:13). Pachacamac iconography meshed elements of several stylistic traditions to form a distinctive and elaborate style that was widely adopted and distributed. One prominent theme was the Pachacamac Griffin (Figure 7.11; Menzel 1964), a unique flying mythical being with a feline body and bird head that meshed Tiwanaku and Wari elements.

Pachacamac-style ceramics and textiles appear in distant regions of the Peruvian coast and highlands (Isbell 1987:188; Shimada 1991: 49). The leapfrog character of Pachacamac influence and the synthetic style of its iconography alludes to forms of interaction distinct from yet coexisting with that of Tiwanaku and Wari. A central part of its influence may have been the establishment of affiliated local shrines (Shimada 1991:50). By the Late Horizon, Pachacamac was the political-ritual center for the Ichma polity and a ceremonial city of pan-Andean renown with numerous satellite settlements. Each satellite acquired a small branch oracle in return for elaborate offerings and generous donations made to the main shrine (Rostworowski 1992). The network was described in intimate family terms. Branch oracles were brothers, wives, sons, or daughters of Pachacamac, the great "world creator," depending on their relative prestige, influence, and generosity to Pachacamac. A similar network focused on the oracle of the Pachacamac Temple may have been in place by the Middle Horizon.

Wari and Pachacamac societies reciprocally supported each other (Kaulicke 2000). While tension undoubtedly punctuated their interlinked histories, Pachacamac's rise was predicated on Wari expansion and protection just as Wari leaders benefited from economic interaction and ideological affiliation with the ceremonial center. In the Late Horizon,

Pachacamac's archipelago-like network thrived within the Inca Empire. The last Inca rulers curried strong connections with Pachacamac priests and had an elaborate temple for Inti, the Inca solar deity, built near the older Pachacamac Temple (Uhle 1991). Rulers such as Tupac Yupanqui regularly consulted with the oracle before embarking on important campaigns (Guaman Poma 1992[1615]:239–240; Rostworowski 1992). It seems likely that a similar relationship held between Pachacamac priests and Wari leaders in the Middle Horizon.

Much of Pachacamac's religious and economic power was tied to the ocean. By aligning with Pachacamac's religious-commercial network, Wari leaders drew on its practical and spiritual power and adapted it to an imperial ideology that linked ancestors and mountains to the generative forces of water. Such an ideology would have resonated particularly well as drought conditions came to an end, thereby legitimizing and perhaps to some degree welcoming Wari imperialism.

Indeed, Pachacamac was most likely the primary source of Spondylus shell offered in ritual contexts at Wari sites, and Wari leaders may have monopolized its acquisition. In sharp contrast to Tiwanaku ritual offerings, Wari offerings commonly included Spondylus shells. The Inca crushed thorny Spondylus shells (*mullu*), considered the "favorite food of the gods," for offerings to invoke rain (Glowacki and Malpass 2003:442), and as material symbols of the sea's life-giving power. To acquire Spondylus, highland leaders traded prized mineral resources of great ritual value such as copper and turquoise with Pachacamac merchants. Thus, if the Wari state drew on Tiwanaku myth and ideology, it also developed in tandem with the extension of Pachacamac's expanding ritual-trade network. Much more work remains to be done regarding this intensive, long-term relationship.

The Wari-Tiwanaku Frontier

Over the past few years, archaeologists have begun to closely examine the relationship between Wari and Tiwanaku in local regions (Figure 7.12). Most critical has been research in the Wari-Tiwanaku border zone, including the regions of Arequipa and Moquegua. Wari occupation in Arequipa was most intensive in the Siguas Valley, the southernmost part of Arequipa (Cardona 2002:71). Here, at 2,900 meters, the settlement of Corralón served as a regional center of Wari cultural influence and agropastoral production. At the center of dispersed household compounds was a central sector of agglutinated structures that included a trapezoidal plaza for communal ceremony and at least one patio group for elite-sponsored feasting. Local communities occupied

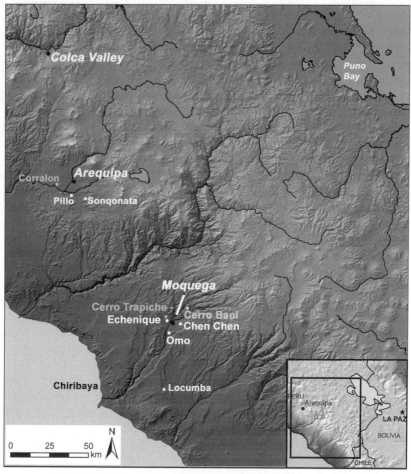

Figure 7.12 The Arequipa and Moquegua regions, showing key
Tiwanaku (in white) and Wari (in gray) sites (base map by Steve
Wernke).

nearby settlements, and some acquired Wari-style ceramic wares and
other goods. Wari occupation in this part of Arequipa was distinct from
that of Tiwanaku, centered to the north and east, which appears to have
been more deeply rooted and culturally influential (Cardona 2002:78–
87). A significant boundary apparently divided the occupations; yet, its
characteristics remain to be clarified.

A clearer Wari-Tiwanaku boundary appears in the Moquegua Valley
further south. During a first wave of Wari imperialism at around AD 650,

Figure 7.13 Cerro Baúl towers prominently over the upper Moquegua valley.

Wari leaders established a colony in the upper sierra of the Moquegua Valley, some 2,000–2,500 meters above sea level (Feldman 1989; Moseley et al. 1991; Nash 2002; Williams 2001). The political center of the colony was perched some 600 meters atop Cerro Baúl, "an impressive mountain that dominates the valley's visual landscape" (Figure 7.13; Williams and Nash 2002:245). Wari occupied the peaks of nearby Cerros Mejia and Petroglifo as well as the lower slopes of all three mountains. Wari essentially created a new settlement system at the upper edges of a fertile valley first occupied by indigenous Huaracane farmers and later dominated by Tiwanaku colonists. The system emphasized key Wari cultural values of surveillance and separation. Not only were key settlements positioned to view and be viewed, but access to Baúl and Mejia was naturally restricted by boundary walls (Nash 2002; Williams and Nash 2002). One massive wall blocked access to Baúl from the west, the area colonized by Tiwanaku-affiliated communities.

While Tiwanaku expanded irrigated farming in the lower sierra pampas on the south side of the valley, Wari created a labor-intensive productive regime focused on steep, terraced hillslopes fed by massive, sinuous canals (Williams 1997). A central trunk in the productive system was the monumental El Paso aqueduct, which could carry massive amounts of

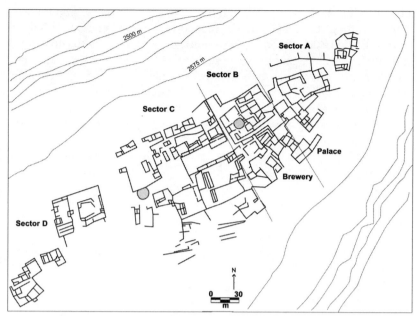

Figure 7.14 Map of the Wari occupation atop Cerro Baúl (D-shaped structures in gray; adapted from Williams and Nash 2002).

water to extensive terraces at a rate of 400 liters per second. Wari's massive irrigation systems may have precipitated tension between the two states in AD 650–800. Considering relatively low rainfall levels in the seventh century, P. Ryan Williams and Donna Nash (2002:256) suggest that Tiwanaku came to view the Wari colonists as "water usurpers."

The impressive mountaintop settlements of Baúl, Mejia, and Petroglifo incorporated characteristic Wari architecture and spatial organization. In each case, key ceremonial structures and high-status residents occupied the summit, while the terraced hillslopes were dedicated to residential occupations, craft specialization, and agricultural concerns. As at many Wari settlements, major constructions on Petroglifo appear not to have been completed (Nash 2002). A massive staircase built of megalithic stones and crowned by a stone gate formed a "monumental passage" up to Cerro Mejia's summit (Williams and Nash 2002:253). Here one found residential compounds clustered around food-production areas, a patio group for elite-sponsored commensalism, and a large trapezoidal plaza for communal events (Nash 2002).

The most significant Wari personnel and elite-sponsored activities were atop Cerro Baúl (Figure 7.14). The site witnessed two phases of construction that correspond with the state's two phases of imperialism, one beginning at AD 650 and the second in the ninth century (Williams 2001). By AD 800–900, the ritual-political center of the site and colony, Sector B, incorporated one of the site's two D-shaped structures for elite rituals and a trapezoidal plaza flanked by galleries for commensalism. The adjacent Sector A housed attached specialists who crafted prized adornments and ritual objects of chrysacolla and lapis lazuli. Children buried under floors wore elaborate necklaces of perforated shell beads, evoking depictions of the adornments found on the necks of elaborate human effigy jars, and apparently marking elite or royal status (Blom, Williams, and Nash 2004).

Elite-sponsored commensalism was a key activity on the summit, and it involved particularly elaborate china, fuels, and cooking techniques (Nash and Williams 2004). Typical drinks included maize and *molle* berry *chicha* served in elaborate Wari and hybrid Wari-Tiwanaku vessels (D. Goldstein and Quispe 2004). Food included a range of local and exotic delicacies, including *quinoa*, cactus fruits, chili peppers, peanuts, beans, camelid meat, guinea pig (*cuy*), *vizcacha*, deer, doves, pigeons, anchovies, and tuna (DeFrance 2004). In the middle of Sector A was an elaborate *chicha* brewery. Patios and orthogonal patio groups for feast preparation and commensalism were distributed over the summit; yet, there was no large plaza for major state-sponsored feasts as there were at other Wari and later Inca sites (Nash and Williams 2004). Feasting was what Dietler terms "diacritical" rather than "reciprocal" (2001), in that it prioritized diplomacy and competition among elites, including invited Tiwanaku leaders (Williams and Nash 2002), more than it did repaying or distributing reciprocal obligations among nonelites. Large-scale state activities involving nonelites most likely occurred elsewhere in Moquegua.

During the first two centuries of Wari occupation in upper Moquegua, a clear spatial and cultural boundary divided the two colonies, insinuating strained détente or tense coexistence. One would expect evidence for interaction between Tiwanaku and Wari colonists. Wari ceramic vessels are known from Tiwanaku cemeteries and at least one hybrid Tiwanaku vessel is known from Cerro Baúl. Yet such cases are rare, indicating that social interaction and cultural synergy were not preponderant. The Wari site complex of Cerro Trapiche occupied the middle Moquegua valley on the north side of the river, high above and opposite the Tiwanaku colonies to the south (P. Goldstein and Carter 2004). Part of the complex occupied an old Huaracane cemetery, and thereby appropriated ancient sacred space and identified its foreign occupants with the valley's ancient and legitimate inhabitants. Its attached agricultural terrace systems differed notably from Tiwanaku's pampa systems in full view on the other side of the valley. In fact, the Tiwanaku colony of Cerro Echenique lay just 2 kilometers or less than a half-hour walk from Trapiche. Echenique was the only Tiwanaku site north of the river, and it is not surprising that a defensive wall protected its nearby fields. Unlike Echenique and other Tiwanaku sites, Trapiche incorporated a patio group for Wari-style communal consumption.

While Tiwanaku colonists fermented and consumed maize *chicha*, Wari colonists at Trapiche and other Wari sites largely fermented and consumed *molle chicha* (D. Goldstein and Quispe 2004; P. Goldstein and Carter Moseley et. al 2005). Processing and consuming *molle* chicha was a recurring practice that marked Wari cultural identity both in the heartland and in valley regions such as Moquegua (Cook and Glowacki 2003; Tung 2003). Its practice here alongside other distinctive aspects of Wari state culture (patio groups, D-shaped buildings, terraced farming), in striking contrast to characteristic Tiwanaku practices (pampa farming, maize cultivation, sunken courts), attests the intractable persistence of a Tiwanaku-Wari social boundary in an otherwise close, interactive milieu. Apparently, profound differences between Tiwanaku and Wari in urban form, ritual practice, subsistence production, and commensalism were forged early on in border zones such as Moquegua and intentionally maintained over generations as an enduring boundary that distinguished two dynamic, internally diversified, yet distinct cultural and political identities.

Sometime after AD 800, local relations between Wari and Tiwanaku appear to have shifted. In patio groups and plazas dating to the tenth century on Cerro Baúl, Tiwanaku vessels were first employed in rituals of consumption (Williams and Nash 2002). At this time, Tiwanaku-affiliated settlements first occupied the upper Moquegua Valley around Cerro Baúl (Goldstein 1993a; Owen 1998; Williams and Nash 2002). These included sites with Tiwanaku-influenced Chen Chen and Tumilaca ceramic wares, the latter of which appeared at sites on Baúl's very slopes. Most obsidian at these sites derived from sources that supplied not Tiwanaku but Wari sites such as Cerro Baúl (Vining 2004). It is likely that these Tiwanaku-affiliated people, who by now may have enjoyed some autonomy in relation to the distant center, interacted intensively with local Wari elites and perhaps worked on their extensive terrace systems in exchange for valued goods.

It would appear that relations between local Wari and Tiwanaku-identified populations had "warmed" to a degree, or at least that more frequent and intensive interaction mediated undercurrents of sociopolitical tension. Likely following confrontations, local Wari and Tiwanaku leaders may have had to accept the idea that the valley would have to be big enough for the two of them. Diplomatic relations may have been made possible or legitimate by the very different styles of political hegemony, productive intensification, and religious ideology fostered by the two polities. By the tenth century, Williams and Nash (2002:261) hypothesize, "institutional relationships were affirmed through ritual feasting and drinking . . . on Cerro Baúl." It is entirely within reason that Tiwanaku hosted similar activities at Omo M10 and that Wari colonists visited and worshiped at the Omo temple that was built during this time. Thus, in AD 800–1000 Moquegua formed an interactive multiethnic colony that accommodated two cultural-political identities and political systems and their constituent, ranked groups.

The timing of changes in Tiwanaku and Wari occupations in Moquegua (~AD 800) correlates well with transformations in both states at panregional scales. Such evidence raises questions that are currently unanswerable: Were profound changes in each polity related to the shifting character of their interaction? Did circumstances in the border zone precipitate those transformations? The timing of massive programs of productive intensification and sociopolitical consolidation across the Andes implicates a profound shift in geopolitical relations between Tiwanaku and Wari. A major confrontation or series of confrontations, quite possibly precipitated in border zones such as Moquegua, may well have provoked the shift.

Alternatively, periodic confrontations during early phases of state expansion, as "citizens" of the two states became feisty neighbors in border zones, may have precipitated a diplomatic relationship of coexistence and interaction by the end of the eighth century. The late appearance of Tiwanaku religious iconography on Wari crafted media and late interethnic interaction in Moquegua allude to such a scenario. Whatever the case, mutual interaction and influence conditioned the future development of both imperial states. Practices and ideals unique to each civilization sharpened and became more self-conscious. That the two identities managed to coexist in close quarters such as Moquegua emphasizes, beyond ancient Andean techniques of diplomacy, the complementary aspects of their hegemonies. Still, harmonious coexistence and a "live and let live" mentality ultimately had its limitations as it does between any two human civilizations. A sharp cultural boundary defined and polarized two enduring and very distinct constellations of traditions, practices, and ideals. Implicit in the geopolitical boundary was some degree of antagonism, intolerance, and opposition that, it may turn out, played a trump card in precipitating the end of the two states.

Conclusions

Much remains to be done in Wari and on the relation between Wari and Tiwanaku as peer-polities. Tiwanaku and Wari were very different types of imperial states, though both maintained congeries of political, economic, and ideological relations with distant regions and shared core elements of a more ancient Andean cosmology that emphasized the spiritual and practical power of mountains, water, and ancestors. The consolidation of each state, furthermore, was predicated on communal consumption and elite-sponsored feasting, which inspired innovative techniques of brewing and food preparation, new types of pottery dedicated to fermentation, storage, and consumption (including mass-produced serving wares), and a new scale of political diplomacy grounded in conspicuous generosity.

Yet from the start, Tiwanaku and Wari were founded in different cultural principles. Different brewing techniques and "brands" of beer – maize *chicha* on the one hand and *molle chicha* on the other – were among the practices that distinguished the two states and formed their cultural boundary. Other practices included Wari use of turquoise and Spondylus shell in ritual offerings, which apparently never occurred in Tiwanaku. More profound differences included distinct iconographic repertories, mortuary rituals, and approaches to urbanism. In establishing regional authority, Wari was interested in rigid spatial order and surveillance. Many regional centers were built according to an abstract plan with minimal attention to local landscape or cultural patterns. Tiwanaku regional influence was built from the ground up in the sense that many local centers were ancient ritual-political centers, and their visual plans drew more explicitly on local traditions. In many cases, local Tiwanaku authority was based on emulation rather than imposition. To caricature the distinctions, we might say that Wari chose the "control freak" path while Tiwanaku opted for the zen road to statecraft.

Yet it would be a mistake to consider Wari an outward-focused and expansive empire that imposed itself on local regions and Tiwanaku as an inward-focused phenomenon that grew through emulation and consensus. Just as Tiwanaku had deeply rooted imperial agendas in specific regions of the south-central Andes and ultimately developed profoundly transformative imperial strategies, Wari expanded as much through local spiritual concerns and affective dimensions of affiliation as it did by imposition. State legitimacy, which was always on the minds of Wari elites and commoners alike if for different reasons, depended on it. Despite rigid ground plans, Wari enclosures incorporated conspicuous local elements just as its woven textiles incorporated pattern-disrupting signatures.

Further, changes in most regions under Wari authority followed local historical trajectories rather than sudden ruptures attendant on Wari conquest. The appearance of ceramic styles such as Cajamarca, Pachacamac, and Nasca at Wari raises the intriguing possibility that, like Tiwanaku, it was a cosmopolitan settlement "colonized" by local groups (see Shimada 1991:49). Wari was more than a religious confederation, though Pachacamac played a heavy hand in Wari expansion and vice versa. It also was more than a network of centers linked by commerce, although acquiring valued symbolic resources such as turquoise and Spondylus was critical. Its true imperial designs like those of many past states have suffered from a heavy dose of the same Western reinterpretation that has distorted many past polities. As much as it was a "despotic" regime that appropriated valued resources and transformed local landscapes and livelihoods, Wari imperialism was highly dynamic, it was as spiritual as it was political, and it developed as a creative integration of diverse cultural elements.

In a bid for legitimacy at around AD 700, just as Wari imperial designs were amplifying, some Wari elites adapted elements of an ancient religious ideology now centered at Tiwanaku to their own. The creative assimilation of Tiwanaku religious iconography and ideology fostered an early archaeological conflation of Tiwanaku and Wari as a widespread "Tiahuanaco Horizon." From the Tiwanaku point of view, Ayacucho (or at least Conchopata) was another far region of cultural influence such as San Pedro de Atacama, where local elites emulated Tiwanaku ritual practices and religious ideals, and grafted a Tiwanaku affiliation to their own intricate webs of long-distance relations and identities. Such a scenario emphasizes the very complementary and interpenetrating character of Tiwanaku and Wari statecraft.

Yet Wari-Tiwanaku interaction was mutual. Quite possibly, massive changes in imperial strategy, spatial organization, and feasting activities in the Tiwanaku realm after AD 800 drew reciprocally on patterns of statecraft already established in Wari. That is, Tiwanaku leaders may have learned a few things about imperialism from their Wari colleagues in Ayacucho. At this time, it appears, Wari-Tiwanaku relations took on a somewhat friendlier face, the product of a new era of diplomacy that followed an era of escalating tension and conflict. More research will be required to address such ideas. What is clear is that the two states were sovereign and mutually influenced one another. Throughout their histories, their respective affiliated populations defined themselves in relation to one another and to their neighboring societies, most intensively so in the borderlands.

8 Collapse and Regeneration

The reasons why civilizations collapse are manifold. We tend to think of collapse as the complete and unfortunate end of a past people. This assumption is continually invoked in popular romantic accounts of the past, including television specials concerned with the "mystery" of Maya collapse or the "discovery" of lost Andean cities. Overly dramatic attempts to box up and sell the past, in most cases a very complex and hazily understood past, mislead. Resonating with our deeply ingrained common sense regarding the past, they promote the idea that such civilizations ended abruptly, taking with them their people and leaving behind only abandoned ruins. Yet the question is not so much what happened to the people- for the distant descendents of many past civilizations continue to thrive around the world -but what happened to the political systems and religious ideals that inspired the exotic, and beautiful monuments that continue to intrigue today.

For years, archaeologists have grappled with collapse. An important conclusion of ongoing research is that the end of a civilization should be distinguished from the collapse of a state (Yoffee and Cowgill 1988). By civilization archaeologists mean a "great tradition," the preeminent cultural elements of an archaic state: extensive urban centers, integrated farming systems, monumental architecture, and finely crafted sculptures and goods. By state collapse, we refer to a "rapid, significant loss of an established level of sociopolitical complexity" (Tainter 1988:4). In separating these dimensions, we distinguish complementary aspects of such a major transformation.

While useful, the term "collapse" is problematic. A state is not a material thing – a gigantic monolith, say – that physically falls, though it may be symbolized as such (in the National Geographic special "Lost Empire of Tiwanaku," Tiwanaku collapse is appropriately symbolized as a falling, shattering *kero*). Rather collapse was most frequently a process of sociopolitical fragmentation. In Tiwanaku, collapse was a process of fragmentation that was neither rapid nor complete. Collapse was a long, volatile process spanning several generations. The polity disintegrated

and a great tradition ended, but in the process – and as *part of* that process – new cultural practices and political ideals were forged. Just as the
Andean Middle Horizon helps us understand the intricacies and variability of past states, so its end opens new paths for understanding collapse
as a global, recurring, cumulative phenomenon.

Collapse is as relevant today as it was a thousand years ago, and recent
research emphasizes two key facets of the process. First, archaeologists are
beginning to examine the internal social processes implicated in state collapse and the rise of post-state societies. In the past, we focused on external processes or "prime removers" such as environmental catastrophe,
mass migration, or military conquest. Like recent research on the Maya,
research on Tiwanaku emphasizes the central role of human agency in
state collapse. Regional environmental and sociopolitical changes played
key roles, but most importantly, they exacerbated social tensions that had
been brewing throughout the Middle Horizon. Second, archaeologists
have tended to ignore the issue of "what happened next" in collapse. The
material culture postdating state collapse is usually far less well crafted
and monumental and thus not as ideal for popular consumption or conventional archaeological interest. Only recently have archaeologists begun
to tackle the process of cultural regeneration that accompanies state collapse and to understand collapse as a process of cultural genesis as much
as the end of a state or civilization. Like recent research on the Maya
(Demarest 2004; O'Mansky and Dunning 2004), research at Tiwanaku
highlights the complex, cumulative shifts and profound continuities that
characterized the emergence of later societies (Janusek 2004a, 2004b,
2004c).

In this chapter, I approach Tiwanaku collapse as a cultural revolution
as much as a "decline and fall." I examine the regional forces and long-
standing tensions that together deflated once-sacred symbols, eroded
once-prestigious ideologies, and forged a new world of symbols, ideals,
and everyday life. Tiwanaku's fate may teach us something about our
own nation-focused identity politics and religious ideals and how they
can foster change for the better or to the detriment of our societies.

In this chapter, I evaluate evidence for Wari collapse and the abandonment of its major centers. Next, I examine evidence for Tiwanaku collapse, including the destruction of major monuments, the abandonment
of cities and major settlements, and the decline of intensive agricultural
regimes. The chapter then turns to the rise of new types of polities, settlement networks, livelihoods, and ritual practices during the Late Intermediate Period in the central Andean Highlands and the altiplano. Finally, I
discuss the relation of Tiwanaku and Wari collapse to the rise of the Inca
state.

Wari Collapse

The reasons for and trajectory of Wari state collapse are unknown. It is likely, Schreiber notes (2001:91), that "the reasons for [Wari] collapse are...numerous and complex" and that they involved shifting environmental, sociopolitical, and ideological climates. For years, archaeologists thought Wari had disappeared from the central Andean highlands by AD 800–850. Ongoing research indicates that the state continued to thrive until much later, perhaps as late as AD 950–1000, right about the time that a major crisis befell Tiwanaku. The city of Wari itself experienced a late and relatively short period of reorganization sometime in the late ninth or early tenth century. In its "Great Walls" phase, many sectors in the north side of the city were leveled and covered with irregularly shaped compounds bounded by thick, massive, curving walls (Figure 7.2a). The emerging urban landscape departed substantially in plan and organization from that of the preceding epoch with its repeating patio groups and D-shaped structures. The new order may well have been an intentional rejection of prior ideological and social principles (Isbell 1997b; Isbell, Brewster-Wray, and Spickard 1991). By this time, most of Wari's known regional enclosures, the extreme materialization of those principles, had been abandoned. A new political faction may have come to power. Isbell (1997b:216) suggests that "the unity of the Wari state expressed in orthogonal cellular architecture was fragmenting into smaller and repetitive power centers," perhaps now focused on the competing kin groups and political factions that had always comprised the Wari political system.

The new political regime was short lived. Sectors in the south half of the city such as Moraduchayoq were inhabited on a smaller scale. Many patio groups were sequentially abandoned and converted into outhouses and trash dumps. Telling, most new compounds in the north were never fully occupied, and several cleared areas were never rebuilt. Most interesting, a long thick pile of rubble that still snakes across the site may have served as a "causeway for transporting workmen and materials" across the city (Isbell 1997b:216). Wari was abandoned under construction.

Wari hegemony over local regions had been continually in flux. Thus, linking state collapse to waning influence in any particular region remains a challenge. Many regional Wari centers were simply abandoned. In the Sondondo Valley, Jincomocco and nearly every Middle Horizon village were depopulated, giving way to fortified settlements at higher elevations. Other sites and regions point to volatile social conditions and conflict. The end of Wari occupation in the Lucre Basin was quick and possibly violent. The administrative centers of Qoripata and Pikillacta were both deserted and finally razed, possibly representing a "major attempt... to expel the [Wari] from Cuzco" (Glowacki and Malpass 2003:275). Pikillacta was abandoned in a particularly meticulous and careful manner (McEwan 1996). Key doorways were blocked, as they had been at Viracochapampa, and rooms were cautiously emptied of their buried offerings and valuable objects. Such precautions suggest to Gordon McEwan (1996:184) that, as in Huamachuco, the inhabitants intended to return to the site. Yet before they returned, the site was completely razed in an intensely hot blaze that completely carbonized the massive beams supporting second-story floors. Wari hegemony near Cuzco had ended and quite possibly at the hands of native populations. An important question is the effect this may have had on the rise of the Inca state in Cuzco two to three centuries later.

The end of Wari occupation in Moquegua was very likely related to interactions with Tiwanaku populations. Overall, "the end of the Middle Horizon occupation of Moquegua was violent and tumultuous" (Williams and Nash 2002:262). It occurred sometime around AD 1000, and possibly later than it had southeast of Cuzco. Tiwanaku-affiliated Chen Chen settlements in the middle valley were completely sacked and destroyed sometime around the end of the tenth century. It remains unclear who perpetrated the thorough destruction that turned Tiwanaku settlements into rubble (Moseley et al. 1991). In light of the interethnic interactions and tensions that had endured centuries in the region, it is possible that local Wari inhabitants, perhaps in alliance with defecting Tiwanaku-derived Tumilaca inhabitants in the upper Valley, were the primary culprits. Yet even if Wari ousted the local Tiwanaku occupation, its victory was short-lived and possibly Pyrrhic. Around the same time, several buildings atop Cerro Baúl were ritually burned and the site was abandoned (Moseley et al. 2005; Williams and Nash 2002:259). This rapid sequence of events hints that the end of the Middle Horizon in Moquegua was not simply a result of conflict between Wari and Tiwanaku. It implicates other pan-regional or local causes that most likely involved profound shifts in human and environmental conditions.

Tiwanaku Collapse

Because of ongoing archaeological and paleoenvironmental research in the Lake Titicaca Basin, we have a firmer foundation for evaluating the causes and trajectory of Tiwanaku state collapse. Past interpretations focused on external processes. Historians and linguists interpreted Tiwanaku collapse as a product of ethnic replacement (Bouysee-Cassagne 1987; Espinoza 1980; Gisbert, Arze, and Cajiás 1987; Torero 1970, 1987). In this view, Tiwanaku, whose populations presumably spoke Pukina (Waldomar Espinoza suggests Tiwanaku be renamed the "Pukina culture"), succumbed to waves of Aymara groups that emigrated either from Ayacucho, Peru, or northern Chile. Such a view assumes that Tiwanaku populations spoke one language and held a single cultural tradition, an assumption that appears overly static in light of our current perspective of Tiwanaku. It assumes an overly simplistic relation between language, culture, and history. Most important, it does not to stand up to recent evidence for collapse.

As noted in Chapter 2, recent paleoecological research in the Lake Titicaca Basin indicates that a severe drought descended on the altiplano at around AD 1100 (Kolata and Ortloff 1996b; Ortloff and Kolata 1993). Unlike normal small-cycle shifts in lake levels, this drought caused a long-term drop in lake levels on the order of 12–17 meters (Binford et al. 1997). This caused the shores of Lake Titicaca to recede many kilometers and water tables to drop precipitously. Lake Wiñaymarka, for centuries at the heart of altiplano cultural development, essentially disappeared. Such conditions left heretofore lacustrine settlements such as Lukurmata in inland locations and, as Alan Kolata and colleagues point out, huge tracts of raised field-farming systems and their intricate hydraulic systems high and dry.

Yet as Clark Erickson (1999) notes, to conclude that environmental catastrophe caused state collapse would be overly simplistic. We potentially fall into the trap of environmental determinism that has plagued conventional archaeology for decades. Others critique the chronological resolution of the lake cores that are at the foundation of the drought hypothesis (Calaway 2005). If we accept the practice-oriented position that humans are dynamic players in history, however disastrous, then we must explore this major cultural and political transformation more deeply. We must consider human ingenuity and its physical environment as mutually dynamic players in history and explore the potentially volatile social context that drought entered and the dynamic trajectory that ensued.

Abandonment and Destruction in Tiwanaku Cities

Tiwanaku's dismantling was by all accounts a long and periodically volatile process. The decline of its two primary urban centers, in particular, had a drawn-out history that commenced during the state's cultural and political apogee in Tiwanaku 2. It was then that an elite class crystallized in Tiwanaku and that the urban core was reconfigured as space dedicated to elite-sponsored ceremonies and feasts. It was also then that Lukurmata declined as Tiwanaku's second city under new policies of state consolidation and agricultural intensification. During this phase, and occurring over several generations, settlement began to disperse in the Tiwanaku Valley. The number of small hamlets and villages had increased by three times their number in Tiwanaku 1, and most large towns grew considerably. By AD 1000, settlement in the valley formed several discrete clusters, each of which appears to have been a semi-autonomous community or sociopolitical unit (Albarracin-Jordan and Mathews 1990; McAndrews, Albarracin-Jordan, and Bermann 1997). Given tighter control over urban livelihoods and increasing opportunities in rural areas, the shift may manifest a growing preference for life outside of the primary city. In this scenario, it involved sociopolitical decentralization and increased local control over productive systems in the Tiwanaku Valley as state leaders sought to control the more fertile Koani Pampa. As an unforeseen consequence of cumulative changes in the polity, and with ominous consequences for the state, the balance of social power was shifting in Tiwanaku's very heartland. As James Mathews puts it (1997:259), "the seeds of Tiwanaku's collapse were sown during [its] apogee."

The decline of the principal city was a drawn-out process. Residential sectors were abandoned not all at once but one sector at a time throughout Late Tiwanaku 2 (AD 1000–1100/1150). In Akapana East, people built small shanty houses over abandoned areas once dedicated to elite-sponsored commensalism, and some sectors were occupied by temporary squatters who built what we might call prehispanic "mobile homes" (Janusek 2004a). Gradually, populations moved out of Tiwanaku, and the prior city shrank to perhaps 3 percent of its former size. It now centered on a low bluff that overlooked the lower valley and the distant lake edge. Major construction in monumental complexes and the sculpting of monolithic portals and monoliths had ceased by AD 1000 (Alconini 1995; Manzanilla 1992; Vranich 1999). By this time, the Akapana and Puma-punku were venerated more as ancient sacred shrines, or *huacas*, than as the living temples they had been since their construction. A ritual offering atop Akapana dating to Late Tiwanaku 2 poignantly emphasizes this transformation. People dumped the remains of numerous llamas around the corner structure of the elite patio group, at a time just after the complex had begun to collapse but before it began to accumulate sediment. The offering marks a moment of crisis and may well represent a prayer or plea to hinder the forces that had begun to sunder Tiwanaku civilization.

Crisis is more directly apparent in the treatment of elite residences and icons of elite ancestry and ritual passage that once dominated Tiwanaku's sacred landscape. At around AD 1000, the Putuni elite residential complex was destroyed. The walls of the West Palace were knocked down and the East Palace was razed to the ground (Couture 2002; Couture and Sampeck 2003). At some point long before the Colonial Period and not unlikely upon Tiwanaku collapse, its cemetery of deceased nobility was looted. Located in the Putuni courtyard, the Putuni Monolith, a small andesite sculpture depicting what was perhaps a deified ancestor for resident elite, was summarily decapitated and buried. Although impossible to prove, this monolith may have been defaced and ritually interred when the Putuni palaces were destroyed.

Whether or not coincident with such events, most of Tiwanaku's stone portals and ancestor effigies were at some point systematically defaced of destroyed. The frieze of an elegantly sculpted gateway lintel in the Kantatayita was hammered vigorously to remove the metal lamina that, held in place by gold pins, had once covered it (Kolata 1993a). The massive portals standing at the east edge of Pumapunku were pushed over and smashed in place (Protzen and Nair 2000, 2002). Many Tiwanaku sculptures show similar patterns of destruction. The feline face of a basalt *chachapuma* recovered from the base of the Akapana, one of several that once flanked its west entrance, had been intentionally mutilated before being buried (Figure 8.1a). Of other sandstone and andesite monoliths, only their pedestals or shattered bodies remain. Most impressive is the massive andesite head of a Tiwanaku ancestral personage that once crowned the so-called Gigantic Monolith, perhaps the largest effigy monolith to have stood in Tiwanaku (Figure 8.1b). Like destruction of the sculpted portals in Pumapunku, ritual decapitation of the Gigantic Monolith would have required a monumental effort on the part of highly motivated zealots.

Who wreaked such havoc, and why? According to written documents, the Inca, who conquered the region some three hundred to four hundred years later, had no reason to destroy the monuments that they held in great esteem. For the Inka, Tiwanaku's stone monoliths represented the original "models" of the humans that Viracocha had created in a primordial epoch (Conklin 2004a). Inca rulers established a political-ritual complex on the old Pumapunku structure, transforming its form and meaning (Cobo 1990:100–101; Moseley 2001). They curated it and other monuments and sculptures to form a living museum – what Jason Yaeger terms a "memory theater" to enact their origin myth and solidify their power and legitimacy (Yaeger and Lopez 2004). The Inca recreated Tiwanaku in their own imaginative image. The form of the Pumapunku may have inspired one of the Inca's principal cosmic symbols (Yaeger 2004), material icons of which were erected in the central plazas of Cuzco and other regional centers. In such ways, the Inca asserted Tiwanaku's cosmic and spatiotemporal primacy in their own built places, incorporated societies, and imperial projects.

Spanish priests, adventurers, and administrators were notoriously less kind. It is likely that a great deal of destruction occurred during the long Colonial Period, in particular with the establishment of "zero-sum" anti-native religious practices after 1570 or after the great native rebellions of the late eighteenth century. Yet evidence for Spanish defacement appears on only two monoliths that remain intact. Both of these, including the great Ponce Monolith, had been interred almost unblemished in what appears to be proper Christian burials (Conklin 2004a). Tiwanaku's destruction has continued into recent times. As noted in Chapter 1, railway employees dynamited several stones and monoliths, and the Bolivian army trained their guns on others for target practice. A simple walk through Tiahuanaco today will convince the most casual tourist that local populations for centuries have mined Tiwanaku's monuments for their elegant, conveniently located carved stones. Colonial and more recent destruction in many cases is apparent, and overall it has been opportunistic.

Much monumental destruction occurred as part of the volatile process of state collapse. Recurring patterns of facial mutilation and decapitation on monoliths indicate that their destruction was highly ritualized rather than opportunistic; icons were ritually "killed" while they still had great meaning and power. More profoundly than the razing of the Putuni Palaces, the ritualized destruction and defacement of icons representing elite ancestors targeted the ideological foundations of power and legitimacy among Tiwanaku's elite. I argue that much of it was wrought just as Tiwanaku populations – elite and commoner – fragmented into conflictive factions, and as powerful gestures of symbolic violence.

Regional Politics, Environment, and Human Agency

Volatile pan-regional political conditions and deteriorating climate, it appears, catalyzed cumulative local tensions that had begun to render fragile Tiwanaku's foundations of state power. Conflict in Moquegua, which by all accounts involved Wari and local populations, resulted in the destruction of Tiwanaku's maize-producing colonies by AD 1000. It remains to be determined whether similar conflicts characterized other Tiwanaku provinces, such as Cochabamba. Whatever the case, the collapse of Wari at roughly the same time strongly suggests that the end of the Middle Horizon was, in part, a powerful, widespread, and cumulative reaction to the centralized imperial structures and policies that had dominated the Andean highlands for several centuries.

Drought in the altiplano rendered raised-field systems unreliable and in many sectors no longer viable, and it diminished supplies of valued

Figure 8.1 Ritually mutilated Tiwanaku sculptures: a basalt *chachapuma* from the base of Akapana's stairway (a); and the "decapitated" head of the Gigantic Monolith (b).

lake resources such as fish and *totora*. Much of the vast agricultural estate of the Koani Pampa, which had subsidized the massive feasts and ceremonies that supported elite power and state hierarchy, now lay interminably fallow. The food and drink that fueled bouts of competition among elite factions and that established working relations of patronage and reciprocity between elites and commoners, dwindled severely. Consumption and commensalism, *collective effervescence* and *communitas*, to borrow, respectively, from Emile Durkheim and Victor Turner, had forged and continually invigorated a shared, prestigious Tiwanaku identity. The consumable goods that facilitated such relations of power and identity were now scarce. The state's very raison d'être, the lifeblood of its unity, was disappearing.

Macro-sociopolitical and environmental transformations did not simplistically cause state collapse. Drought conditions and pan-regional conflict exacerbated an already volatile society and landscape at home. The foundation of state power had been rendered especially fragile over the course of Tiwanaku's later history, as elites sought to establish greater control over urban centers, farming systems, trade networks, ritual centers, and livelihoods. Tiwanaku leaders had seriously strained an enduring etiquette of social values, inciting contradictory consciousness and the potential for symbolic and physical violence. This is not to suggest that it provoked a commoner, or "egalitarian," revolt. The sociopolitical systems that arose out of Tiwanaku's ashes, if not rigidly centralized, were distinctly hierarchical. Rather, this profound negation of Tiwanaku ideals, symbols, and practices was the work of large factions involving people of various roles, statuses, and identities. Regional leaders in the Machaca region to the south, which rose in importance and population, may have played a key role in this transformation. In the upper Moquegua Valley, new Tumilaca sites after AD 1000 may represent a diaspora of defecting, previously Tiwanaku-affiliated populations (Owen 2005). These groups may have played a dynamic role in ending Tiwanaku state influence and destroying earlier settlements in the region.

Disenfranchised groups with ancestry in the Katari Valley, whether residing in their homeland or in diaspora communities, also may have fomented state collapse. It is telling that the ancient boundary between the Tiwanaku and Katari valleys reemerged with a vengeance after, and perhaps in the course of state collapse. In the Taraco hills between them emerged a long line of fortresses and refuge sites that effectively defined in military terms a boundary that had predated Tiwanaku.

As elite power eroded, centralized state hegemony become increasingly untenable. A common identity and an elegant hierarchical cosmology centered on Tiwanaku monuments, symbols, elites, and royal ancestors, once celebrated as the spiritual sources of life and regeneration for all, became increasingly difficult to justify or recreate. Instead, as conditions deteriorated and people's livelihoods were increasingly threatened, the tables turned against Tiwanaku leaders. Groups with revitalized local identities turned away from and to some extent against what were now considered the sources of deteriorating conditions. Life in Tiwanaku's centers gradually became undesirable, and ruling residences and depictions of royal ancestors became the target for violence and destruction.

Tiwanaku had risen as a seductive ritual and political phenomenon grounded in ideals of tolerance, diversity, and consent. Emergent elite groups and shifting regional conditions eroded such ideals in Tiwanaku's later years. Ultimately, it was humans and emerging social tensions that fragmented the state and rendered obsolete its key monuments and symbols. By AD 1200, as a result of natural and social forces, Tiwanaku was no longer a vibrant part of social identity in its own heartland.

Figure 8.2 Guman Poma's rendering of *Auca Runa*, or epoch of
"warlike people" that preceded the Inca Empire (adapted from
Guaman Poma 1992[1615]).

After the State

The Late Intermediate Period

The phases following the collapse of Tiwanaku and Wari remain among
the most mysterious in the culture history of the highland Andes. According to Guaman Poma (1992), the Inca characterized the epoch immedi-
ately preceding their own (that of "the sun"), as *Auca Runa*, or that of
the "warlike people" (Figure 8.2). This idea seamlessly blends myth and

history in setting the stage for the Inca Empire. During this time, Guaman Poma tells us, social organization and technology advanced greatly over that of the previous epoch, *Purun Runa*, or that of the "wild men." *Ayllu* organization first emerged along with its respected leaders, and the world was first divided into four parts, or *suyu*. Yet, as people became increasingly belligerent, cruel, and prone to drunkenness, they abandoned their fertile lowlands for the mountains where they built stone fortresses, or *pukaras*. The myth of the *Auca Runa* casts Inca imperial hegemony in the golden and benevolent light of its sun deity, Inti. It is not unlike the evolutionary schemes that drive Western common sense.

Historical documents and documented myths such as that of *Auca Runa* offer clues to the four-hundred-year period that preceded such documentation. Yet it is easy to fall into the trap of interpreting them too literally. We need archaeology to balance the biases inherent in documents written by people who, like any of us, had personal opinions and wrote for specific political or professional ends. People may lie, but their garbage cannot.

The scope and shape of cultural transformation in the Andes varied greatly according to local conditions and historical circumstances. In the central Andes, an ideology celebrating intensive farming shifted to ideologies emphasizing reciprocal integration between farming and herding communities (Parsons, Hastings, and Matos 1997). Duality is manifest at multiple nested levels. Many settlements were divided in two by internal walls, and settlements of equivalent role and size were frequently "paired," suggesting that they represented complementary halves of larger communities. Walls, ditches, and tombs located at the boundaries of settlements "may have served to formally demarcate moiety boundaries by providing stages for the performance of integrative public ritual" (Parsons, Hastings, and Matos 1997:334), whether mortuary rites or ritual battles. Groups of farmers and herders, in turn, formed encompassing *ayllus*, each with its respective representatives and leaders. Large sites located between farming and herding communities, or between the sierra and *puna* zones, served as political-ritual centers for such *ayllus*. Mortuary rituals recharged group memory and identity, and ceremonies enacted in massive cemeteries may have fortified broad interpolity boundaries.

The altiplano supported a network of independent, interacting polities. By the fifteenth century, these formed a number of interacting kingdoms, or *señorios*, with fluid political boundaries and volatile histories. The best-documented polities were those most critical to Inca hegemony, including the adjacent polities of Colla and Lupaca in the northwest Lake Titicaca Basin. To the south, in regions that included the old Tiwanaku heartland, were the loosely integrated Pacajes federations. Further south, in the dry central altiplano, were polities and confederations such as Carangas, Killakas, Qaraqara, and Charcas. Sometimes hostile and sometimes joining forces to form macrofederations, these polities interacted intensively with each other and with societies in other regions. Their boundaries, like their political structures, were fluid and volatile.

Not even Colla and Lupaca, the most influential polities in the south-central Andes just before the Inca arrived, were archaic states in a strict sense. In fact, the documented fame of Lupaca's leaders Qari and Qusi, and their claims to lands in the warm western valleys, owed greatly to their collaboration with the Inca against their longtime enemies, the Colla (Stanish 1989, 1992; van Buren 1996). While these polities were hierarchical in political structure and wide ranging in interaction and trade, they were also discontinuous in space and shifting through time. In some respects, they are reminiscent of recent chiefly societies in Polynesia and elsewhere.

The fall of the Middle Horizon states fostered and resulted from the rise of these new political systems, interaction networks, and cultural values in the high Andes. Archaeology bears out some of the patterns narrated in the *Auca Runa* myth. Settlement dispersed in the old cores of the Wari and Tiwanaku states as groups abandoned nucleated urban centers. Across the Andes, people eventually began to build mountaintop *pukaras* above nearby towns and villages (Parsons and Hastings 1988; Stanish 2003). *Pukaras* served social integration and identity. Some served as fortresses or refuge camps for locals, others served major ceremonies and ritual battles, and some housed extensive permanent settlement (Figure 8.3). They tended to be located in sight of one another. Such patterns suggest that they served, by means of signal fires, mirrors, or other means, to communicate messages quickly over vast regions, whether calling political meetings, marking the beginning of a festival, or warning of potential attack. Aymara communities continue to conduct similar activities today.

Yet the Late Intermediate Period was not simply a dark age of constant conflict. Three or four generations after collapse in the central and south-central Andes, population density increased in many regions. If hostilities had intensified, they did so in the context of new political systems and vibrant interaction networks. New productive systems were more resilient in the face of much drier conditions, a resilience that had been strained for the sake of intensive farming whether on terraces under Wari or raised fields under Tiwanaku. This is most clear in the post–Tiwanaku Lake Titicaca Basin. Production on raised fields declined but did not end abruptly. Rather raised-field farming continued on a smaller scale, complementing cultivation in *qochas* and irrigation-fed hill slopes.

Figure 8.3 View of the terraced mountaintop site of Pukara de
Khonkho, a densely populated *pukara* in the Machaca region of the
altiplano.

As significant, the relative role of camelid herding increased in importance throughout the region (Graffam 1992; Janusek and Kolata 2003).
Access to ample grazing lands was now paramount, which explains both
the highly dispersed settlement choices of post-Tiwanaku populations
and their renewed interest in the high *puna*. At the Tiwanaku site of
Palermo, Peru, a sunken temple now served as a makeshift corral (Stanish
2003:199). Many groups became mobile pastoralists, traveling seasonally
to higher ground to tend herds or to distant regions to trade for desired
goods. By AD 1450, the Inca considered Collasuyu the most lucrative
Andean region in terms of "wealth on the hoof" (Murra 1980 [1956]).
Following state fragmentation, communities returned to an ideal that
had always proved reliable at local scales: maximizing diversity to minimize risk. Maximizing wealth, an ideal that increasingly gained currency
during the Middle Horizon, had failed. Raised-field segments, and most
likely terrace systems in the central Andes, were now incorporated into
productive regimes that favored more balanced mosaics of agropastoral
enterprises.

Corresponding with such transformations were new social organizations, cultural practices, and religious ideals. The *ayllus* so common until

Figure 8.4 Rectangular *chullpas* in the Carangas region of the Bolivian altiplano. Note the three holes above each of their doorways, in which were fixed wooden ceremonial drinking *keros*.

recently across the highland Andes crystallized during this time. They gained power just as Wari and Tiwanaku collapsed and as people adapted to new social and environmental conditions. This paradigmatic form of Andean social organization emerged not without precedent in the Middle Horizon. *Ayllus* were historically grounded in the urban and rural corporate and regional ethnic groups that for generations had characterized Tiwanaku, and most likely Wari, society. Nested *ayllu* organization as we know it is a resilient, variable social form whose roots are sunk deep in the Andean past, and whose historical form took on new dimensions after state hegemony.

Mortuary rituals now centered on mummified remains housed in aboveground burial chambers, or *chullpas* (Figure 8.4; Isbell 1997a; Rydén 1947; Stanish 2003). Like Middle Horizon burials, *chullpas* were material symbols and places that conjured a group's ancestry and identity. In most regions, in fact, *chullpas* coexisted with subterranean tombs. Unlike subterranean cist burials in Tiwanaku and Wari, a group's *chullpas* were highly visible symbols of its ancestry and identity. Each housed multiple mummy bundles, the ancestors of an entire *ayllu*, on some prominent point in the landscape. *Chullpas* varied greatly in elaboration and style, manifesting both infraregional status distinctions and interregional ethniclike or macro-*ayllu* differences. In the volatile generations following collapse, as land tenure became more volatile and open to question, *chullpas* symbolically fixed a community to the physical landscape.

Ceramic vessels also changed markedly. In the Lake Titicaca Basin, Tiwanaku's sophisticated "technology of consumption" disappeared in favor of a limited range of small bowls (Janusek 2003a). *Keros*, *tazons*, *escudillas*, and a wide range of other forms that had been dedicated to communal consumption disappeared completely. Iconography no longer depicted religious and mythical icons but rather quickly executed images of llamas, corrals, and abstract designs. Large cooking pots and fermentation jars, which had become increasingly significant under Tiwanaku, became uncommon. Most striking about the shift in ceramic technology is that nondecorated domestic ceramic wares changed only minimally. What disappeared, in essence, were the intricate ceramic assemblages that advertised Tiwanaku mythical imagery, facilitated commensalism, and fostered Tiwanaku's composite identity.

In the southern basin, local populations adopted new ceramic styles and new mortuary rites through interaction with other societies and to break with the past. Cultural shift was both adoption and creation. Groups sought to interact and affiliate with other groups in the wake of collapse, while intentionally negating the styles, practices, and ideals that emblemized the state. New ceramic assemblages like new mortuary practices expressed a distinctly non-Tiwanaku (and, to some extent, perhaps, anti-Tiwanaku) ideology.

Society and cosmology transformed as societies became more heterarchical. Duality, an ancient and enduring principle, more than centrality, a principle that had gained currency during the Middle Horizon, took the day as a conceptual foundation for social, political, and cosmic orders. Each macro-*ayllu* community now consisted of asymmetrical, complementary, and competing halves, or moieties. Within each moiety, and forming another ethniclike distinction, were *ayllus* that identified as either Aymara or Uru, depending on their occupation and civility. More broadly, the entire Lake Titicaca Basin was now divided into Urkosuyu and Umasuyu. Geographically, Urkosuyu referred to societies on the west side of the lake, while Umasuyu referred to societies on its east side. To the south, the geopolitical boundary fell between the Tiwanaku and Katari Valleys and may have followed the Taraco Range. It followed a social boundary that not only had figured as a central element in Tiwanaku culture and political structure but may have predated Tiwanaku hegemony. After Tiwanaku, the boundary correlated with the use of Urko and Uma Pacajes vessels, two different styles of serving bowls (Janusek 2003a). Most telling, a line of high-altitude *pukaras* emerged deep in the Taraco hills. In one sense, the old enmity between the Tiwanaku and Katari valleys reemerged. Yet the *pukaras* clearly formed a regional sociopolitical boundary that also, in characteristic Andean fashion, most likely integrated two distinct macrocommunities in reciprocal bonds. In the wake of Tiwanaku state collapse, new forms took on old meanings and old forms new meanings.

Cultural reformulation created new ways of life as much as it literally buried those considered less meaningful. It was the product of continuous human activity on the part of groups whose integrity and identity were built into past urban and rural landscapes. In tandem with balanced productive regimes, a nonintegrated political landscape, and new centers and leaders, groups fashioned new styles and practices to express different, non-Wari and non-Tiwanaku values and ideals. Eventually, Tiwanaku, like Wari, no longer held a central place in local myth and social memory.

Tiwanaku, Wari, and the Inca State

Some archaeologists now acknowledge that the collapse of Middle Horizon states was historically interwoven with the rise of the Inca state a couple of centuries later. Tiwanaku disintegrated only a few generations before the emerging Inca state gained momentum in Cuzco (Bauer 1992; McEwan, Chatfield, and Gibaja 2002). Yet the attitude of the Inca royal dynasty toward Tiwanaku and Lake Titicaca was very different from what it was toward memory of Wari and its inheritors. On the one hand, Inca settlement planning drew heavily on that of Wari. Inca site layout, the use of extensive walled enclosures (what the Inca termed *kanchas*), internal niches, and fieldstone masonry all had precedents in Wari sites. The core of the Inca state was geographically near the old Wari heartland. Recent work in the Cuzco region suggests that a major ethnic component of the emergent Inca were Lucre Basin inhabitants (McEwan, Chatfield, and Gibaja 2002; Moseley 2001:248). Living near the abandoned Wari centers of Huaro and Pikillacta, these people continued to build monumental architecture and craft polychrome ceramic wares throughout the Late Intermediate Period, unlike the Killke who lived near the Inca capital itself. The Inca appear to have co-opted these cultural preferences to craft their early state and, eventually, a pan-Andean empire.

Yet, the Inca made no overt reference to Wari in known myths and histories. It is as if their imperial strategies were best appropriated and their cultural legacy forgotten. Helping explain this conundrum is the fact that the Wari heartland of Ayacucho was the homeland of the Inca's great pre-imperial nemesis, the Chanka. Inca mythical history relays the story of a great battle between the Inca and the Chanka that is reminiscent of biblical Armageddon. Inca victory under the epic leader Pachacuti – in which stones themselves came to life as warriors on their side – gave the Inca a divine mandate to rule the Andes. Yet close reading of the documented history of the great Inca-Chanka war suggests that the two societies, perhaps interlinked as macromoieties in characteristic Andean fashion, engaged in periodic ritualized battle (Urton 1999). Like the fabled holocaust of Sodom and Gomorrah, the Inca-Chanka war narrative perhaps represents not a single historical event but rather a mythicized long-term enmity and ritualized recurrence. From this perspective, the Inca failed to glorify Wari because the Chanka, their nemesis, were Wari's inheritors. The Inca appropriated Chanka's local past as readily as they killed Chanka leaders, but the Wari failed to figure prominently in Inca history. Figuring prominently in Inca mythical history was Tiwanaku's privileged legacy (see Chapter 1).

Conclusions

So what happened to the Tiwanaku? To be sure, their prestigious culture was reformulated, their integrative ideology dissipated, and their centralized political structure dismantled. Still, their descendants lived on in the southern Lake Titicaca Basin and in diasporic communities throughout the south-central Andes. Despite major cultural transformations, including significant depopulation of prior demographic centers, distant descendants of other past civilizations – the Classic Maya, the Pueblo, Imperial Rome – can be found in and near the regions where such civilizations rose and fell. Many of the cultural, religious, and sociopolitical elements that characterized Tiwanaku civilization can be found, if in highly altered form, in the very different communities that inhabit the altiplano landscape today. This is not to suggest that cultural continuity has taken the day in the millennium that has transpired since Tiwanaku collapse. Several successive hegemonic regimes, generations of intermarriage and *creolizing*, and cultural transformations and ethnic reformulations have transformed forever, and continue to transform, south-central Andean cultural history.

Life in the high Andes today is a fine, perilous, and often volatile balance. It balances continuity with native traditions and the changes attendant on globalization; the political power of communities and of nation states; and communal practices and neoliberal policies. Yet as in the past, societies seek to balance egalitarian and hierarchical forces and centripetal and centrifugal tendencies. Livelihoods thrive on a pragmatic balance of secular concerns and ritual practices. People still invoke the chthonic, life-giving powers of earth, water, and mountains for the well-being of humans, their crops, and herds just as they seamlessly seek redemption in the celestial powers of Christianity. As much is clear in ongoing Aymara political movements that challenge state authority and seek to establish a greater role for native voices in contemporary national politics in Bolivia and Peru. It is fascinating, if frightening, to consider what the future in Tiwanaku's old heartland may bring.

9   Conclusion

Men make their own history, but they do not make it just as they please; they do not make it under circumstances chosen by themselves, but under circumstances directly encountered, given and transmitted from the past. The tradition of all the dead generations weighs like a nightmare on the brain of the living.

– Karl Marx 1986[1852]:97

"Rationality is bounded ... because the human mind is socially bounded, socially structured. The individual is always, whether he likes it or not, trapped [within limits ... he owes to his upbringing and training] – *save to the extent that he becomes aware of it* ...

– Pierre Bourdieu and Loïc J. D. Wacquant 1992:126 [emphasis mine]

Tiwanaku was an extremely complex and highly dynamic civilization. Investigators have variously interpreted Tiwanaku as a religious phenomenon, a predatory state, and a political federation. Tiwanaku's religious importance is clear in its Formative origins, monumental temples and monuments, iconographic imagery, and medicinal/ritual complex. Tiwanaku eventually developed into an imperial phenomenon that incorporated and colonized far-flung regions, including the warm valleys of Moquegua and Cochabamba and the cold but mineral-rich landscape of Santiago de Huari. Intensification of political centralization after AD 800 is manifest in many domains of life in its central cities, rural landscapes, and peripheral regions.

Tiwanaku also was a vast community in which people of diverse trades, languages, lifestyles, and homelands invested their hearts, minds, and careers. It consisted of peoples of diverse affiliations and interests who conducted variable livelihoods and participated in overlapping communities of practice. People of diverse backgrounds and languages made Tiwanaku their home. Much like contemporary communities and nations, Tiwanaku was a cosmopolitan and ever-shifting social phenomenon that eludes simplistic interpretation. Above all, it was a project of social integration, and Tiwanaku itself became the most significant – though by no means exclusive -place of social encounter and interaction. Like any civilization that dominates a world region, Tiwanaku promoted its practices and values as utopian and highly redemptive directives for this and the after-life.

In this final chapter, I summarize some of the principal conclusions of this study in relation to a few salient questions that it and past research present for future investigation into Tiwanaku and the Middle Horizon Andes.

Practice Theory and Tiwanaku

A theoretical approach informed by practice theory, one which emphasizes the means of human dwelling in the world, gives particular weight to three interrelated dimensions of Tiwanaku. First, it illuminates the complexity of Tiwanaku's cultural and political integration, particularly in regard to the innumerable households, kin-groups, elite factions, ethnic groups, and polities that composed it, and the multiple strategies of interaction that its leaders juggled to influence or control far-flung regions. Second, it recognizes that human-environment relations were dynamic. This is as clear in Tiwanaku collapse as it is in the ongoing production of anthropogenic landscapes and the cultural incorporation of natural references and celestial cycles. Third, this approach treats history as a complex, cumulative, and fundamentally social phenomenon rather than an inevitable one-way street driven by teleological progress or disembodied process. Enmeshed in traditional practices as Marx famously pointed out, and attuned to shifting environmental and sociopolitical conditions, human activity guided the course of history, even though its consequences were unforeseen, many of its motivations subconscious, and much of it subject to powerful contingencies and unpredictable circumstances.

Social Diversity and State Integration

Tiwanaku was the first – or "pristine" – politically centralized integration of diverse societies and landscapes in the south-central Andes. Nevertheless, spiritual and economic integration in the Lake Titicaca Basin and its environs preceded the Tiwanaku state by several hundred years. The circum-Titicaca Yayamama religious tradition and its attendant multi-centered economic networks fostered the rise of cultural complexes such as Chiripa in the south and Qaluyu in the north. The Late Formative witnessed shifts in agropastoral production and interregional interaction that fostered the rise of interacting communities and regional polities, including multicommunity polities in the south and Pukara in the north.

Tiwanaku coalesced out of a matrix of cultural principles, socioeconomic networks, productive regimes, and religious ideologies that had been developing over centuries. Its creative brilliance rested in a conjunction of cultural syntheses and transformations: the rise of Tiwanaku itself as a center of caravan trade and festival; the coalescence of a flexible, tolerant, and seductive ideology; and the formation of an inclusive domain of cultural affiliation and identity – an encompassing, prestigious imagined community. Tiwanaku became a place of social and ritual encounter for diverse communities. Diversity characterized the social, spatial, and ritual landscapes of the central cities, the productive economies of its hinterland, and the sociopolitical constitution of its peripheries. The social diversity so integral to Tiwanaku's unity remained vital throughout its generations of hegemony. It crystallized fiercely, if founded on new principles, in the state's final decades.

A combination of local social and natural conditions and core interests and strategies shaped Tiwanaku's geopolitical diversity across the south-central Andes. In Tiwanaku 1, state interest in local resources and landscapes varied. Critical resources sought by emergent Tiwanaku elite groups included salt and minerals from Potosi and northern Chile, psychotropic substances and exotic items from the humid valleys east of Lake Titicaca, and maize, coca and other ritual goods from temperate valleys such as Cochabamba and Moquegua. State control over local regions varied according to existing natural and social conditions, but in most cases, it involved some form of incorporative strategy that thrived on interaction with local groups and their neighbors. At the frontiers of colonies such as Cochabamba and Moquegua, local polities such as Mizque and Azapa prospered. Pan-regional cultural development in the south-central Andes developed as much from interaction with Tiwanaku and the local adoption and interpretation of its goods, symbols, and ideals, as it did from Tiwanaku political "expansion" into foreign territories.

In Tiwanaku 2, Tiwanaku's interests became more focused and its strategies more invasive. Tiwanaku also may have developed cozier relations with Wari leaders during this time. To support Tiwanaku's growing elite factions, feasting economy, and consumptive culture, control over maize in temperate valleys and over tubers and quinoa in the Lake Titicaca Basin became critical. Colonization of and control over productive areas in Katari and Moquegua intensified, and the organization of local settlement and production was transformed. Substantial renewal in Tiwanaku's urban core and on the Island of the Sun indicates that religion and ritual practice became more singular and morally dogmatic. Accompanying increasing political and economic centralization was a more rigidly conservative and less tolerant ideological attitude. As questions for future research; Were these changes instigated by intensified interaction between Tiwanaku and Wari? Given that some Wari elites adopted Tiwanaku's religious symbols, did Tiwanaku leaders, and perhaps a new ruling dynasty, reciprocally adopt Wari-style imperial strategies?

Humans and Landscape in the High Andes

Early complex societies in the south-central Andes were autonomous yet mutually interacting communities that practiced a variety of productive regimes. Those regimes varied by society and ecological zone; yet, all involved some fine balance of sedentary and transhumant livelihoods. Emergent complexity not only involved a shift in productive intensity and political structure but also in the way that people viewed and transformed the worlds they inhabited; that is, their sense of being and agency within them. Productive intensification necessitated a new way of seeing the world. It required a shift from a worldview that prioritized the natural environment as something to which one adjusted one's rhythms and skills, to a worldview in which the environment was routinely manipulated and controlled. Attending this shift was an increasing importance for ritual activity and artistic expression, whether focused on domestic settings as in Wankarani communities or on communal settings as in Chiripa.

Throughout the history of the south-central Andes, people apprehended elements of the landscape and incorporated its symbols into monuments and built environments. Yayamama sculptures depicted icons and images that communicated the power of agropastoral cycles, fertility, and ancestors. In the Late Formative, stone sculptures meshed the power of natural forces with community ancestors and emergent high-status lineages. Making reference to the altiplano landscape and natural cycles intensified during the Tiwanaku period, when new generations of artisans carved *totora* reed lintels over the entrance to the Pumapunku and designed intricate water-management networks throughout the urban core. Artisans continued to sculpt representations of natural features and productive elements onto a new style of stone monoliths. These now also featured celestial images of a solar cult that Tiwanaku rulers most likely proselytized, and references to a calendar system kept by priests to efficiently integrate diverse productive regimes and coordinate recurring ritual events. The specific symbols that each monolith depicted and the natural icons that each emphasized were unique. Tiwanaku was a syncretism of religious cults and creeds. Its monuments both valorized and reified the social identities, ecological settings, and livelihoods of the different groups that made up Tiwanaku's increasingly vast community.

Tiwanaku hegemony transformed the altiplano landscape and its environs. It would be difficult to define a truly "natural" landscape in the Lake Titicaca Basin after the sixth century AD (Erickson 2000). On a scale that far surpassed that of previous generations, state imperialism induced major changes in the ecological conditions of the south-central Andes. Increasing population densities and settlement sizes in the Tiwanaku core magnified human exploitation of the environment and its resources. Intensified herding and grazing of camelids taxed pasturage and may have stimulated the construction of corrals, settlements, and irrigation networks in *puna* zones. Research at Iwawe suggests that intensive fishing may have transformed the lake's ecology and fish flocks. Intensification in farming, and especially in raised fields, permanently transformed the ecology of the region. It is possible that, at its peak, raised-field farming raised average temperatures substantially across the basin.

Intriguing questions arise: Did productive intensification instigate collapse by overtaxing the precarious altiplano environment? Overfishing and overhunting can lead to the depletion of animal species; overgrazing can instigate hillside erosion and fallow plots; and the world over, intensive farming notoriously accelerates erosion, nutrient depletion, and especially salinization (Figure 9.1). Such possibilities remain to be thoroughly investigated. It is likely that in Tiwanaku 2, to support Tiwanaku's more centralized political structure, more powerful elite factions, and an ever-growing feasting economy, the altiplano environment was increasingly overworked. Combined with an increasingly demanding and volatile sociopolitical milieu, such intensification may have rendered the region particularly vulnerable to drought and erosion in the eleventh and twelfth centuries. To the extent that intensified production and consumption were macroregional phenomena, increasing sociopolitical complexity may have exacerbated productive problems across the south-central Andes. Once again, testing such possibilities will be the work of future research.

Long-Term History and Cultural Regeneration

A founding point of this study is that social change is circumstantial and cumulative rather than evolutionary or driven by "progress." History is directed neither by abstract teleological forces nor a few good (or bellicose) men. The culture and history of a society are never completely dictated by environment or even its catastrophic shifts, for humans usually act on and adapt to them even in the harshest conditions. Nor can an archaic state and its transformations be explained simply by appeal to externalized, metahistorical processes. Shifts in sociopolitical,

Figure 9.1 Salt-encrusted fossil raised field beds of the Katari Valley.

ideological, and environmental conditions together fostered major historical junctures such as state emergence, consolidation, and collapse. Further exploring these dynamic conjunctions and transformations is a challenge for future research.

The trajectory of Tiwanaku history illuminates the critical roles played by humans acting as members of local groups and communities over the long term. Tiwanaku emerged out of a dynamic cultural and sociopolitical milieu as a socially diversified and spiritually syncretic phenomenon. For all of its later "hardness" and centralization, Tiwanaku remained a vast, prestigious imagined community. Like identification with any nation today, local identification with Tiwanaku as a pan-Andean phenomenon was one of many overlapping identities that an individual or group juggled and internalized. People of diverse backgrounds celebrated massive temples such as the Kalasasaya and Akapana, for it is they who helped build them; it is they, at least as much as high-status leaders and coordinators, who invested their identity, emotions, and spirituality in such monuments. As patent in highlighting the decisive roles of local communities was the increasing importance of consumption in Tiwanaku society, and in particular of lively feasting events. If feasting was partly an elite mechanism for distributing obligations and loyalties, it also was the condition on which people participated in, affiliated with, and subjected themselves to Tiwanaku hegemony. As long as other things remained equal, this condition – this *covenant* – was honored. Once things became alarmingly unequal, it was discarded.

Profound post-Tiwanaku cultural transformations attest Tiwanaku's increasingly centralized and hierarchical character. The ritualized destruction of Tiwanaku monuments indicates that its spirituality and symbolism had become increasingly onerous and anachronistic. Razing elite palaces such as Putuni sent even more direct messages of disaffection. Yet Tiwanaku's collapse was part of a constructive process of creating new domestic and ritual practices, material styles, and ways of living in and interpreting the world. Like Tiwanaku's rise, its collapse was a panregional process of cultural revolution and regeneration. A major lacuna in our archaeological knowledge of the region is a sound understanding of this transformation and the emergence of post-Tiwanaku societies in the Lake Titicaca Basin and across the south-central Andes. Future research must seek to resolve the intricacies of Tiwanaku disintegration and the complex trajectory of post-Tiwanaku cultural regeneration.

Past phenomena such as Tiwanaku are to some extent timeless. Centers of civilization such as Teotihuacan, Uruk, Xian, Cahokia, and Rome all have this in common. Their material ruins and symbolic significance far outlive their time of imperial greatness: The Inca venerated Tiwanaku as their mythical homeland, Spanish zealots derided it for its anti-Christian devils, and state-funded Bolivian archaeologists recreated it as their national patrimony. Today, archaeologists of diverse nationalities earn their livings studying it, "New Agers" consider it a center of spiritual power; and native Aymara have reclaimed it as their native heritage. Tiwanaku remains powerful; it continues to shape culture, knowledge, and history far beyond its immediate landscape and homeland. Indeed, as Marx noted, the traditions of generations long since deceased continue to weigh on the brains of the living, if by complexly interwoven means. Through tourism, archaeology, and fanciful New Age interpretations, Tiwanaku's impact has now reached global proportions.

There is no single and uniquely valid interpretation of or claim to Tiwanaku. In fact, there never was. Like the diverse, partially conflictive interpretations of Tiwanaku that have arisen over the millennium since its collapse, the visions of Tiwanaku held by those who lived in, affiliated with, worshiped in, or fought with ancient Tiwanaku differed phenomenally. In part because of conflicting claims on the past, the fate of Tiwanaku's monuments and progeny remain in the balance. On August 6, 2000, native altiplano communities wrested the ruins from state control and reclaimed the ancient site as their rightful heritage. On December 18, 2005, Bolivia elected its first "native" president, Evo Morales. On January 21, 2006, just a few days after I finished writing this book, the new president, hundreds of participants, and world leaders from several nations traveled to Tiwanaku for his ceremonial inauguration. The main ceremony took place in the sunken court of the Kalasasaya, framed by the Ponce Monolith: an ancient ceremonial space that is politically potent to this day.

Tensions in the disparate and, to some extent, opposed interests of the different communities that stake a claim in Tiwanaku are on the rise, as they are among the nations we inhabit in this world of increasingly global seductions and hegemonies. Tiwanaku ruins, native Andean populations, the Bolivian state, and all of the other nations that constitute the global network, thrive in an entangled and precarious mesh of human interests and social forces. Becoming aware of the transformative power of our everyday thought and activity, as Marx and Bourdieu knew well, is perhaps the first necessary movement toward turning the living and in many ways burdensome past we have inherited into a constructive future.

Glossary

All words are Aymara or Quechua except where indicated as Spanish

achachila: a sacred mountain to which offerings are periodically made, and more specifically, the spiritual force embodied in a particularly imposing snow-capped peak.

altiplano: the Andean high plateau.

ayllu: an indigenous kin-based group or community whose members share common labor obligations, lands, rituals, and/or ancestors.

ayni: kin-based or community aid in labor, which is expected to be reciprocated in kind.

bofedal: (Spanish) spongy, marshy wetland fed either by mountain springs or groundwater.

bola (also *boleadora*): (Spanish) a throwing device made of weights that hang from interconnected cords, designed to capture animals by entangling their appendages. In the past, they also served as weapons in battle.

cacera: a repeat buyer/seller, or a person with whom one regularly conducts business or other transactions, and in return typically gives or receives a *yapa*, or "something extra."

cañiwa: see quinoa

chachapuma: a human or were-feline, typically depicted as a human or human-like being wearing a feline mask and/or accoutrements (see Figure 6.7).

charqui: an Andean jerky made from dried and salted meat, most commonly that of llamas and alpacas.

chicha: (Spanish; *k'usa* or *ch'ua* in Aymara): a native Andean drink most frequently made by fermenting maize, but also made with fermented quinoa, *molle*, or any of several other vegetables and fruits, and often "spiked" with other ingredients, including plants with narcotic or hallucinogenic properties.

ch'iji: (see ichu)

chuño: an eminently storable freeze-dried tuber. *Chuño* is made by leaving potatoes outside for several days so that they freeze at night and dry out in the strong daytime sun (see Figure 2.3). *Tunta* is a similar product made by freeze-drying and then re-hydrating tubers in water.

conquistadores: (Spanish) Spanish conquerors

cordillera: (Spanish) a mountain range

cuy: the guinea pig, domesticated early in the Andes for its tasty meat.

escudilla: see *kero*

ichu: a hard, spiny-tipped bunchgrass that covers vast portions of the altiplano (note *ichu* in the foreground of Figure 2.9). Ch'iji is a smaller, greener grass that grows in relatively low, wet portions of the altiplano.

incensario: an elegantly crafted ceremonial incense burner employed in Tiwanaku ceremonial and mortuary contexts, and frequently modeled in the form of a feline or llama. *Sahumadors* were less elaborate incense burners employed in domestic contexts, and they very likely doubled as lamps.

kero: a ceramic drinking goblet, first made popular during the Middle Horizon in Tiwanaku and Wari cultures (see Figures 4.20 and 4.26). In Tiwanaku, it was used in both ceremonial feasts and quotidian meals. Also common in Tiwanaku was the *tazon* or flaring bowl, most likely used to consume soups and stews. The elegantly crafted, flaring-rim *escudilla* bowl was largely limited to high status and ceremonial activities.

kiswara (Buddleja coriacea): a relatively small evergreen tree or shrub native to the Andes, and that grows up to altitudes of 4400 m.

mallku: a traditional hereditary lord of altiplano polities and macro-*ayllus*. The term also refers to a sacred mountain peak (*apu* in Quecha) and the Andean condor.

marka: this term refers most generally to a people or community, and more specifically to its primary center or town.

mashwa: see *oca*

molle: (*Shinus molle*) a moderately sized (5-18 m. tall) tree or shrub, also known as the pepper tree, that produces a small, bright red aromatic fruit traditionally employed, among other things, to make a fermented drink in some parts of the Andes.

nuña: (Spanish): see *tarwi*

oca: (*Oxalis tuberosa*) an elongated, sweet-tasting tuber that is important to the Andean diet. As important, *ulluco (Ullucus tuberosus)* is a small and brightly colored tuber known as *papa lisa* in Spanish. Only slightly less significant is *mashwa (Tropaeolum tuberosum)*, a small tuber with a somewhat bitter taste that is frequently boiled in stews.

olla: (Spanish) a ceramic cooking vessel.

pampa: the low, flat, and frequently waterlogged portions of the Andean high plateau.

pukara: a fortress, lookout, or place of refuge. *Pukara* most commonly refers to the high-altitude defensive sites established in the Andes after the Middle Horizon.

puna: the high-altitude grasslands of the Andean high plateau, generally over 4000 meters above sea level.

qocha: an artificial sunken basin for capturing and storing water to enhance agropastoral production, particularly in areas distant from substantial lakes or rivers.

quebrada: (Spanish) a ravine or gorge.

quinoa: (*Chenopodium quinoa*) a hardy grain that is well-adapted to high-altitude conditions and is rich in protein. For thousands of years, cultivated quinoa has been a critical part of the Andean diet. Also high in protein, *cañiwa* is even more frost-resistant and can grow at extremely high elevations.

reducciónes: (Spanish) new towns created in the sixteenth century as a pan-Andean Spanish Colonial program to nucleate, control, and effectively tax indigenous populations.

sahumador: see *incensario*

suni: the altitudinal zone of ~3500–4000 meters above sea level that forms the base of the Andean high plateau.

tarwi: (*Lupinus mutabilis*) a hardy Andean legume with large seeds that are extremely high in protein. *Nuña* (*Phaseolus vulgaris*) is a popping variety of common bean that can grow above 2500 meters.

tazon: see *kero*

tinaja: (Spanish) a type of large ceramic vessel used most commonly to store liquids and ferment alcoholic drinks. In Tiwanaku culture, *tinajas* were typically decorated with volute designs that represented the liquid it contained.

thola (t'ula): (*Baccharis incarun*) an aromatic and resinous high altitude plant thought by Aymara to have curative properties, and frequently employed in offerings or made into tea.

tunta: see *chuño*

tupu: a fastening pin, commonly used in reference to the metal pins traditionally used to fasten a woman's woven mantle.

ulluco: see *oca*

yunga: valley, or more generally the warm valley zones east and west of the altiplano (~1000–2500 meters). Today the term is used more specifically to refer to the warm, humid valleys east of the altiplano in the Bolivian Department of La Paz.

References

Abbott, Mark, Michael W. Binford, Mark Brenner, and Kerry Kelts. 1997. A 4500 14C yr high-resolution record of water-level changes in Lake Titicaca, Bolivia-Peru. *Quaternary Research* 47:169–180.

Abercrombie, Thomas A. 1998. *Pathways of memory and power: Ethnography and history among an Andean People.* Madison: University of Wisconsin Press.

Agüero P., Carolina. 2001. Contactos entre el altiplano central de Bolivia y los oasis de Atacama (800–900 DC): El caso de la cueva de Pulacayo. Instituto de Investigaciones Arqueológicas and Museo R. P. Gustavo Le Paige S. J., Universidad Católica del Norte, San Pedro de Atacama.

Albarracin-Jordan, Juan V. 1996a. *Tiwanaku: Arqueología regional y dinámica segmentaria.* La Paz, Bolivia: Plural Editores.

Albarracin-Jordan, Juan V. 1996b. Tiwanaku settlement system: The integration of nested hierarchies in the lower Tiwanaku Valley. *Latin American Antiquity* 7(3):183–210.

Albarracin-Jordan, Juan V. 1999. *The archaeology of Tiwanaku: The myths, history, and science of an ancient civilization.* La Paz, Bolivia: PAP.

Albarracin-Jordan, Juan V., Carlos Lemuz Aguirre, and Jose Luis Paz Soria. 1993. Investigaciones en Kallamarka: Primer informe de prospeccion. *Textos Antropológicos* 6:11–123.

Albarracin-Jordan, Juan V., and James E. Mathews. 1990. *Asentamientos prehispánicos del Valle de Tiwanaku,* Vol. 1. La Paz, Bolivia: CIMA.

Albores, Luis. 2002. Conservación en America Latina. *National Geographic en Español* 10(6):102–107.

Alcock, Susan E., Terence N. D'Altroy, Kathleen D. Morrison, and Carla M. Sinopoli. 2001. *Empires: Perspectives from archaeology and history.* Cambridge: Cambridge University Press.

Alconini Mújica, Sonia. 1995. *Rito, símbolo e historia en la pirámide de Akapana, Tiwanaku: Un análisis de cerámica ceremonial prehispánica.* La Paz, Bolivia: Editorial Acción.

Aldenderfer, Mark S. 1989. The Archaic Period in the south-central Andes. *Journal of World Prehistory* 3(2):117–158.

Aldenderfer, Mark S. 1991. Continuity and change in ceremonial structures at Late Preceramic Asana, Southern Peru. *Latin American Antiquity* 2(3):227–258.

Aldenderfer, Mark S. 1998. *Montane foragers: Asana and the south-central Andean Archaic.* Iowa City: University of Iowa Press.

321

Anders, Martha B. 1986. Wari experiments in statecraft: A view from Azángaro. In *Andean archaeology: Papers in memory of Clifford Evans*. R. Matos M., S. A. Turpin, and H. H. Eling, Jr., eds., pp. 201–224. Institute of Archaeology, University of California at Los Angeles.

Anders, Martha B. 1990. Maymi: Un sitio del Horizonte Medio en el Valle de Pisco. *Gaceta Arqueológica Andina* (17):27–40.

Anders, Martha B. 1991. Structure and function at the planned site of Azángaro: Cautionary notes for the model of Huari as a centralized secular state. In *Huari administrative structure: Prehistoric monumental architecture and state government*. W. H. Isbell and G. F. McEwan, eds., pp. 165–198. Washington, DC: Dumbarton Oaks.

Anders, Martha B., Susana Arce, Izumi Shimada, Victor Chang, Luis Tokuda, and Sonia Quiroz. 1998. Early Middle Horizon pottery production at Maymi, Pisco. *MASCA Research Papers in Science and Archaeology* 15:323–326.

Anderson, Benedict. 1983. *Imagined communities*. London: Verso.

Anderson, Karen. 1999. Tiwanaku political economy: The view from Cochabamba. Paper presented at the 64th annual meeting of the Society for American Archaeology, Chicago.

Anderson, Karen, Ricardo Cespedes Paz, and Ramon Sanzetenea. 1998. The Late Formative to Middle Horizon transition in Cochabamba, Bolivia. Paper presented at the 63rd annual meeting of the Society for American Archaeology, Seattle.

Anello Oliva, S. J., Giovanni. 1998 [1631]. *Historia del reino y provincias del Peru y Vidas de los varones insignes de la compania de Jesus*. Lima: Pontificia Universidad Catolica del Peru.

Angelo Zelada, Dante. 2003. *La cultura Chicha: Aproximación al pasado prehispánico de los valles sur Andinos*. Tupiza, Bolivia: Gobierno Municipal.

Angrand, Leonce. 1866. Lettre sur les Antiquites de Tiaguanaco et l'origine presumable de la plus ancienne civilisation du Haut-Perou. In *Extrait de la Revue Generale de L'architecture et des Travaux Publics*. Paris.

Arellano Lopez, Jorge. 2000. *Arqueologia de Lipes: Altiplano sur de Bolivia*. Quito: Pontificia Universidad Catolica de Ecuador.

Arguedas, Alcides. 1911. *Pueblo Enfermo: Contribución a la sicología de los Pueblos Hispanoamericanos*. Barcelona: Viuda de Luis Tasso.

Arnold, Denise Y. 1992. La casa de adobes y piedras del Inka: Género, memoria y cosmos en Qaqachaka. In *Hacia un orden Andino de las cosas*. D. Y. Arnold and J. de Dios Yapita, eds., pp. 31–108. La Paz: Hisbol/ILCA.

Arnold, Jeanne E. 1996. The Archaeology of complex hunter-gatherers. *Journal of Archaeological Method and Theory* 3:77–126.

Arriaza, Bernardo T. 1995. *Beyond death: The Chinchorro mummies of ancient Chile*. Washington, DC: Smithsonian Institution Press.

Ascher, Marcia, and Robert Ascher. 1997 [1981]. *Code of the Quipu*. New York: Dover.

Aschero, Carlos A. 2000. Figuras humanas, camélidos y espacios en la interacción circumpuneña. In *Arte en las rocas: Arte rupestre, menhires y piedras de colores en Argentina*. M. M. Podesta and M. d. Hoyos, eds., pp. 16–44. Buenos Aires: Sociedad Argentina de Antropologia.

Ashmore, Wendy, and A. Bernard Knapp. 1999. *Archaeologies of landscape: Contemporary perspectives*. Oxford: Blackwell.

Baker, Paul A., Geoffrey O. Seltzer, Sherilyn C. Fritz, Robert B. Dunbar, Matthew J. Grove, Pedro M. Tapia, Scott L. Cross, Harold D. Rowe, and James P. Broda. 2001. The history of South American tropical precipitation for the past 25,000 years. *Science* 291:640–643.

Bandelier, Adolph F. 1904. Aboriginal trephining in Bolivia. *American Anthropologist* 6:440–446.

Bandelier, Adolph F. 1910. *The islands of Titicaca and Koati.* New York: Hispanic Society of America.

Bandelier, Adolph F. 1911. The ruins at Tiahuanaco. *Proceedings of the American Antiquarian Society* 21:218–265.

Bandy, Matthew S. 1999. The Montículo excavations. In *Early settlement at Chiripa, Bolivia: Research of the Taraco Archaeological Project.* C. A. Hastorf, ed., pp. 43–50. Berkeley: Contributions of the University of California Archaeological Research Facility.

Bandy, Matthew S. 2001. Population and history in the ancient Titicaca Basin. Ph.D. dissertation, Department of Anthropology, University of California, Berkeley.

Bandy, Matthew S. 2004. Fissioning, scalar stress, and social evolution in Early Village Societies. *American Anthropologist* 106(2):322–333.

Bandy, Matthew S., Amanda B. Cohen, Paul S. Goldstein, Augusto Cardona R., and Antonio Oquiche H. 1996. The Tiwanaku occupation of Chen Chen (M1): Preliminary report on the 1995 salvage excavations. Paper presented at the 61st annual meeting of the Society for American Archaeology, New Orleans, LA.

Bandy, Matthew S., and Christine A. Hastorf. 2007. An Introduction to Kala Uyuni and the Taraco Peninsula polity. In *Kala Uyuni: An early political center in the southern Lake Titicaca Basin.* M. T. Bandy and C. A. Hastorf, eds., pp. 1–12. Berkeley: University of California Archaeological Research Facility.

Barrett, John C. 1994. *Fragments from antiquity: An archaeology of social life in Britain, 2900–1200 BC.* Oxford: Blackwell.

Barrett, John C. 2000. A thesis on agency. In *Agency in archaeology.* M.-A. Dobres and J. Robb, eds., pp. 61–68. London: Routledge.

Bastien, Joseph W. 1978. *Mountain of the condor: Metaphor and ritual in an Andean ayllu.* New York: West.

Bastien, Joseph W. 1985. Qollahuaya-Andean body concepts: A topographical-hydraulic model of physiology. *American Anthropologist* 87(3):595–611.

Bastien, Joseph W. 1988. *Healers of the Andes: Kallawaya herbalists and their medicinal plants.* Salt Lake City: University of Utah Press.

Bauer, Brian S. 1992. *The development of the Inca state.* Austin: University of Texas Press.

Bauer, Brian S., and Bradford M. Jones. 2003. Early Intermediate and Middle Horizon ceramic styles of the Cuzco Valley. *Fieldiana* 34:1–65.

Bauer, Brian S., and Charles Stanish. 2001. *Ritual and pilgrimage in the ancient Andes.* Austin: University of Texas.

Bawden, Garth. 1996. *The Moche.* Oxford: Blackwell.

Beaule, Christine D. 2002. Late Intermediate Period political economy and household organization at Jachakala, Bolivia. Ph.D. dissertation, Department of Anthropology, University of Pittsburgh.

Beck, Robin A. 2004a. Platforms of power: House, community, and social change in the Formative Lake Titicaca Basin. Ph.D. dissertation, Department of Anthropology, Northwestern University, Chicago.

Beck, Robin A. 2004b. Architecture and polity in the Formative Lake Titicaca Basin, Bolivia. *Latin American Antiquity* 15(3):323–343.

Bellamy, Hans S. 1948. *The Atlantis myth*. London: Faber and Faber.

Benevides C., Mario. 1991. Cheqo Wasi, Wari. In *Huari administrative structure: Prehistoric monumental architecture and state government*. W. A. Isbell and G. McEwan, eds., pp. 55–70. Washington, DC: Dumbarton Oaks.

Benitez, Leonardo. 2005. Time and calendrics at Tiwanaku: An archaeoastronomical study. Paper presented at the 70th annual meeting of the Society for American Archaeology, Salt Lake City.

Benitez, Leonardo. 2006. The temporal framework for a mythological pantheon. Paper presented at the 71st annual meeting of the Society for American Archaeology, San Juan.

Bennett, Wendell C. 1934. Excavations at Tiahuanaco. *Anthropological Papers of the American Museum of Natural History* 34:359–494.

Bennett, Wendell C. 1936. Excavations in Bolivia. *Anthropological Papers of the American Museum of Natural History* 35:329–507.

Bennett, Wendell C. 1953. *Excavations at Wari, Ayacucho, Peru*. New Haven, CT: Yale University Publications in Anthropology.

Bennett, Wendell C., and Junius Bouton Bird. 1964. *Andean culture history: The Archaeology of the central Andes from early man to the Incas*. Garden City, NJ: Natural History Press.

Berenguer R., José. 2004. *Caravanas, interacción, y cambio en el desierto de Atacama*. Santiago; Museo Chileno de Arte Precolombino.

Berenguer R., José, and Percy H. Dauelsberg. 1989. El norte grande en la orbita de Tiwanaku. In *Culturas de Chile: Prehistoria desde sus origines hasta los albores de la conquista*. J. Hidalgo L., V. Schiappacasse, H. Niemeyer F., C. Aldunate del S., and I. Solimano R., eds., pp. 129–180. Santiago: Editorial Andres Bello.

Berenguer R., José, Victoria Castro R., and Osvaldo Silva G. 1980. Reflexiones acerca de la presencia de Tiwanaku en el norte de Chile. *Estudios Arqueológicos* 5:81–92.

Berger, Peter L., and Thomas Luckmann. 1966. *The social construction of knowledge: A treatise in the sociology of knowledge*. New York: Anchor.

Bermann, Marc. 1994. *Lukurmata: Household archaeology in prehispanic Bolivia*. Princeton, NJ: Princeton University Press.

Bermann, Marc. 1997. Domestic life and vertical integration in the Tiwanaku heartland. *Latin American Antiquity* 8(2):93–112.

Bermann, Marc. 2003. The archaeology of households in Lukurmara. In *Tiwanaku and its hinterland: Archaeology and paleoecology of an Andean civilization*, Vol. 2. A. L. Kolata, ed., pp. 327–340. Washington, DC: Smithsonian Institution Press.

Bermann, Marc, and Jose Estevez Castillo. 1993. Jachakala: A new archaeological complex of the Department of Oruro, Bolivia. *Annals of Carnegie Museum* 62(4):311–340.

Bermann, Marc, and Jose Estevez Castillo. 1995. Domestic artifact assemblages and ritual activities in the Bolivian Formative. *Journal of Field Archaeology* 22(3):389–398.

Bertonio, P. Ludovico. 1984 [1612]. *Vocabulario de la Lengua Aymara.* Cochabamba: CERES/IFEA/MUSEF.

Betanzos, Juan de. 1996 [1551–1557]. *Narrative of the Incas.* R. Hamilton and D. Buchanan, trans. Austin: University of Texas Press.

Bhaskar, Roy. 1978. *The possibility of naturalism: A philosophical critique of the contemporary human sciences.* London: Routledge.

Biesboer, David D., Michael W. Binford, and Alan L. Kolata. 1999. Nitrogen fixation in soils and canals of rehabilitated raised fields of the Bolivian altiplano. *Biotropica* 31(2):255–267.

Binford, Michael W., Mark Brenner, and Barbara W. Leyden. 1996. Paleoecology and Tiwanaku agroecosystems. In *Tiwanaku and its hinterland: Archaeology and paleoecology of an Andean civilization,* Vol. 1. A. L. Kolata, ed., pp. 89–108. Washington, DC: Smithsonian Institution Press.

Binford, Michael W., and Alan L. Kolata. 1996. The natural and human setting. In *Tiwanaku and its hinterland: Archaeology and paleoecology of an Andean civilization,* Vol. I. A. L. Kolata, ed., pp. 23–56. Washington, DC: Smithsonian Institution Press.

Binford, Michael W., Alan L. Kolata, Mark Brenner, John W. Janusek, Matthew T. Seddon, Mark Abbott, and Jason H. Curtis. 1997. Climate variation and the rise and fall of an Andean civilization. *Quaternary Research* 47:235–248.

Blacker, Juan Carlos. 2001. Growing up Wari: An analysis of architectural style, technique, and history at the Middle Horizon site of Conchopata, Ayacucho, Peru. Master's thesis, Department of Anthropology, State University of New York, Binghamton.

Blom, Deborah E. 1999. Tiwanaku regional interaction and social identity: A bioarchaeological approach. Ph.D. dissertation, Department of Anthropology, University of Chicago.

Blom, Deborah E. 2005. Embodying borders: Human body modification and diversity in Tiwanaku Society. *Journal of Anthropological Archaeology* 24:1–34.

Blom, Deborah E., Benedikt Hallgrímsson, Linda Keng, María C. Lozada C., and Jane E. Buikstra. 1998. Tiwanaku "Colonization": Bioarchaeological implications for migration in the Moquegua Valley, Peru. *World Archaeology* 30(2):238–261.

Blom, Deborah E., and John W. Janusek. 2004. Making place: Humans as dedications in Tiwanaku. *World Archaeology* 36(1):123–141.

Blom, Deborah E., P. Ryan Williams, and Donna Nash. 2004. Mortuary remains on the mountain. Paper presented at the 69th annual meeting of the Society for American Archaeology, Montreal.

Bourdieu, Pierre. 1990. *The logic of practice.* Stanford: Stanford University Press.

Bourdieu, Pierre, and Loïc J. D. Wacquant. 1992. The purpose of reflexive sociology (the Chicago workshop). In *An invitation to reflexive sociology.* P. Bourdieu and L. J. D. Wacquant, eds., pp. 61–216.

Bouysse-Cassagne, Thérèse. 1986. Urco and Uma: Aymara concepts of space. In *Anthropological history of Andean polities.* J. Murra, N. Wachtel, and J. Revel, eds., pp. 201–227. Cambridge: Cambridge University Press.

Bouysse-Cassagne, Thérèse. 1987. *La identidad Aymara: Aproximación histórica* (Siglo XV, Siglo XVI). La Paz, Bolivia: Hisbol.

Bradley, Richard. 1998. *The significance of monuments: On the shaping of human experience in Neolithic and Bronze Age Europe.* London: Routledge.

Bragayrac D., Enrique. 1991. Archaeological excavations in the Vegachayoq Moqo sector of Huari. In *Huari administrative structure: Prehistoric monumental architecture and state government*. W. H. Isbell and G. F. McEwan, eds., pp. 71–80. Washington, DC: Dumbarton Oaks Research Library and Collection.

Brewster-Wray, Christine C. 1990. Moraduchayoq: An administrative compound at the sites of Huari, Peru. Ph.D. dissertation, Department of Anthropology, State University of New York, Binghamton.

Brockington, Donald L., David M. Pereira, R. Sanzatenea Rocha, and Maria A. Muñoz C. 1995. *Estudios arqueológicos del periodo Formativo en el sur-este de Cochabamba: 1988–89.* Cochabamba: Instituto de Investigaciones Antropologicas and the Universidad Mayor de San Simon.

Brooks, Sarah, Michael Glascock, and Martin Giesso. 1997. Source of volcanic glass for ancient Andean tools. *Nature* 386(6624):449–50.

Browman, David L. 1972. Asiruni, Pucara-Pokotia and Pajano: Pre-Tiahuanaco South Andean monolithic stone styles. Paper presented at the 34th annual meeting of the Society for American Archaeology, St. Louis.

Browman, David L. 1978a. Toward the development of the Tiahuanaco (Tiwanaku) state. In *Advances in Andean archaeology*. D. L. Browman, ed., pp. 327–349. The Hague: Mouton Publishers.

Browman, David L. 1978b. The Temple of Chiripa (Lake Titicaca, Bolivia). In *III Congreso Peruano "El hombre y la cultura Andina,"* Vol. 2. R. Matos, ed., pp. 807–13. Lima.

Browman, David L. 1980. Tiwanaku expansion and altiplano economic patterns. *Estudios Arqueológicos (Antofagasta)* 5:107–120.

Browman, David L. 1981. New light on Andean Tiwanaku. *American Scientist* 69(4):408–419.

Browman, David L. 1987. Pastoralism in highland Peru and Bolivia. In *Arid land use strategies and risk management in the Andes*. D. L. Browman, ed., pp. 121–150. Boulder, CO: Westview Press.

Browman, David L. 1990. High altitude camelid pastorlism of the Andes. In *The world of pastorlism: Herding systems in comparative perspective*. D. L. J. John G. Galaty, ed., pp. 323–352. New York: Guilford Press.

Browman, David L. 1994. Titicaca Basin archaeolinguistics: Uru, Pukina, and Aymara AD 750–1450. *World Archaeology* 26(2):234–250.

Browman, David L. 1997a. Political institutional factors contributing to the integration of the Tiwanaku state. In *Emergence and change in early urban societies*. L. Manzanilla, ed., pp. 229–244. New York: Plenum Press.

Browman, David L. 1997b. Pajano: Nexus of formative cultures in the Titicaca Basin. Paper presented at the 49th International Congress of Americanists, Quito.

Browman, David L. 1998. Lithic provienience analysis and emerging material complexity at Formative Period Chiripa, Bolivia. *Andean Past* 5:301–324.

Brumfiel, Elizabeth M. 1994. Ethnic groups and political development in ancient Mexico. In *Factional competition and political development in the New World*. J. W. Fox, ed., pp. 89–102. Cambridge: Cambridge University Press.

Bruno, Maria C. 2000. Sacred springs: Preliminary investigation of the Choquepacha spring / fountain, Tiwanaku, Bolivia. Paper presented at the 65th annual meeting of the Society for American Archaeology, Philadelphia.

Bruno, Maria C., and William T. Whitehead. 2003. Chenopodium cultivation and Formative Period agriculture at Chiripa, Bolivia. *Latin American Antiquity* 14(3):339–355.

Brush, Stephen. 1977. *Mountain, field, and family: The economy and human ecology of an Andean village*. Philadelphia: University of Pennsylvania Press.

Burger, Richard L., Karen Mohr-Chávez, and Sergio Chávez. 2000. Through the glass darkly: Prehispanic obsidian procurement and exchange in southern Peru and northern Bolivia. *Journal of World Prehistory* 14(3):267–362.

Burger, Richard L., and Frank Asaro. 1977. Trace element analysis of obsidian artifacts from the Andes: New perspectives on pre-Hispanic economic interaction Peru and Bolivia. *Lawrence Berkeley Laboratory Report 6343*. Berkeley: University of California Press.

Burkholder, JoEllen. 1997. Tiwanaku and the anatomy of time. Ph.D. dissertation, Department of Anthropology, State University of New York, Binghamton.

Calaway, Michael J. 2005. Ice cores, sediments and civilisation collapse: a cautionary tale from Lake Titicaca. *Antiquity* 79:778–779.

Capriles Flores, José M. 2005. State of the fish: Characteristics of fish consumption and exploitation in the Tiwanaku Period at Iwawi, Bolivia. In *Advances in the archaeology of the Titicaca Basin*, Vol. 2. C. Stanish and E. E. Klarich, eds., pp. Los Angeles: Cotsen Institute of Archaeology (in press).

Capriles Flores, José M., and Eliana Flores Bedregal. 2000. Identificación de pelos y fibras animales del hallazgo arqueológico de Amaguaya. In *XIII reunion anual de Etnologia*, Tomo 1, Vol. 1. pp. 111–120. Anales de la Renuion Anual de Etnologia. La Paz: MUSEF.

Cardona Rosas, Augusto. 2002. *Arqueología de Arequipa: De sus albores a los Incas*. Arequipa, Peru: CIARGQ.

Carney, Heath J., Michael W. Binford, Ruben R. Marin, and Charles R. Goldman. 1993. Nutrient and sediment retention in Andean raised-field agriculture. *Nature* 364:131–133.

Castelnau, Francis de. 1939 [1850–51]. El pueblo de Tiahuanaco. In *Tiahuanacu: Antologia de los principales escritos de los cronistas coloniales, americanistas e historiadores Bolivianos*. G. Ortrero, ed., pp. 53–66. *Biblioteca Boliviana*, Vol. 2. La Paz: Imprenta Artistica.

de Certeau, Michel. 1984. *The practice of everyday life*. Berkeley: University of California Press.

Céspedes Paz, Ricardo. 2000. Excavaciones arqueológicas en Piñami. *Boletín de Inian-Museo* 9:1–13.

Céspedes Paz, Ricardo, A. Muñoz, and Ramon Sanzetenea. 1998. Excavations at Pinami: Chronological sequences and regional development for the Valle Central in Cochabamba, Bolivia, during the development of Tiwanaku. Paper presented at the 63rd annual meeting of the Society for American Archaeology, Seattle.

Chapman, Robert. 2003. *Archaeologies of complexity*. London: Routledge.

Chávez, Karen L. Mohr. 1977. Marcavalle: The ceramics from an Early Horizon Site in the Valley of Cuzco, Peru, and implications for South Highland socio-economic interaction. Ph.D. dissertation, Department of Anthropology, University of Pennsylvania.

Chávez, Karen L. Mohr. 1985. Early Tiahuanaco related ceremonial burners from Cuzco, Peru. *Diálogo Andino (Arica, Chile)* 4:137–178.

Chávez, Karen L. Mohr. 1988. The significance of Chiripa in Lake Titicaca basin developments. *Expedition* 30:17–26.

Chávez, Sergio Jorge. 1976. The Arapa and Thunderboldt stelae: A case of stylistic identity with implications for Pukara influences in the area of Tiahuanaco. *Ñawpa Pacha* 13:3–25.

Chávez, Sergio Jorge. 1992. The conventionalized rules in Pucara pottery technology and iconography: Implications of socio-political development in the Northern Titicaca Basin. Ph.D. dissertation, Department of Anthropology, Michigan State University.

Chávez, Sergio Jorge. 2002. Identification of the camelid woman and feline man themes, motifs, and designs in Pucara style pottery. In *Andean archaeology II: Art, landscape, and society*. H. Silverman and W. H. Isbell, eds., pp. 35–69. New York: Kluwer Academic/Plenum.

Chávez, Sergio Jorge, and Karen L. Mohr Chávez. 1970. Newly discovered monoliths from the Highlands of Puno, Peru. *Expedition* 12(4):25–39.

Chávez, Sergio Jorge, and Karen L. Mohr Chávez. 1975. A carved stela from Taraco, Puno, Peru and the definition of an early style of stone sculpture from the altiplano of Peru and Bolivia. *Ñawpa Pacha* 13:45–83.

Chávez, Sergio Jorge, and Karen L. Mohr Chávez. 1997. Copia de los informes entrgados a la direccion del INAR. La Paz: Official research report submitted to the Instituto Nacional de Arqueologia (INAR), La Paz.

Childe, V. Gordon, 1936. *Man makes himself.* London: Watts.

Childe, V. Gordon. 1950. The urban revolution. *Town Planning Review* 21(1):3–17.

Choque Canqui, Roberto. 1993. *Sociedad y economía Colonial en el sur Andino.* La Paz: Hisbol.

Choque Canqui, Roberto. 2003. *Jesus de Machaca, La marka rebelde, Vol. 1: Cinco siglos de historia.* La Paz: Plural.

Cieza de León, Pedro de. 1959 [1553]. *The Incas of Pedro de Cieza de León: History of the conquest of Peru.* H. de Onis, trans. Norman: University of Oklahoma Press.

Cobo, Father Bernabé. 1990 [1653]. *Inca Religion and Customs.* (Selections from Historia del Nuevo Mundo). Roland Hamilton, trans. and ed. Austin: University of Texas Press.

Cohen, Amanda B. 2008. Ritualization and architecture in the Titicaca Basin: The development of the sunken court complex in the Formative Period. Ph.D. dissertation, Department of Anthropology, University of California, Los Angeles (in progress).

Comaroff, John, and Jean Comaroff. 1991. *Of revelation and revolution: Christianity, colonialism, and consciousness in South Africa.* Chicago: University of Chicago Press.

Conklin, Beth A. 2001. *Consuming grief: Compassionate cannibalism in an Amazonian society.* Austin: University of Texas Press.

Conklin, William J. 1982. The information system of the Middle Horizon Quipus. In *Ethnoastronomy and archaeoastronomy in the American Tropics.* A. F. Aveni and G. Urton, eds., pp. 261–281. New York: New York Academy of Sciences.

Conklin, William J. 1983. Pucara and Tiahuanaco tapestry: Time and style in a Sierra Weaving tradition. *Ñawpa Pacha* 21:1–45.

Conklin, William J. 1991. Tiahuanaco and Huari: Architectural comparisons and interpretations. In *Huari administrative structure: Prehistoric monumental architecture and state government.* W. H. Isbell and G. F. McEwan, eds., pp. 281–291. Washington, DC: Dumbarton Oaks Research Library and Collection.

Conklin, William J. 2004a. Las piedras textiles de Tiwanaku. In *Tiwanaku: Aproximaciones a sus contextos históricos y sociales.* M. Rivera and A. L. Kolata, eds., pp. 235–264. Santiago: Universidad Boliviariana.

Conklin, William J. 2004b. The Fire Textile: The history and iconography of a "unique" Huari cloth acquired by the TM in Washington, with a conservational account of its treatment. *HALI* 133:94–100.

Conklin, William J., and Michael E. Moseley. 1988. The patterns of art and power in the Early Intermediate Period. In *Peruvian prehistory.* R. Keating, ed., pp. 145–163. Cambridge: Cambridge University Press.

Conrad, Geoffrey 1981. Cultural materialism, split inheritance, and the expansion of ancient Peruvian empires. *American Antiquity* 46:3–26.

Cook, Anita G. 1992. The stone ancestors: Idioms of imperial attire and rank among Huari figurines. *Latin American Antiquity* 3(4):341–364.

Cook, Anita G. 1994. *Wari y Tiwanaku: Entre el estilo y la imagen.* Washington, DC: Pontificia Universidad Catolica del Peru.

Cook, Anita G. 2001. Huari D-shaped structures, sacrificial offerings, and divine rulership. In *Ritual sacrifice in ancient Peru.* E. P. Benson and A. G. Cook, eds., pp. 137–164. Austin: University of Texas Press.

Cook, Anita G., and Mary Glowacki. 2003. Pots, politics, and power: Huari ceramic assemblages and imperial administration. In *The archaeology and politics of food and feasting in early states and empires.* T. L. Bray, ed., pp. 172–202. New York: Kluwer Academic/Plenum.

Corrigan, Philip, and Derek Sayer. 1985. *The Great Arch: English state formation as cultural revolution.* Oxford: Basil Blackwell.

Courty, Georges. 1910. La Question du prehistorique Americain. *Bulletin et Memoires de la Societe d'Anthropologie de Paris* 1(1):189–190.

Couture, Nicole C. 2002. The construction of power: Monumental space and an elite residence at Tiwanaku, Bolivia Ph.D. dissertation, Department of Anthropology, University of Chicago.

Couture, Nicole C. 2003. Ritual, monumentalism, and residence at Mollo Kontu, Tiwanaku. In *Tiwanaku and its hinterland: Archaeology and paleoecology of an Andean civilization,* Vol. 2. A. L. Kolata, ed., pp. 202–225. Washington, DC: Smithsonian Institution Press.

Couture, Nicole C., and Deborah E. Blom. 2004. Informe sobre los trabajos realizados por el Proyecto Jacha Marka en los años de 2001 y 2002. La Paz: Report presented to the Viceministry of Culture, Bolivia.

Couture, Nicole C., and Kathryn Sampeck. 2003. Putuni: A history of palace architecture in Tiwanaku. In *Tiwanaku and its hinterland: Archaeology and paleoecology of an Andean civilization,* Vol. 2. A. L. Kolata, ed., pp. 226–263. Washington, DC: Smithsonian Institution Press.

Créqui-Montfort, George de. 1904. Fouilles de la mission scientifique Française à Tiahuanaco. Ses recherches archéologiques et ethnographiques en Bolivie, au Chile et dans la République Argentine. *Proceedings of the 14th International Congress of Americanists*, Stuttgart, pp. 531–550.

Crumley, Carole. 1987. A dialectical critique of hierarchy. In *Power relations and state Formation*. T. C. Patterson and C. W. Gailey, eds., pp. 155–159. Washington, DC: American Anthropological Association.

Crumley, Carole. 1995. Hetererachy and the analysis of complex societies. In *Heterarchy and the analysis of complex societies*. R. M. Eherenreich, C. L. Crumley, and J. E. Levy, eds., pp. 1–4. Arlington, VA: American Anthropological Association.

D'Altroy, Terence N. 2002. *The Incas*. Oxford: Blackwell.

DeFrance, Susan. 2004. Wari diet in Moquegua: The ordinary and the exotic. Paper presented at the 69th annual meeting of the Society for American Archaeology, Montreal.

Demarest, Arthur A. 1981. *Viracocha: On the nature and antiquity of the Andean High God*. Cambridge, MA: Harvard University Press.

Demarest, Arthur A. 2004. *Ancient Maya: Rise and fall of a rainforest civilization*. Cambridge: Cambridge University Press.

Denevan, William M. 1987. Terrace abandonment in the Colca Valley, Peru. In *Pre-Hispanic agricultural fields in the Andean region*. W. M. Denevan, K. Mathewson, and G. Knapp, eds., pp. 1–43. Oxford: British Archaeological Reports.

Denevan, William M., and B. L. Turner II. 1974. Forms, functions and associations of raised fields in the Old World Tropics. *Journal of Tropical Geography* 39:24–33.

Dietler, Michael. 2001. Theorizing the feast: Rituals of consumption, commensal politics, and power in African contexts. In *Feasts: Archaeological and ethnographic perspectives on food, politics, and power*. M. Dietler and B. Hayden, eds., pp. 65–114. Washington, DC: Smithsonian Institution Press.

Dietler, Michael. 2003. Clearing the table: Some concluding reflections on commensal politics and imperial states. In *The archaeology and politics of food and feasting in early states and empires*. T. L. Bray, ed., pp. 271–284. New York: Kluwer Academic/Plenum.

Dillehay, Tom D. 1984. A late Ice-Age settlement in southern Chile. *Scientific American* 251(4):106–119.

Dillehay, Tom D. 1997. *The archaeological context of Monte Verde: A Late Pleistocene Settlement in Chile*, Vol. 2. Washington, DC: Smithsonian Institution Press.

Dillehay, Tom D., and Lautaro Núñez Atencio. 1988. Camelids, caravans, and complex societies in the south-central Andes. In *Recent studies in pre-Columbian archeology*. N. J. Saunders and O. de Montmollin, eds., pp. 603–634. Oxford: British Archeological Reports.

Donkin, R. 1979. *Agricultural terracing in the aboriginal New World*. Tucson: University of Arizona Press.

Donnan, Christopher B., and Carol J. Mackey. 1978. *Ancient burial patterns of the Moche Valley, Peru*. Austin: University of Texas Press.

d'Orbigny, A. 1944 [1839]. *El hombre Americano, considerado en sus aspectos fisiologicos y morales*. T. Alfredo Cepeda, trans. Buenos Aires: Editorial Futuro.

Durkheim, Emile. 1915. The elementary forms of the religious life. London: George Allen & Unwin.

Earle, Timothy K. 1989. The evolution of chiefdoms. *Current Anthropology* 30:84–88.

Eliade, Mircea. 1959. *The sacred and the profane: The nature of religion.* W. R. Trask, trans. New York: Harcourt, Brace & World.

Erickson, Clark L. 1985. Applications of prehistoric Andean technology: Experiments in raised field Agriculture, Huatta, Lake Titicaca: 1981–1982. In *Prehistoric intensive agriculture in the Tropics.* I. S. Farrington, ed., pp. 209–232. Oxford: British Archaeological Reports.

Erickson, Clark L. 1988. An Archaeological investigation of raised field agriculture in the Lake Titicaca Basin of Peru. Ph.D. dissertation, Department of Anthropology, University of Illinois, Urbana-Champagne.

Erickson, Clark L. 1992. Prehistoric landscape management in the Andean Highlands: Raised field agriculture and its environmental impact. *Population and Environment* 13(4):285–300.

Erickson, Clark L. 1993. The social organization of prehispanic raised field agriculture in the Lake Titicaca Basin. In *Economic aspects of water management in the prehispanic New World.* V. L. Scarborough and B. L. Isaac, eds., pp. 369–426. Greenwich: JAI Press.

Erickson, Clark L. 1999. Neo-environmental determinism and agrarian "collapse" in Andean prehistory. *Antiquity* 73:634–42.

Erickson, Clark L. 2000. The Lake Titicaca Basin: A Precolumbian built landscape. In *An imperfect balance: Landscape transformations in the Precolumbian Americas.* D. L. Lentz, ed., pp. 311–356. New York: Columbia University Press.

Escalante Moscoso, Javier F. 1997. *Arquitectura prehispánica en los Andes Bolivianos.* La Paz: CIMA.

Escalante Moscoso, Javier F. 2003. Residential architecture in La K'arana, Tiwanaku. In *Tiwanaku and its hinterland: Archaeology and paleoecology of an Andean civilization,* Vol. 2. A. L. Kolata, ed., pp. 316–326. Washington, DC: Smithsonian Institution Press.

Espinoza Soriano, Waldemar. 1980. *Los fundamentos lingüísticos de la etnohistoria Andina.* Madrid: Revista Española de Antropología Americana.

Estete, Miguel. 1891 [1534]. La relacion del Viaje que hizo el Señor Capitan Hernando Pizarro por mandado del Senor Gobernador su Hermano, desde el Peblo de Caxamarca a Parcama y de alli a Jauja (1533). In *Verdedera relación de la conquista del Peru y Provincia del Cuzco.* F. de Xerex, ed., pp. 119–149. Sevilla: Concepcion Bravo.

Estevez Castillo, Jose. 1988. Evidencias de asentamientos Precolombinos en las provincias de sud Yungas y Murillo. *Arqueología Boliviana* 3:83–106.

Faldin, Juan D. 1991. La ceramic Chiripa en los valles de Larecaja y Muñecas de La Paz. *Puma Punku (nueva época)* 1(2):119–132.

Faldin, Juan D. 1995. La arqueología de la Provincia de Larecaja y Muñecas y su sistema precolombino. *Arqueología Boliviana* 2:53–74.

Feinman, Gary M. 2000. Corporate/Network: New perspectives on models of political action and the Puebloan southwest. In *Social theory in archaeology.* M. B. Schiffer, ed., pp. 31–51. Salt Lake City: University of Utah Press.

Feinman, Gary M., and Joyce Marcus. 1998. *Archaic states.* Santa Fe: School of American Research.

Feldman, Robert A. 1989. A speculative hypothesis of Wari southern expansion. In *The nature of Wari: A reappraisal of the Middle Horizon Period in Peru*. M. Czwarno, F. M. Meddens, and A. Morgan, eds., pp. 72–97. Oxford: BAR International Series 525.

Fernandez, D. A. 1974. Excavaciones arqueológicas en la cueva de Huachichocana, Departmento de Tumbaya, Prov. de Jujuy. *Relaciones (Buenos Aires)* 8:101–126.

Flannery, Kent V., ed. 1976. *The Early Mesoamerican village*. New York: Academic Press.

Flores-Ochoa, Jorge A. 1987. Cultivation in the qocha of the South Andean Puna. In *Arid land use strategies and risk management in the Andes: A regional anthropological perspective*. D. L. Browman, ed., pp. 271–296. Boulder, CO: Westview Press.

Flores Ochoa, Jorge A., and Magno Percy Paz Flores. 1983. La agricultura en lagunas del altiplano. *Ñawpa Pacha* 21:127–152.

Frame, Mary. 1990. *Andean four-cornered hats*. New York: Metropolitan Museum of Art.

Fried, Morton H. 1967. *The evolution of political society*. New York: Random House.

Frye, Kirk, and Lee Steadman. 2001. Incatunuhuiri: A case for early sociopolitical complexity in the Titicaca Basin. Paper presented at the 66th annual meeting of the Society for American Archaeology, New Orleans.

Gabelmann, Gabi. 2001. Chonqollo: Producción de cerámica a intercambio de bienes durante el Periodo Formativo, un Ejemplo del Valle Santivanez, Cochabamba. *Textos Antropológicos* 13(1–2):197–230.

Garcilaso de la Vega, El Inca. 1966 [1609]. *Royal commentaries of the Incas and general history of Peru*. Harold V. Livermore, trans. Austin: University of Texas Press.

Geertz, Clifford. 1980. *Negara: The theatre state in nineteenth century Bali*. Princeton, NJ: Princeton University Press.

Giddens, Anthony. 1979. *Central problems in social theory: Action, structure and contradiction in social analysis*. Berkeley: University of California Press.

Giddens, Anthony. 1984. *The constitution of society: Outline of the theory of structuration*. Berkeley: University of California Press.

Giesso, Martin. 2000. Stone tool production in the Tiwanaku heartland: The impact of state emergence and expansion on local households. Ph.D. dissertation, Department of Anthropology, University of Chicago.

Giesso, Martin. 2003. Stone tool production in the Tiwanaku heartland. In *Tiwanaku and its hinterland: Archaeology and paleoecology of an Andean civilization*, Vol. 2. A. L. Kolata, ed., pp. 363–383. Washington, DC: Smithsonian Institution Press.

Gillespie, Susan. 2000. Rethinking Maya social organization: Replacing "Lineage" with "House." *American Anthropologist* 102(3):467–484.

Girault, Louis. 1987. *Kallawaya: Curanderos itinerantes de los Andes*. La Paz: UNICEF.

Gisbert, Teresa, Silvia Arze, and Martha Cajiás. 1987. *Arte textil y mundo Andino*. La Paz: Gisbert y Cía.

Glowacki, Mary. 2002. The Huaro archaeological complex. In *Andean archaeology I: Variations in sociopolitical organization*. W. H. Isbell and H. Silverman, eds., pp. 267–286. New York: Kluwer Academic/Plenum.

Glowacki, Mary, and Michael Malpass. 2003. Water, huacas, and ancestor worship: Traces of a sacred Wari landscape. *Latin American Antiquity* 14(4):431–448.

Goldstein, David J., and Rosana Nelly Qusipe Valencia. 2004. Putting the food on the table: Paleoethnobotanical investigations at Cerro Baul, Part 1. Paper presented at the 69th annual meeting of the Society for American Archaeology, Montreal.

Goldstein, Paul S. 1989. Omo, a Tiwanaku provincial center in Moquegua, Peru. Ph.D. dissertation, Department of Anthropology, University of Chicago.

Goldstein, Paul S. 1993a. Tiwanaku temples and state expansion: A Tiwanaku sunken-court temple in Moquegua, Perú. *Latin American Antiquity* 4(1):22–47.

Goldstein, Paul S. 1993b. House, community and state in the earliest Tiwanaku colony: Domestic patterns and state integration at Omo M12, Moquegua. In *Domestic architecture, ethnicity, and complementarity in the south-central Andes*. M. Aldenderfer, ed., pp. 25–41. Iowa City: University of Iowa Press.

Goldstein, Paul S. 1995–96. Tiwanaku settlement patterns of the Azapa Valley, Chile: New Data and the legacy of Percy Dauelsberg. *Diálogo Andino* 14/15:57–73.

Goldstein, Paul S. 2000. Exotic goods and everyday chiefs: Long-distance exchange and indigenous sociopolitical development in the south central Andes. *Latin American Antiquity* 11(4):335–362.

Goldstein, Paul S. 2003. From stew-eaters to maize-drinkers: The chicha economy and the Tiwanuku expansion. In *The archaeology and politics of food and feasting in early states and empires*. T. L. Bray, ed., pp. 143–172. New York: Kluwer Academic/Plenum.

Goldstein, Paul S. 2005. *Andean diaspora: The Tiwanaku colonies and the origins of South American empire*. Gainesville: University Press of Florida.

Goldstein, Paul S., and Tara Carter. 2004. An outpost in Tiwanaku's Valley: The Wari occupation at the Cerro Trapiche Site. Paper presented at the 69th annual meeting of the Society for American Archaeology, Montreal.

Goldstein, Paul S., and Bruce Owen. 2001. Tiwanaku in Moquegua: The altiplano colonies. *Boletín de Arqueología PUCP* 5:169–188.

Gonzales Carre, E., Enrique Bragayrac D., Maria A. Munoz C., V. Tielser, and M. Lopez. 1996. *El templo mayor de la ciudad de Wari*. Ayacucho: Universidad Nacional de San Cristobal de Huamanga.

Gonzales, Rex A. 1998. *La cultura de La Aguada: Arqueología y diseños*. Buenos Aires: Filmediciones Valero.

Gose, Peter. 1993. Segmentary state formation and ritual control of water under the Incas. *Comparative Study of Society and History* 35:480–514.

Gose, Peter. 1996. Oracles, divine kingship, and political representation in the Inka state. *Ethnohistory* 43(1):1–32.

Graffam, Gray C. 1990. Raised Fields without Bureaucracy: An archaeological examination of intensive wetland cultivation in the Pampa Koani Zone, Lake Titicaca, Bolivia. Ph.D. dissertation, Department of Anthropology, University of Toronto.

Graffam, Gray C. 1992. Beyond state collapse: Rural history, raised fields and pastoralism in the South Andes. *American Anthropologist* 94(4):882–904.

Gramsci, Antonio. 1971. *Selections from the prison notebooks*. Edited and translated by Q. Hoare and G. Nowell Smith. New York: International Publishers.

Grossman, Joel W. 1983. Demographic change and economic formation in the south-central highlands of pre-Huari Peru. *Ñawpa Pacha* 21:45–126.

Guaman Poma de Ayala, Felipe. 1992 [1615]. *El primer nueva coronica y buen gobierno*. Mexico City: Siglo Veintiuno.

Guillet, David. 1987. Terracing and irrigation in the Peruvian Highlands. *Current Anthropology* 28(4):409–430.

Hancock, Graham. 1996. *Fingerprints of the gods*. New York: Crown Publishers.

Hastorf, Christine A., ed. 1999. *Early settlement at Chiripa, Bolivia: Research of the Taraco Archaeological Project*. Berkeley: University of California Archaeological Research Facility.

Hastorf, Christine A. 2003. Community with the ancestors: Ceremonies and social memory in the Middle Formative at Chiripa, Bolivia. *Journal of Anthropological Archaeology* 22:305–332.

Hastorf, Christine A. 2005. The Upper (Middle and Late) Formative in the Titicaca region. In *Advances in Titicaca Basin archaeology*, Vol. 1. C. Stanish, A. B. Cohen, and M. S. Aldenderfer, eds., pp. 65–94. Los Angeles: Cotsen Institute of Archaeology.

Hastorf, Christine A., Matthew S. Bandy, William T. Whitehead, and Lee Steadman. 2001. El Periodo Formativo en Chiripa, Bolivia. *Textos Antropológicos* 13(1–2):17–92.

Helms, Mary W. 1993. *Craft and the kingly ideal: Art, trade, and power*. Austin: University of Texas Press.

Hendon, Julia A. 1996. Archaeological approaches to the organization of domestic labor: Household practice and domestic relations. *Annual Review of Anthropology* 25:45–61.

Hesse, Brian. 1982. Animal domestication and oscillating environments. *Journal of Ethnobiology* 2:1–15.

Higueras-Hare, Alvaro. 1996. Prehispanic settlement and land use in Cochabamba, Bolivia. Ph.D. dissertation, Department of Anthropology, University of Pittsburgh.

Higueras-Hare, Alvaro. 2001. La ocupación prehistórica de la región de Cochabamba durante el Periodo Formativo. *Textos Antropológicos* 13(1–2):183–196.

Hirth, Kenneth G. 1993. The household as an analytical unit: Problems in method and theory. In *Prehispanic domestic units in western Mesoamerica: Studies of the household, compound, and residence*. R. S. Santley and K. G. Hirth, eds. pp. 21–36. Boca Raton, FL: CRC Press.

Holland, Dorothy, William Lachicotte Jr., Debra Skinner, and Carole Cain. 1998. *Identity and agency in cultural worlds*. Cambridge, MA: Harvard University Press.

Hyslop, John. 1984. *The Inca road system*. New York: Academic Press.

Ibarra Grasso, Dick Edgar, and Roy Querejazu Lewis. 1986. *30.000 Años de prehistoria en Bolivia*. La Paz, Bolivia: Los Amigos del Libro.

Ingold, Tim. 1993. *Perception of the environment: Essays in livelihood, dwelling, and skill.* London: Routledge.

Isbell, William H. 1977. *The rural foundation for urbanism: Economic and stylistic interaction between rural and urban communities in eighth-century Peru.* Urbana: University of Illinois Press.

Isbell, William H. 1987. City and state in Middle Horizon Huari. In *Peruvian prehistory.* R. W. Keatinge, ed., pp. 164–189. Cambridge: Cambridge University Press.

Isbell, William H. 1989. Honco Pampa: Was it a Huari Administrative Center? In *The nature of Wari: A reappraisal of the Middle Horizon Period in Peru.* R. M. Czwarmo, F. M. Meddens, and A. Morgan, eds., pp. 98–114. London: BAR International Series.

Isbell, William H. 1997a. *Mummies and mortuary monuments: A postprocessual prehistory of central Andean social organization.* Austin: University of Texas press.

Isbell, William H. 1997b. Reconstructing Huari: A cultural chronology for the capital city. In *Emergence and change in early urban societies.* L. Manzanilla, ed., pp. 181–228. New York: Plenum Press.

Isbell, William H. 2000. Repensando el Horizonte Medio: el caso de Conchopata, Ayacucho, Peru. In *Boletín de Arqueología PUCP* 4:9–68.

Isbell, William H. 2004a. Mortuary preferences: A Wari culture case study from Middle Horizon Peru. *Latin American Antiquity* 15(1):3–32.

Isbell, William H. 2004b. Venerated women: Mortuary inferences from Conchopata. Paper presented at the 69th annual meeting of the Society for American Archaeology, Montreal.

Isbell, William H., Christine Brewster-Wray, and Lynda E. Spickard. 1991. Architecture and spatial organization at Huari. In *Huari administrative structure: Prehistoric monumental architecture and state government.* W. H. Isbell and G. F. McEwan, eds., pp. 19–54. Washington, DC: Dumbarton Oaks, Research Library and Collection.

Isbell, William H., and JoEllen Burkholder. 2002. Iwawi and Tiwanaku. In *Andean archaeology I: Variations in sociopolitical organization.* H. Silverman and W. H. Isbell, eds., pp. 199–242. New York: Kluwer Academic/Plenum.

Isbell, William H., and Anita G. Cook. 2002. A new perspective on Conchopata and the Andean Middle Horizon. In *Andean archaeology: Art, landscape, and society.* H. Silverman and W. H. Isbell, eds., pp. 249–306. New York: Kluwer Academic/Plenum.

Isbell, William H., and Gordon F. McEwan. 1991. A history of Huari studies and introduction to current interpretations. In *Huari administrative structure: Prehistoric monumental architecture and state government.* W. H. Isbell and G. F. McEwan, eds., pp. 1–18. Washington, DC: Dumbarton Oaks Research Library and Collection.

Isbell, William H., and Katharina J. Schreiber. 1978. Was Huari a state? *American Antiquity* 43(3):372–389.

Izko, Xavier. 1992. *La doble frontera: Ecología, política y ritual en el altiplano central.* La Paz, Bolivia: Hisbol.

Janusek, John Wayne. 1999. Craft and local power: Embedded specialization in Tiwanaku cities. *Latin American Antiquity* 10(2):107–131.

Janusek, John Wayne, ed. 2000. Desarollo cultural en los Valles Orientales Bolivianos: Informe de los Trabajos en Icla, 1999. Report submitted to the Direccion Nacional de Antroologia y Arqueologia, La Paz, Bolivia.

Janusek, John Wayne. 2001. Asentamiento rural y campos elevados de cultivo en el Valle del Río Katari durante el Periodo Formativo Tardío. *Textos Antropológicos* 13(1–2):111–134.

Janusek, John Wayne. 2002. Out of many, one: Style and social boundaries in Tiwanaku. *Latin American Antiquity* 13(1):35–61.

Janusek, John Wayne. 2003a. Vessels, time, and society: Toward a chronology of ceramic style in the Tiwanaku heartland. In *Tiwanaku and its hinterland: Archaeology and paleoecology of an Andean civilization*, Vol. 2. A. L. Kolata, ed., pp. 30–92. Washington, DC: Smithsonian Institution Press.

Janusek, John Wayne. 2003b. The changing face of Tiwanaku residential life: State and social identity in an Andean city. In *Tiwanaku and its hinterland: Archaeology and paleoecology of an Andean civilization*, Vol. 2. A. L. Kolata, ed., pp. 264–295. Washington, DC: Smithsonian Institution Press.

Janusek, John Wayne. 2004a. *Identity and power in the ancient Andes: Tiwanaku cities through time*. London: Routledge.

Janusek, John Wayne. 2004b. Tiwanaku and its precursors: Recent research and emerging perspectives. *Journal of Archaeological Research* 12(2):121–183.

Janusek, John Wayne. 2004c. Collapse as cultural revolution: Power and identity in the Tiwanaku to pacajes transition. In *Foundations of power in the prehispanic Andes*. K. Vaughn, D. Ogburn, and C. A. Conlee, eds., pp. 175–210. Arlington, VA: American Anthropological Association.

Janusek, John Wayne, ed. 2005a. Khonkho Wankane: Informe de investigaciones en 2001–2002. La Paz: Report submitted to the Viceministry of Culture, Bolivia.

Janusek, John Wayne, 2005b. Of Pots and people: Ceramic style and social identity in Tiwanaku. In *Us and them: Ethnicity in the Andean region*. Richard Reycraft, ed., pp. 34–51. Los Angeles: University of California Press.

Janusek, John Wayne. 2006. The Changing "Nature" of Tiwanaku Religion and the Rise of an Andean State. *World Archaeology* 38(3):469–492.

Janusek, John Wayne. 2007a. Patios hundidios, encuentros rituales, y el auge de Tiwanaku como un centro pan-regional Andino. *Boletin de Arqueología PUCP* 9 (in press).

Janusek, John Wayne. 2007b. Close Encounters of an Andean Kind: Social Diversity, Ritual Encounter, and the Contingent Production of Tiwanaku. In *Visions of Tiwanaku*. C. Stanish and A. Vranich, eds. Los Angeles: Cotsen institute of Archaeology at the University of California, Los Angeles (in press).

Janusek, John Wayne. 2008a. Interacción interregional y desarollo sociopolítico en la región de Icla, Chuquisaca, Bolivia. *Chungará* (in press).

Janusek, John Wayne. 2008b. Contextualizando el sitio de Khonkho Wankane: objectivos, antecedentes, y resultados preliminares del Proyecto Jach'a Machaca. *Nuevos Aportes* 4. Web publication in press.

Janusek, John Wayne, and Deborah E. Blom. 2006. Identifying Tiwanaku urban populations: Style, identity, and ceremony in Andean cities. In *Urbanization in the preindustrial world: Cross-cultural perspectives*. G. Storey, ed., pp. 233–251. Tuscaloosa: University of Alabama Press.

Janusek, John Wayne, and Howard Earnest. 1990. Excavations in the Putuni: The 1988 season. In *Tiwanaku and its hinterland*. Report submitted to the Instituto Nacional de Arqueologia, La Paz, National Science Foundation, and the National Endowment for the Humanities. A. L. Kolata, ed., pp. 236–246. Chicago: University of Chicago.

Janusek, John Wayne, and Alan L. Kolata. 2003. Prehispanic rural history in the Katari Valley. In *Tiwanaku and its hinterland: Archaeology and paleoecology of an Andean civilization*, Vol. 2. A. L. Kolata, ed., pp. 129–172. Washington, DC: Smithsonian Institution Press.

Janusek, John Wayne, and Alan L. Kolata. 2004. Top-down or bottom-up: Rural settlement and raised field agriculture in the Lake Titicaca Basin, Bolivia. *Journal of Anthropological Archaeology* 23:404–430.

Janusek, John Wayne, Arik T. Ohnstad, and Andrew P. Roddick. 2003. Khonkho Wankane and the rise of Tiwanaku. *Antiquity* 77(296), http://antiquity.ac.uk/ ProjGall/janusek/janusek.html (accessed September 20, 2006).

Jennings, Justin. 2004. La chichería y el patron: Chicha and the energetics of feasting in the prehistoric Andes. In *Foundations of power in the prehispanic Andes*. K. Vaughn, D. Ogburn, and C. A. Conlee, eds., pp. 241–260. Arlington, VA: American Anthropological Association.

Joyce, Arthur A., Laura Arnaud Bustamente, and Marc N. Levine. 2001. Commoner power: A case study from the Classic Period collapse on the Oaxaca Coast. *Journal of Archaeological Method and Theory* 8(4):343–385.

Joyce, Rosemary. 1993. Women's work: Images of production and reproduction in pre-Hispanic southern central America. *Current Anthropology* 34:255–274.

Kaulicke, Peter. 2000. La Sombra de Pachacamac: Huari en la costa central. *Boletín de Arqueología PUCP* 4:313–358.

Kertzer, David I. 1988. *Ritual, politics, and power*. New Haven, CT: Yale University Press.

Ketteman, William G. 2002. New dates from the Huari Empire: Chronometric dating of the prehistoric occupation of Conchopata, Ayacucho, Bolivia. Master's thesis, Department of Anthropology, State University of New York at Binghamton.

Kidder, Alfred. 1943. Some early sites in the northern Lake Titicaca Basin. *Papers of the Peabody Museum of American Archaeology and Ethnology* 27(1).

Kidder, Alfred. 1956. Digging in the Titicaca Basin. *University Museum Bulletin* (University of Pennsylvania, University Museum) 20(3):16–29.

Klarich, Elizabeth A. 2005. From the monumental to the mundane: Defining early leadership strategies at Late Formative Pukara, Peru. Ph.D. diss, University of California, Santa Barbara.

Knapp, A. Bernard, and Wendy Ashmore. 1999. Archaeological landscapes: Constructed, conceptualized, ideational. In *Archaeologies of landscape*. W. Ashmore and A. B. Knapp, eds., pp. 1–30. Oxford: Blackwell.

Knobloch, Patricia J. 2000. Wari ritual power at Conchopata: An interpretation of *Anadenanthera colubrina* iconography. *Latin American Antiquity* 11(4):387–402.

Knudson, Kelly J., T. Douglas Price, Jane E. Buikstra, and Deborah E. Blom. 2004. The use of strontium isotope analysis to investigate Tiwanaku migration and mortuary ritual in Bolivia and Peru. *Archaeometry* 46(1):5–18.

Knudson, Kelly J., Tiffiny A. Tung, Kenneth C. Nystrom, T. Douglas Price, and Paul D. Fullagar. 2005. The origin of the Juch'uypampa cave mummies: Strontium isotope analysis of archaeological human remains from Bolivia. *Journal of Archaeological Science* 32:903–913.

Kolata, Alan L. 1986. The agricultural foundations of the Tiwanaku state: A view from the heartland. *American Antiquity* 51:748–762.

Kolata, Alan L. 1991. The technology and organization of agricultural production in the Tiwanaku State. *Latin American Antiquity* 2(2):99–125.

Kolata, Alan L. 1992. Economy, ideology, and imperialism in the south-central Andes. In *Ideology and pre-Columbian civilizations*. A. A. Demarest and G. W. Conrad, eds., pp. 65–85. Santa Fe, NM: School of American Research.

Kolata, Alan L. 1993a. *Tiwanaku: Portrait of an Andean civilization*. Cambridge: Blackwell.

Kolata, Alan L. 1993b. Understanding Tiwanaku: Conquest, colonization, and clientage in the South Central Andes. In *Latin American horizons*. D. S. Rice, ed., pp. 193–224. Washington, DC: Dumbarton Oaks.

Kolata, Alan L. 1996a. Proyecto Wila Jawira: An introduction to the history, problems, and strategies of research. In *Tiwanaku and its hinterland: Archaeology and paleoecology of an Andean civilization*, Vol. 1. A. L. Kolata, ed., pp. 1–22. Washington, DC: Smithsonian Institution Press.

Kolata, Alan L. 1996b. *Valley of the spirits: A journey into the lost realm of the Aymara*. New York: Wiley.

Kolata, Alan L. 2000. Environmental thresholds and the "natural history" of an Andean civilization. In *Environmental disaster and the archaeology of human response*. R. M. Reycraft, ed., pp. 163–178. Albuquerque, NM: Maxwell Museum of Anthropology.

Kolata, Alan L. 2003a. Introduction to the Proyecto Wila Jawira research program. In *Tiwanaku and its hinterland: Archaeology and paleoecology of an Andean civilization*, Vol. 2. A. L. Kolata, ed., pp. 3–17. Anthropological Papers No. 7. Washington, DC: Smithsonian Institution Press.

Kolata, Alan L. 2003b. The social production of Tiwanaku: Political economy and authority in a native Andean State. In *Tiwanaku and its hinterland: Archaeology and paleoecology of an Andean civilization*, Vol. 2. A. L. Kolata, ed., pp. 449–472. Washington, DC: Smithsonian Institution Press.

Kolata, Alan L., and Charles R. Ortloff. 1996a. Tiwanaku raised-field agriculture in the Lake Titicaca Basin of Bolivia. In *Tiwanaku and its hinterland: Archaeology and paleoecology of an Andean civilization*, Vol. 1. A. L. Kolata, ed., pp. 109–152. Washington, DC: Smithsonian Institution Press.

Kolata, Alan L., and Charles R. Ortloff. 1996b. Agroecological perspectives on the decline of the Tiwanaku state. In *Tiwanaku and its hinterland: Archaeology and paleoecology of an Andean civilization*, Vol. 1. A. L. Kolata, ed., pp. 181–202. Washington, DC: Smithsonian Institution Press.

Kolata, Alan L., and Carlos Ponce Sanginés. 1992. Tiwanaku: The city at the center. In *The ancient Americas: Art from sacred landscapes*. R. F. Townsend, ed., pp. 317–334. Chicago: Art Institute.

Kolata, Alan L., and Carlos Ponce Sanginés. 2003. Two hundred years of archaeological research at Tiwanaku: A selective history. In *Tiwanaku and its hinterland: Archaeology and paleoecology of an Andean civilization*, Vol. 2. A. L. Kolata, ed., pp. 18–29. Washington, DC: Smithsonian Institution Press.

Kolata, Alan L., Oswaldo Rivera Sundt, Juan Carlos Ramirez, and Evelyn Gemio. 1996. Rehabilitating raised-field agriculture in the southern Lake Titicaca Basin of Bolivia: Theory, practice, and results. In *Tiwanaku and its hinterland: Archaeology and paleoecology of an Andean civilization*, Vol. 2. A. L. Kolata, ed., pp. 203–230. Washington, DC: Smithsonian Institution Press.

Korpisaari, Antti. 2006. *Death in the Bolivian high plateau: Burials and Tiwanaku society*. Oxford: BAR International Series 1536.

Korpisaari, Antti. 2007. The Tiwanaku portrait vessels, human effigy vessels, and human figurines of the Island of Pariti, Lake Titicaca, Bolivia. Manuscript in possession of the author.

Korpisaari, Antti, and Martti Pärssinen, Eds. 2005. *Pariti: Isla, misterio, y poder*. La Paz: Republics of Bolivia and Finland.

Korpisaari, Anti, and Jedú Sagárnaga Meneses. 2007. "Investigaciones arqueológicas en la isla Pariti, Bolivia: Temporada de campo 2004." In *Actas del simposio internacional de arqueología del área centro sur Andina*. A. Belan Franco, M. Ziolkowski, and J. Jennings, eds. University of Varsovia, Poland (in press).

La Barre, Weston. 1947. The Uru-Chipaya. In *Handbook of South American Indians*. Vol. 2 of The Andean civilizations. J. H. Steward, ed., pp. 585–618. Washington, DC: Smithsonian Institution.

La Barre, Weston. 1948. *The Aymara Indians of the Lake Titicaca Plateau, Bolivia*. American Anthropologist Memoirs No. 68. Menasha, WI: American Anthropological Association.

Lanning, Edward P. 1967. *Peru before the Incas*. Englewood Cliffs, NJ: Prentice Hall.

Larco Hoyle, Rafael. 1948. *Cronología Arqueológica del Norte del Peru*. Buenos Aires: Sociedad Geografica Americana.

Lau, George F. 2002. Feasting and ancestor veneration in Chinchawas, North Highlands of Ancash, Peru. *Latin American Antiquity* 13(3):279–304.

Lave, Jean, and Etienne Wenger. 1991. *Situated learning: Legitimate peripheral participation*. Cambridge: Cambridge University Press.

Lavenu, A. 1992. Formation and geological evolution. In *Lake Titicaca: A synthesis of limnological knowledge*. C. DeJoux and A. Iltis, eds., pp. 3–15. Monographiae Biologicae, Vol. 68. Dordrecht: Kluwer Academic.

Lechtman, Heather. 1997. Arsenic bronze and the Middle Horizon. In *Arqueología, Antropología e historia en los Andes: Homenaje a María Rostworowski*. R. Varón Gabai and J. Flores Espinoza, eds., pp. 153–186. Lima: Instituto de Estudios Peruanos and Banco Central de Reserva del Perú.

Lechtman, Heather. 1998. Architectural cramps at Tiwanaku: Copper-arsenic-nickel bronze. In *Metallurgica Andina: In Honour of Hans-Gert Bachmann and Robert Maddin*. T. Rehren, A. Hauptmann, and J. D. Muhly, eds., pp. 77–92. Bochum: Deutsches Bergbau-Museum.

Lechtman, Heather. 2003. Tiwanaku Period (Middle Horizon) bronze metallurgy in the Lake Titicaca Basin: A preliminary assessment. In *Tiwanaku and its hinterland: Archaeology and paleoecology of an Andean civilization*, Vol. 2. A. L. Kolata, ed., pp. 404–434. Washington, DC: Smithsonian Institution Press.

Lecoq, Patrice. 1987. Caravanes des llamas, sel et echanges dans une communaute de Potosi, en Bolivie. *Bulletin de l'Institut Francais d'Etudes Andines* 16(3–4):1–38.

Lecoq, Patrice. 1999. *Uyuni Préhispanique: Arquéologia de la cordillère intersalar (Sud-Ouest Bolivien)*. Oxford: Archaeopress.

Lemuz Aguirre, Carlos. 2001. Patrones de asentamiento arqueológico en la península de Santiago de Huata, Boliva. Licenciatura thesis, Universidad Mayor de San Andres, La Paz.

Lemuz, Carlos. 2005. Normalizacion de datos de asentamiento en la Cuenca Sur del Lago Titicaca. Report submitted to the Direccion Nacional de Arqueología de Bolivia (DINAR), La Paz.

Lemuz Aguirre, Carlos, and Jose Luis Paz Soria. 2001. Nuevas consideraciones acerca del Periodo Formativo en Kallamarka. *Textos Antropológicos* 13(1–2):93–110.

Lennon, Thomas J. 1983. Pattern analysis of prehispanic raised fields of Lake Titicaca, Peru. In *Drained field agriculture in Central and South America*. J. Darch, ed., pp. 183–200. BAR International Series.

Leoni, Juan B. 2004. Ritual, place, and memory in the construction of community identity: A diachronic view from Ñawimpukyo (Ayacucho, Peru). Ph.D. dissertation, Department of Anthropology, State University of New York, Binghamton.

Le Paige, Gustavo. 1961. Cultura de Tiahuanaco en San Pedro de Atacama. *Rivista Anales Universidad del Norte (Chile)* 1:7–96.

Le Paige, Gustavo. 1965. San Pedro de Atacama y su Zona (14 temas). *Revista Anales de la Universidad del Norte (Chile)* 4.

Lima Torrez, M. del Pilar. 2000. Ocupación Yampara en Quila Quila? Cambios socio-políticos de una sociedad prehispánica durante el Horizonte Tardío. Licenciatura thesis, Universidad Mayor de San Andres, La Paz.

Lizárraga, F. R. de. 1909[1605]. Descripción breve de toda la tierra del Perú, Tucumán, Río de la Plata y Chile. *Historiadoras de Indias*, Vol. 2 (Madrid): 485–660.

Llagostera Martinez, Agustin. 1995. Art in the snuff trays of San Pedro de Atacama (Northern Chile). In *Andean art: Visual expression and its relation to Andean beliefs and values*. P. Dransart, ed., pp. 51–77. Aldershot: Avebury.

Lozada, Maria Cecilia. 1998. The seniorio of Chiribaya: A bioarchaeological study in the Osmore drainage of southern Peru. Ph.D. dissertation, Department of Anthropology, University of Chicago.

Lozada, Maria Cecilia, and Jane E. Buikstra. 2002. *El Seniorio Chiribaya en la Costa Sur del Peru*. Lima: Instituto de Estudios Peruanos.

Lumbreras, Luis G. 1974. *The peoples and cultures of ancient Peru*. B. J. Meggars, trans. Washington, DC: Smithsonian Institution Press.

Lumbreras, Luis G. 1981. *Arqueología de la América Andina*. Lima: Editorial Milla Batres.

Lumbreras, Luis G. 2000. *El imperio Wari*. Lima: Lluvia.

Lynch, Thomas F. 1983. Camelid pastoralism and the emergence of Tiwanaku civilization in the south-central Andes. *World Archaeology* 15(1):1–14.

Mackey, Carol J. 1982. The Middle Horizon as viewed from the Moche Valley. In *Chan Chan: Andean desert city*. M. E. Moseley and K. C. Day, eds., pp. 321–331. Albuquerque: University of New Mexico Press.

Manzanilla, Linda. 1992. *Akapana: Una pirámide en el centro del mundo*. Mexico City: Universidad Nacional Autónoma de México, Instituto de Investigaciones Antropológicas.

Manzanilla, Linda, and Eric Kenneth Woodard. 1990. Restos humanos asociados a la pirámide de Akapana (Tiwanaku, Bolivia). *Latin American Antiquity* 1(2):133–149.

Markham, Clements R. 1862. *Travels in Peru and India while superintending the collection of Chinchona plants and seeds in South America, and their introduction into India.* London: J. Murray.

Martinez, Gabriel. 1989. *Espacio y pensamiento I: Andes meridionales.* La Paz: Hisbol.

Marx, Karl. 1986 [1852]. The eighteenth brumaire of Louis Bonaparte. In *Karl Marx and Frederick Engels: Selected works*, pp. 95–180. New York, International Publishers.

Marx, Karl. 1986 [1888]. Theses on Feuerbach. In *Karl Marx and Frederick Engels: Selected works*, pp. 28–30. New York, International Publishers.

Mathews, James E. 1992. Prehispanic settlement and agriculture in the Middle Tiwanaku Valley, Bolivia. Ph.D. dissertation, Department of Anthropology University of Chicago.

Mathews, James E. 1997. Population and agriculture in the emergence of complex society in the Bolivian altiplano: The case of Tiwanaku. In *Emergence and change in early urban societies.* L. Manzanilla, ed., pp. 245–274. New York: Plenum Press.

Mathews, James E. 2003. Prehistoric settlement patterns in the Middle Tiwanaku Valley. In *Tiwanaku and its hinterland: Archaeology and paleoecology of an Andean civilization*, Vol. 2. A. L. Kolata, ed., pp. 112–128. Washington, DC: Smithsonian Institution Press.

McAndrews, Timothy L. 2001. Organización y crecimiento de los sistemas de asentamiento tempranos basados en aldeas en el altiplano Andino del Sur Central. *Textos Antropológicos* 13(1–2):135–146.

McAndrews, Timothy L. 2005. *Wankarani settlement systems in evolutionary perspective.* Pittsburgh and La Paz: University of Pittsburgh and Plural.

McAndrews, Timothy, Juan Albarracin-Jordan, and Marc Bermann. 1997. Regional settlement patterns in the Tiwanaku valley of Bolivia. *Journal of Field Archaeology* 24(1):67–84.

McEwan, Gordon F. 1991. Investigations at the Pikillacta site: A provincial Huari center in the valley of Cuzco. In *Huari administrative structure: Prehistoric monumental architecture and state government.* W. A. Isbell and G. McEwan, eds., pp. 93–119. Washington,: Dumbarton Oaks.

McEwan, Gordon F. 1996. Archaeological investigations at Pikillacta, a Wari Site in Peru. *Journal of Field Archaeology* 23(2):169–186.

McEwan, Gordon F. 1998. The function of niched halls in Wari architecture. *Latin American Antiquity* 9(1):68–86.

McEwan, Gordon F., Melissa Chatfield, and Arminda Gibaja. 2002. The archaeology of Inca origins: Excavations at Choquepuquio, Cuzco, Peru. In *Andean Archaeology I: Variations in sociopolitical organization.* W. H. Isbell and H. Silverman, eds., pp. 287–302. New York: Kluwer Academic/Plenum.

McEwan, Gordon F., and Nicole C. Couture. 2005. Pikillacta and its architectural typology. In *Pikillacta: The Wari empire in Cuzco.* G. F. McEwan, ed., pp. 11–28. Iowa City, University of Iowa Press.

Mendelssohn, Karl. 1971. A scientist looks at the pyramids. *American Scientist* 59:210–220.

Menzel, Dorothy. 1964. Style and time in the Middle Horizon. Ñawpa Pacha 2:1–105.

Menzel, Dorothy. 1968. New data on the Huari Empire in Middle Horizon Epoch 2A. Ñawpa Pacha 6:47–114.

Menzel, Dorothy. 1977. The archaeology of ancient Peru and the work of Max Uhle. Berkeley: R. H. Lowie Museum Anthropology, University of California.

Mercado de Peñalosa, Pedro. 1965 [1583]. Relación de la provincia de los Pacajes. In Relaciones geográficas de Indias – Perú, Biblioteca de Autores Españoles (t. 183). M. Jiménez de la Espada, ed., pp. 334–341. Madrid: Ediciones Atlas.

Metraux, Alfred. 1945. The story of South America's Chipaya Indians. Natural History 54:425–431.

Metraux, A., and H. Lehmann. 1937. Archeologie de la province d'Oruro, Bolivie (Mounds de Belen). Journal de la Societe des Americanistes 29:147–155.

Molina, Cristobal de. 1916 [1553]. Relación de las fábulas y ritos de los Incas. Lima: San Marti y Cia.

Money, Mary. 1991. El "tesoro de San Sebastian:" Una tumba importante de la cultura Tiwanaku. Kava, Beitrage zur Allgemeinen und Vergleichenden Archaeologie 1:189–198.

Moore, Jerry D. 1996. The archaeology of plazas and the proxemics of ritual: Three Andean traditions. American Anthropologist 98(4):789–802.

Moore, Katherine M., David Steadman, and Susan DeFrance. 1999. Herds, fish, and fowl in the domestic and ritual economy of formative Chiripa. In Early settlement at Chiripa, Bolivia: Research of the Taraco archaeological project. C. A. Hastorf, ed., pp. 105–116. Berkeley: Contributions of the University of California Archaeological Research Facility.

Morell, Virginia. 2002. Empires across the Andes. National Geographic Magazine 201:106–129.

Morris, Craig, and Donald E. Thompson. 1985. Huánuco Pampa: An Inca city and its hinterland. London: Thames and Hudson.

Moseley, Michael E. 2001. The Incas and their ancestors (revised edition). New York: Thames and Hudson.

Moseley, Michael E., Robert A. Feldman, Paul S. Goldstein, and Luis Watanabe. 1991. Colonies and conquest: Tiahuanaco and Huari in Moquegua. In Huari administrative structure: Prehistoric monumental architecture and state government. W. H. Isbell and G. F. McEwan, eds., pp. 121–140. Washington, DC: Dumbarton Oaks.

Moseley, Michael E., Donna Nash, Patricck Ryan Williams, Susan DeFrance, Ana Miranda, and Mario Ruales. 2005. Burning down the brewery: Excavation and evacuation of an ancient imperial colony at Cerro Baúl, Peru. Proceedings of the Nacional Academy of Sciences 102(48):17264–17271.

Mujica, Elías. 1978. Nueva hipótesis sobre el desarrollo temprano del altiplano, del Titicaca y de sus areas de interacción. Arte y Arqueología 5–6:285–308.

Mujica, Elías. 1985. Altiplano-coast relationships in the south-central Andes: From indirect to direct complementarity. In Andean ecology and civilization. S. Masuda, I. Shimada, and C. Morris, eds., pp. 103–140. Tokyo: University of Tokyo.

Muñoz Ovalle, Iván. 1987. Enterramientos en túmulos en el valle de Azapa: Nuevas evidencias para definir la fase Alto Ramirez en el extremo norte de Chile. *Chungará* 19:93–127.

Muñoz Ovalle, Iván. 1995–1996. Poblamiento humano y relaciones interculturales en el valle de Azapa: Nuevos hallazgos en torno al Período Formativo y Tiwanaku. *Diálogo Andino* 14/15:241–276.

Murra, John V. 1972. El "control vertical" de un máximo de pisos ecológicos en la economía de las sociedades andinas. In *Visita de la Provincia de León de Huánuco en 1562*, Vol. 2. J. V. Murra, ed., pp. 429–76. Huánuco: Universidad Nacional Hermilio Valdizán.

Murra, John V. 1975. Maiz, tubérculos, y ritos agrícolas. In *Formaciones económicas y políticas del mundo Andino*. J. V. Murra, ed., pp. 45–57. Lima: Instituto de Estudios Peruanos.

Murra, John V. 1980 [1956]. *The economic organization of the Inka state*. Greenwich, CT: JAI Press.

Nadaillac, M. de. 1939 [1883]. La prehistoria de Tiahuanacu. In *Tiahanacu: Antologia de los principales escritos de los cronistas coloniales, Americanistas, e historiadores Bolivianos*. G. Otrero, ed., pp. 67–76. *Biblioteca Boliviana*, Vol. 2. La Paz: Imprenta Artistica.

Nash, Donna. 2002. The archaeology of space: Places of power in the Wari Empire. Ph.D. dissertation, Department of Anthropology, University of Florida.

Nash, Donna, and P. Ryan Williams. 2004. Fine dining and fabulous atmosphere: Feasting facilities and political interaction in the Wari realm. Paper presented at the 69th annual meeting of the Society for American Archaeology, Montreal.

Nielson, Axel E. 2001. Ethnoarchaeological perspectives on caravan trade in the south-central Andes. In *Ethnoarchaeology of Andean South America*. L. A. Kuznar, ed., pp. 163–201. Ann Arbor: International Monographs in Prehistory.

Nuñez Atencio, Lautaro A. 1964. Influencia de Tiahuanaco en la talla de madera del norte de Chile. *Boletín de la Universidad de Chile* 50:51–56.

Nuñez Atencio, Lautaro A. 1976. Geoglifos y tráfico de caravanas en el desierto Chileno. In *Homaje al Dr. R. P. Gustavo Le Paige S. J.* L. Nuñez, ed., pp. 147–201. Antofagasta: Universidad del Norte.

Nuñez Atencio, Lautaro A. 1985. Petroglifos y tráfico en el desierto. In *Estudios en arte rupestre*. C. Aldunate de S., J. Berenguer R., and V. Castro R., eds., pp. 243–263. Santiago: Museo Chileno de Arte Precolombino.

Núñez Atencio, Lautaro A., and Thomas C. Dillehay. 1995 [1979]. *Movilidad Giratoria, armonía social y desarrollo en los Andes Meridionales: Patrones de tráfico e interacción económica*. Antofagasta: Universidad Católica del Norte.

Nuñez Mendiguiri, Mario, and Rolando Paredes. 1978. Esteves: Un sitio de ocupación Tiwanaku. In *III Congreso Peruano del hombre y la cultura Andina*. R. Matos M., ed., pp. 757–764. Lima.

Oakland, Amy S. 1986. Tiwanaku textile style from the south central Andes, Bolivia and North Chile. Ph.D. dissertation, Department of Anthropology, University of Texas.

Oakland Rodman, Amy. 1992. Textiles and ethnicity: Tiwanaku in San Pedro de Atacama, North Chile. *Latin American Antiquity* 3(4):316–340.

Ochatoma Paravicino, Jose, and Martha Cabrera Romero. 2001. *Poblados rurales Huari: una vision desde Aqo Wayqo*. Lima: CANO.

Ochatoma Paravicino, Jose, and Martha Cabrera Romero. 2002. Religious ideology and military organization in the iconography of a D-shaped ceremonial precinct at Conchopata. In *Andean archaeology II: Art, landscape, and society*. H. Silverman and W. H. Isbell, eds., pp. 225–248. New York: Kluwer Academic/Plenum.

O'Mansky, Matthew, and Nicholas P. Dunning. 2004. Settlement and Late Classic political disintegration in the Petexbatun Region, Guatemala. In *The terminal classic in the Maya Lowlands: Collapse, transition, and transformation*. A. A. Demarest, P. M. Rice, and D. S. Rice, eds., pp. 83–101. Boulder: University Press of Colorado.

Orlove, Benjamin S. 1991. Mapping reeds and reading maps: The politics of representation in Lake Titicaca. *American Ethnologist* 18(1):3–38.

Orlove, Benjamin S. 2002. *Lines in the water*. Berkeley: University of California Press.

Ortloff, Charles R. 1996. Engineering aspects of Tiwanaku groundwater-controlled agriculture. In *Tiwanaku and its hinterland: Archaeology and paleoecology of an Andean civilization*, Vol. 1. A. L. Kolata, ed., pp. 153–168. Washington, DC: Smithsonian Institution Press.

Ortloff, Charles R., and Alan L. Kolata. 1989. Hydraulic analysis of Tiwanaku aqueduct structures at Lukurmata and Pajchiri, Bolivia. *Journal of Archaeological Sciences* 16:513–535.

Ortloff, Charles R., and Alan L. Kolata. 1993. Climate and collapse: Agroecological perspectives on the decline of the Tiwanaku state. *Journal of Archaeological Science* 20:195–221.

Owen, Bruce D. 1998. A Tiwanaku IV temple at Cerro Baúl: Evidence and implications. Paper presented at the 38th annual meeting of the Institute of Andean Studies, Berkeley, CA.

Owen, Bruce D. 2005. Distant colonies and explosive collapse: The two stages of the Tiwanaku diaspora in the Osmore drainage. *Latin American Antiquity* 16(1):45–80.

Parejas Moreno, Alcides, and Carola Muñoz Reyes de Pareja. 2002. Noticias sobre arqueología boliviana en la obra de d'Orbigny. In *El Naturalista Francés Alcide d'Orbigny en la visión de los Bolivianos*. R. D. Arze Aguirre, ed., pp. 267–294. La Paz, Bolivia: Plural.

Pari Flores, Romulo Elias. 1987. El proceso histórico social de los Tiwankau y su implicancia en el valle de Moquegua. Licenciatura thesis, Universidad Catolica Santa Maria.

Parsons, Jeffrey R. 1968. An estimate of size and population for Middle Horizon Tiahuanaco, Bolivia. *American Antiquity* 33:243–45.

Parsons, Jeffrey R. 1976. Settlement and population history in the basin of Mexico. *Annual Review of Anthropology* 1:127–150.

Parsons, Jeffrey R., and Charles Hastings. 1988. The Late Intermediate Period. In *Peruvian prehistory*. R. Keatinge, ed., pp. 190–229. Cambridge: Cambridge University Press.

Parsons, Jeffrey R., Charles M. Hastings, and Ramiro Matos M. 1997. Rebuilding the state in Highland Peru: Herder-cultivator interaction during the Late Intermediate Period. *Latin American Antiquity* 8(4):317–341.

Pärssinen, Martii. 1992. *Tawantinsuyu: The Inka state and its political organization.* Helsinki: Societas Historica Finlandiae.

Pauketat, Timothy R. 2000. The tragedy of the commoners. In *Agency in archaeology.* M.-A. Dobres and J. Robb, eds., pp. 123–139. London: Routledge.

Pauketat, Timothy R., and Susan M. Alt. 2005. Agency in a post-mold? Physicality and the archaeology of culture-making. *Journal of Archaeological Method and Theory* 12(3):213–236.

Paz Flores, M. Percy. 1988. Ceremonias y pinturas rupestres. In *Llamichos y paqocheros: Pastores de llamas y alpacas.* J. A. Flores Ochoa, ed., pp. 217–223. Cusco: Editorial Universitaria.

Paz Flores, M. Percy. 2000. Los llameros de Qochauma y sus viajes a Markapata. In *Pastorea Andino: Realidad, sacralidad, y posibilidades.* J. A. F. Ochoa and Y. Kobayashi, eds., pp. 135–149. La Paz: Plural-MUSEF.

Paz Soria, Jose Luis. 2000. Transición Formativo-Tiwanaku en el sitio de Corralpata, Bolivia. Licenciatura thesis, Universiadad Mayor de San Andres, La Paz.

Paz Soria, Jose Luis, and Maria Soledad Fernandez. 2007. Excavations in the KU (Kala Uyuni) Sector. In *Kala Uyuni: An early political center in the southern Lake Titicaca Basin.* M. T. Bandy and C. A. Hastorf, eds., pp. 25–34. Berkeley: University of California Archaeological Research Facility.

Pereira Herrera, David M., Ramon Sanzetenea Rocha, and Donald L. Brockington. 2001. Investigaciones del proyecto arqueológico Formativo en Cochabamba, Bolivia. *Textos Antropológicos* 13(1–2):183–196.

Perez, Adolfo E. 2004. Autonomía y dinámica social en los Andes: Proceso y desarollo socioeconómico en Irohito, Bolivia. Licenciatura thesis, Universidad Mayor de San Andres.

Perez, Ismael. 2000. Estructuras megalíticas funerarias en el complejo Huari. *Boletín de Arqueología PUCP* 4:505–548.

Perez, Maribel. 2005. Características de la economía de subsistencia en contextos de los periodos Formativo y Tiwanaku en el sitio de Irohito, Bolivia. Licenciatura thesis, Universidad Mayor de San Andres.

Platt, Tristan. 1987. Entre Ch'axwa y Muxsa: Para una historia del pensamiento político Aymara. In *Tres reflexiones sobre el pensamiento Andino.* T. Bouysse-Cassagne, O. Harris, T. Platt, and V. Careceda, eds., pp. 61–132. La Paz: Hisbol.

Plourde, Aimee, and Charles Stanish. 2001. Formative period settlement patterning in the Huancané-Putina River Valley, northeastern Titicaca Basin. Paper presented at the 60th annual meeting of the Society for American Archaeology, New Orleans.

Ponce Sanginés, Carlos. 1961. *Informe de Labores.* La Paz: Centro de Investigaciones Arqueologicas en Tiwanaku.

Ponce Sanginés, Carlos. 1970. *Las culturas Wankarani y Chiripa y su relación con Tiwanaku.* La Paz, Bolivia: Academia Nacional de Ciencias de Bolivia.

Ponce Sanginés, Carlos. 1978a. *El Instituto nacional de arqueología de Bolivia: Su organización y proyecciones.* La Paz: Instituto Nacional de Arqueologia.

Ponce Sanginés, Carlos. 1978b. *Apuntes sobre desarrollo nacional y arqueología.* La Paz: Instituto Nacional de Arqueologia.

Ponçe Sanginés, Carlos. 1980. *Panorama de la Arqueología Boliviana,* 2nd ed. La Paz, Bolivia: Librería Editorial Juventud.

Ponce Sanginés, Carlos. 1981. *Tiwanaku: Espacio, tiempo, y cultura: Ensayo de síntesis arqueológica.* La Paz, Bolivia: Los Amigos del Libro.

Ponce Sanginés, Carlos. 1990. *Descripción sumaria del Templete Semisuterraneo de Tiwanaku.* La Paz: Juventud.

Ponce Sanginés, Carlos. 1991. El urbanismo de Tiwanaku. *Pumapunku: Nueva Época* 1:7–27.

Ponce Sanginés, Carlos. 1993. La cerámica de la época I (aldeana) de Tiwanaku. *Pumapunku: Nueva Época* 4:48–89.

Ponce Sanginés, Carlos. 1995. *Tiwanaku: 200 años de investigaciones arqueológicas.* La Paz: Producciones CIMA.

Ponce Sanginés, Carlos, Arturo Castaños Echazú, Waldo Avila Salinas, and Fernando Urquidi Barrau. 1971. *Procedencia de las areniscas utilizadas en el templo precolombino de Pumapunku (Tiwanaku).* La Paz: Academia Nacional de Ciencias de Bolivia.

Ponce Sanginés, Carlos, Johan Reinhard, Max Portugal, Eduardo Pareja, and Leocadio Ticlla. 1992. *Arqueología subacuática en el Lago Titicaca.* La Paz: Editorial La Palabra.

Ponce Sanginés, Carlos, and G. Mogrovejo Terrazas. 1970. *Acerca de la presencia del material lítico de los monumentos de Tiwanaku.* Laz Paz: Academia Nacional de Ciencias de Bolivia.

Portugal Ortiz, Max. 1992. Trabajos arqueológicos de Tiwanaku, Pt. 1. *Textos Antropológicos* 4:9–50.

Portugal Ortiz, Max. 1998a. Cultura Chiripa: Proto-estado del Altiplano. *Textos Antropológicos* 9:21–46.

Portugal Ortiz, Max. 1998b. *Escultura prehispánica Boliviana.* La Paz: UMSA.

Portugal Ortiz, Max, and Maks Portugal Zamora. 1975. Investigaciones arqueológicas en el valle de Tiwanaku. In *Arqueología en Bolivia y Perú*, Vol. 2. pp. 243–283. La Paz, Bolivia: Instituto Nacional de Arqueología.

Portugal Zamora, Maks. 1980. Petroglifos en el valle de Tiwanaku. El Diario, October 19.

Posnansky, Arthur. 1914. *Una metrópoli prehistórica en la América del sud* (Eine Praehistorische Metropole in Südamerika). Berlin: Editor, Dietrich Reimer (Ernest Vohsen).

Posnansky, Arthur. 1945. *Tihuanacu: The cradle of American man*, Vols. 1 and 2. New York: J. J. Augustin.

Pozzi-Escot B., Denise. 1991. Conchopata: A community of potters. In *Huari administrative structure: Prehistoric monumental architecture and state government.* W. A. Isbell and G. McEwan, eds., pp. 81–92.

Protzen, Jean-Pierre, and Stella E. Nair. 2000. On reconstructing Tiwanaku architecture. *Journal of the Society of Architectural Historians* 59(3):358–371. Washington, DC: Dumbarton Oaks.

Protzen, Jean-Pierre, and Stella Nair. 2002. The Gateways of Tiwanaku: Symbols or Passages? In *Andean archaeology II: Art, landscape, and society.* H. Silverman and W. H. Isbell, eds., pp. 189–223. New York: Kluwer Academic/Plenum.

Prümers, Heiko. 1993. Die ruinen von Tiahuanaco im Jahre 1848: Zeihnungen und notizen von Leonce Angrand. *Beitrage zur Allgemeinen und Vergleichenden Archaologie* 13:385–478.

Prümers, Heiko, Alexandre Chevalier, Jochen Gorsdorf, Redegund Hoffbauer, Irmtrud B. Wagner, Gunther A. Wagner, and Joachim Wahl. 2002. Pailon: Asentamientos prehispanicos en el Depto. Sta. Cruz, Bolivia. *Kava, Beitrage zur Allgemeinen und Vergleichenden Archaeologie* 22(95–242).

Querejazu Lewis, Roy. 1983. *El Mundo arqueólogico del Cnl. Frederico Diez de Medina*. La Paz: Los Amigos del Libro.

Randall, Robert. 1993. Los dos vasos: Cosmovisión y política de la embriaguez desde el inkanato hasta la colonia. In *Borrachera y memoria: la experiencia de lo sagrado en los Andes*. T. Saignes, ed., pp. 73–112. La Paz: Hisbol.

Rasnake, Roger Neil. 1988. *Domination and cultural resistance: Authority and power among Andean people*. Durham, NC: Duke University Press.

Ravines, Roger. 1967. El Abrigo de Caru y sus relaciones culturales con otros sitios tempranos del sur del Peru. *Ñawpa Pacha* 5:39–57.

Ravines, Roger. 1972. Sequencias y cambios en los artefactos líticos del sur del Peru. *Revista del Museo Nacional (Lima)* 28:133–184.

Reinhard, Johan. 1992. Underwater archaeological research in Lake Titicaca, Bolivia. In *Ancient America: Contributions to New World archaeology*. N. Saunders, ed., pp. 117–143. Oxford: Oxford Books.

Rendon Lizarazu, Pablo. 2000. La Tableta de Rape de Amaguaya. In *XIII reunion anual de etnología*, Tomo 1., Vol. 1., pp. 89–96. Anales de la Renuion Anual de Etnologia. La Paz: MUSEF.

Renfrew, Colin. 1986. Introduction: Peer polity interaction and socio-political change. *In Peer polity interaction and socio-political change*. C. Renfrew and J. F. Cherry, eds., pp. 1–26. Cambridge: Cambridge University Press.

Reycraft, Richard M. 2005. Style, change and ethnogenesis among the Chiribaya of far south Coastal Peru. In *Us and them: Archaeology and ethnicity in the Andes*. R. M. Reycraft, ed., pp. 54–72. Los Angeles: Cotsen Institute of Archaeology.

Rick, John. 2004. The evolution of authority and power at Chavin de Huantár, Peru. In *Foundations of power in the prehispanic Andes*. Kevin J. Vaughn, Dennis Ogburn, and Christine A. Conlee, eds., pp. 71–90. Arlington, VA: American Anthropological Association.

Rivera Casanovas, Claudia S. 2003. Ch'iji Jawira: *A case of ceramic specialization in the Tiwankau urban periphery*. In *Tiwanaku and its hinterland: Archaeology and paleoecology of an Andean civilization*, Vol. 2. A. L. Kolata, ed., pp. 296–315. Washington, DC: Smithsonian Institution Press.

Rivera, Mario A. 1991. The prehistory of northern Chile: A synthesis. *Journal of World Prehistory* 5(1):1–47.

Rivera, Mario A. 2002. *Historias del desierto: Arqueologia del norte de Chile*. La Serena, Chile: Editorial del Norte.

Rivera Sundt, Oswaldo. 1989. Resultados de la excavación en el centro ceremonial de Lukurmata. In *Lukurmata*, Vol. 2. A. L. Kolata, ed., pp. 59–88. La Paz: Instituto Nacional de Arqueología.

Roche, Michele A., Jacques Bourges, Jose Cortes, and Roger Matos. 1991. Climatología e hidrología de la cuenca del Lago Titicaca. In *El Lago Titicaca*. C. Dejoux and A. Iltis, eds., pp. 83–104. La Paz: Hisbol.

Rockman, Marcy. 2003. Knowledge and learning in the archaeology of colonization. In *Colonization of unfamiliar landscapes: The archaeology of adaptation*. M. Rockman and J. Steele, eds., pp. 3–43. New York: Routledge.

Rose, Courtney E. 2001a. Household and community organization of a Formative Period, Bolivian settlement. Ph.D. dissertation, Department of Anthropology, University of Pittsburgh.

Rose, Courtney E. 2001b. Organizacion residencial en una aldea del Periodo Formativo temprano: El stio Wankarani de La Barca, Oruro. *Textos Antropológicos* 13(1–2):147–166.

Rostworowski de Diez Canseco, María. 1989. *Costa Peruana Prehispánica*. Lima: Instituto de Estudios Peruanos.

Rostworowski de Diez Canseco, María. 1992. *Pachacamac y el Señor de los Milagros: Una Trayectoria Milenaria*. Lima: Instituto de Estudios Peruanos.

Rowe, John H. 1946. Inca culture at the time of the Spanish conquest. In *The Andean civilizations: Handbook of South American Indians*, Vol. 2. J. H. Steward, ed., pp. 183–330. Washington, DC: Smithsonian Institution Press.

Rowe, John H. 1956. Archaeological explorations in southern Peru. *American Antiquity* 22(2):120–137.

Rowe, John H. 1960. Cultural unity and diversification in Peruvian archaeology. In *Men and cultures*. A. F. Wallace, ed., pp. 627–631. Philadelphia: University of Pennsylvania Press.

Rowe, John H. 1963. Urban settlements in ancient Peru. *Ñawpa Pacha*. 1:1–25.

Rowe, John H., Donald Collier, and Gordon R. Willey. 1950. Reconnaissance notes on the site of Wari, near Ayacucho, Peru. *American Antiquity* 16(2):120–137.

Rydén, Stig. 1947. *Archaeological researches in the highlands of Bolivia*. Göteborg: Elanders Boktryckeri Aktiebolag.

Rydén, Stig. 1957. *Andean excavations 1: The Tiahuanaco era east of Lake Titicaca*. Ethnographical Museum of Sweden, Monograph Series No. 4. Stockholm: Ethnographical Museum of Sweden.

Rydén, Stig. 1959. *Andean excavations 2: Tupuraya and Cayhuasi, Two Tiahuanaco sites*. Ethnographical Museum of Sweden, Monograph Series No. 6. Stockholm: Ethnographical Museum of Sweden.

Sagárnaga Meneses, Jedú Antonio. 1987. *Fritz Buck: Un hombre, una colección*. La Paz: Los Amigos del Libro.

Sahlins, Marshall. 1985. *Islands of history*. Chicago: University of Chicago Press.

Sahlins, Marshall. 1996. The sadness of sweetness: The native anthropology of western cosmology. *Current Anthropology* 37(3):395–428.

Saignes, Thierry. 1993. Estar en otra cabeza: tomar en los Andes. In *Borrachera y memoria: la experiencia de lo sagrado en los Andes*. T. Saignes, ed., pp. 11–21. La Paz: Hisbol.

Salazar-Soler, Carmen. 1993. Embriaguez y visiones en los Andes: Los Jesuitas "borracheras" indígenas en el Peru (Siglos XVI y XVII). In *Borrachera y memoria: la experiencia de lo sagrado en los Andes*. T. Saignes, ed., pp. 23–42. La Paz: Hisbol.

Sanchez de Lozada, David. 1996. Heat and moisture dynamics in raised fields of the Lake Titicaca region, Bolivia. Ph.D. dissertation, Department of Anthropology, Cornell University.

Santoro, C., and Lautaro A. Nuñez Atencio. 1987. Hunters of the dry puna and salt puna in northern Chile. *Andean Past* 1:57–110.

Sarmiento de Gamboa, Pedro. 1999[1572]. *History of the Incas*. Sir Clements Markham, trans. Mineola, NY: Dover.

Sartre, Jean-Paul. 1992 [1956]. *Being and Nothingness: A phenomenological essay on ontology.* New York: Washington Square Press.

Sawyer, Alan R. 1977. Paracas and Nazca iconography. In *Pre-Columbian art history: Selected readings.* A. Cordy-Collins and J. Stern, eds., pp. 393–406. Palo Alto: Peek.

Schreiber, Katharina. 1987. From state to empire: The expansion of Wari outside the Ayacucho Basin. In *The origins and development of the Andean state.* J. Haas, S. Pozorski, and T. Pozorski, eds., pp. 91–96. New York: Cambridge University Press.

Schreiber, Katharina. 1992. *Wari imperialism in Middle Horizon Peru.* Ann Arbor: Museum of Anthropology, University of Michigan.

Schreiber, Katharina. 1999. Regional approaches to the study of prehistoric empires: Examples from Ayacucho and Nasca, Peru. In *Settlement pattern studies in America: Fifty years since Virú.* B. R. Billman and G. M. Feinman, eds., pp. 160–171. Washington, DC: Smithsonian Institution Press.

Schreiber, Katharina. 2001. The Wari empire of Middle Horizon Peru: The epistemological challenge of documenting an empire without documentary evidence. In *Empires: Perspectives from archaeology and ethnohistory.* S. E. Alcock, ed., pp. 70–92. New York: Cambridge University Press.

Schüler, Wolfgang. 1988. Close encounters: Andean ritual battles. Master's thesis, London School of Economics.

Scott, James C. 1990. *Domination and the arts of resistance: Hidden transcripts.* New Haven, CT: Yale University Press.

Seddon, Matthew T. 1994. Excavations in the raised fields of the Río Catari sub-basin, Bolivia. Master's thesis, University of Chicago.

Seddon, Matthew T. 1998. Ritual, power, and the development of a complex society. Ph.D. dissertation, Department of Anthropology, University of Chicago.

Service, Elman R. 1975. *Origins of the state and civilization: The process of political evolution.* New York: Norton.

Sewell, Jr., William H. 1992. A theory of structure: Duality, agency, and transformation. *The American Journal of Sociology* 98(1):1–29.

Shady, Ruth. 1981. Intensificacion de contactos entre las sociedades andinas como preludio al "Movimiento Huari" del Horizonte Medio. *Boletín del Museo Nacional de Antropología y Arqueología* (Lima) 7.

Shady, Ruth. 1989. Cambios significativos ocurridos en el mundo andino. In *The nature of Wari: A reappraisal of the Middle Horizon Period in Peru.* R. M. Czwarno, F. M. Meddens, and A. Morgan, eds. pp. 1–22. London, BAR Internacional Series 525.

Shady, Ruth, and Artuto Tuiz. 1979. Evidence of interregional relationships during the Middle Horizon on the north-central coast of Peru. *American Antiquity* 44:676–684.

Shea, Daniel. 1969. Wari Wilka: A central Andean oracle center. Ph.D. diss, University of Wisonsin–Madison.

Shimada, Izumi. 1991. Pachacamac archaeology: Retrospect and prospect. In *Pachacamac: A reprint of the 1903 edition by Max Uhle.* I. Shimada, ed., pp. xv–lxvi. Philadelphia: University of Pennsylvania.

Shimada, Izumi, Crystal Baker Schaaf, Lonnie G. Thompson, and Ellen Mosley-Thompson. 1991. Cultural impacts of severe droughts in the prehistoric Andes:

Application of a 1500-year ice core precipitation record. *World Archaeology* 22(3):247–270.

Silverblatt, Irene. 1987. *Moon, sun, and witches: Gender ideologies and class in Inca and Colonial Peru.* Princeton, NJ: Princeton University Press.

Silverman, Helaine, and Donald A. Proulx. 2002. *The Nasca.* Oxford: Blackwell.

Smith, Adam T. 2003. *The political landscape: Constellations of political authority in Early Complex polities.* Berkeley: University of California Press.

Smith, C. T., W. Denevan, and P. Hamilton. 1968. Ancient ridged fields in the region of Lake Titicaca. *Geographical Journal* 134:353–367.

Squier, Ephriam G. 1878. *Peru: Incidents of travel and exploration in the land of the Incas.* New York: Harper.

Stanish, Charles. 1989. An archaeological evaluation of an ethnohistorical model in Moquegua. In *Ecology, settlement and history in the Osmore Drainage, Perú,* Vol. 1. D. Rice, C. Stanish, and P. Scarr, eds., pp. 303–321. Oxford: British Archaeological Reports.

Stanish, Charles. 1992. *Ancient Andean political economy.* Austin: University of Texas Press.

Stanish, Charles. 1994. The hydraulic hypothesis revisited: Lake Titicaca Basin raised fields in theoretical perspective. *Latin American Antiquity* 5(4):312–332.

Stanish, Charles. 1999. Settlement pattern shifts and political ranking in the Lake Titicaca Basin, Peru. In *Settlement pattern studies in the Americas.* B. R. Billman and G. M. Feinman, eds., pp. 116–128. Washington, DC: Smithsonian Institution Press.

Stanish, Charles. 2002. Tiwanaku political economy. In *Andean Archaeology I: Variations in sociopolitical organization.* H. Silverman and W. H. Isbell, eds., pp. 169–198. New York: Kluwer Academic/Plenum.

Stanish, Charles. 2003. *Ancient Titicaca: The evolution of social complexity in southern Peru and northern Bolivia.* Los Angeles: University of California Press.

Stanish, Charles, Edmundo de la Vega M., Lee Steadman, Cecilia Chávez Justo, Kirk Lawrence Frye, Luperio Onofre Mamani, Matthew T. Seddon, and Percy Calisaya Chuquimia. 1997. *Archaeological survey in the Juli-Desaguadero region of the Lake Titicaca Basin, southern Peru.* Chicago: Field Museum of Natural History.

Stanish, Charles, and Lee Steadman. 1994. *Archaeological research at Tumatumani, Juli, Peru.* Chicago: Field Museum of Natural History.

Steadman, Lee. 1995. Excavations at Camata: An early ceramic chronology for the Western Titicaca Basin, Peru. Ph.D. dissertation, Department of Anthropology, University of California at Berkeley.

Steadman, Lee. 1997. Ceramic perspectives on the Yaya-Mama religious tradition. Paper presented at the 62nd annual meeting of the Society for American Archaeology, Nashville, TN.

Steadman, Lee. 1999. The ceramics. In *Early settlement at Chiripa, Bolivia: Research of the Taraco archaeological project.* C. A. Hastorf, ed., pp. 61–72. Berkeley: Contributions of the University of California Archaeological Research Facility.

Stein, Gil J. 1998. Heterogeneity, power, and political economy: Some current research issues in the archaeology of Old World Complex societies. *Journal of Archaeological Research* 6:1–44.

Stone-Miller, Rebecca. 2002. *Art of the Andes: From Chavin to Inca*. London: Thames and Hudson.

Stone-Miller, Rebecca, and Gordon McEwan. 1990/1991. The representation of the Wari state in stone and thread. *Res* 19/20:53–79.

Stovel, Emily Mary. 2002. The importance of being Atacameño: Political identity and mortuary ceramics in northern Chile. Ph.D. dissertation, Department of Anthropology, State University of New York, Binghamton.

Stübel, Moritz, and Max Uhle. 1892. *Die Ruinstaette von Tiahuanaco in Hochlande des Alten Peru: Eine Kulturgeschichtliche Studie*. Leipzig: Verlag von Karl W. Heirsermann.

Sutter, Richard C. 2000. Prehistoric genetic and cultural change: A bioarchaeological search for pre-Inka altiplano colonies in the coastal valleys of Moquegua, Peru, and Azapa, Chile. *Latin American Antiquity* 11:43–70.

Tainter, Joseph A. 1988. *The collapse of complex societies*. Cambridge: Cambridge University Press.

Tarrago, Myriam N. 1989. Contribucion al conocimiento arqueológico de las poblaciones de los oasis de San Pedro de Atacama en relación con los otros pueblos puneños, en especial, el sector septentrional del valle Calchaqui. Ph.D. diss, Departments de Antropología, Universidad de Rosario.

Thompson, Lonnie G., Ellen Mosely-Thompson, J. F. Bolzan, and B. R. Koci. 1985. A 1500-year record of tropical precipitation in ice cores from the Quelccaya Ice Cap, Peru. *Science* 229:971–973.

Thompson, Lonnie G., M. E. Davis, Ellen Mosely-Thompson, and K.-B. Liu. 1988. Pre-Incan agricultural activity recorded in dust layers in two tropical ice cores. *Nature* 336:763–765.

Tomczak, Paula D. 2001. Prehistoric socio-economic relations and population organization in the Lower Osmore Drainage of southern Peru. Ph.D. dissertation, Department of Anthropology, University of New Mexico.

Topic, John R. 1991. Huari and Huamachuco. In *Huari administrative structure: Prehistoric monumental architecture and state government*. W. H. Isbell and G. F. McEwan, eds., pp. 141–164. Washington, DC: Dumbarton Oaks Research Library and Collection.

Topic, John R., and Theresa Lange Topic. 1992. The rise and decline of Cerro Amaru: An Andean shrine during the Early Intermediate Period and Middle Horizon. In *Ancient image, ancient thought: The archaeology of ideology*. Proceedings of the 23rd annual conference of the Archaeological Association of the University of Calgary. A. Sean Goldsmith, S. Garvie, D. Selin, and J. Smith, eds., pp. 167–180. Calgary: University of Calgary Archaeological Association.

Topic, John R., and Teresa Lange Topic. 2000. Hacia una comprensión del fenómeno Huari: Una perspectiva norteña. *Boletín de Arqueología PUCP* 4:181–217.

Topic, Theresa Lange. 1991. The Middle Horizon in Northern Peru. In *Huari administrative structure: Prehistoric monumental architecture and state government*. W. H. Isbell and G. F. McEwan, eds., pp. 233–246. Washington, DC: Dumbarton Oaks Research Library and Collection.

Torero, Alfredo. 1970. Lingüística e historia en la sociedad Andina. *Anales Científicos de la Universidad Nacional Agraria* 8(3/4):231–64.

Torero, Alfredo. 1987. Lenguas y pueblos altiplánicos en torno al Siglo XVI. *Revista Andina* 5(2):329–405.

Torres, Constantino. M. 1987. *The iconography of South American snuff trays and related paraphernalia*. Etnologiska Studier. Etnografisca Museum, Goteborg 37.

Torres, Constantino M. 2001. Iconografía Tiwanaku y en la parafenalia inhalatoria de los Andes centro-sur. *Boletín de Arqueología PUCP* 5:427–454.

Torres, Constantino M., and William J. Conklin. 1995. Exploring the San Pedro de Atacama/Tiwanaku Relationship. In *Andean art: Visual expression and its relation to Andean beliefs and values*. P. Dransart, ed., pp. 78–108. Aldershot: Avebury.

Torres-Rouf, Christina. 2002. Cranial vault modification and ethnicity in Middle Horizon San Pedro de Atacama, Chile. *Current Anthropology* 43:163–171.

Tourtellot, Gair. 1988. Developmental cycles of households and houses at Seibal. In *Household and community in the Mesoamerican past*. R. R. Wilk and W. Ashmore, eds., pp. 97–120. Albuquerque; University of New Mexico Press.

Trouillot, Michel-Rolph. 1995. *Silencing the past: Power and the production of history*. Boston: Beacon Press.

Tschopik Jr., H. 1946. The Aymara. In *The Andean civilizations: Handbook of South American Indians*, Vol. 2. J. H. Steward, ed., pp. 501–573. Washington, DC: Smithsonian Institution.

Tung, Tiffiny A. 2003. A bioarchaeological perspective on Wari imperialism in the Andes of Peru: A view from heartland to hinterland skeletal populations. Ph.D. dissertation, Department of Anthropology, University of North Carolina.

Tung, Tiffiny A. 2007. From corporeality to sanctity: transforming bodies into trophy heads in the Prehispanic Andes. In *The taking and displaying of human trophies by Amerindians*. R. J. Chacon and D. H. Dye, eds., pp. 477–500. New York: Springer Press.

Tung, Tiffiny A., and Anita G. Cook. 2006. Intermediate elite agency in the Wari Empire: The bioarchaeological and mortuary evidence. In *Intermediate elite agency in precolumbian states and empires*. C. Elson and A. R. Covey, eds., pp. 68–93. Tucson: University of Arizona Press.

Tung, Tiffiny A., and Kelly J. Knudson. 2006. Identifying the origin of Wari trophy heads in the ancient Andes using bioarchaeology and archaeological chemistry. Paper presented at the 75th annual meeting of the American Association of Physical Anthropology, Anchorage.

Turner, Terence. 1993. Social complexity and recursive hierarchy in indigenous south American societies. *Journal of the Steward Anthropological Society* 24(1–2):37–59.

Turner, Victor. 1969. *The ritual process: Structure and anti-structure*. Ithaca, NY: Cornell University Press.

Uhle, Max. 1895. Fieldnotes of the second official visit to Bolivia, sent from La Paz to the Department of Archaeology and Paleontology, University of Pennsylvania, October 18.

Uhle, Max. 1903. Ancient South American civilization. *Harper's Monthly Magazine* 107:780–786.

Uhle, Max. 1912. Review of A. Posnansky, Guía general ilustrada para la investigación de los monumentos prehistóricos de Tihuanacu é Islas del Sol y la Luna. *Revista Chilena de Historia y Geografía* 2:467–79.

Uhle, Max. 1991 [1903]. Pachacamac: report of the William Pepper, M.D., LL.D., Peruvian expedition of 1896. In *Pachacamac: A reprint of the 1903 edition by Max Uhle*. I. Shimada, ed., pp. 1–103. Philadelphia: University Museum of Archaeology and Anthropology, University of Pennsylvania.

Urton, Gary. 1999. *Inca myths*. Austin: University of Texas Press.

Urton, Gary. 2003. *Signs of the Inca Quipu*. Austin: University of Texas.

Van Buren, Mary. 1996. Rethinking the vertical archipelago: Ethnicity, exchange, and history in the south central Andes. *American Anthropologist* 98(2):338–351.

van Kessel, Juan. 1992. *Cuando arde el tiemo sagrado*. La Paz: Hisbol.

Verano, John W., Alexei Vranich, and Kristen Gardella. 2006. Skeletal remains from a unique dedicatory offering at Tiwanaku. Paper presented at the 25th Northeast Conference on Andean Archaeology and Ethnohistory, Philadelphia.

Vining, Benjamin R. 2004. Lithic materials and social contexts at the Middle Horizon Huari site of Cerro Baul, Peru. Paper presented at the 69th annual meeting of the Society for American Archaeology, Montreal.

von Däniken, Arich. 1971. *Chariots of the gods? Unresolved mysteries of the past*. New York: Bantam Books.

von Humboldt, Alexander. 1878. *Sitios de las cordilleras y monumentos de los pueblos indigenas de America (1814)*. T. B. B. Giner, trans. Madrid: Imprenta y Libreria de Gaspar.

Vranich, Alexei. 1999. Interpreting the meaning of ritual Spaces: The temple complex of Pumapunku, Tiwanaku, Bolivia. Ph.D. diss., University of Pennsylvania.

Vranich, Alexei. 2001. The Akapana pyramid: Reconsidering Tiwanaku's monumental center. *Boletín de Arqueología PUCP* 5:295–308.

Wachtel, Nathan. 1982. The Mitimas of the Cochabamba Valley: The colonization policy of Huayna Capac. In *The Inca and Aztec states, 1400–1800: Anthropology and history*. G. A. Collier, R. I. Rosaldo, and J. D. Wirth, eds., pp. 199–235. New York: Academic Press.

Wachtel, Nathan. 1994. *Gods and vampires: Return to Chipaya*. C. Volk, trans. Chicago: University of Chicago Press.

Wachtel, Nathan. 2001. *El regreso de los antepasados: Los indios Urus de Bolivia, del siglo XX al XVI, ensayo de historia regresiva*. L. Ciezar, trans. Mexico City: El Colegio de Mexico.

Wallace, Dwight T. 1957. The Tiahuanaco Horizon styles in the Peruvian highlands. Ph.D. dissertation, Department of Anthropology, University of California, Berkeley.

Walter, Heinz. 1966. *Beitrage zur archaologie Boliviens: Die Grabungen des Museums fur Volkerkunde Berlin im Jahre 1958*. Berlin: Dietrich Reimer.

Walter, Heinz. 1994 [1966]. Excavación mound Huancarani. In *Invesitigaciones de arqueólogos alemanes en Bolivia: Heinz Walter y Hermann Trimborn*. H. Walter and H. Trimborn, eds., pp. 9–96. Buenos Aires: Centro Argentino de Etnología Americana.

Wassén, S. Henry. 1972. *A medicine-man's implements and plants in a Tiahuanacoid tomb in highland Bolivia*. Etnologiska Studier 32. Göteborg: Elanders Boktryckeri Aktiebolag.

Wasson, John. 1967. Investigaciones preliminares de los "Mounds" en Oruro. *Khana* 1(38):145–156.

Weber, Max. 1930. *The Protestant ethic and the spirit of capitalism.* London: Unwin.

Webster, Ann DeMuth. 1993. The role of the South American camelid in the development of the Tiwanaku state. Ph.D. dissertation, Department of Anthropology, University of Chicago.

Webster, Ann DeMuth, and John Wayne Janusek. 2003. Tiwanaku camelids: Subsistence, sacrifice, and social reproduction. In *Tiwanaku and its hinterland: Archaeology and paleoecology of an Andean civilization*, Vol. 2. A. L. Kolata, ed., pp. 343–362. Washington, DC: Smithsonian Institution Press.

Wernke, Steven A. 2003. An archaeo-history of Andean community and landscape: The Late Prehispanic and Early Colonial Colca Valley, Peru. Ph.D. dissertation, Department of Anthropology, University of Wisonsin–Madison.

Willey, Gordon R. 1953. *Prehistoric settlement patterns in the Virú Valley, Peru.* Washington, DC: Smithsonian Institution Press.

Williams, Patrick Ryan. 1997. The role of disaster in the development of agriculture and the evolution of social complexity in the south-central Andes. Ph.D. dissertation, Department of Anthropology, University of Florida.

Williams, Patrick Ryan. 2001. Cerro Baúl: A Wari Center on the Tiwanaku frontier. *Latin American Antiquity* 12(1):67–83.

Williams, Patrick Ryan, and Donna J. Nash. 2002. Imperial interaction in the Andes: Huari and Tiwanaku at Cerro Baúl. In *Andean archaeology I: Variations in sociopolitical organization*. H. Silverman and W. H. Isbell, eds., pp. 243–266. New York: Kluwer Academic/Plenum.

Williams, Patrick Ryan, and Donna Nash. 2006. Sighting the *apu*: A GIS analysis of Wari imperialism and the worship of mountain peaks. *World Archaeology* 38(3):455–468.

Wilson, David. J. 1988. *Prehispanic settlement patterns in the Lower Santa Valley, Peru.* Washington, DC: Smithsonian Institution Press.

Wilson, David J. 1999. *Indigenous South Americans of the past and present.* Boulder, CO: Westview Press.

Winterhalder, Bruce P., and R. B. Thomas. 1978. *Geoecology of South Highland Peru: A human adaptation perspective.* Boulder: University of Colorado, Institute of Arctic and Alpine Research.

Wirrmann, Denis, Philippe Mourguiart, and Luis Fernando de Oliveira Almeida. 1990. Holocene sedimentology and ostracod distribution in Lake Titicaca: Paleohydrological interpretations. In *Quaternary of South America and Antarctic Peninsula*. J. Rabassa, ed., pp. 89–128. Rotterdam: Backema.

Wise, Karen. 1993. Late Intermediate Period architecture of Lukurmata. In *Domestic architecture, ethnicity, and complementarity in the South-Central Andes.* M. S. Aldenderfer, ed., pp. 103–113. Iowa City: University of Iowa Press.

Wright, Henry T. 1984. Prestate political formations. In *On the evolution of complex societies: Essays in honor of Harry Hoijer.* T. K. Earle, ed., pp. 43–77. Malibu, CA: Undena Press.

Wright, Henry T., and Gregory A. Johnson. 1975. Population, exchange and early state formation in southwestern Iran. *American Anthropologist* 77:267–289.

Wright, Melanie F., Christine A. Hastorf, and Heidi Lennstrom. 2003. Pre-Hispanic agriculture and plant use at Tiwanaku: Social and political implications. In *Tiwanaku and its hinterland: Archaeology and paleoecology of an Andean civilization*, Vol. 2. A. L. Kolata, ed., pp. 384–403. Washington, DC: Smithsonian Institution Press.

Wright, Rita. 1991. Women's labor and pottery production in prehistory. In *Engendering archaeology: Women and prehistory*. J. M. Gero and M. W. Conkey, eds., pp. 194–223. Oxford: Blackwell Press.

Wylie, Allison. 2002. *Thinking from things: Essays in the philosophy of archaeology.* Berkeley: University of California Press.

Yaeger, Jason. 2004. Tiwanaku and the construction of Inka imperial ideology. In *SAR annual report*. J. Stoker, ed., pp. 17. Santa Fe: School of American Research.

Yaeger, Jason, and Jose Maria Lopez Bejarano. 2004. La reconfiguracíon de un espacio sagrado: Los Inkas y la pirámide Pumapunku en Tiwanaku, Bolivia. *Chungará* 36(2):335–348.

Yates, Donna, and Jonah Augustine. 2006. New discoveries and unexpected contexts: Continued excavations to the west of the Akapana Pyramid, Tiwanaku, Bolivia. Paper presented at the 71st annual meeting of the Society for American Archaeology, San Juan.

Yoffee, Norman. 2005. *Myths of the archaic state.* Cambridge: Cambridge University Press.

Yoffee, Norman, and George L. Cowgill. 1988. *The collapse of ancient states and civilizations.* Tucson: University of Arizona Press.

Young-Sanchez, M. 2004. The Art of Tiwanaku. In *Tiwanaku: Ancestors of the Inca*. M. Young-Sanchez, ed., pp. 24–69. Denver Art Museum, University of Nebraska Press, Lincoln and London.

Zuidema, R. Tom. 1990. *Inca civilization in Cuzco.* J.-J. Decoster, trans. Austin: University of Texas Press.

Zuidema, R. Tom. 1999. Pilgrimage and ritual movements in Cuzco and the Inca Empire. Paper presented at the International Workshop, The Cosmology and Complexity of Pilgrimage, New Delhi.

Index